THE COMPLETE

REFERENCE

GUIDE TO

BIBLE
PROPHECY

RON RHODES

HARVEST PROPHECY
AN IMPRINT OF HARVEST HOUSE PUBLISHERS

Scripture versions used in this book are listed at the back of the book.

Cover design by Bryce Williamson

Cover images © BlackJack3D / Getty Images

Interior design by Janelle Coury Illustration and Design

For bulk, special sales, or ministry purchases, please call 1-800-547-8979.
Email: CustomerService@hhpbooks.com

This logo is a federally registered trademark of the Hawkins Children's LLC. Harvest House Publishers, Inc., is the exclusive licensee of this trademark.

The Complete Reference Guide to Bible Prophecy

Published by Harvest House Publishers
Eugene, Oregon 97408
www.harvesthousepublishers.com

ISBN 978-0-7369-8655-7 (pbk)
ISBN 978-0-7369-8656-4 (eBook)

Library of Congress Control Number: 2024931009

Printed in the United States of America

24 25 26 27 28 29 30 31 32 / LB / 10 9 8 7 6 5 4 3 2 1

To him who loves us and has freed us from our sins by his blood
and made us a kingdom, priests to his God and Father,
to him be glory and dominion forever and ever.
Amen.

Behold, he is coming with the clouds,
and every eye will see him,
even those who pierced him,
and all tribes of the earth will wail on account of him.
Even so. Amen.

Revelation 1:5-7

Acknowledgments

Words cannot adequately convey the immense appreciation I have for the unwavering love and encouragement I receive from my incredible wife, Kerri, and our two amazing adult children, David and Kylie. In addition, our delightful grandsons, Carter and Bennett, fill my life with constant laughter and joy. My heart truly overflows with gratitude! Praise be to the Lord for giving me such an extraordinary family.

My deepest gratitude also goes out to all my friends at Harvest House Publishers, especially Bob Hawkins and Steve Miller. The dedication and tireless efforts of the entire staff are truly appreciated! Each of you has glorified God in a wonderful way through your commitment to publishing excellence.

Lord Jesus, I want to thank You yet again for the opportunity to serve You through the written word. In this book, I strive to showcase Your greatness, yet I humbly acknowledge that my efforts capture only a single drop from the boundless ocean of Your divine magnificence. May this humble literary endeavor bring glory to Your awesome Name.

Come soon, Lord!

Contents

Introduction: The Complete Reference Guide
to Bible Prophecy. 9

Part 1—Understanding Prophets, Prophecy, and Prophetic Covenants

1. Demystifying Prophets and Prophecy. 16

2. The Vital Importance of Prophecy 24

3. God's Covenants: The Cornerstone of Bible Prophecy 31

4. Essential Prophetic Passages You Need to Know. 38

Part 2—Interpreting Prophecy

5. A Mini-Survey of 16 Debated Issues. 52

6. Why a Literal Approach Is Best 67

7. Fundamentals of Prophecy Interpretation 74

8. The Striking Connection Between Jesus, Paul, and John. . . . 80

Part 3—Israel and the Church

9. Distinguishing Israel and the Church. 88

10. Clarifying Misunderstood Verses About
Israel and the Church. 97

Part 4—God's Purpose for the Present Age

11. The Course of the Present Age 104

12. The Remarkable Rebirth of Israel 112

Part 5—Current Events and the Signs of the Times

13. Deciphering the Signs of the Times 120

14. The Rebuilding of the Jewish Temple 129

15. The Rising Tide of Apostasy 135

16. The Decline of the United States 143

Part 6—The Rapture of the Church

17. Millions Vanish in the Blink of an Eye 152

18. Exploring Alternative Perspectives on the Rapture 161

19. Investigating Historical Claims
    About the Origin of the Rapture 170

20. Frequently Asked Questions About the Rapture 178

21. The Mysterious Withdrawal of "He Who Now Restrains" . . 186

22. Christians Face the Judgment Seat of Christ in Heaven 192

23. The Sacred Union: The Marriage of the Lamb 199

Part 7—The Ezekiel Invasion

24. The Emerging End-Times Military Coalition
    Against Israel 206

25. The Timing of the Invasion 214

26. The Epic Defeat of the Invaders 228

Part 8—The First Half of the Tribulation Period

27. The Rise of a Revived Roman Empire 238

28. Menacing Features of the Tribulation Period 245

29. The Stranglehold of Religious New Babylon on the World . . 253

30. The 144,000 Courageous Jewish Evangelists 260

31. God's Two Miracle-Working Prophetic Witnesses 267

32. The Cataclysmic Unleashing of the Seal Judgments 274

Part 9—The Antichrist and the False Prophet

33. The Antichrist's Ascent to Global Power 286

34. The Emergence of the Insidious False Prophet 295

Part 10—The "Great Tribulation"

35. The Wounding and "Resurrection" of the Antichrist 304

36. 666 and the Mark of the Beast 310

37. Religious New Babylon Falls,
    Commercial New Babylon Rises 316

38. The Terrifying Trumpet Judgments Are Unleashed 322

39. Darkness Descends: The Antichrist Is Worshiped 329

40. The Onset of the "Great Tribulation" 335

41. The Catastrophic Unleashing of the Bowl Judgments 341

42. Armageddon Ignites 349

43. The Collapse of Commercial New Babylon 355

44. Jerusalem Is Besieged, the Jewish Remnant Is Imperiled 363

Part 11—The Awe-Inspiring Second Coming of Christ

45. The Glorious Appearing 370

46. The Subsequent 75-Day Transition Period 380

Part 12—The Millennial Kingdom

47. Bountiful Spiritual and Material Blessings in the
    Millennial Kingdom 388

48. Satan's Dramatic Final Act: The Climactic Uprising 396

Part 13—The Great White Throne Judgment and the Lake of Fire

49. The Divine Reckoning: The Wicked Face the Great White Throne Judgment 404

50. The Divine Retribution: The Lake of Fire Is Populated 410

Part 14—The Eternal State for Believers: All Things Made New

51. The Majestic New Heavens—the Pristine New Earth 418

52. The Resplendently Glorious New Jerusalem 424

Part 15—Living in the Light of Bible Prophecy

53. Living Expectantly 436

54. Living Righteously 444

55. Living with an Eternal Perspective 452

Postscript: The Grand Reversal 459

Appendix A: A Concise Outline of the End Times in Chronological Order 462

Appendix B: A Simplified Glossary of Prophetic Terms 488

Bibliography 497

Notes 502

INTRODUCTION

The Complete Reference Guide to Bible Prophecy

It has been my privilege to write dozens of books dealing with various facets of Bible prophecy. These books cover a range of topics, including the chronology of the end times, lively debates on topics such as the timing of the rapture, and contemporary trends as they relate to Bible prophecy. Other areas explored include the antichrist, the false prophet, Israel's role in prophecy, the Ezekiel invasion of Israel, the rise of New Babylon, Jesus' teachings on the end times, high technology and the end times, and frequently asked questions about Bible prophecy.

Added to this collection are expository books such as *40 Days through Revelation* and *40 Days through Daniel*, which are designed to help readers understand these two apocalyptic books of the Bible. Each of my previous prophecy books has been a joy for me to write because they each contain important prophetic truths that Christians need to know about.

The advantage of the present book—*The Complete Reference Guide to Bible Prophecy*—is that I cover all of these topics and more. All of my previous books have helped me prepare for this one. All the research that went into writing those books has now been compiled into a single, cohesive volume. This book could be considered a one-stop shop for information on Bible prophecy. It is my sincere hope that it will become your trusted prophecy companion for many years to come. And I pray that it will bless you.

You will find that the book contains a considerable amount of descriptive text on many topics. But interspersed throughout are some special features—that will benefit you in your study of prophecy. These special features include:

- *Charts:* There are charts on all sorts of subjects. Examples include charts on messianic prophecies, conditional versus unconditional covenants, and a comparison of the various future judgments.

- *Fast Facts:* These are useful summaries of some of the most important aspects of prophecy. Examples include:

  · Fast facts on apostasy in the United States
  · Fast facts on the man of sin
  · Fast facts on Babylon in Revelation

- *Christ in Prophecy:* Jesus is the heart and center of Bible prophecy. For example:

  · Jesus will come for us at the rapture (1 Thessalonians 4:13-17).
  · He will unleash judgments upon the earth during the tribulation period (Revelation 6).
  · He will return at the second coming (Revelation 19:11-21).
  · He will reign during the millennial kingdom (Revelation 20:2-5).

- *Personality Profiles:* Included are profiles of:

  · Gog,
  · Satan,
  · the antichrist,
  · the false prophet,
  · the 144,000 Jewish evangelists,
  · and God's two prophetic witnesses.

- *You May Be Interested to Know...:* These are little tidbits of interesting information. Here are a few examples:

  · Twenty-eight percent of the Bible is prophetic.
  · Thirty-five percent of Americans now pay greater attention to how the daily news might relate to the end of the world.
  · Israel's rebirth as a nation in 1948 sets the stage for other prophecies to be fulfilled—including these two:
    1. The antichrist will sign a covenant with Israel.
    2. The Jewish temple will be rebuilt.

- *Lexical Nuggets:* These are insights from the original Hebrew and Greek languages. An example is how the word *delivers* in the phrase "delivers us from the wrath to come" literally means "snatch from" (1 Thessalonians 1:10). Christians will be *snatched* from the earth before the wrathful tribulation period begins.

- *Frequently Asked Questions:* These are common questions that people ask. Among them:

  · Will little children participate in the rapture?

  · Do departed believers look over heaven's balcony to observe us?

  · How can a good God cast people into the lake of fire?

- *Historical Insights:* Bible history helps us to better understand prophecy. For example:

  · Discoveries of sealed scrolls from Bible times give us insight into the seal judgments.

  · The discovery of a Bema seat (elevated seat) in Corinth gives us insight into the judgment seat of Christ. In Corinth, these "seats" were used to distribute victor's crowns to winners of athletic contests.

- *Geography in the End Times:* These features focus on areas such as Israel and Jerusalem, the revived Roman Empire, New Babylon, Russia, and various Muslim nations that will attack Israel in the end times.

- *Numbers in Prophecy:* There are many references to numbers in the book of Revelation. These include seven years, 1,260 days, "time, times, and half a time," 144,000 Jewish witnesses (12,000 from each tribe), two prophets, seven seal judgments, seven trumpet judgments, seven bowl judgments, and 666 in reference to the antichrist.

- *Cross-References:* These cross-references focus on major prophetic topics such as the rapture, the tribulation period, the antichrist, the second coming, the millennial kingdom, and the judgments.

- *Interesting Quotes:* There are many interesting quotations from both ancient and modern authors. They help bring clarity—*and enrichment*—to our study of prophecy.

- *A Lesson to Learn:* These are simple life-change lessons—applicational truths that are spiritually beneficial.

Of course, not every chapter will have all of these (and other) special features. But some will be included in each chapter. I think you will find the book very informative, *but it will also be fun to read.*

A Heartfelt Exhortation

Allow me to emphasize right from the beginning—in the very introduction of the book—that Bible prophecy is worthy of your trust because it comes directly from God Himself. Scripture reveals that God knows all things, both actual and possible (Matthew 11:21-24). He knows all things past (Isaiah 41:22), present (Hebrews 4:13), and future (Isaiah 46:10). There can be no increase or decrease in His knowledge, for He knows all things. Psalm 147:5 affirms that God's understanding "is beyond measure." His knowledge is infinite (Psalms 33:13-15; 139:11-12; 147:5; Proverbs 15:3; Isaiah 40:14; 46:10; Acts 15:18; 1 John 3:20; Hebrews 4:13). I encourage you to read these verses—they will inspire you and bless you!

God wants us to have a high degree of confidence in the accuracy of Bible prophecy. He doesn't want us to doubt it. He assures us: "I am God, and there is no other; I am God, and there is none like me, declaring the end from the beginning and from ancient times things not yet done, saying, 'My counsel shall stand, and I will accomplish all my purpose'…I have spoken, and I will bring it to pass; I have purposed, and I will do it" (Isaiah 46:9-11).

When I first became a Christian, the thing that convinced me of the trustworthiness of Bible prophecy was that more than 100 messianic prophecies in the Old Testament were precisely fulfilled in the first coming of Jesus. You might say they were fulfilled to the crossing of the *t* and the dotting of the *i*. For example, the Old Testament prophesied that the Messiah would be from the seed of a woman (Genesis 3:15), the offspring of Abraham (Genesis 12:3), from the tribe of Judah (Genesis 49:10), the son of David (Jeremiah 23:5-6), conceived of a virgin (Isaiah 7:14), born in Bethlehem (Micah 5:2), the heralded Messiah (Isaiah 40:3), the coming King (Zechariah 9:9), the sacrificial lamb who would be crucified for our sins (Isaiah 53), the one who would be pierced in His side (Zechariah 12:10), the one who would die around AD 33 (Daniel 9:24-25), and the one who would rise from the dead (Psalms 2; 16). These—and a multitude of others—were literally fulfilled in Jesus' first coming.

Because this is true, you can also trust what the prophetic Scriptures reveal about Christ's second coming and all the prophetic events leading up to it. Never doubt it! Put the stake in the ground today. I urge you to affirm with me:

> *I am confident that Bible prophecies about the future are accurate because God has been 100-percent accurate in all His prophecies in the past. He has set an unbroken precedent. I will never question Him. I will take Him at His word. All that remains is for me to learn what the Bible teaches about prophecy. Once I learn it, it will immediately become a firm conviction in my mind. I will trust what I learn from the Bible about prophecy because I believe in a trustworthy God. The matter is settled! There is absolutely no hesitation.*

As is true with all of my writings, I hope that this book will not only inform your mind, but also touch your heart. Christian theology that does not touch the heart has failed in its task. I am convinced that this book will touch your heart because the truths it contains have already touched mine.

It is my prayer that this book will cause a paradigm shift in the way you view the present world. The more you think about the glorious truths of the prophetic future, the more you will gain an eternal perspective that will help you deal with the difficult situations you will inevitably face during this short earthly life.

May it be so!

PART 1

Understanding Prophets, Prophecy, and Prophetic Covenants

IN THIS SECTION

1—Demystifying Prophets and Prophecy—16

2—The Vital Importance of Prophecy—24

3—God's Covenants: The Cornerstone of Bible Prophecy—31

4—Essential Prophetic Passages You Need to Know—38

1

Demystifying Prophets and Prophecy

God has revealed everything He wants us to know about Himself and how to have a relationship with Him through the Scriptures. He is the One who caused the Bible to be written. He speaks to us through the words of the Bible, just as He did to ancient people when those words were first given.

One of the most intriguing aspects of the Bible is its abundance of prophecies concerning the future. God reveals a great deal about the end times, particularly in apocalyptic books such as Revelation and Daniel.

YOU MAY BE INTERESTED TO KNOW...
Twenty-Seven Percent of the Bible Is Prophetic

> Of the 23,210 verses of the Old Testament, 6,641 are prophetic. This is 28.5 percent.

> Of the 7,914 verses of the New Testament, 1,711 are prophetic. This is 21.5 percent.

> When the Old and New Testaments are combined, 8,352 of the 31,124 verses in the Bible are prophetic.

> This is 27 percent of the Bible.

🕮 LEXICAL NUGGET: *Prophet*

The English word *prophet* comes from the Hebrew word *nabi*. It means "God's spokesman."

1. Prophets sometimes spoke of God's predictions of future events.

2. Other times, they spoke God's Word on contemporary issues.

Major Prophets and Minor Prophets
There are two categories of prophets:

The *major prophets* were Isaiah, Jeremiah, Ezekiel, and Daniel. These guys were the "big wheels."

The *minor prophets* were Hosea, Joel, Amos, Obadiah, Jonah, Micah, Nahum, Habakkuk, Zephaniah, Haggai, Zechariah, and Malachi. These men were the "small fries." Yet, their words were as divinely inspired as those of the major prophets. God spoke through all of them.

It is interesting to note that in the Old Testament, God's human messenger spoke a prophetic word, and in the New Testament, those words are said to have come from God Himself. This shows that God was the ultimate source of their prophetic words.

OLD TESTAMENT REFERENCE	NEW TESTAMENT REFERENCE
The psalmist said (Psalm 95:7)	The Holy Spirit said (Hebrews 3:7)
The psalmist said (Psalm 45:6)	God said (Hebrews 1:8)
The psalmist said (Psalm 102:25, 27)	God said (Hebrews 1:10-12)
Isaiah said (Isaiah 7:14)	The Lord spoke by the prophet (Matthew 1:22-23)
Hosea said (Hosea 11:1)	The Lord spoke by the prophet (Matthew 2:15)
Eliphaz's words (Job 5:13)	God's Words (1 Corinthians 3:19)

FAST FACTS ON GOD'S PROPHETS

- God personally chose His prophets (Jeremiah 1:5; Luke 1:13-16).
- They came from all walks of life—from farmers to princes (Amos 7:14; Genesis 23:6).
- They often prefaced their words with "Thus saith the Lord."
- Their words were not their own, but those of God.

- As a result, their messages—including their prophecies of the distant future—were supernatural rather than natural.
- God's prophets were always 100 percent accurate.

Some Bible scholars define prophecy as "history written in advance." It is more accurate to say that prophecy is *God's revelation* regarding history in advance, since only God, in His omniscience, knows the future. God claimed this in Isaiah 46:9-10: "I am God, and there is no other; I am God, and there is none like me, declaring the end from the beginning and from ancient times things not yet done, saying, 'My counsel shall stand, and I will accomplish all my purpose.'"

The word *prophesy* (as opposed to *prophecy*) means to set forth prophecies. Everything that God prophesies will come to pass. You can be sure of that. God said this in Isaiah 48:3: "The former things I declared of old; they went out from my mouth, and I announced them; then suddenly I did them, and they came to pass."

He likewise affirms in Isaiah 42:8-9: "I am the LORD; that is my name; my glory I give to no other, nor my praise to carved idols. Behold, the former things have come to pass, and new things I now declare; before they spring forth I tell you of them."

These verses show that God controls the course of human history. He alone can reveal the future to us. His predictions (or prophecies) are always accurate.

"History is a story written by the finger of God."

—C.S. Lewis[1]

"What has happened in the past, what is happening now, and what will happen in the future is all evidence of the unfolding of the purposeful plan devised by the personal God of the Bible. All the circumstances of life—past, present, and future—fit into the sovereign plan like pieces of a puzzle."

—Robert Lightner[2]

The biblical prophets made very specific predictions about the future. As Mark Hitchcock put it, "The biblical prophets did not peddle predictions that were so vague and general that they could be adapted to any situation. The prophecies recorded in the Bible are very precise and so specific that when they are fulfilled, it's very clear there's something unique and special about them."[3]

For example, in the Old Testament, God's prophets predicted (1) Jesus' birth in Bethlehem (Micah 5:2), (2) His conception by a virgin (Isaiah 7:14), and (3) His crucifixion (Isaiah 53:12; Zechariah 12:10). These predictions are very specific. There is no ambiguity. These three—and more than a hundred others—were explicitly fulfilled in Christ.

The prophecies of the end times are equally specific. These include prophecies concerning the rapture of the church, the rise of the antichrist, the false prophet, the tribulation period, the second coming of Christ, the millennial kingdom, the great white throne judgment, and the eternal state.

CHRIST IN PROPHECY
Jesus Fulfilled the Three Offices of Prophet, Priest, and King

As a Prophet, Jesus gave major discourses:

> the Upper Room Discourse (John 14–16),

> the Olivet Discourse (Matthew 24–25),

> and the Sermon on the Mount (Matthew 5–7).

Understanding Prophetic Terminology

Eschatology. The term *eschatology* comes from two Greek words: *eschatos,* meaning "last" or "last things," and *logos,* meaning "study of." Eschatology is the study of last things. It is the study of the end times. It is pronounced es-kuh-TOL-uh-jee.

The doctrine of eschatology can be divided into two distinct categories:

- *Personal eschatology* deals with an individual's death, future judgment, and heavenly or hellish destiny.
- *General eschatology* deals with more general topics, such as the rapture, the tribulation period, the second coming, and the millennial kingdom.

Apocalyptic literature. Apocalyptic literature is a unique form of literature that reveals or unveils the future through divine revelations. (In Greek, *apocalypse* means "revelation" or "unveiling.") Daniel and Revelation are the two apocalyptic books of the Bible. It is beneficial to study these books simultaneously.

The last days. One would assume that the term "last days" is equivalent to "end times." But this is not the case. The New Testament reveals that the term can be applied to our present church age: "Long ago, at many times and in many ways, God spoke to our fathers by the prophets, but in these last days he has spoken to us by his Son" (Hebrews 1:1-2). This indicates that people from the time of the New Testament to the present day are already living in the "last days" (see also 1 Peter 1:20).

The term is used differently throughout the Old Testament. It often refers prophetically to Israel during the seven-year period of tribulation, after which the divine Messiah will return and establish His millennial kingdom on earth: "When you are in tribulation, and all these things come upon you in the latter days, you will return to the LORD your God and obey his voice" (Deuteronomy 4:30).

▦ NUMBERS IN PROPHECY: *The Seven-Year Tribulation Period*

> The tribulation period will last "one week" of years, which is seven years (Daniel 9:27).

> Prophetic Scripture refers to *half* of the tribulation period in various ways:

» 42 months (Revelation 13:5), which is three-and-a-half years.

» 1,260 days (Revelation 11:3), which is three-and-a-half years.

» time, times, and half a time (Daniel 7:25), which is three-and-a-half years. ("Time" is one year; "times" is two years; "half a time" is half a year.)

The end times. The end times is a broad term that encompasses a variety of events that take place in the prophetic future. These events include the rapture, the judgment seat of Christ, the tribulation period, Armageddon, the second coming of Christ, the millennial kingdom, and the great white throne judgment. Also included are heaven (for believers) and hell (for unbelievers).

Pretribulationism. This is the theological view that the rapture will take place before the tribulation period. (This is my position.)

Midtribulationism. This is the theological view that the rapture will occur at the midpoint of the tribulation period.

Posttribulationism. This is the theological view that the rapture will occur after the tribulation period.

The pre-wrath theory. This is the theological view that the rapture will occur before the final portion of the tribulation, when God's wrath will be unleashed.

The partial-rapture theory. This is the theological view that only those who are prepared and waiting for Christ will be raptured. As Christians become purified and found worthy, they too will be raptured at various times throughout the tribulation.

Preterism. This is the theological view that the majority of the prophecies in the book of Revelation (especially chapters 6–18) and in Christ's Olivet Discourse (Matthew 24–25) were fulfilled in AD 70 when Rome overran Jerusalem.

Amillennialism. This is the theological position that there is no future millennial kingdom. Christ simply reigns over the church from heaven.

Postmillennialism. This is the theological position that Christ's second coming will occur after a long period of time—metaphorically described as 1,000 years—during which the church will Christianize the entire world.

Premillennialism. This is the theological position that Christ will return prior to the millennial kingdom, which will feature a 1,000-year rule of Christ on earth. (This is my position.)

Don't worry if you can't remember all these definitions. Appendix B: "A Simplified Glossary of Prophetic Terms" is always available to you.

The Personal Blessing of Prophetic Scripture

- God's prophetic plan includes not only the whole world, but also each and every one of us.
- God has His eyes on us and has a wonderful plan for our future (Jeremiah 29:11; Psalm 32:8; Proverbs 3:5-6; Romans 8:28).
- It is beneficial to begin each day with this thought.

FREQUENTLY ASKED QUESTIONS

Did God's prophets ever make mistakes?

No, not when speaking on behalf of God. However, some have tried to argue that Jonah made a false prophecy. After all, Jonah proclaimed that in 40 days Nineveh would be overthrown by God. But Jonah's prediction of Nineveh's destruction did not come to pass. Nevertheless, Jonah did not make a mistake. He told the Ninevites exactly what God had told him to say (Jonah 3:1-2). A repentance clause was built into Jonah's prophecy: "If at any time I declare concerning a nation or a kingdom, that I will pluck up and break down and destroy it, and if that nation, concerning which I have spoken, turns from its evil, I will relent of the disaster that I intended to do to it" (Jeremiah 18:7-8). The Ninevites understood that *if they did not repent*, Nineveh would fall in 40 days (Jonah 3:5-9). Because they repented, God withheld judgment.

Are there any prophets today?

Some Christians claim that there are prophets in the church today. However, the Bible indicates that the church was "built on the foundation of the apostles and prophets" (Ephesians 2:20). Once a foundation is laid, it is permanent. Therefore, there is no need to lay a new foundation with new apostles and prophets. Today's self-proclaimed prophets do not have the predictive abilities of Isaiah, Ezekiel, and Daniel. Instead, they simply proclaim the Word of God. Therefore, they are called "prophets" in a very loose sense.

Will there be any prophets in the future?

During the tribulation period, God will raise up two mighty prophetic witnesses with the same miraculous abilities as Moses and Elijah (Revelation 11:1-15). I will address these prophets later in the book.

CROSS-REFERENCES
Prophecy

A gift of the Holy Spirit—1 Corinthians 12:10

Not based on the will of man—2 Peter 1:21

Certainty of God's Word—Ezekiel 12:26-28

God declares things before they occur—Isaiah 42:9

God declares the end from the beginning—Isaiah 46:10-11

God declares what is to come—Isaiah 44:7

God fulfills the prophet's message—Isaiah 44:26

Is a sure word—2 Peter 1:19

Prime purpose of prophecy—John 13:19

Prophetic visions and dreams—Numbers 12:6

Qualification for a prophet—1 Samuel 10:12

2

The Vital Importance of Prophecy

Some Bible students may be unaware of the vital importance of Bible prophecy. They might assume that the sole function of prophecy is to inform us of the future.

Truth be told, Bible prophecy is full of benefits for those who look beyond that single purpose. These benefits make the study of prophecy invaluable.

1. Prophecy Proves that the God of the Bible Is the One True God

In Isaiah 41:21-23, God challenges the people to prove that their idols are indeed gods:

> Set forth your case, says the LORD;
> bring your proofs, says the King of Jacob.
> Let them bring them, and tell us
> what is to happen.
> Tell us the former things, what they are,
> that we may consider them,
> that we may know their outcome;
> or declare to us the things to come.
> Tell us what is to come hereafter,
> that we may know that you are gods.

Obviously, these idols and false gods could not oblige because they do not even exist. In contrast, the true God says of Himself, "Behold, the former things have come to pass, and new things I now declare; before they spring forth I tell you of them" (Isaiah 42:9). This verse expresses the idea, "Everything I predicted in the past has come to pass, and I will now predict additional future events."

God also later affirmed: "I am God, and there is no other; I am God, and there is none like me, declaring the end from the beginning and from ancient times things not yet done, saying, 'My counsel shall stand, and I will accomplish all my purpose'" (Isaiah 46:9-10). When God says, "There is none like me, declaring the end from the beginning," it expresses the idea, "*No one else can predict the future before it occurs like I can.*"

2. Prophecy Proves the Bible Is the Word of God

Just as Bible prophecy demonstrates that the God of the Bible is the only true God, it also demonstrates that the Bible is the only true "holy book." No other holy book, including the Muslim Qur'an, Hindu Vedas, or any New Age text, can compete with the Bible. The fulfillment of prophecy proves that the Bible is indeed the Word of God and can be relied upon.

COMPELLING EVIDENCE FOR THE BIBLE

1. God alone knows the prophetic future.

2. The Bible is the *only* holy book that contains God's many specific prophecies about the future.

3. More than 100 Old Testament messianic prophecies of Christ's first coming were fulfilled in the pages of the New Testament, demonstrating God's perfect accuracy in predicting the future.

4. Prophecy, then, is compelling evidence that the Bible is God's Word.

3. Prophecy Is a Powerful Tool of Evangelism

Evangelism and prophecy can be an effective combination. Peter's sermon on the day of Pentecost illustrates this. Several supernatural events had just occurred. Therefore, Peter addressed the large crowd about what was happening in their midst. He began his message by discussing a prophecy concerning the outpouring of the Holy Spirit upon the people: "What you see was predicted long ago by the prophet Joel" (Acts 2:16 NLT). After discussing the prophecy, Peter launched into his evangelistic pitch, culminating with this invitation: "Everyone who calls on the name of the Lord will be saved" (verse

21 NLT). *The result?* "Those who believed what Peter said were baptized and added to the church that day—about 3,000 in all" (verse 41 NLT). Prophecy can be an important component in evangelism.

A TESTIMONY

My family regularly attended a liberal church in the 1970s. Liberal churches typically teach that the Bible is man-made, the miracles in the Bible never happened, Jesus is not really God, and Jesus is not the only way to salvation.

I had no idea that I was attending a false church. I was biblically illiterate. Then I started reading some books on Bible prophecy. These books caused a major paradigm shift in my life. As a direct result of prophecy, I became a Christian, left the liberal church, joined a good biblical church, eventually attended Dallas Theological Seminary, received both a master of theology degree and a doctor of theology degree, and have been serving the Lord ever since.

I am a living testimony of how prophecy can be used in evangelism. Bible prophecy has completely changed the course of my life.

4. Prophecy Comforts Us When We Lose a Loved One in Death

In the early history of the church, the Thessalonian believers lost some family members in death. The apostle Paul had previously explained to them how living believers would one day be caught up in the rapture. But what about deceased believers? This was the question they posed to Paul.

Paul explained in 1 Thessalonians 4:13-17 that the dead in Christ would first be resurrected, and then living Christians would be translated into their glorified bodies. Both groups would then instantly be caught up to meet Christ in the air and taken to heaven (John 14:1-3; 1 Corinthians 15:51-54). Paul said, "Therefore encourage one another with these words" (1 Thessalonians 4:18).

Of course, it is natural for us to continue to grieve after the death of a

Christian loved one. However, we do not "grieve as others who have no hope" (1 Thessalonians 4:13). We know that a reunion is imminent. We will be with our Christian loved ones again. We will once again see their faces, hear their voices, and exchange hugs with them. Someone once said, "No two Christians will ever meet for the last time." I believe this to be true.

HISTORICAL INSIGHT
Prophecy Was a Great Comfort to the Early Christians

> The original readers of Revelation were Christians who lived about 65 years after Jesus' crucifixion and resurrection.

> These second-generation Christians faced tremendous obstacles.

> Because of Roman hostility toward Christianity, their lives had become increasingly difficult.

> Many of them suffered persecution and some were even martyred (Revelation 2:13).

> Revelation was written to provide these believers with a strong sense of hope that would enable them to patiently endure their suffering.

> *The big lesson:* Human suffering is temporary. Eternal life with God is forever.

5. Prophecy Demonstrates that God Will Triumph Over Evil

A new day will soon come. The antichrist, the false prophet, Satan, and all anti-God human rebels will be quarantined forever in the lake of fire (Revelation 19:20; 20:10). Meanwhile, resurrected believers will dwell directly in God's presence for all eternity in the New Jerusalem, the city of the redeemed. As the Scriptures state:

> Behold, the dwelling place of God is with man. He will dwell with them, and they will be his people, and God himself will be with them as their God. He will wipe away every tear from their eyes, and death shall be no more, neither shall there be mourning, nor crying, nor pain anymore, for the former things have passed away.

And he who was seated on the throne said, "Behold, I am making all things new" (Revelation 21:3-5).

Evil will no longer exist!

YOU MAY BE INTERESTED TO KNOW...
Americans Are Increasingly Interested in the End of the World

> Thirty-five percent of Americans are now paying more attention to how the news—mostly *bad* news—relates to the end of the world.

> Seventeen percent believe the end of the world will happen in their lifetime.

> Fifty-nine percent believe the prophecies of the book of Revelation will be fulfilled.[1]

6. Prophecy Is a Source of Spiritual Blessing

Revelation 1:3 states unequivocally: "Blessed is the one who reads aloud the words of this prophecy, and blessed are those who hear, and who keep what is written in it, for the time is near." This is the first of seven special pronouncements of blessing in the book of Revelation (see also 14:13; 16:15; 19:9; 20:6; 22:7-14).

People like to read about the blessings, but they often overlook the part about obedience. The blessed are "those who hear, *and* who keep what is written in it." We recall the exhortation of James: "Be doers of the word, and not hearers only, deceiving yourselves" (James 1:22).

Read the prophetic Word, obey the Word, and be blessed!

7. Prophecy Has Contemporary Relevance

A final reason Bible prophecy is vitally important is that a number of ancient prophecies appear to be coming to pass in our time, or at least the stage is being set for their fulfillment. These include:

• the rebirth of Israel as a nation,

• a falling away from the truth,

• the widespread acceptance of doctrinal error,

- a significant moral decline,
- a growing tolerance for all things evil,
- a widespread outbreak of sexual sins and perversions,
- a steady decline in religious freedom,
- increased worldwide persecution of God's people,
- ever-escalating conflict in the Middle East,
- efforts to rebuild the Jewish temple,
- the stage being set for a massive Russian/Muslim invasion of Israel,
- the steady rise of globalism,
- political and economic moves toward the establishment of a revived Roman Empire,
- and the emergence of a cashless world in preparation for the antichrist's control of the world economy during the tribulation period.

It is sobering to think about how all of these are trending in varying degrees in our present day—sure indicators that we are living in the end times. This makes prophecy vitally important.

CHRIST IN PROPHECY
Jesus Addressed Many Prophetic Issues

- > The Olivet Discourse is so named because Jesus delivered it while seated on the Mount of Olives (Matthew 24:3).
- > The disciples asked Jesus, "Tell us, when will these things be, and what will be the sign of your coming and of the end of the age?" (Matthew 24:3).
- > The Olivet Discourse is Jesus' answer to this question.
- > Jesus foretold false christs, wars, famines, earthquakes, the desecration of the Jewish temple, cosmic upheavals (Matthew 24:4-28), the sign of His coming (verses 29-31), and how the end times would resemble the days of Noah (verses 36-39).

FREQUENTLY ASKED QUESTIONS

Does the study of Bible prophecy distract Christians from more important matters, such as fulfilling the Great Commission?

No. In fact, Bible prophecy aids in the fulfillment of the Great Commission. As Peter demonstrated when he preached on the day of Pentecost (Acts 2), prophecy can play a significant role in evangelism. In keeping with this, Matthew's Gospel contains many quotations and allusions to Old Testament messianic prophecies in order to demonstrate to the Jews that Jesus is the promised Jewish Messiah. In addition, more than a quarter of the Bible is prophetic. This is too large a portion of the Bible to ignore.

Are liberal critics correct in claiming that messianic prophecies of Christ's first coming were inserted into the Bible after the fact, and are therefore untrustworthy?

No. Nearly all scholars agree that the Old Testament prophetic writings were completed at least 400 years before the birth of Christ, with many books dating back to the eighth and ninth centuries BC. The exception is the book of Daniel, which some scholars date to 167 BC. A critically important manuscript copy of Isaiah dates to 150 BC, which is 150 years before the birth of Christ. This means that all of the specific prophecies of the coming divine Messiah found in Isaiah—for example, that Jesus would be born of a virgin (7:14), be named Immanuel (7:14), be anointed by the Holy Spirit (11:2), have a ministry in Galilee (9:1-2), have a ministry of miracles (35:5-6), be silent before His accusers (53:7), be crucified with thieves (53:12), accomplish a sacrificial atonement for humankind (53:5), and then be buried in a rich man's tomb (53:9)—could not possibly have been recorded after the fact.

You can trust Bible prophecy!

3

God's Covenants: The Cornerstone of Bible Prophecy

Covenants were common in biblical times. Nations made covenants with other nations (1 Samuel 11:1), just as individuals made covenants with other individuals (Genesis 21:27).

There were many kinds of covenants. In some cases, nations made covenants in the form of treaties or alliances. People sometimes signed friendship pacts as covenants (1 Samuel 18:3-4). A person could even make a covenant with himself. This is illustrated by Job: "I made a covenant with my eyes not to look with lust at a young woman" (Job 31:1 NLT). He made a pact with himself in order to help him avoid immorality.

This chapter focuses on the major covenants God made with His people. These include His covenant promises to Abraham (Genesis 15:12-21; 17:1-14), David (2 Samuel 7:13; 23:5), and the people of God under the new covenant (Hebrews 8:5-13). These covenants are the cornerstone of Bible prophecy. They demonstrate that God is a God of promises.

YOU MAY BE INTERESTED TO KNOW...
God Is a Promise Keeper

> - Numbers 23:19 tells us that "God is not man, that he should lie, or a son of man, that he should change his mind. Has he said, and will he not do it? Or has he spoken, and will he not fulfill it?"

> - An aged Joshua declared, "Not one word of all the good promises that the LORD had made to the house of Israel had failed; all came to pass" (Joshua 21:45).

> - Joshua, near the time of his death, later affirmed: "And now I am about to go the way of all the earth, and you know in your hearts

and souls, all of you, that not one word has failed of all the good things that the LORD your God promised concerning you. All have come to pass for you; not one of them has failed" (Joshua 23:14).

> Solomon later proclaimed, "Blessed be the LORD who has given rest to his people Israel, according to all that he promised. Not one word has failed of all his good promise, which he spoke by Moses his servant" (1 Kings 8:56).

6∂ UNDERSTANDING OUR TERMS: *Covenant*

Simply put, a covenant is a promissory agreement between two parties.

In biblical times, there were two types of covenants: conditional and unconditional. A *conditional covenant* is similar to a contract with an "if" clause. Conditions had to be met for the promises to be fulfilled.

A conditional covenant between God and humans required that humans meet specific requirements before God was obligated to fulfill His promise. Such a covenant might be as simple as, "Obey Me, and I will bless you." If the conditions are not met ("obey me"), God is not obligated to fulfill His promises ("I will bless you").

The fulfillment of an *unconditional covenant* was not contingent on any conditions; no "ifs" were attached. This form of covenant involved God's firm and unbreakable promises regardless of the merit (or lack thereof) of the humans to whom God made the promises.

Some Christians like to call this a *unilateral covenant* instead of an unconditional one. "Unilateral" means that one person (in this case, God) does something without putting any conditions on the other party (for example, Israel). Other Christians prefer the designation *one-sided covenant* or *divine commitment covenant*.

CONDITIONAL COVENANT	UNCONDITIONAL COVENANT
Two-sided covenant	One-sided covenant
Entails human and divine commitment	Entails divine commitment alone
Conditions attached	No conditions attached

| Blessing hinges on human merit | God blesses regardless of merit |
| Blessings are earned | Blessings are freely given |

The Abrahamic covenant, the Davidic covenant, and the new covenant are three of the most important biblical covenants that God made with human beings. The Abrahamic and Davidic covenants have significance for Israel's future (especially the land and throne promises), but the spiritual blessings of the covenants extend to the Gentiles as well. The new covenant has both present and future applications for all believers, Jews and Gentiles. (More on this shortly.)

The Abrahamic Covenant

God's covenant with Abraham was unconditional (Genesis 12:1-3; 15:18-21). According to Genesis 12, God made seven prophetic promises to Abraham (then named Abram) in this covenant:

1. *I will make you a great nation (12:2).* From Abraham's perspective, this was an extraordinary promise. He and Sarai had not yet had a child. They were also old. It seemed unlikely that the Jewish nation would come from him and his wife. With God, however, all things are possible (Mark 10:27).

2. *I will bless you (12:2).* God blessed Abraham with great wealth (13:2) and substantial material possessions (24:35). God favored Abraham (21:22).

3. *I will make your name great (12:2).* God made Abraham famous and gave him an excellent reputation. Both the Old and New Testaments testify to this. Abraham was known as a "prince of God" (Genesis 23:6), "a friend of God" (James 2:23), and the founder of the Jewish nation (Genesis 15:1-6; Romans 4:1). Abraham is a well-known figure today among Jews, Christians, and others around the world.

4. *I will bless those who bless you (12:3).* Abraham's relationship with God was so close that to bless him was to bless God. Friends of the Jewish people are considered to be friends of God and thus receive His blessing.

5. *I will curse those who curse you (12:3).* Anti-Semites are ultimately hostile to God and will be punished accordingly.

6. *All peoples on earth will experience blessing through you (12:3)*. This blessing was realized with the birth of Abraham's descendant, Jesus Christ, the Savior of humanity (Galatians 3:8, 16).

7. *I will give you and your descendants the land of Canaan (12:1; 15:18-21)*. This is "the Promised Land" (Psalm 47:4).

These land promises to Israel will be fulfilled in the millennial kingdom, which will come after the second coming of Christ. This means that God's promise will be fulfilled thousands of years after He made it. Israel will one day possess the land, just as God foretold! God is faithful.

God later reaffirmed this covenant with Isaac, Abraham's son (17:21; 26:2-5), because it was so important to Israel's future. He also reaffirmed it with Jacob, the son of Isaac (28:10-17; 35:12-14). The Bible describes this covenant as an *everlasting* covenant (Genesis 17:7-8; 1 Chronicles 16:17; Psalm 105:7-11; Isaiah 24:5).

The Davidic Covenant

God's covenant with David was unconditional. God promised that a descendant of David would rule forever (2 Samuel 7:12-13; 22:51). This covenant contains three notable words: *throne, house*, and *kingdom*—words that point to a royal dynasty. This covenant is fulfilled in Jesus Christ, who was born of the royal line of David (Matthew 1:1).

Christ will reign as Monarch from the throne of David in Jerusalem during the future 1,000-year millennial kingdom (Micah 4:15; Zephaniah 3:14-20; Zechariah 14:18-21). This reign will extend beyond the Jews to include the Gentile nations. Christ's authority will extend "from sea to sea...to the ends of the earth!" (Psalm 72:8). Daniel 7:14 states, "All peoples, nations, and languages" will serve Him.

CHRIST IN PROPHECY
Matthew's Genealogy

> - Matthew begins his Gospel by alluding to the Abrahamic and Davidic covenants.

> - He opens with the words: "The book of the genealogy of Jesus Christ, the son of David, the son of Abraham" (Matthew 1:1).

> - Matthew thus emphasizes that Jesus came to fulfill the unconditional covenants God made with David and Abraham.

HISTORICAL INSIGHT
Mary and the Davidic Covenant

> Mary, the mother of Jesus, quickly realized that her unborn child would fulfill the Davidic covenant.

> The angel Gabriel appeared to her and said, "The Lord God will give to him the throne of his father David, and he will reign over the house of Jacob forever, and of his kingdom there will be no end" (Luke 1:32-33).

> Notice the three key words—*throne, house,* and *kingdom.* These are the three key words God used in His covenant with David (2 Samuel 7:16).

The New Covenant

The new covenant is a vital, unconditional covenant made by God. In it, God promised to provide for the forgiveness of sins solely through the sacrifice of Jesus Christ and His resurrection from the dead (Jeremiah 31:31-34). Under the old covenant, worshipers did not receive complete forgiveness. Under the new covenant, Christ our High Priest has provided that complete forgiveness: "God made Christ, who never sinned, to be the offering for our sin, so that we could be made right with God through Christ" (2 Corinthians 5:21 NLT).

When Jesus ate the Passover meal with His disciples in the Upper Room, He spoke of "the new covenant between God and his people—an agreement confirmed with my blood, which is poured out as a sacrifice for you" (Luke 22:20 NLT). Our forgiveness was accomplished through the once-for-all sacrifice of Jesus on the cross.

This covenant revolutionizes our relationship with God. Without these wonderful promises in the new covenant, neither you nor I would have any hope of an afterlife in paradise in the direct presence of God.

A LESSON TO LEARN

If there is one thing we have learned about God in this chapter, it's that He keeps His promises. So today, drive the stake into the ground. You should have unwavering faith that God will fulfill all that is promised in the prophetic Scriptures. Let there be no doubt in your mind (1 Kings 8:56).

This chapter demonstrates that one of God's promises is that Jesus will rule from the throne of David during the millennial kingdom. This will not happen until after the second coming of Christ. However, today Christ must also reign supreme upon the throne of our hearts. He must have complete control over all aspects of our lives (John 14:23-24).

Hold nothing back!
Refuse all compromise!

FREQUENTLY ASKED QUESTION
How do we know the Abrahamic covenant was unconditional?

In ancient Judaism, parties to a conditional covenant would divide an animal into two halves and walk between the halves. This was a picture of how each party was held accountable for keeping their promises (Jeremiah 34:18-19). When God made His covenant with Abraham in Genesis 15, only God walked between the two halves after Abraham was put to sleep (verses 12, 17). This visually illustrates that God's promises to Abraham in the covenant were unconditional and depended on God alone.

CROSS-REFERENCES
Jesus, the Messianic King

> Authority over everything—Matthew 11:27
> Bless the King—Luke 19:38
> Complete authority—Matthew 28:18
> David's throne established forever—2 Samuel 7:16
> Everlasting kingdom—Daniel 2:44; 7:14; Luke 1:33
> Father installs Son as King—Psalm 2:6
> Government will rest on His shoulders—Isaiah 9:6
> Jesus, King of kings—Revelation 19:16
> Kingship—John 18:37
> Magi worshiped the child King—Matthew 2:1-2, 11
> Everlasting dominion—Daniel 7:13-14

Land Promises to Israel

> Land promised to Abraham and his descendants—Genesis 11:31; 12:7
> Parameters of land promises—Genesis 15:18-21

Promises passed to Isaac's line—Genesis 26:3-4

Promises passed to Jacob's line—Genesis 28:13-14

Promises reaffirmed—Psalm 105:8-11

Land permanently restored to Israel—Deuteronomy 30:5; Isaiah 11:11-12; Jeremiah 23:3-8; Ezekiel 37:21-25; see also Isaiah 60:18, 21; Jeremiah 23:6; 24:5-6; 30:18; 31:31-34; 32:37-40; 33:6-9; Ezekiel 28:25-26; 34:11-12; 36:24-26; 37; 39:28; Hosea 3:4-5; Joel 2:18-29; Amos 9:14-15; Micah 2:12; 4:6-7; Zephaniah 3:19-20; Zechariah 8:7-8; 13:8-9

4

Essential Prophetic Passages You Need to Know

This chapter contains a concise summary of the major prophecies of the Bible. These summaries are introductory. I will discuss these passages in much greater detail throughout the rest of the book. But I wanted to include this chapter early in the book for two reasons:

1. It will familiarize you with the most important prophecy passages in the Bible.

2. It will give you the "big picture" of Bible prophecy before we delve into the finer details.

I recommend that you review this chapter periodically. Doing so will help you to increasingly think *biblically* about prophecy-related issues. The more that these passages are imprinted upon your mind, the stronger your confidence will be in your understanding of the prophetic future.

THE REBIRTH OF ISRAEL—EZEKIEL 37:1-6

The vision of the dry bones shows the Lord putting bones back together into a skeleton. It is then covered with muscles, tendons, and skin. God then breathes life into the body. This metaphorically refers to Israel becoming a nation again (see verse 11). This became a reality in 1948!

END-TIMES DOCTRINAL AND MORAL APOSTASY—1 TIMOTHY 4:1-2; 2 TIMOTHY 4:3-4

The apostle Paul lamented, "The Spirit expressly says that in later times some will depart from the faith by devoting themselves to deceitful spirits and teachings of demons" (1 Timothy 4:1-2). He warned, "The time is coming when people will not endure sound teaching, but having itching ears they will accumulate for themselves teachers to suit their own passions, and will turn away from listening to the truth and wander off into myths" (2 Timothy 4:3-4).

THE RAPTURE—1 THESSALONIANS 1:10; 4:13-18; 5:9

First Thessalonians 1:10 affirms that Jesus "delivers us from the wrath to come," which is the wrathful time of the tribulation. "Deliver" has the literal meaning of "snatch away." The dead will be resurrected, and the living will experience an instant transformation into their glorified bodies. Both groups will be "snatched" from the earth to meet Christ in the air (4:13-18). After all, "God has not destined us for wrath" (5:9).

THE RAPTURE—REVELATION 3:10

Jesus promises in Revelation 3:10, "I will keep you from the hour of trial that is coming on the whole world, to try those who dwell on the earth." This means that Christ will keep us from the time of tribulation.

THE RAPTURE—1 CORINTHIANS 15:50-58

"We shall all be changed, in a moment, in the twinkling of an eye" (verse 51). The rapture will happen instantly. Believers who have died will be resurrected—"the dead will be raised imperishable" (verse 52). Believers still alive will be transformed into glorified bodies—"we shall be changed" (verse 52). Death will thus be defeated (verse 55).

THE RAPTURE—JOHN 14:1-3

Christ pledges to "take you to myself" (John 14:3). This is how He "delivers us from the wrath to come" (1 Thessalonians 1:10) and "will keep you from the hour of trial" (Revelation 3:10). Christ will snatch us from the earth and transport us straight to heaven—the "Father's house."

THE EZEKIEL INVASION—EZEKIEL 38:1-6

The prophet Ezekiel said that in the end times, the Jews would be brought back to the land of Israel from "many nations" (Ezekiel 36–37). Sometime after this, a powerful military leader named Gog would lead Russia and a group of Muslim nations—Iran, Sudan, Turkey, Libya, and other Islamic nations—in an overwhelming military attack on Israel (38:1-6). Their goal will be the complete annihilation of the Jews. God will turn the tables and destroy the invading army (39).

HISTORICAL INSIGHT
God Is the Protector of Israel

1. From Old Testament times to the prophetic future, God is the Protector of Israel.

2. He watches over Israel: "Behold, he who keeps Israel will neither slumber nor sleep" (Psalm 121:4).

3. He promises the Jews that "no weapon that is fashioned against you shall succeed" (Isaiah 54:17).

4. He promised Abraham, "I will bless those who bless you, and him who dishonors you I will curse" (Genesis 12:3).

FREQUENTLY ASKED QUESTION
Is "Gog" another term for the antichrist?

No, it is not. The antichrist will lead a revived Roman Empire (Daniel 2, 7), while Gog will lead an invading force comprising Russia and some Muslim nations (Ezekiel 38:1-6). God will destroy the invading force (Ezekiel 39), ending Gog's brief time in the spotlight. However, the antichrist will remain in power throughout the seven-year tribulation period (Revelation 4–18).

THE EMERGENCE OF A REVIVED ROMAN EMPIRE—DANIEL 2; 7

We read about Nebuchadnezzar's prophetic dream in Daniel 2. This passage depicts the end-times revived Roman Empire as a combination of iron and clay. Daniel, the great dream interpreter, understood this to mean that, just as iron is strong, so too would the Roman Empire of the end times be strong. However, just as iron and clay do not naturally mix, the end-times Roman Empire would have some internal divisions. Complete integration would be missing.

Daniel 7 reveals that this empire would comprise ten nations ruled by ten monarchs. Out of this ten-nation alliance, another monarch—the antichrist—will emerge. He will start small, but he will soon become strong enough to overthrow three of the existing monarchs. Eventually, he will acquire power and authority over the entire revived empire.

THE SEVENTIETH WEEK OF DANIEL (THE TRIBULATION PERIOD)—DANIEL 9:20-27

Daniel 9 shows that the prophetic calendar for Israel is divided into 70 groups of seven years. This totals 490 years. The first 69 seven-year periods (totaling 483 years) ended with the first coming of Jesus the Messiah (Daniel 9:25). The prophetic clock then stopped. There is a gap between these 483 years and the last seven years of the prophetic timeline for Israel. During this interval, several events were predicted to occur:

- The Messiah would be killed.

- Jerusalem and its temple would be destroyed, which occurred in AD 70.

- From then on, the Jews would experience tribulation and distress (Daniel 9:26).

The final "week" of seven years for Israel will begin when the antichrist confirms a seven-year covenant with Israel (Daniel 9:27). The signing of this peace treaty will signal the beginning of the tribulation period.

CHRIST'S OLIVET DISCOURSE (THE TRIBULATION PERIOD)—MATTHEW 24–25

This discourse is known as the Olivet Discourse because Jesus "sat on the Mount of Olives" when He delivered it (Matthew 24:3). The disciples had asked, "Tell us, when will these things be, and what will be the sign of your coming and of the close of the age?" The Olivet Discourse is Jesus' answer to this question.

In the Olivet Discourse, Jesus predicted the destruction of the Jewish temple (Matthew 24:1-2). He then addressed the signs of the end of the age—including the appearance of false christs, wars, earthquakes, famines, the abomination of desolation, cosmic upheavals (verses 4-28), and the sign of

His coming (verses 29-31). Jesus compared the end times to the days of Noah (verses 36-39) and urged His followers who are alive during the tribulation period to prepare for His return (verses 32-35, 45-51; see also 25:1-13, 14-30). Finally, He discussed the judgment of the nations that will occur after His return (verses 31-46).

RELIGIOUS NEW BABYLON DOMINATES THE WORLD—REVELATION 17

Religious New Babylon is portrayed as a "religious prostitute" that will influence the entire world during the first half of the tribulation period (verse 1). This idolatrous and apostate religion will exercise powerful political clout (verses 12-13). It will seem outwardly glorious while being inwardly corrupt (verse 4). It will persecute believers in Jesus around the world (verse 6).

THE RISE OF THE ANTICHRIST—REVELATION 13:1-4

The beast, known as the antichrist, emerges from "the sea." The sea symbolizes the Gentile nations (Revelation 17:15). This suggests that the antichrist will be a Gentile.

The prefix *anti* can mean "instead of," "against," or "opposed to." Therefore, the term *antichrist* can mean "instead of Christ," "opposed to Christ," or "against Christ." Perhaps each of these nuances is appropriate for this diabolical leader.

THE MAN OF LAWLESSNESS (THE ANTICHRIST)—2 THESSALONIANS 2:1-12

The terms "man of lawlessness" (2 Thessalonians 2:3) and "lawless one" (verse 8) indicate that the antichrist will pay no heed to God's laws and commandments. The antichrist "shall do as he wills" (Daniel 11:36), not as God wills.

THE ANTICHRIST—DANIEL 11:36-45

Instead of pursuing God's will, the antichrist will be driven by his own desires. He will also do what Satan desires (2 Thessalonians 2:9). The antichrist, energized by Satan, will seek worship by claiming to be God. He will say many things against the one true God.

THE BLASPHEMY OF THE ANTICHRIST—REVELATION 13:5-10

The antichrist will commit grievous blasphemy against the true and only God. He will relentlessly deify and exalt himself. He is truly "anti-Christ," putting himself in Christ's place. During the tribulation, he will wage war against God's people and persecute them.

THE RISE OF THE FALSE PROPHET—REVELATION 13:11-14

A supreme false prophet will arise as the antichrist's right-hand man and first lieutenant during the tribulation. The antichrist will be a military and political leader, while the false prophet will be a religious leader. He will promote the worship of the antichrist. Those who refuse to comply will be executed.

THE 144,000 JEWISH EVANGELISTS BEGIN MINISTRY EARLY IN THE TRIBULATION—REVELATION 7:1-8

God chose the Jews to be His witnesses. They were tasked with spreading God's good news to all other nations (Isaiah 42:6; 43:10). The Jewish people were tasked with representing God to the Gentile nations of the world. They failed in this endeavor because they did not even recognize Jesus as the divine Messiah. Early in the tribulation, the 144,000 Jews who accept Jesus as the divine Messiah will begin their ministry, and they will finally fulfill this divine mandate.

THE TWO PROPHETIC WITNESSES BEGIN MINISTRY EARLY IN THE TRIBULATION—REVELATION 11:1-6

Early in the tribulation, God will raise up two mighty prophetic witnesses who will bear amazing testimony to the true God. The power of these witnesses is reminiscent of Elijah (1 Kings 17; Malachi 4:5) and Moses (Exodus 7–9). In Bible times, two witnesses were required to confirm a testimony (see Deuteronomy 17:6; 19:15; Matthew 18:16; John 8:17; Hebrews 10:28).

THE FIRST SIX SEAL JUDGMENTS ARE UNLEASHED—REVELATION 6:1-17

Human suffering will steadily increase throughout the tribulation. Early in the tribulation period, the seal judgments will be the first set of judgments to be unleashed on the earth. These include carnage and war, famine, death, economic upheaval, a large (and catastrophic) earthquake, and cosmological disturbances.

THE SEVENTH SEAL JUDGMENT—REVELATION 8:1-6

Christ's opening of the seventh seal inaugurates a whole new series of judgments known as the trumpet judgments. When this seal is broken, heaven is silent for half an hour. The inhabitants of heaven get a sense of what is in store for everyone on earth.

THE FIRST FOUR TRUMPET JUDGMENTS—REVELATION 8:7-13

The seal judgments were terrible enough. The trumpet judgments are even worse. The first trumpet judgment brings blood-infused hail and fire upon the earth. One-third of the earth and trees, as well as all the grass, will be burned. In the second trumpet judgment, something like a flaming mountain is hurled into the sea, killing one-third of all marine life. One-third of the sea becomes blood. The third trumpet judgment results in a giant meteor or asteroid striking the earth, thereby rendering one-third of the world's water unfit for human consumption. The fourth trumpet judgment dramatically reduces the amount of sunlight reaching the earth.

THE FIFTH AND SIXTH TRUMPET JUDGMENTS—REVELATION 9

The fifth trumpet judgment releases demons from the bottomless pit. They inflict excruciating pain on human victims for five months. The sixth trumpet judgment sees the destruction of one-third of humanity by four fallen angels.

THE GREAT MULTITUDE OF BELIEVERS—REVELATION 7:9-17

The tribulation period will see many people become believers in Jesus. Upon witnessing the miraculous departure of millions of Christians from the earth at the rapture, many people will undoubtedly become convinced of the truth of Christianity. (Bibles and Christian literature will be left behind to explain the event.) Numerous conversions will also come through the ministry of the 144,000 Jewish evangelists described in Revelation 7 and 14. Add to this the miraculous ministry of the two witnesses of Revelation 11—prophets whose powers are comparable to those of Moses and Elijah—and it is understandable why "a great multitude that no one could number" will become believers during the tribulation period (Revelation 7:9-17).

THE MESSAGE OF THE LITTLE SCROLL—REVELATION 10

John was told to take the scroll from an angel and "eat" it. The symbolism is profound. John described the scroll as tasting like honey when he ate it. This symbolizes how John found great joy and pleasure in God's Word because it was rich in God's glorious promises. After John ate the scroll, his stomach quickly soured. This symbolizes how sickening it is for unbelievers to understand the doom and gloom that the prophetic Scriptures proclaim for those who reject God.

THE DEATH, RESURRECTION, AND ASCENSION OF THE TWO WITNESSES—REVELATION 11:7-14

At the midpoint of the tribulation period, the antichrist will execute the two prophetic witnesses. The inhabitants of the world will celebrate this in Christmas-like fashion by exchanging gifts (Revelation 11:10). After lying dead in the streets for three-and-a-half days, the prophets are resurrected by God. As the lifeless corpses suddenly rise in full view of live television and internet feeds, the Christmas-like celebrations quickly give way to global terror. The resurrection and ascension of the two witnesses will serve as a resounding exclamation point to their prophecies throughout their three-and-a-half-year ministry.

THE FALL OF RELIGIOUS NEW BABYLON—REVELATION 17

At the midpoint of the tribulation period, the antichrist and the ten kings under his authority will destroy the false world religion, the idolatrous "prostitute" of the end times. The false religious system that flourished during the first half of the tribulation period will be obliterated because the antichrist will now be on the religious center stage. The final global religion will consist solely of worship of the antichrist. No competing religious system will be tolerated.

THE RISE OF COMMERCIAL NEW BABYLON—REVELATION 18

New Babylon will now transition from a religious center to a commercial center. World leaders will be instrumental in making commercial New Babylon a worldwide powerhouse, motivated by the wealth it brings them. New Babylon will also enjoy widespread support from international business leaders because of its unparalleled potential for financial success. Anyone associated with the business of New Babylon will live in luxury. The antichrist, a business wizard influenced by Satan, will rule over the bustling commercial metropolis of New Babylon.

THE OUTBREAK OF WAR IN HEAVEN—REVELATION 12

Still at the midpoint of the tribulation period, war now breaks out in heaven between God's holy angels and the evil angels. Satan and his fallen angels are no match for the angelic legions of God, led by the archangel Michael. Satan once had access to heaven, as described in the book of Job. But that access ends abruptly at this point. Satan is enraged and will now unleash his unrestrained wrath on earth's inhabitants through the antichrist.

THE MARK OF THE BEAST—REVELATION 13:15-18

The false prophet will attempt to force people worldwide to worship the antichrist, the man of sin. He will force them to receive the mark of the beast. Without this mark, no one can buy or sell (Revelation 13:16-17). This "squeeze play" effectively means that people will either worship the antichrist or starve.

THE SEVENTH TRUMPET JUDGMENT—REVELATION 11:15-19

Things continue to unravel during the second half of the tribulation period, going from bad to worst. The seventh trumpet inaugurates the seven bowl judgments toward the end of the tribulation period.

THE BOWL JUDGMENTS—REVELATION 16:1-21

The third and final set of God's judgments is now unleashed upon the world. These are God's final judgments on earth's inhabitants. These judgments include horribly painful sores on humans, more bodies of water turning to blood, the death of all sea creatures, people being scorched by the sun, rivers drying up, total darkness descending upon the land, a catastrophic earthquake, and widespread destruction, among other things (Revelation 16). Such is God's judgment on a world that rejects Christ.

THE FALL OF COMMERCIAL BABYLON—REVELATION 18:1-24

God will cause a military force to attack the headquarters of the antichrist in Babylon. Just as God used the Babylonians to punish Israel in the Old Testament, He now uses a northern alliance to punish Babylon. God shows no mercy to Babylon, just as Babylon showed no mercy in its oppression of Israel. However, the antichrist will not be in the city when the attack occurs. He will be with his armies preparing for his own attack against Jerusalem.

THE CAMPAIGN OF ARMAGEDDON—REVELATION 19:17-21

The campaign of Armageddon begins with the assembling of the antichrist's allies who are bent on eradicating the Jews (Psalm 2:1-6; Joel 3:9-11; Revelation 16:12-16). Jerusalem will be attacked and ravaged (Micah 4:11–5:1; Zechariah 12–14). The forces of the antichrist then move against the Jewish remnant in the wilderness (Jeremiah 49:13-14). The remnant has no hope of survival. But then a wonderful thing happens. These Jews finally believe in Jesus as the Messiah and cry out to Him for deliverance. Christ responds immediately. From Bozrah to Jerusalem, all the antichrist's forces will be decimated at the second coming of Christ (Joel 3:12-13; Zechariah 14:12-15; Revelation 14:19-20). The believing remnant will then be invited into Christ's millennial kingdom.

THE SECOND COMING OF CHRIST—REVELATION 19:11-16

Christ will return as "King of kings and Lord of lords" (verse 16), and "on his head are many diadems" (verse 12). "From his mouth comes a sharp sword with which to strike down the nations" (verse 15)—He will essentially tell the invaders to "drop dead," and the forces of the antichrist will be decimated.

THE JUDGMENT OF THE NATIONS—MATTHEW 25:31-46

Believers and unbelievers from among the Gentile nations are depicted as sheep and goats (Matthew 25:31-46). They will be judged based on how they treated Christ's "brothers" (the 144,000 Jewish witnesses) during the tribulation period. Those found to be believers (the sheep) will be invited into Christ's millennial kingdom. The goats (unbelievers) go on into punishment.

CHRIST'S MILLENNIAL KINGDOM—REVELATION 20:1-6

The devil will be chained in the bottomless pit just before Christ's millennial kingdom begins. This quarantine will effectively remove a powerful destructive and deceptive force from all areas of human life and thought.

The millennial kingdom of Christ will be magnificent. During this time, righteousness will blossom and flourish (Isaiah 11:3-5), peace will spread throughout the world (2:4), and the earth's productivity and fruitfulness will skyrocket (35:1-2).

SATAN'S FINAL REBELLION—REVELATION 20:7-10

Satan will be released from the bottomless pit at the end of Christ's 1,000-year kingdom. He will have one last chance to deceive the nations. God's purpose appears to be to demonstrate once and for all that every human being is desperately evil. Even in the most favorable environment (Christ's kingdom), the fallen human nature is relentlessly inclined toward sin.

The final defeat of Satan will see him thrown into the lake of fire. The antichrist and the false prophet have already been there, suffering for 1,000 years.

THE GREAT WHITE THRONE JUDGMENT—REVELATION 20:11-15

The wicked of all ages will face Christ at the great white throne judgment. They will be resurrected to take part in this judgment (John 5:28-29). Warren Wiersbe explains, "There will be a Judge but no jury, a prosecution but no defense, a sentence but no appeal. No one will be able to defend himself or accuse God of unrighteousness."[1]

THE NEW JERUSALEM AND THE ETERNAL STATE—REVELATION 21–22

You will notice that the Bible begins with paradise, but it is soon lost. The Bible ends with paradise being restored. Fire will destroy the present earth and heavens to make way for the new heavens and earth. Following the cleansing of the present universe, God will construct a new heavens and earth. The remnants of the curse and Satan's extended presence will be completely removed. There will be no more curse, no more bad germs, and no more sickness. No more sorrow, tears, or death. A glorified humanity will inhabit a glorified, re-created earth.

The remaining chapters of this book will provide an in-depth examination of each of these topics.

PART 2

Interpreting Prophecy

IN THIS SECTION

5——A Mini-Survey of 16 Debated Issues—52

6——Why a Literal Approach Is Best—67

7——Fundamentals of Prophecy Interpretation—74

8——The Striking Connection Between Jesus, Paul, and John—80

A Mini-Survey of 16 Debated Issues

There are a variety of Bible prophecy enthusiasts out there. Many hold to different views on major aspects of Bible prophecy. For example:

- There are three views of the millennium: premillennialism, amillennialism, and postmillennialism.
- There are five different views of the rapture: pretribulationism, midtribulationism, posttribulationism, partial rapture, and pre-wrath.
- Some Christians hold to dispensationalism while others hold to covenant theology.

It is not a problem if you are unfamiliar with some (or all) of these terms. I will not bury you in unnecessary details in this book. But I'd like to briefly summarize 16 debates you probably need to know about. My discussion of each debate will necessarily be brief. This chapter is not intended to be a comprehensive analysis of each position. Further clarification of each of these issues will be provided in subsequent chapters of the book. This chapter is basically the "big picture" on the "big debates."

DEBATE 1—THE INTERPRETATION OF PROPHECY

The most important debate concerns the proper method of interpreting Bible prophecy: literal versus allegorical interpretation. A person's position on this issue will affect their entire prophetic viewpoint. Indeed, a person's chosen method of interpretation will determine:

- whether the millennial kingdom of Christ in Revelation 20 is a real future kingdom or Christ's present control of the church from heaven;

- whether the 144,000 Jews are meant to be taken literally or as a metaphor for the church;
- whether the two prophetic witnesses in Revelation 11 are to be taken literally or as a metaphor for the church;
- or whether God's covenant promises are to be taken literally in reference to Israel or figuratively in reference to the church.

Depending on one's chosen method of interpretation, one can come to very different conclusions about Bible prophecy.

The allegorical view is held by many people today. This school of thought interprets the prophetic Scriptures metaphorically. It looks for hidden, symbolic meanings in the biblical text. Such allegorism is fundamental to both amillennialism and postmillennialism.

Others, me included, hold to a literal interpretation of prophecy. The term *literal* comes from the Latin *sensus literalis*, which refers to seeking a plain, straightforward sense of the text.

> "The literal method of interpretation is the method that gives each word the same exact basic meaning it would have in normal, ordinary, customary usage, whether employed in writing, speaking, or thinking."
>
> —J. Dwight Pentecost[1]

Since all the Old Testament prophecies concerning Christ's first coming were fulfilled in a literal manner, we have good reason to expect that the prophecies concerning Christ's second coming will also be fulfilled in a literal manner.

DEBATE 2—THE CHURCH AND ISRAEL

Allegorical interpreters of prophecy see the church as the "new Israel." They believe that all the prophetic promises made to Israel in the Old Testament are fulfilled in the New Testament church.

Literal interpreters of prophecy, on the other hand, make a distinction between the church and Israel. They are seen as two distinct entities in God's prophetic plan.

Two considerations are particularly relevant:

1. The distinction between the church and Israel is evident throughout the New Testament (see 1 Corinthians 10:32). In the book of Acts alone, the word *Israel* is used 20 times, and the word *church* 19 times.

2. Paul told the Jews that God still had a plan for them (Romans 9–11). Paul, a Jew himself, believed that Israel would eventually fulfill God's ancient covenants. So the church *does not* fulfill prophetic promises made to Israel in the Old Testament.

Years of research into Bible prophecy emboldens me to state with confidence:

> In the study of prophecy, Israel is always Israel, and the church is always the church.

DEBATE 3—DISPENSATIONALISM VERSUS COVENANT THEOLOGY

Dispensationalism is a theological framework defined by its emphasis on the following three tenets: (1) a literal interpretation of the Bible, (2) a clear distinction between Israel and the church, and (3) God's glory as the ultimate goal in all things.

Dispensationalism views the world as a household run by God. In this household, God gives people specific responsibilities. God promises blessings to those who obey Him during each respective dispensation. He threatens judgment when people disobey Him. Each dispensation is characterized by the testing of humanity, its failure, and the resulting judgment. Then, as events continue to unfold, God progressively reveals His purpose for human history. (This is known as "progressive revelation.")

Traditional dispensationalism features seven dispensations:

1. the dispensation of innocence (Genesis 1:28–3:6),

2. the dispensation of conscience (Genesis 3:7–8:14),

3. the dispensation of human government (Genesis 8:15–11:9),

4. the dispensation of promise (Genesis 11:10–Exodus 18:27),

5. the dispensation of law (Israel) (Exodus 19–John 14:30),

6. the dispensation of grace (the church) (Acts 2:1–Revelation 19:21),

7. and the dispensation of the kingdom (Revelation 20:1-16).

In contrast to dispensationalism, covenant theology rejects a literal reading of prophecy. The New Testament church, believed to be God's spiritual Israel, supposedly fulfills all the Old Testament promises. Instead of a literal 1,000-year reign of Christ, the millennium is simply a metaphor for the present church age.

Covenant theology takes its name from the so-called covenant of works and the covenant of grace. God supposedly made a covenant of works with Adam, promising him eternal life in exchange for obedience. Adam failed. God then made a second covenant with Adam, the covenant of grace. In it, God promised eternal life to those who believed in Jesus.

Dispensationalists respond that neither the covenant of works nor the covenant of grace is explicitly mentioned in the Bible. They would say covenant theologians are fixated on allegory, and they read the New Testament back into the Old Testament.

DEBATE 4—THE UNITED STATES IN PROPHECY

Many theories have been proposed over the years as to whether the United States is mentioned in Bible prophecy. Some of these theories have been speculative and far-fetched, while others have taken a more reasoned approach.

There are two broad perspectives regarding the United States in Bible prophecy:

1. Some people believe that the United States is only indirectly mentioned in Bible prophecy. Some proponents of this view believe that the US may be one of "the nations" mentioned in prophecy (Haggai 2:6-7; Zechariah 12:3). Others are more specific,

suggesting that the US is the Babylon of Revelation 17–18, the land divided by rivers of Isaiah 18:1-7, or perhaps the land of Tarshish of Ezekiel 38:13.

2. The second major perspective is that the United States is completely absent from Bible prophecy. If this is true, then the question becomes: *Why isn't* the United States mentioned in prophecy? Various explanations have been offered. Some say that the United States will suffer a moral collapse. Others say the US economy will collapse. Still others suggest a possible nuclear or electromagnetic pulse attack. Many Christians wonder if God will punish the United States for its heinous misdeeds. Those who don't think this is a possibility should read what the apostle Paul says in Romans 1:18-28.

FREQUENTLY ASKED QUESTIONS

Is it possible that the United States will turn its back on Israel in the end times, resulting in God's punishment?

Yes, it is. Let's not forget God's promise to Abraham and his descendants in Genesis 12:3: "I will bless those who bless you, and him who dishonors you I will curse." God has never revoked or abrogated this ancient promise. Woe to the United States if it ever turns its back on Israel! God is a promise-keeper!

Is it possible that the rapture of the church could cause the decline of the United States?

Most certainly! Given the high concentration of Christians in this country, it seems reasonable to conclude that the United States will be more adversely affected by the rapture than most other nations.

The rapture will result in the sudden departure of many workers of all kinds from their jobs. Debts and mortgages will not be paid. Numerous college tuitions and student loans will go unpaid. Countless business leaders will no longer be around to run their respective companies. Many law enforcement officials won't be around to keep things in order, leading to more crime. The escalating panic caused by the sudden disappearance of millions of people will likely cause the stock market to drop significantly. This and much more could damage the United States after the rapture.

DEBATE 5—THE EZEKIEL INVASION: PAST OR FUTURE?

Ezekiel 38:1-6 foretells an invasion of Israel by Russia, allied with some Muslim nations, including Iran, Sudan, Turkey, and Libya. The main point of contention among Bible students is whether this invasion has already occurred in the past or will occur in the future.

I believe it is best to view the invasion as still in the future. Among the reasons:

1. Israel has never experienced an invasion of the magnitude described in Ezekiel 38–39. Furthermore, the specific nations mentioned in this passage have never invaded Israel in the past. Because it has not yet happened, its fulfillment must be in the future.

2. Ezekiel said that the events he was predicting would take place "in the latter years" (Ezekiel 38:8) and "in the last days" (38:16). Such phrases point to the end times.

3. Because many of the nations mentioned in Ezekiel 38–39 are geographically distant from one another, an alliance between them may not have made sense in Ezekiel's day. However, today, it's perfectly reasonable considering the majority of the coalition's member nations are Islamic. (Islam did not exist in Ezekiel's day, but rather, emerged in the seventh century AD.) Muslim countries have made no secret of their hatred of Israel.

4. Ezekiel said that the invasion would occur after Israel had been regathered from many countries around the world (Ezekiel 38:8, 12). This never happened during Bible times. Yet, since 1948, when Israel regained its national identity, Jews have immigrated to Israel from all over the world.

DEBATE 6—THE TIMING OF THE RAPTURE

Christians are deeply divided over the timing of the rapture. Sometimes the debate generates more heat than light. There are five main points of view:

1. *Pretribulationism* holds that the rapture will take place before the tribulation period. (This is my view.)

2. *Midtribulationism* holds that the rapture will occur in the middle of the tribulation.

3. *Posttribulationism* holds that the rapture will occur after the tribulation.

4. The *pre-wrath view* says that the rapture will occur near the end of the tribulation, before God's great wrath is unleashed.

5. The *partial-rapture view* says that only faithful and watchful Christians will be raptured. Unfaithful Christians will be left behind to endure the tribulation.

A literal interpretation of prophecy naturally leads to pretribulationism.

DEBATE 7—THE IDENTITY OF BABYLON

Numerous theories have been proposed regarding the identity of Babylon in Revelation 17–18. Following are the major ones:

Rome. Rome was filled with rampant idolatry and persecuted Christians relentlessly. It was a "great city" in that it ruled over multiple geographical territories. (Babylon is called a "great city" in Revelation 17:18 and 18:10.) Rome must therefore be Babylon.

The Roman Catholic Church. Babylon is described as a prostitute in Revelation 17:1. Just as a prostitute is sexually unfaithful, the Roman Catholic Church is said to be unfaithful to the truth of Christianity. Since Roman Catholicism is a perversion of Christianity, the term "Babylon" is appropriate. In addition, the prostitute's clothes (as described in Revelation) look like those of Catholic popes and cardinals.

Apostate Christianity. Similar to how a prostitute is sexually unfaithful, apostate Christianity is unfaithful because it has abandoned the truth of Christianity (Revelation 17:1, 3).

New York City. Babylon and New York City both have sins "piled as high as heaven" (Revelation 18:5), are sources of global immorality (18:2-9), and are incredibly wealthy and dominant economic powers (18:11-20). New York is also a "great city." Given all this, New York City must be Babylon.

Jerusalem. Preterists say that the Old Testament often depicts Israel as a prostitute because of her covenant unfaithfulness to God (Isaiah 1:21; Jeremiah 2:20-24, 30-33; 3:1-3, 8; Ezekiel 16; 23; Hosea 9:9). In light of this, Jerusalem must be Babylon the harlot (Revelation 17:1).

A Literal Revived City of Babylon. Babylon refers to a literal city in Revelation 17–18 for several compelling reasons: (1) All other locations listed in the book of Revelation are literal, including the cities of the seven churches in Revelation 2–3. (2) Throughout the rest of the Bible, Babylon is always referred to as a literal, godless pagan city. This is the case with all the references to Babylon in the Old Testament. Because the book of Revelation draws so heavily from the Old Testament, it is reasonable to assume that the term has the same literal meaning in Revelation as it does in the Old Testament. (This is my view.)

▥ GEOGRAPHY IN THE END TIMES: *New Babylon*

> New Babylon is said to be along the Euphrates River in Revelation 9:14 and 16:12.

> It is unwise to ignore well-known geographical markers.

> This literal geographical marker indicates that New Babylon is a literal city in the end times.

A literal city of Babylon (aka, New Babylon) makes good sense when you think about it. New Babylon will be the epitome of iniquity in the end times, just as Babylon was during Old Testament times. Just as Babylon spread false religion during Old Testament times, New Babylon will do the same in the end times.

The debate continues!

DEBATE 8—THE MILLENNIAL KINGDOM

There are three main schools of thought on the millennial kingdom:

> *Amillennialism* holds that there is no future millennial kingdom on earth. Christ rules only from heaven over the church.

> *Postmillennialism* holds that Christ's second coming will occur after a long period of time—metaphorically called a "thousand years"— during which the church will Christianize the entire world.

> *Premillennialism* holds that Christ will return before the literal millennial kingdom, which will last for 1,000 years on earth.

A literal interpretation of prophecy easily leads to premillennialism (my view).

DEBATE 9—APPROACHES TO THE BOOK OF REVELATION

There are four major approaches to the book of Revelation:

1. The *historicist view* says that the book of Revelation spans church history from the first century to the second coming of Christ.

2. The *idealist view* says that the book of Revelation is a symbol of the ongoing conflict between God and the devil, between good and evil. Revelation has no historical or future significance.

3. The *preterist view* holds that most of the prophecies in Revelation and Christ's Olivet Discourse have already been fulfilled. The prophecies were fulfilled in the year AD 70, when General Titus and his Roman armies invaded Jerusalem and destroyed the Jewish temple. Therefore, the book of Revelation has no relevance for the future.

4. The *futurist view* (my view) says that most of the events in the book of Revelation and Christ's Olivet Discourse will take place in the end times, just before Christ's return. This view respects the book's claim to be prophecy (Revelation 1:3; 22:7, 10, 18-19). We recall that Jesus told John, "I will show you what must take place after this" (Revelation 4:1). The events that take place "after this" relate to future prophecy.

DEBATE 10—THE IDENTITY OF THE RESTRAINER

Prophetic Scripture reveals that the antichrist cannot appear until "he who now restrains" is removed (2 Thessalonians 2:7-8). *Who is the restrainer?*

Rome. Some church fathers believed that the Roman Empire was the restrainer mentioned in 2 Thessalonians 2:7-8. They believed that the restraining power was embodied in the Roman emperor. However, the Roman Empire fell from power in the fifth century AD, and the antichrist has not yet been revealed. This view is therefore disqualified.

Human Government. This view asserts that the enforcement of law by human government restrains lawlessness. A problem with this view is whether the people who make up the human government can stand up to the antichrist, who will be empowered by Satan.

The Holy Spirit. Many theologians (with whom I agree) believe that only God Almighty is capable of restraining both Satan and the antichrist. The restrainer is interpreted to be the Holy Spirit who indwells the church. We recall 1 John 4:4, which states, "He who is in you is greater than he who is in the world." When the church is raptured, the Holy Spirit (or restrainer) will be "taken out of the way."

DEBATE 11—THE ANTICHRIST: JEW, MUSLIM, OR GENTILE?

Some speculate that the antichrist will be a Jew. An ancient tradition held that the antichrist would come from the Jewish tribe of Dan, which had fallen into apostasy and idolatry (Judges 18:30). This view is problematic because the antichrist is shown to be the greatest enemy of the Jews during the tribulation period (Jeremiah 30:7; Matthew 24:15-21; Revelation 12:6, 13-14). One must ask: *Why would a Jew persecute his own people and seek to eradicate them?*

Others claim that the antichrist will be a Muslim. This Muslim will be a political, military, and religious leader who will seek to subjugate the globe and establish an Islamic world order. He will attempt to impose Sharia law and Islam on the entire world. Those who resist will be beheaded. This leader will ruthlessly persecute the Jews and Christians. A major flaw in this view relates to the antichrist's claim to be God. No Muslim who believes in the Qur'an would ever make such a claim. Qur'an-believing Muslims would seek to behead any infidel who claimed equality with Allah.

The strongest biblical evidence suggests that the antichrist will be a Gentile (my view). The antichrist is described in Revelation 13:1 and 17:15 as coming up out of the sea. In the Bible, "sea" refers to the Gentile nations. Daniel 11 also describes Antiochus Epiphanes (a paganized Gentile) as foreshadowing the future Gentile antichrist.

DEBATE 12—THE MARK OF THE BEAST

Some claim that the mark of the beast will be an implanted chip or microchip. However, it seems preferable to distinguish between the mark of the beast and the technology that enables its enforcement.

THE MARK

> ‣ Revelation 14:9 specifies that the mark will be "on" the forehead or "on" the hand.

> ‣ It does not state that the mark will be "in" the forehead or "in" the hand.

> ‣ The mark of the beast could be a barcode tattoo.

It appears that individuals, like animals today and slaves in the past, will be branded in the future. Since the antichrist will claim to be God, receiving the mark of the beast will be a sign of ownership and submission, religious devotion, and "religious orthodoxy" in worshiping the antichrist.

This mark could likely be enforced around the world using cutting-edge technology such as chip implants, scan technology, and biometrics.

DEBATE 13—THE ANTICHRIST'S RESURRECTION

Bible interpreters debate whether the antichrist will actually rise from the dead. Some say it will be a hoax. Others say it will be authentic.

Some prophecy experts say that the antichrist will suffer a head wound that is usually fatal, but in this case, Satan will heal it and allow him to live on. In line with this, the Bible affirms that the antichrist "*seemed* to have a mortal wound" (Revelation 13:3, emphasis added), or "*appeared* to be fatally wounded" (CSB, emphasis added), or "*as if* it had been fatally wounded" (NASB, emphasis added). The antichrist may appear to be slain when in fact he is still alive. Perhaps Satan will heal him with a "Grade-B" miracle, making it appear to the world that he has risen from the dead.

Other prophecy experts believe that the antichrist will receive a fatal head wound, but Satan will resurrect him. One difficulty with this view is that only God has infinite power (omnipotence), while Satan has finite power. God alone can create life (Genesis 1:1, 21; Deuteronomy 32:39); the devil cannot (Exodus 8:19). Only God has the power to raise the dead (John 10:18; Revelation 1:18). Furthermore, this view seems to contradict the biblical affirmation that the antichrist merely "appeared" or "seemed" to have been killed.

In any case, the biblical text reveals that during the tribulation people will *believe* that he has been resurrected. Therefore, he will be worshiped by people all over the world.

DEBATE 14—THE FIRST AND SECOND RESURRECTIONS

According to Revelation 20:5, believers who perish during the tribulation period "came to life" and participated in the "first resurrection." Some argue that because this is called the "first" resurrection, and because it occurs after the tribulation period, a resurrection cannot have occurred seven years earlier, before the tribulation period, in conjunction with a pretribulational rapture. This would seem to support posttribulationism.

Both pretribs and posttribs agree that Revelation 20:4-6 says that a resurrection will take place after the tribulation, before the beginning of the millennial kingdom. Moreover, they both agree that this will be a part of the "first resurrection." But pretribs also say that not all Christians will be resurrected at the same time. The rapture occurs before the tribulation period, and dead believers—from the day of Pentecost up until the day of the rapture—will be raised from the dead at that time (1 Thessalonians 4:13-17). Then, after the seven years of tribulation are over, those who became believers during the tribulation and died will be resurrected (Revelation 20:4-6). Both of these resurrections are a part of "the first resurrection."

Allow me to clarify. Posttribulationists interpret the phrase "first resurrection" in a strictly chronological sense. In contrast, pretribulationists interpret the phrase "first resurrection" as a *type* of resurrection. Scripture identifies two different types of resurrection. The first resurrection is appropriately referred to as the "first resurrection" (Revelation 20:5), as well as the "resurrection of life" (John 5:29), the "resurrection of the just" (Luke 14:14), and the "better resurrection" (Hebrews 11:35). The "second resurrection" is the final resurrection (Revelation 20:5; see also verses 6, 11-15), also known as the resurrection of condemnation (John 5:29; Daniel 12:2; Acts 15). In short, the first resurrection is the resurrection of believers, while the second is the resurrection of unbelievers.

To clarify further, the term "first resurrection" refers to all the resurrections of the righteous (see John 5:29; Luke 14:14), even though they are separated in time. One resurrection of the righteous occurs at the rapture before the tribulation (1 Thessalonians 4:13-17), another occurs during the tribulation (the two witnesses—Revelation 11:3, 11), and another occurs after the tribulation. They all are "first" in the sense of being a part of the resurrection of believers. Accordingly, the term "first resurrection" applies to all the resurrections of the saints regardless of when they occur, including the resurrection of Christ Himself—the "firstfruits" (see 1 Corinthians 15:23).

The "second" or last resurrection will be a terrifying event to behold. After Christ's millennial kingdom, all the lost people in history will be raised from the dead, judged at the great white throne judgment, and then cast into the lake of fire (Revelation 20:11-15).

DEBATE 15—THE JUDGMENTS

Some people combine the many end-time judgments into one big judgment. For example, some believe that the judgment of the nations in Matthew 25:31-46 is identical to the great white throne judgment in Revelation 20:11-13. A comparison of these judgments makes this view untenable:

> *Different time.* The judgment of the nations takes place at Christ's second coming (Matthew 25:31), while the great white throne judgment follows Christ's millennial kingdom (Revelation 20:11-12).

> *Different scene.* While the judgment of the nations takes place on the earth (Matthew 25:31), the great white throne judgment takes place far from the earth (Revelation 20:11).

> *Different subjects.* Three groups of people are mentioned at the judgment of the nations: the sheep, the goats, and the brothers (Matthew 25:32, 40). The unredeemed of all ages will be judged at the great white throne (Revelation 20:12).

> *Different basis.* The basis of judgment at the judgment of the nations is how people treated Christ's "brothers" (Matthew 25:40); the basis of judgment at the great white throne is a person's works (Revelation 20:12).

> *Different result.* The judgment of nations has two results: the righteous are granted entry into Christ's millennial kingdom, while the unrighteous are punished. The great white throne judgment has only one outcome: the wicked dead are cast into the lake of fire. The righteous are not even mentioned.

> We also notice that no resurrection is mentioned in connection with the judgment of the nations. However, the wicked are resurrected as a prelude to their judgment before the great white throne (Revelation 20:13).

A plain reading of the biblical text makes it clear that these judgments are not the same.

DEBATE 16—HELL

Most Christians believe that wicked unbelievers will suffer eternally in the lake of fire. Others reject the idea of endless torment and adhere to the doctrine of annihilationism. This theory holds that the wicked are completely destroyed and have no conscious existence after death.

Annihilationism is contrary to Scripture. In Matthew 25:46, Jesus said that the unsaved would go into eternal punishment, but the righteous would go into eternal life. There is no way that Jesus' punishment could be some form of nonsuffering extinction of consciousness. If there is no real suffering, then there is no punishment. Punishment requires suffering. And suffering necessarily requires consciousness.

One can exist without being punished, but one cannot be punished without existing. Annihilation refers to the eradication of existence and everything associated with it, including punishment. Punishment is avoided rather than encountered through annihilation.

ETERNAL PUNISHMENT

> Jesus said that the punishment of the wicked is "eternal" (Matthew 25:46).

> The literal translation of the adjective *aionion* in this verse is "everlasting, without end."

> In Romans 16:26, Hebrews 9:14, 13:8, and Revelation 4:9, the same adjective describes God (the "eternal" God).

> The punishment of the wicked is just as eternal as our eternal God.

Notice that there are no levels of extinction or annihilation. Either one is annihilated, or one is not. Whether you are Hitler or a non-Christian moralist, you will be equally annihilated. The Bible, on the other hand, teaches that there will be varying degrees of conscious punishment in hell (see Matthew 10:15; 11:21-24; 16:27; Luke 12:47-48; Hebrews 10:29; Revelation 20:11-15). The various degrees of punishment are proportional to one's degree of depravity. Therefore, such punishment is completely just.

Diversity and Unity

Despite our many disagreements about some aspects of Bible prophecy, there are nevertheless some core prophetic beliefs that can unite us.

UNITY ON CORE PROPHETIC BELIEFS

Christ is going to come back.

When Christ comes again, He will overthrow all evil.

We will all receive incredible resurrected/glorified bodies.

We are all accountable to God and will face judgment for how we lived on earth.

Christians will live face to face with God forever.

Christians will experience no more sin, suffering, Satan, or death in the afterlife.

6

Why a Literal Approach Is Best

We noted in the previous chapter that some Christians believe Bible prophecy should be interpreted allegorically. Others believe it should be interpreted literally. This has been a point of contention since the earliest days of Christianity.

An allegorical school of interpretation originated in Alexandria, Egypt, around AD 190, which is 150 years after the time of Christ. This school consistently applied a nonliteral interpretation of Scripture. Symbolic meanings of Bible verses became the norm.

The allegorical approach became immensely popular. The literal approach faded into obscurity. Unfortunately, the early adoption of the allegorical method profoundly affected subsequent generations.

HISTORICAL INSIGHT
The Influence of Augustine

> Augustine lived from AD 354–430. He was the bishop of Hippo Regius in Numidia, Roman North Africa.

> Augustine interpreted most of the Bible in a literal and natural way. However, his interpretation of prophecy was inconsistent.

> He was convinced of the literal return of Christ. He also believed in a literal heaven and a literal hell.

> However, he concluded that the millennial kingdom was not literal. Using an allegorical method, he proposed that the church was already in the millennium as part of God's spiritual kingdom. He claimed that Christ is presently ruling over the hearts of Christians. He denied that Christ would ever rule a literal kingdom on earth.

> The Roman Catholic Church adopted Augustine's perspective as its own.

> Several well-known luminaries of the Reformation, including Martin Luther and John Calvin, also embraced his viewpoint.

> Because such well-known theologians in church history adopted the allegorical method of interpreting millennial prophecies, many today hold to the same position.

> The allegorical method is now being used to interpret other areas of Bible prophecy, not just the millennium.

The Wisdom of a Literal Approach

Unlike the allegorical method, the literal approach to interpreting Bible prophecy takes the standard, common understanding of each word in Scripture. The meaning of words in the Bible is like that found in everyday communication. It is the basic or plain way of interpreting a passage. Bible scholar David Cooper helps us to understand the literal method:

"Take every word at its primary, ordinary, usual, literal meaning, unless the facts of the immediate context, studied in the light of related passages and [self-evident] and fundamental truths, indicate clearly otherwise."

—David Cooper[1]

The Bible itself demonstrates that a literal interpretation of God's Word was the accepted norm. I am referring to how later biblical texts take earlier biblical texts literally.

Later Bible Texts Take Earlier Texts as Literal

> Exodus 20:10-11 takes the creation events in Genesis 1–2 literally.

> Matthew 19:6 and 1 Timothy 2:13 take the creation account of Adam and Eve literally.

> Romans 5:12-14 takes the fall of Adam and his consequent death literally.

> Matthew 24:38 takes Noah's flood literally.

> Matthew 12:40-42 takes the account of Jonah in the big fish literally.

> First Corinthians 10:2-4 takes the account of Moses literally.

> *Hence—The literal approach to interpreting Scripture is demonstrated within the biblical text itself.*

Further confirmation of the literal method is found in the Old Testament messianic prophecies of Christ's first coming. More than 100 prophecies of the Messiah in the Old Testament found *literal fulfillment* with the first coming of Christ. I addressed some of these prophesies previously in the book (Genesis 3:15; 4:25; 9:26; 12:3; 49:10; Psalms 2; 16; Jeremiah 23:5-6; Isaiah 7:14; 40:3; 53; Daniel 9:24-25; Micah 5:2; Zechariah 9:9; 12:10). Here are some more examples:

TOPIC	OT PROPHECY	JESUS FULFILLS
Escape into Egypt	Hosea 11:1	Matthew 2:14
Called "Immanuel"	Isaiah 7:14	Matthew 1:23
Miracles	Isaiah 35:5-6	Matthew 9:35
Sold for 30 shekels	Zechariah 11:12	Matthew 26:15
Forsaken	Zechariah 13:7	Mark 14:50
Silent	Isaiah 53:7	Matthew 27:12-19
Hands/feet pierced	Psalm 22:16	John 20:25
Crucified	Isaiah 53:12	Matthew 27:38
No bones broken	Psalm 22:17	John 19:33-36
Suffered thirst	Psalm 69:21	John 19:28
Vinegar offered	Psalm 69:21	Matthew 27:34
Scourging/death	Isaiah 53:5	John 19:1, 18
His "forsaken" cry	Psalm 22:1	Matthew 27:46
Ascension	Psalm 68:18	Luke 24:50-53
Right hand of God	Psalm 110:1	Hebrews 1:3

Since every one of these messianic prophecies has been fulfilled to the letter, we can rest assured that the same will be true of the prophecies concerning the second coming and the events leading up to it.

The Precedent Has Been Set

"In the interpretation of unfulfilled prophecy, fulfilled prophecy forms the pattern...The logical way to discover how God will fulfill prophecy in the future is to discover how He fulfilled it in the past. If the hundreds of prophecies concerning Christ's first coming were fulfilled literally, how can anyone reject the literal fulfillment of the numerous prophecies concerning His second coming and reign on the earth?"

—Charles C. Ryrie[2]

The Angel Gabriel's Prophetic Words About the First and Second Comings—Literally Fulfilled

"Take the words of Gabriel in the first chapter of Luke where he foretells of the birth of Christ. In keeping with the angel's words, Mary literally conceived in her womb; literally brought forth a son; His name was literally called Jesus; He was literally great; and He was literally called the Son of the Highest. Will it not be as literally fulfilled that [as Gabriel told Mary] God will yet give to Christ the throne of His father David, that He will reign over the house of Jacob forever, and that of His glorious kingdom there shall be no end?"

—Charles Feinberg[3]

Five Reasons for Adopting a Literal Method of Interpretation

1. A literal interpretation is the conventional method of understanding the meaning of all languages.

2. The vast majority of the Bible makes perfect sense when interpreted literally.

3. A literal approach allows for metaphorical or symbolic interpretations when the context requires it. This is often the case in apocalyptic literature such as Daniel and Revelation.

4. The literal method is the only reliable check on the subjective human imagination.

5. The literal method is the only approach consistent with the idea that the very words of Scripture are "God-breathed" or inspired (2 Timothy 3:16). A symbolic approach to interpreting all Scripture undermines the idea that all Scripture originates from God.

YOU MAY BE INTERESTED TO KNOW...
An Allegorist's Concession

> Even advocates of the allegorical approach admit that a literal approach to the study of Bible prophecy leads to the conclusion that the Bible teaches a literal 1,000-year reign of Christ on earth.

> Amillennialist Floyd Hamilton affirms, "We must frankly admit that a literal interpretation of the Old Testament prophecies gives us just such a picture of an earthly reign of the Messiah as the premillennialist pictures."[4]

FREQUENTLY ASKED QUESTIONS
How can the literal approach to Bible prophecy be correct when the book of Revelation has so many symbols?

The book of Revelation does indeed have many symbols. But every symbol points to something literal.

Typically, symbols in the book of Revelation are defined in the book itself:

- The "seven stars" in Christ's right hand represent "the angels of the seven churches" (Revelation 1:20).
- The "seven gold lampstands" represent "the seven churches" (1:20).
- The "golden bowls full of incense" represent "the prayers of the saints" (5:8).
- "The waters" represent "peoples and multitudes and nations and languages" (17:15).

Every symbol represents something literal. Insights into other symbols can be found either in Revelation or other parts of the Bible—particularly the Old Testament. J. Dwight Pentecost, author of the modern classic *Things to Come*, once said that if you have six months to study the book of Revelation, spend at least the first month studying the Old Testament. Many of the symbols of Revelation are found there.

How can the literal approach to Bible prophecy be correct when Jesus often used nonliteral parables to communicate prophetic truth?

A parable is a story-based teaching tool. Jesus often used parabolic stories to illustrate spiritual truths. Word images help people better understand spiritual teachings.

There is always a literal truth being communicated in parables. For example, the parable of the weeds illustrates the literal fact that a false counter-sowing will duplicate the sowing of the gospel seed (Matthew 13:24-30). The parable of the mustard seed illustrates the literal truth that God's spiritual kingdom had a tiny beginning, much like a mustard seed. But by the time of the second coming, it will have spread all over the world (Matthew 13:31-32).

YOU MAY BE INTERESTED TO KNOW...
References to Parables and Allegories Support a Literal Approach

> The Bible specifically identifies parables (Matthew 13:3) and allegories (Galatians 4:24) within the biblical text.

> By doing so, the Bible shows that the ordinary meaning is literal.

📖 LEXICAL NUGGET: *"Rightly handling"*

> Second Timothy 2:15 says that we should handle the word of truth rightly.

> The phrase "rightly handling," in the Greek, means "cutting straight."

> The Greek term pictures a tentmaker who makes straight cuts rather than wavy cuts in his material.

> It describes a builder who lays bricks in straight rows.

> It describes a farmer plowing a straight furrow.

> We can best meet the requirements of 2 Timothy 2:15 by using the literal method of interpretation.

> The allegorical method, by contrast, zigzags subjectively around the interpretive canvas of the Bible.

Wisest Approach: Use the literal method to interpret prophecy correctly.

7

Fundamentals of Prophecy Interpretation

I f you want to interpret Bible prophecy successfully, it is essential that you follow the rules of interpretation. Otherwise, you may fall prey to unbalanced ideas about Bible prophecy. Seven principles have served me well over the years:

1. When the Plain Sense Makes Good Sense, Seek No Other Sense, Lest You End Up in Nonsense.

"Unless the text indicates clearly that it should be taken symbolically, the passage should be understood literally."

—Arnold Fruchtenbaum[1]

When God created Adam, He endowed Adam (and all subsequent human beings) with intelligible speech. This enabled Adam to communicate objectively with his Creator and with other human beings (Genesis 1:26; 11:1, 7). God used human language as a means of direct communication, often through the "Thus saith the Lord" pronouncements of the prophets (for example, Isaiah 7:7; 10:24; 22:15; 28:16; 30:15; 49:22; 51:22; 52:4).

If God created language so that He could speak to people and so that people could speak to each other, then it stands to reason that God would most often use language in its ordinary and plain sense and that people would do the same. Without this approach, no one could be sure what was being communicated. This leads me to say that when the simple, literal understanding of Scripture makes good sense, there's no need to look for another meaning.

A good example relates to the land promises made to Israel in the Abrahamic covenant (Genesis 12:1-3; 15:18-21; 17:21; 35:10-12). The plain meaning of these verses makes perfect sense. There is no good reason to suppose that the church replaces Israel and that the promises made to Israel will find some kind of allegorical or spiritual fulfillment in the church.

2. It Is Wise to Submit All Personal Theological Preunderstandings to Scripture.

A preunderstanding is a previously formed doctrinal opinion—perhaps based on a book, a sermon, or a radio broadcast.

Of course, all interpreters are influenced to some degree by personal, theological, denominational, and political biases. None of us approaches Scripture in a "chemically pure" way. Therefore, care must be taken to ensure that preconceived notions are compatible with the written Word and subject to its correction. Only preunderstandings that are compatible with Scripture are valid. We must not allow our preconceptions to interfere with the proper interpretation of Scripture.

An illustration might be the widespread belief that the tribulation period will commence immediately following the rapture. Many Christians seem to approach the prophetic Scriptures with this preunderstanding. The problem is that there isn't a single Bible verse that says the tribulation period begins immediately after the rapture. As Daniel 9:27 demonstrates, the tribulation period begins when the antichrist signs a covenant with Israel. Furthermore, there will likely be a window of time between the rapture and the tribulation period that will allow for other prophecies to be fulfilled in the meantime. It is possible that the Ezekiel invasion of Israel will occur during this time.

3. It Is Wise to Carefully Consider the Context of Each Bible Prophecy.

Each word in the Bible is part of a sentence.

Each sentence is part of a paragraph.

Each paragraph is part of a book.

Each book is part of the whole of Scripture.

A prophecy must not be read in a way that contradicts the overall teaching of the Bible. Individual verses and prophecies are not isolated fragments, but rather, components of a larger whole. Therefore, the interpretation of these verses must be in harmony with the whole of Scripture. *Scripture interprets Scripture.*

> *"The entire Holy Scripture is the context and guide for understanding the particular passages of Scripture."*
>
> —Bernard Ramm[2]

Jesus' prophecy in Matthew 24:34 illustrates the importance of context: "Truly I say to you, this generation will not pass away until all these things take place." Did Jesus mean that all end-time predictions had to be fulfilled in the first century, as modern preterists believe? No, I don't think so. The context of Matthew 24 indicates that Christ was saying that those who witnessed the signs mentioned earlier in Matthew 24 would still be alive when the remaining end-time prophecies were fulfilled. These signs include the abomination of desolation (verse 15), the great tribulation like no other (verse 21), and the sign of the Son of Man in heaven (verse 30). Because the tribulation lasts seven years (Daniel 9:27; Revelation 11:2), Jesus would be saying that the "generation" alive at the beginning of the tribulation would still be alive at its end. Context clarifies everything.

4. It Is Important to Consider Genre When Interpreting Individual Bible Verses and Prophecies.

The Bible has many literary genres, each with its own unique characteristics that must be recognized in order to properly understand the text. Incorrect identification of genre will lead one far astray in the interpretation of Bible prophecy.

A SAMPLING OF BIBLICAL GENRES	
Historical	Acts
Dramatic epic	Job
Poetry	Psalms
Wise sayings	Proverbs
Apocalyptic writings	Daniel, Revelation

We can illustrate the importance of genre by looking at biblical poetry. The Psalms refer to God as a Rock (Psalm 18:2; 19:14). The genre of psalms is characterized by a high degree of symbolism. Therefore, the reference to God as a rock should not be taken literally, but as a symbol of God's sturdiness: God is our rock-solid foundation.

Despite the wide range of literary genres in the Bible, the biblical authors most often employed literal statements to express their ideas. And wherever they used literal statements to express their thoughts, the Bible student must take a literal approach to explain them. A literal interpretation of Scripture means that every word in the text has the same basic meaning as it would have in regular, usual, common usage, whether written or spoken.

5. The Skilled Interpreter Is Guided by History and Culture.

We must strive to transcend the limitations of our Western mindset and embrace an ancient Jewish mindset, paying particular attention to Jewish marriage rites, burial rites, family practices, agricultural practices, business practices, the monetary system, methods of warfare, slavery, the treatment of captives, the use of covenants, and religious practices. This wealth of historical data makes it easier to interpret the Bible accurately as we gain a deeper understanding of the world of the biblical writers.

HISTORICAL INSIGHT
The Importance of History Is Illustrated by "the Little Horn"

> A study of Jewish history can help us better understand the biblical reference to the antichrist as the "little horn" in Daniel 8:9.

> The ancient Jews understood that the horn of an animal was used as a weapon by that animal (Genesis 22:13; Psalm 69:31).

> Consequently, the horn came to be seen as a sign of power and strength.

> As an extension of this symbol, horns were sometimes used in biblical times as an emblem of dominion, denoting kingdoms and kings, as in the books of Daniel and Revelation (see Daniel 7–8; Revelation 12:13; 13:1, 11; 17:3-16).

> We conclude that since the antichrist is a "little horn," he will start out small in terms of local dominion, but eventually become large in terms of global dominion (Revelation 13).

"When we claim biblical authority for an idea, we must be prepared to show from the grammar, the history, the culture, and the context that the writer in fact taught that idea. Otherwise, the Bible is not used but abused."

—Gordon Lewis[3]

6. Whenever You Read Prophecy, It Is A Good Idea to Pay Attention to the "Law of Double Reference."

FAST FACTS ON THE LAW OF DOUBLE REFERENCE

- A single passage of prophetic Scripture may refer to two prophetic events that are separated by a significant period of time.
- In that passage, the separate events are blended into one picture, obscuring the intervening period.
- While the gap in time is not perceived within this text, the gap becomes apparent when other prophetic verses are consulted.

The law of double reference could be illustrated by telling someone on a Monday morning, "Next Sunday, our pastor will talk about the roles of husbands and wives in marriage." This might be taken to mean that the pastor will address all of this in a sermon on Sunday morning. But in fact, he will discuss the role of husbands in marriage during the morning service and the role of wives during the evening service. Therefore, the statement contains a double reference. Although the time difference is not apparent in the original statement, the schedule in the church bulletin clarifies the matter.

We can illustrate this law from the Bible by reading Zechariah 9:9-10: "Rejoice greatly, O daughter of Zion! Shout aloud, O daughter of Jerusalem! Behold, your king is coming to you; righteous and having salvation is he, humble and mounted on a donkey, on a colt, the foal of a donkey...He shall speak peace to the nations; his rule shall be from sea to sea." This verse speaks of both Christ's first coming ("mounted on a donkey") and His second coming, which will issue in His universal millennial reign ("his rule shall be from sea to sea").

7. It Is Wise to Keep Jesus in Mind When Interpreting Bible Prophecy.

After all, the central theme of Bible prophecy is Jesus. The Bible is a Jesus book from beginning to end—from Genesis to Revelation. Jesus once said to some Jews, "You search the Scriptures because you think they give you eternal life. But the Scriptures point to me! Yet you refuse to come to me to receive this life" (John 5:39-40 NLT).

Luke 24 tells us that after His resurrection, Jesus appeared to two disciples on the road to Emmaus. He told them things about Himself from the writings of Moses and all the prophets (Luke 24:27). Jesus claimed that the Scriptures were "written about me" (Luke 24:44; see also Hebrews 10:7). *Jesus is truly the heart and center of the Scriptures.*

This means that the interpreter of Bible prophecy must always look for Jesus in the text. Our interpretation of prophetic Scripture ought to be *Christocentric*—centered on Christ.

CHRIST IN PROPHECY
The Christocentric Nature of Bible Prophecy

Jesus is constructing a new dwelling place for us in heaven, the New Jerusalem.	John 14:1-3; Revelation 21
Jesus will retrieve us at the rapture.	1 Thessalonians 4:13-17
Jesus will preside over the judgment of Christians in heaven.	2 Corinthians 5:10
Jesus will unleash judgments upon the earth during the tribulation period.	Revelation 6
Jesus will return at the second coming.	Revelation 19:11-21
Jesus will be the judge of all the nations.	Matthew 25:31-46
Jesus will reign during His millennial kingdom.	Revelation 20:2-5
Jesus will preside over the judgment of the wicked.	Revelation 20:11-15

Applying the seven interpretive principles outlined in this chapter will facilitate a more efficient and effective exploration of the prophetic Scriptures. ***Guaranteed!***

The Striking Connection Between Jesus, Paul, and John

The apostle John, the apostle Paul, the ancient prophets, and Jesus all agree on matters of Bible prophecy. This gives us great confidence in the accuracy of prophecy.

Parallels Between John's Revelation and Jesus' Olivet Discourse

There is a good reason that Jesus and the apostle John agreed prophetically. Revelation was written by John. In Revelation 1:1-2, we read, "This is a revelation from Jesus Christ, which God gave him to show his servants the events that must soon take place. He sent an angel to present this revelation to his servant John, who faithfully reported everything he saw" (NLT).

▨ LEXICAL NUGGET: *"From" or "About"*

> The phrase "revelation *from* Jesus Christ" (Revelation 1:1 NLT) can also be translated "revelation *about* Jesus Christ."

> Both senses are probably intended in this verse.

> The book of Revelation contains prophetic truths that are *from* Jesus and also *about* Jesus.

Notice that God the Father gave this revelation to Jesus Christ (Revelation 1:1). We might say that the *source* of prophetic revelation is the Father while the *revealer* of prophetic revelation is the Son. This reminds us of John 12:49, where Jesus affirmed, "I have not spoken on my own authority, but the Father who sent me has himself given me a commandment—what to say and what to speak."

Because this revelation "from Jesus Christ" was given to John, we would expect the book of Revelation to be in complete agreement with Jesus' teachings on prophecy in the Olivet Discourse (Matthew 24–25). And indeed, that is exactly what we find!

For example, Jesus warned against the appearance of false christs during the tribulation period: "See that no one leads you astray. For many will come in my name, saying, 'I am the Christ,' and they will lead many astray" (Matthew 24:4-5; see also 2 Corinthians 11:4). Christ's warning against false christs in the Olivet Discourse seems to be analogous to what we learn about the first seal judgment, where John foretells the coming of the antichrist—the ultimate false christ (Revelation 6:1-2).

In the Olivet Discourse, Jesus also prophesied, "You will hear of wars and rumors of wars. See that you are not alarmed, for this must take place, but the end is not yet. For nation will rise against nation, and kingdom against kingdom" (Matthew 24:6-7). This is similar to the second seal judgment in the book of Revelation, where peace is removed from the earth and people slaughter each other (Revelation 6:3-4).

In the Olivet Discourse, Jesus further prophesied, "There will be famines and earthquakes in various places" (Matthew 24:7). Jesus' prophecy of famine is analogous to the third seal judgment in Revelation where we read of rampant inflation. This will be a time of economic ruin. The purchasing power of money will be greatly diminished. The cost of food will increase exponentially. People will need an entire day's pay to buy a few meals. Famine will be the inevitable result (Revelation 6:5-6).

There is an important observation we can make here: Those who refuse to receive the mark of the beast will not be able to buy or sell, so they will have less to eat than everyone else (Revelation 13:16-17). Christians will go hungry during the tribulation because they will be economic outcasts.

Just as Jesus prophesied earthquakes in the Olivet Discourse (Matthew 24:7), so John, in Revelation 6:12 says, "There was a great earthquake. The sun became as dark as black cloth, and the moon became as red as blood" (NLT). The great earthquake will apparently cause a massive amount of dust to saturate the atmosphere, blocking out sunlight and turning the moon red.

Jesus predicted in the Olivet Discourse that Christians would be persecuted, imprisoned, and killed (Matthew 24:9). Also, countless unbelievers throughout the world will perish. This is consistent with the book of Revelation, where we read of widespread death (Revelation 6:7-8). The death predicted here seems to be a result of the three previous judgments: the appearance of the antichrist, war, and famine. The death toll will be catastrophic, representing a quarter of the world's population.

A comparison of Matthew 24 with Revelation 6 shows that these terrible events occur during the first half of the tribulation period.

Comparing the Olivet Discourse and the Seal Judgments

OLIVET DISCOURSE (MATTHEW 24)	SEVEN SEAL JUDGMENTS (REVELATION 6)
the rise of false christs (verses 4-5)	first seal: the rise of the antichrist (verses 1-2)
wars and rumors of wars (verse 6)	second seal: peace is taken from the earth (verses 3-4)
famines (verse 7)	third seal: escalation of food costs, famine (verses 5-6)
earthquakes (verse 7)	sixth seal: a great earthquake (verses 12-14)

Parallels Between Jesus and Paul

Jesus' teachings on the rapture are strikingly similar to those of the apostle Paul. One can see such parallels by comparing the prophetic words of Jesus in John 14:1-3 with the prophetic words of Paul in 1 Thessalonians 4:13-18:

> ➤ John 14:3 describes Jesus as coming to the earth ("I will come"), which clearly involves a descent from heaven. In 1 Thessalonians 4:16, Paul said that Christ "will descend from heaven."

> ➤ In John 14:3, Jesus told believers: "I...will take you to myself." Paul revealed in 1 Thessalonians 4:17 that believers will be "caught up" to meet Christ in the air.

> ➤ In John 14:3, Jesus revealed that believers will be with Him ("where I am you may be also"). In 1 Thessalonians 4:17, Paul affirmed that believers "will always be with the Lord."

> ➤ In John 14:1, Jesus revealed the purpose of His revelation about the rapture: "Let not your hearts be troubled." Likewise, in 1 Thessalonians 4:13, 18, Paul revealed the purpose of his revelation about the rapture: "that you may not grieve as others do" and "encourage one another with these words."

It is not surprising that the teachings of Jesus and Paul share some common ground. After all, Jesus said that Paul was "a chosen instrument of mine" who would bring the Lord's message to both Gentiles and Jews (Acts 9:15). We surmise that Paul's words about the rapture were part of Christ's message. Paul was only a messenger—an "instrument"—for Christ.

YOU MAY BE INTERESTED TO KNOW...
Paul Was Consistent in His Prophetic Teachings
The apostle Paul was perfectly consistent when he spoke of the rapture of the church:

1 THESSALONIANS 4:16-18	1 THESSALONIANS 5:10-11
the dead in Christ	those who are "asleep"
we who are alive	those who are "awake"
Encourage one another with these words	Encourage one another and build one another up

Agreement with the Old Testament Prophets
The apostle Peter spoke of the prophets and their words about salvation through Christ: "This salvation was something even the prophets wanted to know more about when they prophesied about this gracious salvation prepared for you. They wondered what time or situation the Spirit of Christ within them was talking about when he told them in advance about Christ's suffering and his great glory afterward" (1 Peter 1:10-11 NLT).

📖 LEXICAL NUGGET: *"Spirit of Christ"*

> ➤ Scholars have debated the meaning of the phrase "Spirit of Christ."
> ➤ Grammatically, the phrase may refer to Christ Himself (as the spirit *of* Christ), or it could refer to the Holy Spirit (as the Spirit *from* Christ).
> ➤ In either case, the form of the word is the same in the original Greek text.[1]

A number of scholars have concluded that it was indeed Christ's prophetic spirit that was at work in the prophets.[2] Based on this verse, Clement of Alexandria suggested that Jesus was "the Prophet of prophets, and Lord of all the prophetical spirit."[3]

> "Christ's revealing work covers a wide span of time and forms. He first functioned in a revelatory fashion even before his incarnation. As the Logos, he is the light which has enlightened everyone coming into the world; thus, in a sense all truth has come from and through him (John 1:9). There are indications that Christ himself was at work in the revelations which came through the prophets who bore a message about him...(1 Peter 1:11). Although not personally incarnate, Christ was already making the truth known."
>
> —Millard Erickson[4]

> In 1 Peter 1:11, "the deity and the pre-existence of Christ are involved: Christ's Spirit testified in advance about Christ's sufferings and glories, that is, when as the incarnate Logos he would suffer in his humiliation and after that be crowned with glories in his exaltation."
>
> —R.C.H. Lenski[5]

I am convinced that this view is correct. However, an additional consideration is worth mentioning. Even if the term is rendered "Spirit *from* Christ," referring to the Holy Spirit, we must acknowledge that the Holy Spirit was carrying out Christ's will in the prophets by providing prophetic truth on Christ's behalf. In John 16:14, Jesus affirmed of the Holy Spirit, "He will glorify me, for he will take what is mine and declare it to you."

> The ancient prophets and Jesus, as well as John and Paul, are in prophetic agreement because Christ is the ultimate source of all prophetic revelation.

CROSS-REFERENCES
The Prophets Spoke for God

Controlled by Holy Spirit—Luke 1:67; Acts 1:16; 11:28; 28:25; 2 Peter 1:21

Messengers of the Lord—Isaiah 44:26

Spoke in the name of the Lord—2 Chronicles 33:18; Ezekiel 3:11; James 5:10

Jesus—Prophet, Priest, and King

As the divine Messiah, Jesus fulfilled the primary functions of Prophet, Priest, and King when He came to earth. As a Prophet, Jesus delivered major discourses, including the Upper Room Discourse (John 14–16), the Olivet Discourse (Matthew 24–25), and the Sermon on the Mount (Matthew 5–7). He also often prophetically addressed the kingdom of God.

As a Prophet, Jesus is omniscient, unlike human prophets who were merely God's messengers. He knows the future as fully as He knows the past. Anyone who spent any time with Jesus soon surmised that He knew everything there was to know. The apostle John said of Jesus, "He knew all people and needed no one to bear witness about man, for he himself knew what was in man" (John 2:24-25). Jesus' disciples said, "Now we know that you know all things" (16:30). After His resurrection from the dead, when Jesus asked Peter for the third time if he loved Him, Peter responded, "Lord, you know everything" (21:17).

Thomas Schultz provides a great overview of the scriptural support for Christ's omniscience:

First, He knows the inward thoughts and memories of man, an ability peculiar to God (1 Kings 8:39; Jeremiah 17:9-16). He saw the evil in the hearts of the scribes (Matthew 9:4); He knew beforehand those who would reject Him (John 6:64) and those who would follow Him (John 10:14). He could read the hearts of every man and woman (Mark 2:8; John 1:48; 2:24-25; 4:16-19; Acts 1:24; 1 Corinthians 4:5; Revelation 2:18-23). A mere human can no more than make an intelligent guess as to what is in the hearts and minds of others.

Second, Christ has knowledge of other facts beyond the possible comprehension of any man. He knew just where the fish were in the water (Luke 5:4, 6; John 21:6-11), and He knew just which fish contained the coin in its mouth (Matthew 17:27). He knew future events (John 11:11; 18:4), details that would be encountered (Matthew 21:2-4), and He knew that Lazarus had died (John 11:14).

Third, He possessed an inner knowledge of the Godhead showing the closest possible communion with God as well as perfect knowledge. He knows the Father as the Father knows Him (Matthew 11:27; John 7:29; 8:55; 10:15; 17:25).

The fourth and consummating teaching of Scripture along this line is that Christ knows all things (John 16:30; 21:17), and that in Him are hidden all the treasures of wisdom and knowledge (Colossians 2:3).

—Thomas Schultz[6]

Jesus, as omniscient deity, has complete knowledge of the future. He knows what He's talking about. And since He spoke through the ancient prophets, through John, through Paul, and others, the prophetic revelations of the future are consistent and are reliable.

You can count on it!

PART 3

Israel and the Church

IN THIS SECTION

9—Distinguishing Israel and the Church—88

10—Clarifying Misunderstood Verses About Israel and the Church—97

9

Distinguishing Israel and the Church

In this chapter and the next, we will look at what Scripture says about the people of God—both Israel and the church.

🔎 UNDERSTANDING OUR TERMS: *Israel*

The Jewish patriarch Jacob was given the name Israel at Peniel because he wrestled with God (Genesis 32:28). "Israel" literally means "one who wrestles with God." The name came to represent Jacob's descendants, the Jews. His descendants were called Israelites (Joshua 3:17; 7:25; Judges 8:27; Jeremiah 3:21) and the house of Israel (Exodus 16:31; 40:38). The term came to represent the Jewish homeland.

🔎 UNDERSTANDING OUR TERMS: *The Church*

The church was founded on the day of Pentecost, unlike Israel, which dates to Old Testament times. The universal church is the ever-expanding body of born-again believers throughout the world, who constitute the body of Christ and over whom Jesus rules as Lord. Local churches are distinct from this universal church. There is only one universal church, but members of the universal church worship in countless local churches scattered throughout the world.

📖 GEOGRAPHY IN THE END TIMES: *Israel and Jerusalem*

> Israel is only 8,000 square miles.
> It is tiny compared to the 5,000,000 square miles of hostile Arab real estate that surrounds it.

> The city name *Jerusalem* literally means "City of Peace" in Hebrew.

> But peace has been elusive in Jerusalem in modern times.

> Jerusalem has been a sore spot in the world, just as Scripture prophesied would be the case in the end times (Zechariah 12:2).

> The stage is being set for the antichrist's covenant with Israel (Daniel 9:27).

> There will be no true and lasting peace until Christ returns and establishes His millennial kingdom (Revelation 20:1-3; see also Isaiah 25:7-8; 30:26; 51:11-16; 52:1-12; 65:17-19; Ezekiel 36:24-38; 37:1-28; Hosea 2:16-17, 19-23; Zechariah 8:1-17; 9:11-17; Romans 11:25-27; Ephesians 3:11-13).

YOU MAY BE INTERESTED TO KNOW...

There Are Notable Similarities Between Israel and the Church:

> Israel and the church are both a part of God's people.

> Both are part of God's spiritual kingdom.

> They both enjoy the spiritual benefits of the Abrahamic and new covenants.

Despite their shared core similarities, Israel and the church are also different.

HISTORICAL INSIGHT

The New Testament Distinguishes the Church from Israel

> First Corinthians 10:32 instructs us to "give no offense to Jews or to Greeks or to the church of God." This verse clearly distinguishes between Jews and the church.

> The book of Acts distinguishes between Israel and the church—mentioning Israel 20 times, and the church 19 times.

> The term *Israel* appears 73 times in the New Testament, each time referring to ethnic Israel, as distinct from the church.

> These factors show that the church was not seen as the new Israel or spiritual Israel during New Testament times.

> *These biblical facts are important because they refute the position of "replacement theologians" who say that the church "replaces" Israel— that is, the church is the new Israel or spiritual Israel.*

Scriptural Indicators that the Church Is Distinct from Israel

The church was established on the day of Pentecost, not in Old Testament times	Acts 1:5; 1 Corinthians 12:13
Israel is made up of Jews, while the church is made up of redeemed Jews and Gentiles	Ephesians 2:15
Israel is an earthly political entity; the universal church is the invisible spiritual body of Christ	Exodus 19:5-6; Ephesians 1:3
National Israel will be restored before Christ returns	Romans 11:1-2, 29
One becomes a Jew by birth; one becomes a member of the church by spiritual birth	John 3:3
The land and throne promises in the Abrahamic and Davidic covenants will be fulfilled in Israel, not the church	Genesis 13:1-7; 2 Samuel 7:12ff

The New Testament depicts the church as a new entity:

1. The resurrection of Jesus Christ is the foundation of the church. This indicates that the church could not have existed before the resurrection of Jesus (Ephesians 1:19-20).

2. Jesus said in Matthew 16:18 that He "will" build His church (future tense). When Jesus made this statement, the church did not yet exist.

3. The church is described as a "mystery" that was first revealed in the New Testament, not in the Old Testament (Ephesians 3:3-5, 9; Colossians 1:26-27).

4. The church is metaphorically referred to as a "new man" in Ephesians 2:15.

5. Every believer in the church age is baptized into the body of Christ (1 Corinthians 12:13). Since this happened for the first time on

the day of Pentecost, the church age must have begun on that day (Acts 2; see also 11:15-16).

In light of these theological considerations, it is evident that the church was established on the day of Pentecost. We have been living in the church age ever since.

The present church age will continue until the church is raptured prior to the tribulation period. Following the resurrection of the dead in Christ, all living believers will be transformed into their glorified bodies (1 Thessalonians 4:13-17; 1 Corinthians 15:50-58). The two groups make up the universal church, and they will meet Christ in the air. When this happens, the church age will be over.

CROSS-REFERENCES

Israel

Abraham's countless descendants—Genesis 15:5
Israelites were fruitful and multiplied—Genesis 47:27
The Shema, a Jewish confession of faith—Deuteronomy 6:4
God has not rejected Israel—Romans 11:1-36
Paul's love for Israel—Romans 9:1-33
Israel and the Ezekiel invasion—Ezekiel 38:1–39:29
Israel in tribulation—Matthew 24:14-42
144,000 Jewish witnesses—Revelation 7:1-8
Jerusalem, a cup of staggering—Zechariah 12:1-14
Distinct from the church—1 Corinthians 10:32
God still has a plan for the Jews—Romans 9–11
God redeems Israel—Psalm 25:22
Redeemer of Israel—Isaiah 49:7
Mosaic covenant—Exodus 19:3-6
New covenant—Jeremiah 31:31-34
Palestinian covenant—Deuteronomy 30
Abrahamic covenant—Genesis 12:3
Davidic covenant—2 Samuel 7:5-17

The Church

A "new man"—Ephesians 2:15
Equality in the church—Galatians 3:26-28

The body of Christ—Colossians 1:18
The bride of Christ—Revelation 21:2
Will reign with Christ—Revelation 20:4, 6
God's temple—1 Corinthians 3:16
Jesus builds it—Matthew 16:18
Jesus purchased it—Acts 20:28
God's household—Ephesians 2:19-20; 1 Timothy 3:14-15
One body, many members—Romans 12:4-5; 1 Corinthians 12:12
A spiritual house—1 Peter 2:4-5

FREQUENTLY ASKED QUESTION

It is one thing to say that Israel and the church are distinct. But what about the local church and the universal church? Are they distinct as well?

"Distinct" may not be the best word. They are *different*. Here's why:

LOCAL CHURCH	UNIVERSAL CHURCH
Membership can include both saved and lost people.	Membership includes only saved people.
Includes only living people.	Includes living and dead believers in Christ, from Pentecost to the rapture.
Local churches are scattered throughout the world.	There is only one universal church.
Local churches are categorized into many different denominations.	The universal church is not denominational. All who trust in Christ for salvation are members, regardless of denominational affiliation.
Includes only part of the body of Christ (living believers).	Includes the entire body of Christ (dead and living members).
Local churches operate under different forms of church government—including congregational, presbyterian, and episcopal.	Christ alone is the head of the universal church.

The universal church is made up of people from all walks of life. They differ in age, sex, race, wealth, social status, and ability, but they are all *one people* (Galatians 3:28). All believers share the *same Spirit* and serve the *same Lord* (Ephesians 4:3-6). The body of Christ is made up entirely of believers in Christ. The only requirement for membership in this universal body is faith in Christ (Acts 16:31; Ephesians 2:8).

📖 LEXICAL NUGGET: *Church*

The English word *church* derives from the Greek term *ekklesia*. This Greek word, in turn, derives from two smaller words. The first is *ek*, which means "out of" or "from among." The second is *klesia*, which means "to call." Combining the two words, *ekklesia* means "to call out from among." The universal church is made up of Jews and Gentiles whom God has called from the world. God has summoned individuals from diverse backgrounds. All are welcome in Christ's church.

We are blessed to be living during the church age.

🕑 UNDERSTANDING OUR TERMS: *The Church Age*

The church age extends from the day of Pentecost (Acts 2) to the day of the rapture (1 Thessalonians 4:13-18).

YOU MAY BE INTERESTED TO KNOW...
The Ages Are Distinct

> There was an Old Testament AGE OF THE LAW before the church age. That dispensation was distinguished by God's provision of the law to Israel to govern all aspects of its existence.

> The millennial kingdom—or KINGDOM AGE—will follow the church age. Christ will reign on the throne of David for a thousand years. The church will reign with Christ as His bride.

CROSS-REFERENCES
The Church Age

Yet future from Jesus' perspective—Matthew 16:18
Inaugurated after Jesus' resurrection—Ephesians 1:20-22
Inaugurated after Jesus' ascension—Ephesians 4:7-12
Began on the day of Pentecost—Acts 2; 11:15-16
Closes at the rapture—1 Corinthians 15:50-58; 1 Thessalonians 4:13-17

CHRIST IN PROPHECY
Christ and the Church

> Christ is building the church (Mathew 16:18).

> Christ will rapture the church from the earth at the end of the church age (1 Thessalonians 4:13-17).

> Christ promised: "If I go and prepare a place for you, I will come again and will take you to myself, that where I am you may be also" (John 14:3).

Meanwhile: The Church Is Called to Holiness

Church members are called to live righteous, holy lives (2 Peter 3:11) and avoid contamination from the world (verse 14).

> *"It is right for the Church to be in the world; it is wrong for the world to be in the Church. A boat in water is good; that is what boats are for. However, water inside the boat causes it to sink."*
>
> —Harold Lindsell[1]

Lindsell makes a good point. The Bible warns, "All that is in the world—the desires of the flesh and the desires of the eyes and pride of life—is not from the Father but is from the world" (1 John 2:16). Such things can be a malignancy for the church. The church cannot fulfill its mission if it resembles the world.

> *"The church's service and mission in the world is absolutely dependent on its being different from the world, being* in *the world but not* of *the world."*
>
> —Jim Wallis[2]

Believers who comprise the church are not to be "of the world" (John 17:16). Scripture warns that "friendship with the world is enmity with God," and "whoever wishes to be a friend of the world makes himself an enemy of God" (James 4:4).

God's Purpose for the Church

God has a specific purpose for the church in this age. Members of the church are called to:

- be Christ's witnesses (Luke 24:45-49; Acts 1:7-8),
- build up the body of Christ (Ephesians 4:11-13),
- do good to all people (Galatians 6:10; Titus 3:14),
- exercise spiritual gifts (Romans 12:6-8),
- financially support God's work (1 Corinthians 16:1-3),
- help brothers and sisters in need (1 John 3:16-18),
- love one another (Hebrews 13:1-3, 16),
- extend hospitality to one another (1 Peter 4:9-11),
- make disciples of all nations (Matthew 28:19-20),
- and preach the Word of God (Mark 16:15-16; 1 Timothy 4:6, 13).

Many local churches may fall short in one or more of these tasks. Nevertheless, this is God's mandate for the church.

The Church in Prophecy

The prophetic Scriptures tell us a lot about the future of the church. Here's a brief summary:

The church will be raptured before the tribulation period.	1 Thessalonians 4:13-17
The tribulation will unfold on the earth while the church is in heaven.	Revelation 6–18
Members of the church will face the judgment seat of Christ in heaven.	2 Corinthians 5:10
The church, as the bride of Christ, will become married to Christ and participate in the marriage supper of the Lamb.	Revelation 19:7

Members of the church will reign with Christ.	2 Timothy 2:12; Revelation 20:6
The church will reside in the New Jerusalem for all eternity.	Revelation 21; see also John 14:1-3

Prophecies like these should motivate Christians to live in righteousness as they await the arrival of the Messiah at the rapture. The church is destined for glory.

FREQUENTLY ASKED QUESTION
Is church attendance required?

The New Testament encourages Christians to attend church regularly. Hebrews 10:25 instructs us explicitly not to forsake gathering together. The Christian life is to be lived in the context of God's family, not in isolation (Acts 2; Ephesians 3:14-15). In addition, attending church equips us for ministry (Ephesians 4:12-16). The Bible does not approve of "lone ranger" Christians. An old proverb says: *Many logs together burn brightly, whereas solitary embers die out* (see Ephesians 2:19; 1 Thessalonians 5:10-11; and 1 Peter 3:8). It is in our own best interest to attend church.

Clarifying Misunderstood Verses About Israel and the Church

t is essential to "rightly divide" Israel and the church. Failure to do so will lead to significant errors in the interpretation of prophecy. God has made prophetic promises to both Israel *and* the church. As noted in the previous chapter, advocates of "replacement theology" say that the church is a continuation of Old Testament Israel. They say the church is the "new Israel" or "spiritual Israel." They contend that Israel's sin and failure caused God to replace national Israel with the church. Thus, the Old Testament promises made to Israel have been transferred to the church. The church is now the "people of God" instead of Israel.

Four scriptures are thought to support this: Galatians 3:29, 6:16, Philippians 3:3, and Joshua 21:43-45. We will now focus our attention on these.

Galatians 3:29—Abraham's Offspring

Replacement theologians believe that Galatians 3:29 supports the idea that the church has replaced Israel. This verse states, "If you are Christ's, then you are Abraham's offspring, heirs according to the promise." Since church members are "Abraham's offspring," it follows that the church must be the new Israel.

Several biblical factors argue against this interpretation. We begin with the interpretive principle, "Scripture interprets Scripture." This principle says that if we interpret one part of Scripture in a way that contradicts another part of Scripture, we have erred. The claim that Galatians 3:29 proves that the church is the new Israel is unfounded because the same apostle Paul who wrote this verse also wrote Romans 9–11, in which he asserted that God still has a prophetic purpose for ethnic Israel outside of the church. At the end of the tribulation period, a remnant of Israel will exercise faith in Jesus, the

Jewish Messiah. The remnant will be invited into Christ's millennial kingdom. In view of this, it is implausible to claim that the church is the "new Israel."

So what does Galatians 3:29 mean? It simply means that Christians, when they believe in Jesus, become spiritual descendants of Abraham and beneficiaries of some of God's promises to him. We are Abraham's "spiritual children" because we have followed his pattern of faith. Like Abraham, we are *justified by faith*. Once justified by faith, believers benefit from some of God's promises to Abraham.

> *"God promised some things to all the physical descendants of Abraham (e.g., Gen. 12:1-3,7). He promised other things to the believers within that group (e.g., Rom. 9:6,8). He promised still other things to the spiritual seed of Abraham who are not Jews (e.g., Gal. 3:6-9). Failure to distinguish these groups and the promises given to each has resulted in much confusion."*
>
> —Thomas Constable[1]

There is one more observation we can make here. Notice that our text says, "If you are Christ's, then you are Abraham's offspring" (Galatians 3:29). The Amplified Bible translates this, "If you belong to Christ [if you are in Him], then you are Abraham's descendants."

The *NIV Application Commentary* tells us why this is important:

> *"Since the Galatian believers are 'in Christ' and since Christ is the Seed of Abraham (v. 19), then it follows that the Galatian believers are also Abraham's seed. And if they are Abraham's seed, then they also inherit Abraham's promise."*
>
> —Scot McKnight[2]

In light of this, it is clear that Galatians 3:29 does not teach that the church is the new Israel. Rather, the church enjoys some of the spiritual benefits of the Abrahamic covenant. Pure and simple!

Philippians 3:3—The Circumcision

Another verse often cited to support the idea that the church is the new Israel is Philippians 3:3. In this verse, believers are referred to as "the circumcision," a Jewish term.

HISTORICAL INSIGHT
Circumcision Was a Sign of the Covenant

> - *Circumcision* literally means a "cutting around."
> - The Jewish ritual of circumcision in the Old Testament involved removing the foreskin of the male organ with a pointed knife or stone (Exodus 4:25; Joshua 5:2).
> - It was a symbol of the covenant that God made with Abraham (Genesis 15).

In Philippians 3:3, Paul was not referring to physical circumcision as practiced by the Jews, but rather to the circumcision of the heart that occurs when a person places his faith in Christ for salvation.

> *"Paul states that we (true believers) are the circumcision—not those born of Jewish parents or who have been literally circumcised, but those who realize that the flesh profits nothing, that man can do nothing in his own strength to win God's smile of approval."*
>
> —William MacDonald[3]

> *"Writing to Gentiles, Paul clarified that he and they were the true circumcision. This was because they had no confidence in the flesh and instead worshiped by the Spirit of God and gloried in Christ Jesus alone."*
>
> —Robert P. Lightner[4]

> *"The true circumcision are not those who want to inflict pain. The truly spiritual man is one who worships God in the spirit, rejoices in Christ Jesus, and has no confidence in the flesh. True circumcision is not a mark on the flesh; it is a mark in the heart."*
>
> —Jon Courson[5]

Therefore, Philippians 3:3 does not teach that the church is the new Israel.

Galatians 6:16—The Israel of God

Another verse often cited to support the idea that the church is the new Israel or spiritual Israel is Galatians 6:16. Paul speaks of believers in Christ as "the Israel of God."

Contrary to the replacement view, Paul is referring to individual Jews who have put their faith in Jesus for salvation. This is in contrast to Jews who seek salvation through obedience to the law. Paul, a Jew who came to faith in Christ on the road to Damascus, is a perfect example of "the Israel of God." He placed his hope for salvation in Christ alone.

> The fact that some Jews have put their faith in Jesus does not invalidate God's promises to national Israel.

> Remember that more than 70 times in the New Testament, the word "Israel" refers to physical Jews.

> Galatians 6:16 does not indicate that the phrase should be interpreted otherwise.

> Paul consistently distinguished between the church and Israel (see Romans 9–11; 1 Corinthians 10:32).

> Therefore, Galatians 6:16 does not support the idea that the church is the new Israel. Rather it speaks of ethnic Jews who have trusted in Jesus for salvation.

YOU MAY BE INTERESTED TO KNOW...
Saved Jews Become Members of the Church

• Some Bible students are curious about the relationship between saved Jews and the church.

• A Jew who professes faith in Christ during the present church age is incorporated into the body of Christ and is considered a member of the church (see Romans 10:12-13; Galatians 3:28).

• However, God still has prophetic plans for ethnic Israel in the future (Romans 9–11).

"For all his demoting of the law and the customs, Paul held good hope of the ultimate blessing of Israel."

—F.F. Bruce[6]

Joshua 21:43-45—God's Promises to Israel Have Been Fulfilled

Replacement theologians often cite Joshua 21:43-45 as proof that the church replaces Israel, since all of God's promises to Israel have been fulfilled in the past:

> Thus the LORD gave to Israel all the land that he swore to give to their fathers. And they took possession of it, and they settled there. And the LORD gave them rest on every side just as he had sworn to their fathers. Not one of all their enemies had withstood them, for the LORD had given all their enemies into their hands. Not one word of all the good promises that the LORD had made to the house of Israel had failed; all came to pass.

On the basis of this passage, proponents of replacement theology claim that all of God's land promises to Israel have been fulfilled. After all, the text affirms that "not one word of all the good promises that the LORD had made to the house of Israel had failed; all came to pass." The modern state of Israel, it is claimed, has no biblical basis. In fact, the existence of Israel is not seen as a fulfillment of Bible prophecy because all the land promises had already been fulfilled in the past.

Several pertinent factors argue against this interpretation of Joshua 21:43-45. God gave the Jews the Promised Land, but the Jews failed to take full advantage of what God had given them. Even though the land was a divine gift, the Canaanites were not completely removed. The land was there for the taking. But the Jews had failed to fully "receive" God's gift by conquering and entering the *entire* land.

> "There were still enemies within the land; not all the Canaanites had been destroyed. But that was not God's fault; He fulfilled His promise by defeating every foe against which the Israelites fought. If there were still undefeated foes and pockets of resistance, it was because Israel did not claim God's promise."
>
> —William MacDonald[7]

Numerous prophecies written long after the time of Joshua predict Israel's future possession of the land in fulfillment of God's covenant with Abraham. This refutes the claim that there are no other land promises to be fulfilled for

Israel. (For example, see Isaiah 60:18, 21; Jeremiah 23:6; 24:5-6; 30:18; 31:31-34; 32:37-40; 33:6-9; Ezekiel 28:25-26; 34:11-12; 36:24-26; 37; 39:28; Hosea 3:4-5; Joel 2:18-29; Amos 9:14-15; Micah 2:12; 4:6-7; Zephaniah 3:19-20; Zechariah 8:7-8; and 13:8-9.) This makes it impossible for God's land promises to Abraham to have been wholly fulfilled in Joshua 21:43-45.

Furthermore, it is obvious that although they possessed some of the land in Joshua's day, they were later *dispossessed*. But the Abrahamic covenant (Genesis 17:8) stipulates that Israel would keep the land *forever*. This alone renders untenable the replacement interpretation of Joshua 21:43-45. This permanent possession of the land will not occur until the future 1,000-year millennial kingdom of Christ.

Conclusion

In the previous chapter, we considered numerous affirmative evidences for the distinction between the church and Israel. The present chapter shows that the four primary verses used by replacement theologians in support of the idea that the church is the new Israel have been misconstrued. A "right dividing" of these verses (2 Timothy 2:15) preserves the distinction between the church and Israel.

PART 4

God's Purpose for the Present Age

IN THIS SECTION

11—The Course of the Present Age—104

12—The Remarkable Rebirth of Israel—112

The Course of the Present Age

Christ gives us insight into the characteristics that will dominate the present age. He does this through His instructive prophetic parables found in Matthew 13.

> ### 📖 LEXICAL NUGGET: *Parable*
>
> The word *parable* means "a placing alongside of" for the purpose of comparison.

YOU MAY BE INTERESTED TO KNOW...
Parables Are a Great Teaching Tool

> - Jesus often used real-life examples—such as a woman who lost a coin, a shepherd watching his flock, and a vineyard laborer—to illustrate spiritual truths.
> - Comparing these stories to spiritual truths enhances our understanding of those truths.

A number of Jesus' parables reveal prophetic truths about the nature of the kingdom from the time of Christ to the end of the age. This shows that Christ's prophetic foresight encompasses all of human history, not just the distant end times.

FREQUENTLY ASKED QUESTION
When Jesus taught parables, why did He say to His followers: "To you it has been given to know the secrets of

the kingdom of heaven, but to them it has not been given"
(Matthew 13:10-11)?

Examining the context enables us to understand why Jesus taught in this manner. In Matthew 13, Jesus is depicted as addressing a diverse group of believers and unbelievers. He did not separate them and teach only the believers. Instead, He structured His teaching so that only believers would understand what He was saying. He did this by using parables.

In Matthew 13:11, the phrase "secrets of the kingdom of heaven" carries the meaning of "mysteries of the kingdom of heaven." The term *mystery*, as used in the Bible, refers to a truth that cannot be discovered by human investigation alone, but rather requires special revelation from God. The term refers to a truth that was unknown to the people of Old Testament times but has since been revealed by God (Matthew 13:17; Colossians 1:26). Thus, Jesus communicates previously unrevealed information about the kingdom of heaven through His parables (Matthew 13).

Hardened unbelievers who had rejected Jesus' previous teachings were unable to understand these parables. Jesus was apparently following a command He had given earlier in the Sermon on the Mount: "Do not give dogs what is holy, and do not throw your pearls before pigs, lest they trample them underfoot and turn to attack you" (Matthew 7:6). In other words, do not share these sacred truths with those who, because of their open and sometimes violent hostility to God, will treat them with contempt and disdain.

It is also possible that there is a component of grace in Christ's actions. Perhaps He did not want to burden unbelievers with additional responsibility by imparting new truths for which they would be held accountable at the final judgment.

FAST FACTS ON HOW PARABLES COMMUNICATE LITERAL TRUTH

- Jesus often used parables that were not meant to be taken literally.
- However, the story in each parable conveys a literal truth.
- That Jesus wanted His parables to be understood by those who were open to them is demonstrated by the care with which He explained two of them to His disciples: the parable of the sower (Matthew 13:3-9, 18-23) and the parable of the weeds (verses 24-30, 36-43).

- His intention was not only to provide clarity as to their correct meaning, but also to instruct believers in the proper method of interpreting the remaining parables.
- Jesus' choice not to interpret His subsequent parables indicates that He fully expected believers to grasp the literal truths He intended by the method He demonstrated.

HISTORICAL INSIGHT
The Jewish Rejection of Christ in the First Century

> Christ found it necessary to address the characteristics of the present age because of the rejection He experienced from the Jews.

> As the Jewish Messiah, He offered the kingdom to the Jewish people (Matthew 11–12).

> The Jewish leaders not only rejected Jesus, but they also said that He performed miracles by the power of Satan (Matthew 12:22-32).

> This marked a decisive turning away from Christ, the Jewish Messiah. As a result, Israel has experienced judicial blindness and hardening as a divine judgment (Romans 11:25).

> God's kingdom program was thereby altered.

> Specifically, the offered kingdom was postponed until the 1,000-year millennial kingdom following Christ's second coming.

> In light of this delay, Jesus informed His disciples what the present age would be like until His second coming, after which He would establish His millennial kingdom.

> These insights were provided in the parables of Matthew 13.

The Parable of the Wheat and Weeds

Jesus spoke these words in Matthew 13:24-30:

> The kingdom of heaven may be compared to a man who sowed good seed in his field, but while his men were sleeping, his enemy came and sowed weeds among the wheat and went away. So when the plants came up and bore grain, then the weeds

appeared also. And the servants of the master of the house came and said to him, "Master, did you not sow good seed in your field? How then does it have weeds?" He said to them, "An enemy has done this." So the servants said to him, "Then do you want us to go and gather them?" But he said, "No, lest in gathering the weeds you root up the wheat along with them. Let both grow together until the harvest, and at harvest time I will tell the reapers, 'Gather the weeds first and bind them in bundles to be burned, but gather the wheat into my barn.'"

Jesus later explained the meaning of this parable to His disciples:

The one who sows the good seed is the Son of Man. The field is the world, and the good seed is the sons of the kingdom. The weeds are the sons of the evil one, and the enemy who sowed them is the devil. The harvest is the end of the age, and the reapers are angels. Just as the weeds are gathered and burned with fire, so will it be at the end of the age. The Son of Man will send his angels, and they will gather out of his kingdom all causes of sin and all law-breakers, and throw them into the fiery furnace. In that place there will be weeping and gnashing of teeth. Then the righteous will shine like the sun in the kingdom of their Father. He who has ears, let him hear (Matthew 24:37-43).

This parable teaches that good and evil, true and false believers, will coexist and intermingle in the world until the final judgment. They will then be separated at the end of the age.

The Parable of the Mustard Seed

Jesus stated in Matthew 13:31-32: "The kingdom of heaven is like a grain of mustard seed that a man took and sowed in his field. It is the smallest of all seeds, but when it has grown, it is larger than all the garden plants and becomes a tree, so that the birds of the air come and make nests in its branches."

This parable reveals that the onset of the kingdom of heaven will be almost imperceptible. The kingdom was indeed modest at the time of Christ and His disciples. But just as a tiny mustard seed can grow into a large plant that can reach more than fifteen feet in height, the kingdom would begin very small but grow very large. By the time of Christ's second coming, the kingdom would cover the whole world.

The Parable of the Leaven

According to Matthew 13:33, Jesus said, "The kingdom of heaven is like leaven that a woman took and hid in three measures of flour, till it was all leavened." There are different views of what Jesus was saying here. Some people think Jesus was predicting evil because leaven, or yeast, is often used in the Bible to represent evil (Matthew 16:12; Mark 8:15; Luke 12:1; 1 Corinthians 5:6-8; Galatians 5:9). Perhaps He is referring to the large number of people who claim to be Christians but lack true faith.

Others suggest it would be wrong to assume that because leaven represents evil in other verses that it must represent evil in Matthew 13. It may be that leaven is used here in a positive sense to represent the dynamic expansion of the kingdom of God as a result of the penetrating power of the gospel of Christ and the supernatural work of the Holy Spirit.

To elaborate on this meaning, we know that when leaven is added to baking flour, a steady, continuous, and irreversible process begins. Considering this, the present parable may be intended to teach that the combination of the gospel of Christ and the supernatural power of the Holy Spirit will result in a continuous and unstoppable process of kingdom expansion.

Both views are plausible.

The Parables of the Hidden Treasure and the Pearl

Jesus spoke two parables in Matthew 13:44-46:

> The kingdom of heaven is like treasure hidden in a field, which a man found and covered up. Then in his joy he goes and sells all that he has and buys that field.

> Again, the kingdom of heaven is like a merchant in search of fine pearls, who, on finding one pearl of great value, went and sold all that he had and bought it.

Both of these parables emphasize the immense value of the kingdom of heaven. Those who recognize its value will do everything in their power to acquire it. They will allow nothing to stand between them and their goal.

To be clear, these parables do not imply that one can buy entrance into the kingdom of heaven with material wealth. Such a conclusion would violate the intent of the parables. In context, the parables simply emphasize the inestimable value of the kingdom and the willingness to sacrifice everything to obtain it.

The Parable of the Fishing Net

Jesus stated in Matthew 13:47-50:

> Again, the kingdom of heaven is like a net that was thrown into the sea and gathered fish of every kind. When it was full, men drew it ashore and sat down and sorted the good into containers but threw away the bad. So it will be at the end of the age. The angels will come out and separate the evil from the righteous and throw them into the fiery furnace. In that place there will be weeping and gnashing of teeth.

Jesus teaches here that true and false (professing) Christians will coexist in the kingdom until His second coming. The righteous will be separated from the unrighteous at the end of the age. The righteous, or true believers, will be invited into Christ's millennial kingdom, while the unrighteous, or false believers, will be excluded from the kingdom and sent to a place of punishment.

Fishermen can attest that when a net is pulled out of the water, it contains a variety of fish, some of which are desirable and worth keeping while others are completely worthless. The fishermen sort the fish, keeping only the desirable specimens and discarding the rest. At the end of the age, Christ will separate the good from the evil, the true Christians from the false Christians, the righteous from the unrighteous.

Continued Opportunities for Repentance and Conversion

We can make some other observations about the course of the present age that are not related to the parables of Christ. For example, Christians sometimes wonder why Christ hasn't returned yet. There is a good reason for this. Second Peter 3:9 instructs, "The Lord is not slow to fulfill his promise as some count slowness, but is patient toward you, not wishing that any should perish, but that all should reach repentance." God is patient and provides ample time for people to repent.

This is consistent with God's long-standing pattern of being very patient before bringing people to judgment (see Joel 2:13, Luke 15:20; Romans 9:9). It is not surprising, therefore, that He continues to show such patience in this present age.

Sadly, even though God is patient and does not want anyone to perish

(2 Peter 3:9), many people will refuse to turn to God. This means that they will be separated from Him for eternity (Matthew 25:46).

Although God desires all human beings to be saved (1 Timothy 2:4), not all will receive God's gift of salvation (Matthew 7:13-14). They choose to remain rebels against God. This is one reason why so many terrible judgments will fall on the unbelieving world during the tribulation period (Revelation 6–18). However, even then, the gospel of the kingdom will be preached and many will turn to God during this time (Revelation 7:9-17).

The Mission of the Church

Meanwhile, the church has a specific mission that God has assigned to it in the present church age. Members of the church are called to be witnesses for Christ (Luke 24:45-49; Acts 1:7-8), to build up the body of Christ (Ephesians 4:11-13), and to do good to all people (Galatians 6:10; Titus 3:14). In addition, they are to use their individual spiritual gifts for the benefit of others in the body of Christ (Romans 12:6-8). They are to financially support God's work (1 Corinthians 16:1-3), help brothers and sisters in need (1 John 3:16-18), show affection for one another (Hebrews 13:1-3, 16), and extend hospitality to one another (1 Peter 4:11). They are to make disciples of all nations (Matthew 28:19-20). And they are to proclaim the Word of God (Mark 16:15-16; 1 Timothy 4:6, 13). Church members are called to be *active participants* in the church age!

A Summary of What to Expect in the Present Age

In summary, the church age will be characterized by the following features:

The Parable of the Wheat and Weeds	True believers and false believers will coexist and mingle until the time of the final judgment, when they will be separated.
The Parable of the Mustard Seed	The kingdom began small, but it will grow to be very large.
The Parable of the Leaven	The kingdom will experience continual growth and expansion throughout history.
The Parables of the Hidden Treasure and the Pearl	The value of the kingdom is incalculable.

The Parable of the Fishing Net	Both true and false Christians will coexist in the kingdom until the time of Christ's return, at which time they will be separated.
2 Peter 3:9	Christ provides ample time for repentance in the present age.
Luke 24:45-49 and other verses	The church has a specific mission that God has assigned to it.

12

The Remarkable Rebirth of Israel

The modern state of Israel was born as a self-governing nation in 1948. This historic event marked the beginning of the fulfillment of specific Bible prophecies regarding an international regathering of Jews in unbelief prior to the judgments that will descend upon the world during the future tribulation. This regathering was predicted to occur after centuries of exile in numerous countries spread across the world.

God promised the Jewish people in Ezekiel 36:10 that in the last days, "I will multiply people on you, the whole house of Israel, all of it. The cities shall be inhabited and the waste places rebuilt." God also promised, "I will take you from the nations and gather you from all the countries and bring you into your own land" (36:24).

During biblical times, Israel was enslaved by individual nations, including the Egyptians, the Babylonians, and the Assyrians. In each case, God eventually delivered them. But never in biblical history were the Israelites delivered "out of the nations" and "all the countries." That event did not occur until 1948, when Israel became a nation again. And Jews have been returning to their homeland ever since, literally from "all the countries" of the world.

The vision of the dry bones in Ezekiel 37 speaks of Israel's rebirth as a nation. In this prophetic passage, the Lord is portrayed as miraculously reassembling scattered bones into a skeleton. The skeleton is wrapped in muscles, tendons, and flesh, and God breathes life into the body. The subject of this chapter is undoubtedly Israel, for we read that "these bones are the whole house of Israel" (verse 11). This chapter portrays Israel as a living, breathing nation that has been brought back from the dead.

YOU MAY BE INTERESTED TO KNOW...
The Vision of the Dry Bones Reveals a Process

The vision of the dry bones is presented as a process, not an instantaneous event:

> First, the scattered bones are reassembled to form a skeleton.

> Then the bones are wrapped in muscle.

> Finally, the breath of life is infused.

> This metaphor points to the process of Israel's rebirth and new growth:

  » Israel became a nation in 1948.

  » Since then, the process has continued as Jews, with each passing year, continue to return to the Holy Land from all over the world.

1948 is a memorable year. In AD 70, Titus and his Roman warriors trampled on and destroyed Jerusalem, conclusively ending Israel as a political entity. Since then, the Jews have been scattered throughout the world for many centuries. In 1940, it was inconceivable that Israel would regain its status as a sovereign state within a decade. Yet it happened. Since 1948, when Israel achieved statehood, Jews have been returning to their homeland.

FREQUENTLY ASKED QUESTIONS

Is it possible that the Old Testament prophecies of the Jewish return to the land were already fulfilled in Old Testament times?

There are compelling reasons why this is not the case. Contextually, the broader prophecy of Israel's rebirth and eventual attack by a northern coalition takes place in the "latter years" (Ezekiel 38:8) and "latter days" (verse 16). These terms point to the end times. Notice also that the regathering of the Jews is "from all the countries" of the world (Ezekiel 36:24). In biblical history, the Jews were never delivered "from all the countries" of the world. That didn't happen until 1948, when Israel became a nation again and Jews from all over the world began to return to Israel.

Is there any real demographic evidence that Jews have been returning to the Holy Land continuously since 1948?

Yes. Israel's population was 806,000 when it declared independence on May 14, 1948. By the end of 2005, Israel was home to nearly seven million people, 5.6 million of whom were Jews.[1] In the years since 2005, many Jews have continued to immigrate to Israel. Anti-Semitism, which is at an all-time high, is the main reason Jews are returning to Israel.

YOU MAY BE INTERESTED TO KNOW...
Israel's Rebirth Sets the Stage for the Fulfillment of Other Prophecies

The rebirth of Israel sets the stage for the fulfillment of other Bible prophecies before and during the tribulation. For example:

> Ezekiel predicts that in the end times, Russia and a coalition of Muslim nations—Iran, Sudan, Turkey, Libya, Kazakhstan, Kyrgyzstan, Uzbekistan, Turkmenistan, Tajikistan, Armenia, and possibly northern Afghanistan—will launch a massive attack against Israel (Ezekiel 38–39). It is obvious that Israel cannot be invaded unless it first exists as a nation.

> The rebirth of Israel is also a prerequisite for the covenant that the antichrist will make with Israel (Daniel 9:27). How could the antichrist make a covenant with Israel if Israel didn't already exist?

> Prophetic Scripture foretells that the Jewish temple in Jerusalem will be rebuilt at the beginning of the tribulation period (Matthew 24:15-16; 2 Thessalonians 2:4). The rebirth of Israel as a nation is a prerequisite for the rebuilding of this temple.

> Jesus prophesies that at the midpoint of the tribulation, when the antichrist establishes his headquarters in Jerusalem, a remnant of Jews will flee the city. The rebirth of Israel as a nation is a prerequisite for these Jews to leave Jerusalem during the tribulation.

An Interpretive Challenge
A Regathering in Unbelief

The fact that Jewish people have returned to the Holy Land does not mean that they now believe in Jesus as their Messiah. This regathering is characterized by unbelief. Jews are going back to the Holy Land even though they don't believe in Jesus.

In the future, however, a Jewish remnant will experience a spiritual revival (Joel 2:28-29). Armageddon, which takes place at the end of the tribulation period, will be the historical context in which Israel will finally be converted (Zechariah 12:2–13:3).

FREQUENTLY ASKED QUESTION
Does the Bible predict that Israel will remain an international sore spot in the end times?

- Yes, it most certainly does.

- In Zechariah 12:2, God declares, "Behold, I am about to make Jerusalem a cup of staggering to all the surrounding peoples." The NIV puts it: "I am going to make Jerusalem a cup that sends all the surrounding peoples reeling."

- The nations surrounding Israel are Islamic. There is a lot of stumbling and reeling in the Middle East these days.

- Those who stumble are anti-Semitic.

Four More Steps to Israel's End-Times Restoration

1. The Jewish remnant will be in danger at the end of the tribulation period (Zechariah 12:2–13:1). The forces of the antichrist will be poised for an attack, intent on exterminating them.

2. God will remove the spiritual blindness that was long ago imposed on the Jews as a punishment. The Jewish remnant will confess their sins, repent, and turn to Jesus as their new Messiah (Leviticus 26:40-42; Jeremiah 3:11-18; Hosea 5:15). This will fulfill Paul's prophecy that Israel will be saved (Romans 11:25-27).

3. The Jews will ask their new Messiah to rescue them from the forces of the antichrist (Zechariah 12:10; Matthew 23:37-39; see also Isaiah 53:1-9; Romans 10:14). Jesus will immediately return (at the second coming) and defeat the forces of the antichrist (Revelation 19:11-16).

4. The Jewish remnant will be welcomed into Christ's millennial kingdom. Israel will then enjoy complete possession of the Promised Land and the Davidic throne will be reestablished, thereby fulfilling God's promises in the Abrahamic and Davidic covenants (Genesis 12:1-3; 15:18-21; 2 Samuel 7:5-17). It will also be a time of physical and spiritual prosperity, thereby fulfilling the

new covenant (Jeremiah 31:31-34). (More on all this later in the book.)

FAST FACTS ON THE CERTAINTY OF THE ABRAHAMIC COVENANT

> > God made His covenant with Abraham around 2100 BC, in which He made specific land promises to Abraham (Genesis 15:18-21).
>
> > The land promises in this covenant were so important that they were passed on to Abraham's son, Isaac (Genesis 26:3-4).
>
> > The land promises were so sure that they were then passed from Isaac to Jacob (Genesis 28:13-14).
>
> > God's covenant land promises are so important that He reaffirmed them later in the Bible. In Psalm 105:8-11 we read that God "remembers his covenant forever, the word that he commanded, for a thousand generations, the covenant that he made with Abraham, his sworn promise to Isaac, which he confirmed to Jacob as a statute, to Israel as an everlasting covenant, saying, 'To you I will give the land of Canaan as your portion for an inheritance.'"
>
> > The constant repetition of these land promises to the Jews demonstrates their inviolable certainty.
>
> > We can therefore affirm with absolute certainty that the entrance of the Jewish remnant into the millennial kingdom—with the subsequent blessings of the Abrahamic, Davidic, and new covenants—is not just a pipe dream. God will fulfill His promises.

The Big Picture: A Summary of Israel in Prophecy

I will provide details on various aspects of Israel in prophecy in the remaining chapters of this book. For now, I want to summarize "the big picture."

Ezekiel prophesied that Israel would be reborn as a nation in the end times. This prophecy was fulfilled in   Ezekiel 36–37
1948.

Zechariah prophesied that Israel would become a sore spot in the world in the end times.	Zechariah 12:2-3
Ezekiel prophesied that a northern military coalition would invade Israel in the end times. This coalition will consist of Russia and a group of Muslim nations.	Ezekiel 38–39
God will deliver Israel from the northern military coalition.	Ezekiel 39
The antichrist's covenant with Israel will provide temporary protection and security. The ratification of this covenant will signal the beginning of the tribulation period.	Daniel 9:27
The Jewish temple will be rebuilt near the beginning of the tribulation period.	Matthew 24:1-2, 15, 27-31; Daniel 9:26-27; 11:31
The antichrist will break his covenant with Israel in the middle of the tribulation period and make Jerusalem his throne.	Daniel 11:40-45
The Jewish temple will be desecrated by the antichrist.	2 Thessalonians 2:1-4
A remnant of Jews will flee Jerusalem.	Matthew 24:16-22
At the end of the tribulation period, when the Jewish remnant is in danger of being destroyed by the antichrist, they will turn to Jesus as their Messiah. Jesus will return at the second coming to destroy the forces of the antichrist, saving the Jewish remnant. The remnant will be invited into the millennial kingdom where unimaginable blessings await them.	Zechariah 12:2–13:1; Romans 11:25-27

PART 5

Current Events and the Signs of the Times

IN THIS SECTION

13 —— Deciphering the Signs of the Times—120

14 —— The Rebuilding of the Jewish Temple—129

15 —— The Rising Tide of Apostasy—135

16 —— The Decline of the United States—143

Deciphering the Signs
of the Times

We must take into view what Scripture tells us will be characteristic of the "latter days."

> ### 🔊 UNDERSTANDING OUR TERMS: *Sign of the Times*
>
> A sign of the times is a prophetically significant event that points to the end times. We might say that the signs of the times are God's "intel in advance" about how the world will appear as we approach the end times.

AN EXTREME TO AVOID

> Some people interpret almost everything that happens in the world as a sign of the times—"Sign, Sign, Everywhere a Sign."

> The problem is that when *everything* seems to be a sign, *nothing* is genuinely a sign.

> When people label so many things as "signs," the signs lose their significance.

> We should only call a "sign" what prophetic Scripture indicates is a "sign."

For the sake of simplicity, I've divided the biblical signs of the times into six categories: the rebirth-of-Israel sign, moral signs, religious signs, realignment-of-nations signs, technological signs, and earth and sky signs. These signs confirm that we are in the end times.

THE REBIRTH-OF-ISRAEL SIGN

Scripture prophesies that after the rebirth of Israel as a nation, the Jews will be gathered from the "four corners of the earth" (Isaiah 11:12). God promised in Ezekiel 36:24, "I will take you from the nations and gather you from all the countries and bring you into your own land." Since 1948, when Israel achieved statehood after a long and worldwide dispersal, more and more Jews have been returning to the Holy Land every year. This is a super-sign of the end times, as it paves the way for the fulfillment of other crucial prophecies.

MORAL SIGNS

The prophetic Scriptures reveal that there will be notable moral signs in the end times (Matthew 23:3). For example, we read in 2 Timothy 3:1-5:

> Understand this, that in the last days there will come times of difficulty. For people will be lovers of self, lovers of money, proud, arrogant, abusive, disobedient to their parents, ungrateful, unholy, heartless, unappeasable, slanderous, without self-control, brutal, not loving good, treacherous, reckless, swollen with conceit, lovers of pleasure rather than lovers of God, having the appearance of godliness, but denying its power.

A COMPARISON WITH TODAY

> - "Lovers of self" is comparable to humanism.
> - "Lovers of money" is comparable to materialism.
> - "Lovers of pleasure" is comparable to hedonism.
> - Three of the most popular philosophical ideas in the world today are humanism, materialism, and hedonism.
> - They often complement each other.

Jesus Himself warned about moral indicators of the end times:

> Because lawlessness will be increased, the love of many will grow cold...For as were the days of Noah, so will be the coming of

the Son of Man. For as in those days before the flood they were eating and drinking, marrying and giving in marriage, until the day when Noah entered the ark, and they were unaware until the flood came and swept them all away, so will be the coming of the Son of Man (Matthew 24:12, 37-39).

Although this passage speaks of the future tribulation, we can see the attitude Jesus described in our own day. People go about their business without caring about the things of God.

FAST FACTS ON AMERICA'S MORAL CRISIS

- More than 63 million unborn children have been murdered via abortion as a result of *Roe v. Wade*.[1]
- Millions of people are enslaved by pornography, which is easily accessible online.
- Substance addiction and alcoholism are rampant among both teenagers and adults.
- Sexual promiscuity, fornication, and adultery have reached unprecedented levels, resulting in the devastating effects of sexually transmitted diseases.
- The family unit is deteriorating, with an estimated 50 percent divorce rate.
- Many people now live together outside of marriage.
- With 40 percent of mothers not being married, the rate of unwed births has reached an all-time high.[2]

RELIGIOUS SIGNS

Prophetic Scripture identifies specific religious signs that will dominate in the end times. These include, but are not limited to, the following:

False Christs. Jesus warned in Matthew 24:24: "False christs and false prophets will arise and perform great signs and wonders, so as to lead astray, if possible, even the elect" (see also Mark 13:22). The apostle Paul also warned of a different Jesus (2 Corinthians 11:4). The danger is obvious: a counterfeit Jesus preaching a counterfeit gospel yields a counterfeit salvation (see Galatians 1:8).

Today, there are more and more false Christs and self-proclaimed messiahs associated with the kingdom of the cults and the occult. This will undoubtedly continue to escalate as the end times progress.

False Prophets and Teachers. Jesus warned, "Beware of false prophets, who come to you in sheep's clothing but inwardly are ravenous wolves" (Matthew 7:15). This warning is important because even God's own people can be deceived (Ezekiel 34:17; 2 Corinthians 11:2-3; Acts 20:28-30). The Bible, therefore, calls on believers to test those who claim to be prophets (1 John 4:1ff).

RECOGNIZING A FALSE PROPHET

False prophets make inaccurate predictions that do not come true.	Deuteronomy 18:21-22
They encourage people to follow false gods or idols.	Exodus 20:3-4; Deuteronomy 13:1-3
They often deny that Jesus is God.	Colossians 2:8-9
They often promote immoral behavior.	Jude 4-7
They often promote strict self-denial.	Colossians 2:16-23
The general rule is that if a "prophet" says something contrary to God's Word, he should be rejected.	Acts 17:11; 1 Thessalonians 5:21

The proliferation of false christs and false prophets in our day will pave the way for the ultimate false christ (the antichrist) and the ultimate false prophet. This is a time for discernment.

False Apostles. False apostles are "deceitful workmen, disguising themselves as apostles of Christ" (2 Corinthians 11:13). This verse identifies two important characteristics of false apostles: (1) False apostles deceive people. (2) False apostles imitate the true apostles of Jesus Christ. Christ commends those who oppose fraudulent apostles in Revelation 2:1.

Increased Apostasy. The end times will witness widespread apostasy from the truth (2 Thessalonians 2:3; see also Matthew 24:10-12). First Timothy 4:1 forewarns, "The Spirit expressly says that in later times some will depart from the faith by devoting themselves to deceitful spirits and teachings of demons." Similarly, 2 Timothy 4:3-4 warns, "The time is coming when people will not endure sound teaching, but having itching ears they will accumulate for themselves teachers to suit their own passions, and will turn away from listening to the truth and wander off into myths." Can anyone doubt that these things are happening in our own day?

VARIETIES OF APOSTASY

A denial of God	2 Timothy 3:4-5
A denial of Christ	1 John 2:18
A denial of Christ's return	2 Peter 3:3-4
A denial of the faith	1 Timothy 4:1-2
A denial of sound doctrine	2 Timothy 4:3-4
A denial of morals	2 Timothy 3:1-8
A denial of authority	2 Timothy 3:4

The subject of apostasy is so important that I will discuss it in detail in a separate chapter.

REALIGNMENT-OF-NATIONS SIGNS

A "United States" of Europe will emerge in the end times, consisting of ten nations that will form a revived Roman Empire (Daniel 2:41-44; 7:7, 23-24; Revelation 17:12-13). There will also be a military coalition consisting of Russia, Iran, Sudan, Turkey, Libya, and other Muslim nations against Israel in the end times (Ezekiel 38–39).

When this northern military coalition moves against Israel, no country on earth, not even the United States, will come to Israel's aid. It is possible that the United States will weaken in the end times. This could be due to a number of factors, such as the prospect of a nuclear attack, EMP attack, implosion due to moral depravity, economic collapse, or even the rapture. The United States may also become a strategic partner of the revived Roman Empire.

It appears that the stage is being set for some of these alignments in our day. For example, the military coalition of Ezekiel 38–39 seems to be forming before our very eyes. And the present European Union (EU) may be the forerunner of the revived Roman Empire.

EARTH AND SKY SIGNS

Prophetic Scripture reveals that frightening cosmic signs will be manifested on the earth or in the heavens during the end times. For example, during the seven-year tribulation period, earthquakes will increase in frequency and severity (Matthew 24:3, 7). Luke 21:11 states, "There will be great earthquakes, famines and pestilences in various places, and fearful events and great signs from heaven." These are the beginnings of "birth pangs" (Matthew 24:8). Like labor pains, these signs will increase in frequency and intensity.

Many Christians are curious about the "fearful events" mentioned in Luke 21:11. Scripture does not provide an explanation. But in the original Greek, "fearful events" carries the idea of "terror," "sights of terror," or "terrifying things." Could this refer to the continuing rise of global terrorism, which has never been more prevalent than it is today? The escalating threat of terrorism seems certain to continue for the foreseeable future.

The signs in the heavens could include a variety of phenomena, including strange weather patterns, falling stars, a darkening of the moon and other celestial bodies (specifically during the tribulation), and large objects striking the earth (Revelation 8:10-12).

Some scholars suggest that a reduction in sunlight (and a reduction of light from other celestial bodies) may occur because of volcanoes, as well as large bodies striking the earth. After such catastrophes, dust is thrown into the atmosphere, obscuring the light (see Revelation 8:12).

TECHNOLOGICAL SIGNS

There are specific prophecies of the tribulation period which, in order to be fulfilled, require technological advances (Matthew 23:3). We may refer to these as technological signs of the times. Many prophecy scholars believe that the necessary technology is now in place for these events to occur.

For example:

- Matthew 24:14 reveals that the gospel will be preached to every nation before Christ's second coming. Modern technology, such as satellites, the internet, global media, translation technologies, artificial intelligence, publishing technologies, and rapid transportation, now make all this possible.

- Revelation 13:16-17 predicts that the antichrist will wield economic control over the entire world. Advances in technology such as the internet, supercomputers, biometric identification procedures, RFID devices, and smart card technology make this possible.

- Revelation 8:7 predicts that much of the earth will be consumed by fire. Today's nuclear weapons make this possible.

- Revelation 16:2 predicts that people all over the world will get horrible and malignant sores. Is this a result of the radiation damage caused by the blasts of nuclear weapons?

- The technology that makes a world government possible (Revelation 13:3-18)—including instant global media via television and radio, cyberspace, and supercomputers—is also now in place. Technology has thus "greased the skids" for the emergence of globalism in our day.

A WARNING TO THE WISE

> Jesus rebuked the Jewish authorities of His day for failing to recognize the signs of the times that pointed to His first coming (Matthew 16:1-3).

> The lesson we draw from this passage is that Jesus calls us to be attentive to the signs of the times and to engage in thoughtful observation of the world.

FREQUENTLY ASKED QUESTION

Because we are witnessing the foreshadowing of future prophetic events, is it possible for us to estimate the dates of future prophetic events?

It would be foolish to even attempt to do so. In Matthew 24:36, Jesus admonished, "Concerning that day and hour no one knows, not even the angels of heaven, nor the Son, but the Father only." In Acts 1:7, He likewise asserted, "It is not for you to know times or seasons that the Father has fixed by his own authority." Despite our inability to set specific dates, however, we can discern that we are now in the general season of the Lord's return (Matthew 24:32-33).

FAST FACTS ON THE RAPTURE AS A *SIGNLESS EVENT*

- In discussing the signs of the times, it is wise to note one particular prophetic event that is not preceded by any signs.

- No signs precede the rapture of the church.

- The Bible presents the rapture as an imminent event.

- This means the rapture is "ready to take place" or "impending."

- There is nothing that must be prophetically fulfilled before the rapture occurs (see 1 Corinthians 1:7; 16:22; Philippians 3:20; 4:5; 1 Thessalonians 1:10; Titus 2:13; Hebrews 9:28; James 5:7-9; 1 Peter 1:13; Jude 21).

- This is in contrast to the second coming of Christ, which will be preceded by seven years of signs (see Revelation 4–18; Matthew 24:3; Luke 21:25).

CROSS-REFERENCES

Signs of the Times

Apostasy—Matthew 24:3, 10; 2 Timothy 4:3-4

Appearance of Antichrist—Matthew 24:5, 23-24, 26; Luke 21:8; 2 Thessalonians 2:1-10; 1 John 2:18-23; 4:3; 2 John 7; Revelation 13:1-8; 19:20

Betrayal—Mark 13:3-4, 12; Luke 21:16

Departure from the faith—1 Timothy 4:1

Earthquakes—Matthew 24:7; Mark 13:8

False christs—Matthew 24:24-25; Mark 13:5, 21-23; Luke 21:8; John 5:41-44

False prophets—Matthew 24:11; Mark 13:6, 21-23

False signs and miracles—Matthew 24:24; Mark 13:22; Luke 21:8; 2 Thessalonians 2:9-10; Revelation 19:20

Famines—Matthew 24:7; Mark 13:8; Revelation 6:5-6

Increase of evil—Matthew 24:12; 2 Timothy 3:1-5; 2 Peter 3:3-4

Innumerable vices—2 Timothy 3:1-5

International strife—Matthew 24:7; Mark 13:8; Luke 21:10; Revelation 6:3-4

Lawlessness—Matthew 24:12

Many fall away—Matthew 24:10

Persecution of believers—Matthew 24:8-9; Mark 13:9-11, 13; Luke 21:12-17

Pestilence—Luke 21:11; Revelation 6:7-8

Tribulation, death, and hatred of believers—Matthew 24:9

Unparalleled distress—Matthew 24:21; Mark 13:17-19; Luke 21:23

Wars, rumors of wars—Matthew 24:6; Mark 13:7; Luke 21:9

Worldwide proclamation of the gospel—Matthew 24:14; Mark 13:10; Revelation 14:6-7

The Rebuilding of the Jewish Temple

The Jewish temple played a pivotal role in the religious lives of the Jewish people during Bible times. It also plays a crucial role in the end times.

HISTORICAL INSIGHT
The Significance of the Temple

> The temple has played a crucial role in the lives of the Jews throughout history.

> Throughout biblical history, the temple was the heart and center of religious worship for the Jewish people.

> The glory of God dwelt within it (Ezekiel 10:4). God was truly among His people during Old Testament times through the temple.

> The temple, as God's dwelling place, was located in Jerusalem. Jews outside of Jerusalem therefore prayed in the direction of Jerusalem.

> Israel has had three different temples throughout its history.

The First Temple

David the shepherd-king desired to build the first temple for God. His status as a warrior disqualified him from undertaking the task. His son Solomon eventually built the temple (1 Kings 6–7; 2 Chronicles 3–4).

Solomon's temple had a holy place and a Holy of Holies. The holy place was the main outer room. It contained the golden incense altar, the table of showbread, five pairs of lampstands, and utensils used for sacrifice. Double doors led into the Holy of Holies, where the Ark of the Covenant was kept. The Ark was placed between two wooden cherubim angels, each ten feet high. God revealed Himself in the Holy of Holies in a cloud of glory (1 Kings 8:10-11).

The temple was eventually destroyed by Nebuchadnezzar and the Babylonians in 587 BC.

The Second Temple

After the Babylonian exile ended, many Jews returned to Jerusalem. They rebuilt the temple on a smaller, leaner scale. King Cyrus of Persia granted permission for their return and the rebuilding of the temple. These Jews were allowed to bring back the temple vessels that Nebuchadnezzar had previously looted.

The returned exiles made a good start in 538 BC. But they soon ran out of steam. The prophets Haggai and Zechariah inspired them to persevere. This second temple was finally completed in 515 BC.

The problem was that it lacked the splendor of Solomon's temple (see Ezra 3:12). It was a shadow of its former glory and a pale imitation of the original. The Ark of the Covenant, never recovered, was missing from this temple. It also had only one seven-branched lampstand, as opposed to Solomon's temple, which had five. This temple lasted around 500 years.

The Third Temple

The third temple in Jerusalem was built by King Herod the Great in 19 BC. Herod thought that this building project would be a good way to obtain favor with the Jews and to impress the Roman authorities.

The construction of the temple was completed in AD 64. The structure was larger and more impressive than Solomon's temple, with a greater proportion of gold. During the day, an enormous, cream-colored temple shone with dazzling brilliance. It measured 490 yards from north to south and 325 yards from east to west.

This temple, however, did not last for long. Only six years after the temple was completed, General Titus and his Roman troops destroyed it, along with the rest of Jerusalem. It is ironic that the very people Herod wanted to impress in Rome were the ones who destroyed the temple!

The Tribulation Temple

A new temple will be built during the coming seven-year tribulation period. With regard to prophetic chronology, several essential factors must be considered:

1. Primarily, Israel must be back in its homeland as a nation. This became a reality in 1948. Jews from all over the world have since returned to the Holy Land (see Ezekiel 36–37). It is obvious that there cannot be a Jewish temple without a Jewish land—a reborn Israel—in which to build it.

2. The temple must be rebuilt by the middle of the seven-year tribulation period because Jesus warned in His Olivet Discourse that there would be a desecration of this temple at the midpoint of the tribulation: "When you see the abomination of desolation spoken of by the prophet Daniel, standing in the holy place (let the reader understand), then let those who are in Judea flee to the mountains" (Matthew 24:15-16). This "abomination of desolation" refers specifically to the antichrist's erecting of an image of himself within the temple, which desecrates the temple. This means that the temple must be built before this time. However, it appears that it will be built even earlier.

3. Daniel 9:27 indicates that animal sacrifices will be permitted during the first half of the tribulation. This means that the temple must exist during the first half of the tribulation because sacrifices must take place in a temple setting. Later, at the midpoint of the tribulation, the antichrist will bring an end to the sacrifices. We know this because the antichrist "shall make a strong covenant with many *for one week*, and for *half of the week* he shall put an end to sacrifice and offering" (Daniel 9:27, emphasis added). This "week" refers to the seven years of the tribulation period. For half of the week—the final three-and-a-half years of the tribulation period—sacrifices will not be permitted in the temple. This implies that sacrifices *will* be permitted during the first half of the tribulation.

This expression ["for half of the week he shall put an end to sacrifice and offering"] refers to the entire Levitical system, which suggests that Israel will have restored that system in the first half of the 70th seven. After this ruler acquires worldwide political power, he will assume power in the religious realm as well and will cause the world to worship him (2 Thes. 2:4; Rev. 13:8). To receive such worship, he will terminate all organized religions. Posing as the world's rightful king and God and as Israel's prince of peace, he will then turn against Israel and become her destroyer and defiler.

—John F. Walvoord[1]

YOU MAY BE INTERESTED TO KNOW...
The Antichrist's Covenant May Allow for the Rebuilding of the Temple

> The covenant agreement signed by the antichrist with Israel may allow for the rebuilding of the Jewish temple and animal sacrifices within the temple (Daniel 9:27).

> Because the antichrist will have great power his covenant will carry considerable weight, even among Muslims who despise Israel.

> The military might of the antichrist will give pause to anyone who might be tempted to violate the covenant.

YOU MAY BE INTERESTED TO KNOW...
Christ and the Antichrist Are Polar Opposites Regarding the Temple

> Christ cleansed the temple (John 2:14, 16).

> The antichrist will defile the temple (Matthew 24:15).

> The antichrist is the *antithesis* of Christ.

THE ANTICHRIST WILL SIT IN THE TEMPLE

> Second Thessalonians 2:4 affirms that the antichrist ultimately "opposes and exalts himself against every so-called god or object of worship, so that he takes his seat in the temple of God, proclaiming himself to be God."

> The antichrist is energized and motivated to do this by Satan himself. Second Thessalonians 2:9 tells us, "The coming of the lawless one [the antichrist] is by the activity of Satan."

> We recall that in the past, Satan once sought the throne of God for himself (Isaiah 14:12-15).

HISTORICAL INSIGHT
Antiochus Epiphanes Prefigured the Antichrist

> The Seleucid Empire was led by Antiochus Epiphanes, who ruled from 175 BC until the time of his death in 164 BC.

> He was the son of King Antiochus III the Great, and the brother of Seleucus IV Philopator.

> He was vile, vengeful, and cruel.

> He was a "type" of the antichrist (he *prefigured* the antichrist) in at least three ways:

  1. Both persecute the Jewish people and seek their destruction.

  2. Both are self-exalted and demand worship.

  3. Both set up an image in the Jewish temple, causing an abomination of desolation.

> Antiochus Epiphanes is thus an idolatrous precursor to the final antichrist (see Daniel 11:31; Matthew 24:15).

Preparations for the Tribulation Temple in the Present Day

Although the temple has not yet been rebuilt, efforts are underway to undertake such a project in the near future. Jewish people and organizations, such as the Temple Institute, have been working behind the scenes to prepare the priestly garments, temple tapestries, and worship implements required for the future temple. These items are being prefabricated in order to ensure that everything will be ready when the temple is rebuilt.

A recent video from the Temple Institute has proposed the rebuilding of the temple. The video tells us that the Temple Institute is committed to doing everything possible to rebuild the temple on the Temple Mount. "It is incumbent on every one of us, at all times, to prepare for the rebuilding of the Holy Temple. With the work of the Temple Institute over the last three decades, preparation for the Temple is no longer a dream, it's a reality, in which everyone can play a part."[2]

The 2004 re-establishment of the Sanhedrin after a 1,600-year hiatus is a significant indicator of the imminent rebuilding of the temple. In Bible times, the Sanhedrin was the highest court and legislative body of the Jews. It consisted of 71 rabbis. According to Thomas Ice, "The reinstitution of the Sanhedrin is seen as a harbinger for the rebuilding of the Temple and the coming of Messiah. Orthodox Jews believe that a body like the Sanhedrin is needed today to oversee the rebuilding of the Temple and to identify Messiah should he appear on the scene."[3] The Sanhedrin convened in October 2004, and now meets monthly in Jerusalem. Presumably, the council will strive to become Israel's highest governing body.

The groundwork is now being laid for the imminent rebuilding of the Jewish temple. According to Arnold Fruchtenbaum, "The Temple Institute in Jerusalem has reconstructed the instruments for Jewish Temple worship; Jewish men determined to be descendants of Aaron, known as the Kohanim, are being trained in ritual practices to serve as Temple priests; and now we have the establishment of an authoritative body to speak to the nation of Israel on matters of Jewish religion."[4] It is all coming together in our day.

Significantly, the new Sanhedrin has requested architectural designs for the temple's rebuilding.[5] To accomplish this, "the group will establish a forum of architects and engineers to begin plans for rebuilding the Temple—a move fraught with religious and political volatility."[6] Meanwhile, they are "calling on the Jewish people to contribute toward the acquisition of materials to rebuild the Temple—including the gathering and preparation of prefabricated, disassembled portions to be stored and ready for rapid assembly, 'in the manner of King David.'"[7]

Consider the following: If the temple is to be rebuilt before (or at the very beginning of) the tribulation period, and if significant preparations for the rebuilding of the temple are being made even now, then the tribulation period must be imminent. And since the rapture precedes the tribulation period, the rapture must be all the nearer.

15

The Rising Tide of Apostasy

A postasy is a significant religious sign of the times.

The Bible contains several notable examples of apostasy. The Israelites of the Old Testament are a classic example of *collective* apostasy, as seen in Joshua 22:22; 2 Chronicles 33:19; Jeremiah 2:4; and 5:6. They abandoned their commitment to the Lord and disobeyed Him. As a result, they experienced several exiles—the Assyrian exile in 722 BC and the Babylonian exile in 605–586 BC.

Another classic example of apostasy is Judas Iscariot, who betrayed Jesus for 30 pieces of silver (Matthew 26:14-25, 47-57; 27:3-10). He strayed from the truth for financial gain. He later hanged himself in remorse (Matthew 27:5), after which his body fell headfirst and "burst open in the middle and all his bowels gushed out" (Acts 1:18). Apostasy can have terrible consequences.

Hymenaeus and Alexander are another well-known example. They experienced a "shipwreck" of their faith and engaged in blasphemy. The apostle Paul delivered them over to Satan (1 Timothy 1:19-20).

Another example is Demas, who turned away from the apostle Paul because of his affection for this present world. Paul stated, "Demas, in love with this present world, has deserted me" (2 Timothy 4:10).

These examples show how money and worldly pursuits can distract people from their commitment to God. The consequences are always serious and sometimes fatal. Thus, the apostles frequently warned of the dangers of apostasy (Hebrews 6:5-8; 10:26).

In light of these dangers, the apostle Paul warned the elders of the church in Ephesus that after his death, false teachers would try to lead church members astray: "I know that after my departure fierce wolves will come in among you, not sparing the flock" (Acts 20:29). Paul warned that men would arise "speaking twisted things, to draw away the disciples after them" (verse 30). Paul took precautions to prevent apostasy.

Apostasy in the End Times

The apostle Paul foretold that there would be greatly increased apostasy in the end times. First Timothy 4:1-2 warns, "The Spirit expressly says that in later times some will depart from the faith by devoting themselves to deceitful spirits and teachings of demons, through the insincerity of liars whose consciences are seared."

It is alarming that a number of cults and false religions have emerged as a direct result of "deceitful spirits and teachings of demons." In each case, they began when the leaders of these groups purportedly received a revelation from an "angel"—who was actually a fallen angel impersonating one of God's angels (2 Corinthians 11:14). For example, Mormonism was founded by Joseph Smith after he received a revelation from the supposed angel Moroni. Islam is rooted in the revelations Muhammad received from the angel "Gabriel." This is not the Gabriel of the Bible, but a diabolical imposter.

The apostle Paul warns: "The time is coming when people will not endure sound teaching, but having itching ears they will accumulate for themselves teachers to suit their own passions, and will turn away from listening to the truth and wander off into myths" (2 Timothy 4:3-4). Who can doubt that these words accurately characterize the present day? Channel surfing on television in the evening will inevitably reveal false teachers preaching doctrines that appeal to people's passions, such as the health and wealth gospel. Some prominent Christian leaders have even claimed that God is not omnipotent, that He is not omniscient, that Jesus made mistakes while on earth, and that Jesus is not the only means of salvation.

The apostle Paul warns that both doctrinal and moral apostasy will escalate in the end times. Moral apostasy involves a departure—a "falling away"—from morality. It refers to the moral corruption that typically develops in those who abandon God and His Word. Paul says in 2 Timothy 3:1-8:

> Understand this, that in the last days there will come times of difficulty. For people will be lovers of self, lovers of money, proud, arrogant, abusive, disobedient to their parents, ungrateful, unholy, heartless, unappeasable, slanderous, without self-control, brutal, not loving good, treacherous, reckless, swollen with conceit, lovers of pleasure rather than lovers of God, having the appearance of godliness, but denying its power. Avoid such people. For among them are those who creep into households and capture weak women, burdened with sins and led astray by various passions, always learning and never able to arrive at a knowledge of the truth. Just as Jannes and Jambres opposed Moses, so these men also oppose the truth, men corrupted in mind and disqualified regarding the faith.

HISTORICAL INSIGHT
Apostasy During Times of Trial

> ➤ Apostasy has consistently been promoted by false teachers throughout biblical history (Matthew 24:11; Galatians 2:4).

> ➤ We detect the pattern of apostasy increasing during times of trial (Matthew 24:9-10; Luke 8:13).

> ➤ This is prophetically significant, for the future tribulation period will be a time of unprecedented trial, and many will fall prey to the teachings of the false prophet, the antichrist's right-hand man.

Apostasy will reach a fever pitch during the tribulation period. Second Thessalonians 2:3 warns, "Let no one deceive you in any way. For that day will not come, unless the rebellion comes first." Many believe this refers to a rebellion against the truth.

Matthew 24:10-12, a passage about the tribulation period, warns that "many will fall away," and "many false prophets will arise and lead many astray." We are told that "the love of many will grow cold." Again, there will be both doctrinal and moral apostasy during the tribulation period.

Some sobering days are ahead.

FAST FACTS ON APOSTASY IN MODERN CULTURE

- Apostasy is rampant in the United States.

- The more than 150 million unchurched people in America are best described as "de-churched."[1] They were churchgoers in the past but have since left the faith community.

- Fifty-nine percent of Americans between the ages of 15 and 29 have disconnected from church life altogether.[2]

- Participation in religious activities such as small groups, Bible study, and even prayer has declined significantly over the past decade.

- Colleges provide our youth with all the justifications they need to reject the Bible, Christianity, and "extremist" Christian morality.

- Many are leaving the Christian church because they find it restrictive, overprotective, judgmental on sexual issues, unwelcoming to skeptics, and hostile to science.

- One-third of college-aged adults want nothing to do with religion.[3]

YOU MAY BE INTERESTED TO KNOW...
Many Americans Hold the Bible in Low Esteem

- The Bible has been reduced to a mere footnote in American life.

- Every year, the number of Christians who think the Bible is just another book written by human beings increases.

- Americans no longer view the Bible as a guide to living a meaningful life.

- Fewer than half of the American population can identify the four Gospels.[4]

- The Bible is said to be "everywhere and nowhere." There are copies of the Bible everywhere. But it is "nowhere" in the sense that it is ignored and left untouched.

- Many churches have downgraded the importance of the Bible in worship and congregational life.

- Sixty-five percent of Christians no longer share the gospel with unbelievers.[5]
- Fewer than one-fifth of Christians are engaged in Bible-based spiritual growth.[6]

YOU MAY BE INTERESTED TO KNOW...
Some Pastors Are Defecting from the Faith

- A number of pastors are abandoning their Christian faith.
- Some renounce their faith because of the prevalence of evil in the world.
- Others turn from their faith because they no longer believe in the supernatural.
- Still others leave because they no longer believe Jesus is the only means of salvation.
- Today, resources and websites are being created to help pastors and Christian leaders adjust to their new lives after abandoning their faith. These websites also teach former pastors how to "come out" and tell others about their decision.

SPIRITUAL WARFARE IN THE END TIMES
Christian Hybrid Religions Are on the Rise

- The formation of hybrid religious movements is increasing at an alarming rate.
- Christian Wicca is an amalgamation of Christianity and witchcraft.
- Christian paganism combines Christianity with pagan ideas, such as the "mother goddess."
- Christian spiritism combines Christian beliefs with attempts to communicate with the dead. There are even "Christian psychics."

> Chrislam says that Christianity and Islam are compatible and that it is possible to be both a Christian and a Muslim at the same time.

> These views are good examples of "doctrines of demons" (1 Timothy 4:1).

When it comes to religion, people today often base their beliefs on emotion and affection. They don't pay much attention to rational thinking. Evidence-based faith has been replaced by experience-based faith. Mysticism is widespread. Consequently, it is not surprising to find yoga, chanting, the use of mantras, and contemplative prayer (mystical prayer) in many churches.

Unfortunately, many Christian leaders are trying to reinvent Christianity to make it more palatable to people. They reject the idea that Jesus is the only means of salvation. They suggest that everyone will be saved unless they deliberately "opt out" of God's salvation offer. This idea is obviously contrary to the Bible (John 14:6; Acts 4:12; 1 Timothy 2:5).

PROPHETIC WARNING: Apostasy will explode geometrically once the church is raptured.

FREQUENTLY ASKED QUESTION
What are some specific ways people can apostatize?

People can apostatize by denying:

- God—2 Timothy 3:4-5
- Christ—1 John 2:18-23
- Christ's return—2 Peter 3:3-4
- "The faith," or body of New Testament Christian doctrine—1 Timothy 4:1-2
- Sound doctrine—2 Timothy 4:3-4
- Christian morality—2 Timothy 3:1-8
- Authority—2 Peter 2:10

CROSS-REFERENCES

Apostasy

Apostles warned of—Hebrews 6:5-8; 10:26

Demas turned away from the apostle Paul—2 Timothy 4:10

Departure from the faith, doctrines of demons—1 Timothy 4:1-2

End times apostasy—2 Thessalonians 2:3; see also Matthew 24:10-12

Escalates during times of trial—Matthew 24:9-10; Luke 8:13

False teachers encourage apostasy—Matthew 24:11; Galatians 2:4

Hymenaeus and Alexander experienced a "shipwreck" of faith—1 Timothy 1:19-20

Judas betrayed Jesus—Matthew 26:14-25, 47-57; 27:3-10

Sound teaching ignored—2 Timothy 4:3-4

"Apostasy must be called what it is—spiritual adultery."

—Francis Schaeffer[7]

Schaeffer's observation is insightful. We should always be faithful (Proverbs 3:3; 2 Timothy 3:14), even in small things (Luke 16:10), and remain loyal to the Lord in all situations (Philippians 1:2). Both doctrinal and moral apostasy constitute spiritual infidelity against the Lord (1 Timothy 4:12; 2 Timothy 2:18).

CRITICAL LESSONS ABOUT APOSTASY FROM FIVE BOOKS OF THE BIBLE

> **Second Chronicles** teaches us that instability and apostasy bring a people down, but reformation and repentance lift them back up.

> **Matthew** (in Christ's Olivet Discourse) teaches us that believers should guard against being led astray by false doctrine.

> **Galatians** teaches us to guard against falling away from the right understanding of the gospel.

> **Second Thessalonians** teaches us that there will be a great rebellion against the truth in the end times.

> **First Timothy** teaches us to beware of false teachers and apostasy.

CROSS-REFERENCES

Beware of False Doctrine

Another gospel—Galatians 1:6-8

Deceptive philosophy—Colossians 2:8

Different Jesus, different Spirit, different gospel—2 Corinthians 11:4

Don't get carried away by strange teachings—Hebrews 13:9

Do not be deceived—Colossians 2:4

Do not be led astray—Colossians 2:8

Do not distort God's Word—2 Corinthians 4:2

Do not tolerate false teachers—2 John 10

Doctrines of demons—1 Timothy 4:1

Encourage by sound doctrine; refute opposers—Titus 1:9

False prophets—2 Peter 2:1

False teachers deceive—Matthew 24:5; 1 Timothy 6:3

Guard what God has entrusted to you—1 Timothy 6:20

Hold steadfastly—2 Timothy 1:13

Many deceivers in the world—2 John 7

Some have wandered from the faith—1 Timothy 6:21

Spirit of the antichrist—1 John 4:3

Teach sound doctrine—Titus 2:1

Turned away from the truth—Titus 3:10-11

16

The Decline of the United States

Many students of prophecy wonder what will happen to the United States in the end times. They search the prophetic Scriptures for clues to the fate of this country. Many have engaged in speculation. Others have taken a more reasoned approach.

Bible prophecy indicates that the balance of power in the end times will shift toward a revived Roman Empire, or what we might call the "United States" of Europe. This empire will be a political and economic superpower in the end times (Daniel 2:2, 7). Given this, it is likely that the United States will weaken during (or before) this time. There are several scenarios that could explain how this might happen.

The Possibility of Moral Implosion

One possibility is that the United States could weaken and implode because of ever-increasing moral and spiritual degeneration. The demise of this country is only a matter of time if its moral fiber continues to deteriorate.

God often brings judgment upon nations that exhibit a persistent pattern of immorality. For decades, Christian leaders have warned that the United States is ripe for judgment. Their warnings usually fall on deaf ears, just as prophets were often ignored in Old Testament times.

FAST FACTS ON GOD'S SOVEREIGN CONTROL OF NATIONS

- God is sovereign over human affairs (Psalms 50:1; 66:7; 93:1; Proverbs 19:21; Isaiah 14:24; 46:10).

- In keeping with His sovereignty, God blesses nations that submit to His authority and destroys those that oppose Him:
  - In the book of Job, we read, "He makes nations great, and he destroys them; he enlarges nations, and leads them away" (Job 12:23).

> · Daniel 2:20-21 tells us that God "removes kings and sets up kings."
> · We are told that "from one man he created all the nations through-out the whole earth. He decided beforehand when we should rise and fall, and he determined their boundaries" (Acts 17:26 NLT).
> • God asserts, "My purpose will stand, and I will do all that I please" (Isaiah 46:10 NIV).
> • God assures us, "Surely, as I have planned, so it will be, and as I have purposed, so it will stand" (Isaiah 14:24).

YOU MAY BE INTERESTED TO KNOW...
The United States Is Virtually Inviting Judgment from God

> > We have seen that God is sovereign over the nations.
> > The Old and New Testaments affirm that God is a God of judgment.
> > God has a long track record of judging unrepentant immorality.
> > The United States is presently in "free fall"—morally and spiritually plummeting without contrition.
> > Therefore, it is quite possible that God will judge America for turning away from Him.

A SAMPLING OF MORAL PROBLEMS
IN THE UNITED STATES[1]

> > The majority of Americans believe that sexual fantasies (59 percent) and cohabitation (60 percent) are "morally acceptable" activities.
> > Nearly one-half of Americans believe that having an abortion (45 percent) and having a sexual relationship with someone of the opposite sex other than one's spouse (42 percent) are morally acceptable.
> > One-third of Americans approve of pornography (38 percent), profanity (36 percent), drunkenness (35 percent), and homosexual intercourse (30 percent).

> Meanwhile, lawlessness is rampant throughout the country.

> Many Americans openly embrace false religions while rejecting the Bible and Christianity.

It would be wise to consider the words of the apostle Paul in Romans 1:18-28:

> The wrath of God is revealed from heaven against all ungodliness and unrighteousness of men, who by their unrighteousness suppress the truth. For what can be known about God is plain to them, because God has shown it to them. For his invisible attributes, namely, his eternal power and divine nature, have been clearly perceived, ever since the creation of the world, in the things that have been made. So they are without excuse. For although they knew God, they did not honor him as God or give thanks to him, but they became futile in their thinking, and their foolish hearts were darkened...Therefore God gave them up in the lusts of their hearts to impurity, to the dishonoring of their bodies among themselves, because they exchanged the truth about God for a lie and worshiped and served the creature rather than the Creator, who is blessed forever!...For this reason God gave them up to dishonorable passions. For their women exchanged natural relations for those that are contrary to nature; and the men likewise gave up natural relations with women and were consumed with passion for one another, men committing shameless acts with men and receiving in themselves the due penalty for their error. And since they did not see fit to acknowledge God, God gave them up to a debased mind to do what ought not to be done.

This passage shows that when a nation willfully rejects God and His Word and turns its back on His moral requirements, God will eventually unleash His wrath upon that nation. God has a long history of retribution against wicked nations. One way God reveals His wrath is by allowing the people of that nation to experience the full brunt of the devastating consequences of their sin.

It is a sobering historical reality that many great nations have risen and fallen throughout human history. In each case, the nation did not anticipate its imminent demise. The mentality of those who lived in these nations was that their nation could never fall. But the harsh reality of documented history is that great nations do fall—*and they fall hard*.

HISTORICAL INSIGHT
Nations that Fell Hard

> The Babylonians never imagined that Babylon would fall, but it did in less than a century.

> The Persians never expected the Persian Empire to fall, but it did after about two centuries.

> The Greeks never expected their empire to fall, but it did in less than three centuries.

> No one thought the Roman Empire would ever fall, but it did after nine centuries.

> In each case, a gross moral decline preceded the fall of the respective empires.

FAST FACTS ON US VULNERABILITY

- Citizens of the United States think they are "special"—that they will succeed where others have failed.
- Such a mentality can be as arrogant as it is foolish.
- Many civilizations that have fallen throughout history also believed they were superior to their neighbors.
- Few of their citizens could have imagined that their society would one day collapse.
- Scholars have different opinions about the average lifespan of civilizations, some say 250 years, others say up to 421 years.
- Either way, US citizens should take notice.

YOU MAY BE INTERESTED TO KNOW...
There is Great Danger in Deserting Israel

> The chances of God's judgment against the United States will escalate dramatically if this country ever turns its back on Israel.

> In Genesis 12:3, God promised Abraham and his descendants: "I will bless those who bless you, and him who dishonors you I will curse."

> God keeps His promises.

> A superpower that turns its back on Israel could face super-deadly consequences.

Nuclear Detonation

One frightening possibility is that the United States could be weakened by a nuclear explosion on its soil. Could this attack come from Russia? From China? North Korea? Iran? An alliance of some of these nations? There are many possibilities.

The prospect of the United States being completely destroyed by a nuclear strike is unlikely. But it would be devastating to the already fragile and debt-ridden US economy if a major city like New York, Los Angeles, Chicago, or Dallas were nuked.

> Islamic jihad could lead to a nuclear detonation on US soil.

> Some contemporary Muslim leaders believe that jihad is a foreign policy option that can contribute to the global expansion of Islamic authority.

> Many Shiite Muslims believe that a massive armed jihad will lead to the subjugation of the entire world to Islam at the end of the world.

Electromagnetic Pulse (EMP) Attack

Another frightening possibility is that an electromagnetic pulse (EMP) attack could incapacitate the United States. A single nuclear weapon delivered by missile a few hundred miles above the United States would cause catastrophic damage. This missile could easily be launched from a cargo ship off the coast of the United States. As the detonation altitude is increased, the geographic area affected increases. At 300 miles high, the entire United States and parts of Canada and Mexico would be exposed.

Such an electromagnetic pulse would wreak havoc on electrical power systems, electronics, and information systems on which Americans depend.

AT HIGH RISK FROM AN EMP ATTACK:

Electronic control • Infrastructure for handling electric power • Sensors and protective systems of all kinds • Computers • Cell phones • Telecommunications • Cars • Boats • Airplanes • Trains • Transportation • Fuel and energy • Banking and finance • Emergency services • Food and water

American society would be particularly vulnerable to an EMP attack because our civilian and military infrastructure is almost entirely powered by electricity and electronic components. It could take months or years to fully recover from such an attack.

The Rapture of the Church

Another scenario is that the United States might weaken after the rapture. Perhaps the United States will be more affected by the rapture than many other countries because of its large Christian population. Many factory workers (and workers of all kinds) will not show up for work after the rapture. Many outstanding debts and mortgages will go unpaid. Many college tuitions and student loans will go unpaid. Many business leaders won't be around to run their companies. There will be fewer law enforcement personnel patrolling the streets, which will allow for an increase in crime. The stock market will inevitably crash due to the panic caused by the sudden disappearance of millions of people.

A COMPOSITE SCENARIO

Any one of these scenarios, or a combination of them, could weaken the United States. To illustrate, the United States is undoubtedly ripe for God's judgment. But there are also many Christians in the United States. Perhaps the Lord will first rapture the church, and then unleash judgment.

FREQUENTLY ASKED QUESTION

Will the United States be in league with the antichrist in the end times?

It is a distinct possibility. Ultimately, the antichrist will establish a global government, and the United States will likely be absorbed into this global empire. Our current political leadership seems to be moving away from US national sovereignty and is becoming more open to globalism.

It is disconcerting to consider Zechariah 12:3, which states that "all the nations of the earth" will gather against Israel during the tribulation period (compare with Zechariah 14:2). "All the nations of the earth" would certainly include the United States (see Revelation 16:14).

Some people may be reluctant to accept the idea that the United States could possibly be involved in a military operation against Israel. Keep in mind, however, that after the rapture there will be no Christians left on earth, including in the United States. Christians who have long supported Israel will have disappeared and will now be in paradise with the Lord. It is not difficult to imagine that a United States without Christians would ally itself with the revived Roman Empire and join the antichrist against Israel.

PART 6

The Rapture of the Church

IN THIS SECTION

17—Millions Vanish in the Blink of an Eye—152

18—Exploring Alternative Perspectives on the Rapture—161

19—Investigating Historical Claims
About the Origin of the Rapture—170

20—Frequently Asked Questions About the Rapture—178

21—The Mysterious Withdrawal of "He Who Now Restrains"—186

22—Christians Face the Judgment Seat of Christ in Heaven—192

23—The Sacred Union: The Marriage of the Lamb—199

17

Millions Vanish in the Blink of an Eye

n the next few chapters, we will be discussing different facets related to the rapture.

🔎 UNDERSTANDING OUR TERMS: *Rapture*

> The word *rapture* comes from the Latin translation of the Bible (*rapio*) and means "caught up."

> The rapture is that glorious event when Christ will descend from heaven, the dead in Christ will be resurrected, and living Christians will be instantly translated into their glorified bodies. Both groups will be caught up to meet Christ in the air and then taken back to heaven (1 Thessalonians 4:13-17; John 14:1-3; 1 Corinthians 15:51-54).

There will be one generation of Christians who will never pass through death's door. One moment they will be on earth, and the next moment they will be with Christ in the air.

"TAKEN UP"—"CAUGHT UP"

The Bible contains numerous examples of individuals being "taken up" or "caught up," often to heaven. The following are just a few examples (with key words in italics):

- The apostle Paul was "*caught up* to the third heaven" (2 Corinthians 12:2).

- The ascension of Jesus is metaphorically described in Revelation 12:5 as a male child who was "*caught up* to God."
- We read that "the Spirit of the Lord *carried* Philip away" (Acts 8:39).
- Likewise, at the rapture, "We who are alive, who are left, will be *caught up* [same Greek word as the previous verses] together with them in the clouds to meet the Lord in the air" (1 Thessalonians 4:17).

The Rapture Is a "Mystery"

- Biblically, a *mystery* is a truth that cannot be known by human investigation alone.
- It requires special revelation from God.
- The word often refers to a truth that was unknown to people in Old Testament times but is now being revealed to humankind by God (Matthew 13:17; Colossians 1:26).
- The rapture is called a mystery in 1 Corinthians 15:51-55.
- While the doctrine of the resurrection was revealed in Old Testament times, the translation of living believers into their glorified bodies was strictly a New Testament revelation.

YOU MAY BE INTERESTED TO KNOW...
There are Five Stages of the Rapture in 1 Thessalonians 4:13-17

1. The Lord Jesus will descend from heaven with a shout and with the sound of a trumpet.
2. The dead in Christ will rise first.
3. Then we who are alive and remain on the earth will be caught up in the clouds with them.
4. We shall all meet the Lord in the air.
5. We shall be with him forever.[1]

How wonderful that day will be!

The Church Is Absent from Tribulation Passages

Pretribulationism holds that Christ will rapture the entire church before any part of the tribulation begins. Consistent with this, no Bible passage about the tribulation mentions the church:

> ➤ No Old Testament passage about the tribulation mentions the church (Deuteronomy 4:29-30; Jeremiah 30:4-11; Daniel 8:24-27; 12:1-2).

> ➤ No New Testament passage about the tribulation mentions the church (Matthew 13:30, 39-42, 48-50; 24:15-31; 1 Thessalonians 1:9-10; 5:4-9; 2 Thessalonians 2:1-11).

> ➤ The first three chapters of Revelation contain 19 references to the word "church." However, it is not mentioned a single time in chapters 6 through 18, which address the tribulation.

The Church Is Not Appointed to Wrath

The church is not appointed to wrath (Romans 5:9; 1 Thessalonians 1:9-10; 5:9). This indicates that the church will not experience the "Great Day of Wrath" during the tribulation period (Revelation 6:17).

First Thessalonians 1:10 specifically promises that Jesus "delivers us from the wrath to come." The Greek word used for "delivers" means to "draw or snatch away, rescue, save, or preserve." Jesus will "snatch away" all Christians to "preserve" them from the horrors of the tribulation period.

God Has a Track Record of Protecting His People

Throughout Scripture, God is seen protecting His people before His judgments fall (see 2 Peter 2:5-9).

- Enoch was transferred to heaven before the judgment of the flood.
- Noah and his family were in the ark before the flood.
- Lot was taken out of Sodom before the judgment of Sodom and Gomorrah.
- The blood of the Paschal lamb protected the firstborn of the Hebrews in Egypt before judgment fell.

- The Hebrew spies were safely out of Jericho and Rahab was safe before judgment fell on Jericho.

- So too, will the church be secured safely (*via the rapture*) before judgment falls in the tribulation period.

KEPT FROM THE HOUR OF TRIAL

> Jesus promised, "Because you have kept my word about patient endurance, I will keep you from the hour of trial that is coming on the entire world, to try those who dwell on the earth" (Revelation 3:10).

> This verse shows that believers will be saved "out of" or "from" (Greek: *ek*) the actual time (hour) of the tribulation.

> This is consistent with God's promise to deliver the church from the wrath to come (1 Thessalonians 1:10; 5:9).

LEXICAL NUGGET: *Definite Articles*

> Notice the definite article before the word *hour* in Revelation 3:10 ("*the* hour of trial").

> In the Greek language, definite articles can indicate specificity.

> The definite article in Revelation 3:10 seems to refer to a specific period of time, not just any hour of trial.

> Contextually, it refers to the future tribulation period—a seven-year "hour of trial"—that is described in Revelation 6–18.

> It is from this time of testing that the church is to be kept.

The Twinkling of an Eye

- In 1 Corinthians 15:51-52, Paul says that the rapture will happen "in the twinkling of an eye."

- The fluttering of an eyelid, the blinking of an eye, is exceedingly fast.

- The bodily transformation that believers will experience at the rapture will be almost instantaneous.

- One moment they will be on earth in mortal bodies. The next moment, they will meet Christ in the clouds, instantly transformed into their glorified bodies.

The Blessed Hope

The term *blessed hope* is a general reference to the rapture of the church. This event is "blessed" because it will bring tremendous blessings to believers. The term evokes a sense of eager anticipation. Believers cannot wait for it to happen! Titus 2:13 urges believers to look "for the blessed hope and the appearing of the glory of our great God and Savior, Christ Jesus."

At this momentous event, those who have died in Christ will be resurrected, and those who are still alive on earth will be instantly translated into their glorified bodies (see Romans 8:22-23; 1 Corinthians 15:51-58; Philippians 3:20-21; 1 Thessalonians 4:13-18; 1 John 3:2-3).

THE RAPTURE IS A **BLESSED** HOPE BECAUSE:

> Our new bodies will be free from sickness, pain, and death.

> We will be face to face with Jesus.

> We will be face to face with our Christian loved ones.

FAST FACTS ON THE RAPTURE VERSUS THE SECOND COMING

The "glorious appearing" (the second coming) is different from the rapture of the church.

- Every eye will see Jesus at the second coming (Revelation 1:7), but the rapture is never described as being visible to the entire globe.

- Jesus will return *for* His church at the rapture (John 14:1-3; 1 Thessalonians 4:13-17), while He will return *with* His church at the second coming (Colossians 3:4; Jude 14; Revelation 19:14).

- Christians meet Jesus in the air at the rapture (1 Thessalonians 4:13-17), whereas Jesus' feet touch the Mount of Olives at the second coming (Zechariah 14:4).

- At the rapture, Christians are caught up to meet Christ in the air, while unbelievers are left behind on earth to go through the tribulation period (1 Thessalonians 4:13-17).

- At the second coming, unbelievers are taken away in judgment (Luke 17:34-36) while mortal believers are left behind on earth to enter Christ's millennial kingdom (Matthew 25:31-46).

- Jesus will receive His bride at the rapture (John 14:1-3), whereas He will execute judgments at the second coming (Matthew 25:31-46).

- The rapture will take place in the twinkling of an eye (1 Corinthians 15:52), whereas the second coming will be more protracted, and every eye will see Him (Matthew 24:30; Revelation 1:7).

QUICK REVIEW
Contrasting the Rapture and the Second Coming

THE RAPTURE	THE SECOND COMING
1. Christ will come for believers in the air.	1. Christ will come to earth with believers.
2. All living Christians will be translated into new glorified bodies.	2. There will be no translation of living Christians.
3. Christians will be taken to the Father's house in heaven.	3. Christians will leave the Father's house to accompany Christ back to earth.
4. There will be no judgment upon the earth.	4. Christ will judge the inhabitants of the earth.
5. It could happen at any time (it is imminent).	5. It cannot take place until the end of the seven-year tribulation period.
6. No prophetic signs precede it.	6. Seven years of signs will precede it.
7. It will affect only believers.	7. It will affect all of humanity.
8. It will occur before the "day of wrath."	8. It will occur after the "day of wrath."
9. It will be followed by the seven-year tribulation period.	9. It will be followed by the millennial kingdom.

Key Verses

THE RAPTURE

John 14:1-3; Romans 8:19; 1 Corinthians 1:7-8; 15:51-53; 16:22; Philippians 3:20-21; 4:5; Colossians 3:4; 1 Thessalonians 1:10; 2:19; 4:13-18; 5:9, 23; 2 Thessalonians 2:1, 3; 1 Timothy 6:14; 2 Timothy 4:1, 8; Titus 2:13; Hebrews 9:28; James 5:7-9; 1 Peter 1:7, 13; 5:4; 1 John 2:28–3:2; Jude 21; Revelation 2:25; 3:10.

THE SECOND COMING

Daniel 2:44-45; 7:9-14; 12:1-3; Zechariah 12:10; 14:1-15; Matthew 13:41; 24:15-31; 26:64; Mark 13:14-27; 14:62; Luke 21:25-28; Acts 1:9-11; 3:19-21; 1 Thessalonians 3:13; 2 Thessalonians 1:6-10; 2:8; 1 Peter 4:12-13; 2 Peter 3:1-14; Jude 14-15; Revelation 1:7; 19:11–20:6; 22:7, 12, 20.

FAST FACTS ON NEW "SAINTS" DURING THE TRIBULATION PERIOD

- It is sometimes claimed that because there are "saints" in the tribulation period, the rapture cannot take place before the tribulation period.
- However, these people become saints *during* the tribulation period, sometime *after* the rapture.
- They might become convinced of the truth of Christianity:
  - after witnessing millions of Christians supernaturally vanish at the rapture;
  - as a result of the ministry of the 144,000 Jewish evangelists (Revelation 7);
  - as a result of the miraculous ministry of the two prophetic witnesses of Revelation 11.
- The book of Revelation indicates that many people will respond to the gospel of the kingdom during the tribulation (Revelation 7:9-10).

FAST FACTS ON IMMINENCE

- The term *imminent* means "ready to take place" or "impending."
- The New Testament teaches that the rapture is imminent; there is nothing that must be prophetically fulfilled before the rapture occurs (1 Corinthians 1:7; 16:22; Philippians 3:20; 4:5; 1 Thessalonians 1:10; Titus 2:13; Hebrews 9:28; James 5:7-9; 1 Peter 1:13; Jude 21).
- The rapture is a *signless* event that can occur at any moment.
- This is in contrast to the second coming, which is preceded by seven years of signs in the tribulation period (see Revelation 6–18).
- The fact that the rapture is a signless event that could occur at any time should motivate Christians to live in purity and righteousness (see Titus 2:13-14).

FREQUENTLY ASKED QUESTIONS

Will people who miss the rapture have another opportunity to believe in Christ during the tribulation period?

Yes, I believe they will. Revelation 7:14 speaks of a great multitude of believers in the Lord Jesus: "These are the ones coming out of the great tribulation. They have washed their robes and made them white in the blood of the Lamb." I believe that many of these will become believers as a direct result of the ministry of the 144,000 Jewish witnesses (Revelation 7; 14) as well as the two prophets of Revelation 11.

Other Christians deny this, claiming that once the tribulation period begins, all further opportunities to believe in Jesus for salvation are gone forever. People in the tribulation will supposedly fall prey to the great deception that God sends upon those who hear the truth of the gospel and then reject it. They base their view largely on 2 Thessalonians 2:9-12:

> The coming of the lawless one is by the activity of Satan with all power and false signs and wonders, and with all wicked deception for those who are perishing, because they refused to love the truth and so be saved. Therefore God sends them a strong delusion, so that they may believe what is false, in order that all may be condemned who did not believe the truth but had pleasure in unrighteousness.

I believe that this verse refers to people living *during* the tribulation who reject God's truth and choose to follow the antichrist instead. These people will be deceived by the message of the antichrist and will be lost. As Mark Hitchcock puts it:

> Many who have rejected the gospel before the Rapture will undoubtedly continue to reject it after the Rapture. However, to say, based on this verse, that no one who has clearly heard the claims of Christ before the Rapture and rejected them can receive God's mercy during the Tribulation is making this verse say much more than the context allows.[2]

If I am dead at the time of the rapture, and if my body has been cremated, will that in any way hinder my resurrection?

Cremation is presented in the Bible as a method of disposing of a body only on exception. Most often, cremation took place in the midst of unusual circumstances. For example, in 1 Samuel 31:11-12 we read about the "inhabitants of Jabesh-gilead" (verse 11) who burned the bodies of Saul and his sons to prevent the Philistines from desecrating their bodies.

Cremation is not mentioned in the New Testament. Burial is the usual method. Moreover, the church fathers preferred burial.

However, there is no prohibition against cremation in Scripture. And if a Christian is cremated, it is no problem for God to raise that person's body from the dead (1 Corinthians 15:42-44).

We read in 2 Corinthians 5:1, "We know that if the tent that is our earthly home is destroyed, we have a building from God, a house not made with hands, eternal in the heavens." It does not matter how our earthly "tent" (body) is destroyed; all that matters is that God will raise it from the dead. Even those who are buried eventually dissolve into dust and bones. So, whether we're buried or cremated, we can all look forward to a permanent resurrection body that will never be subject to death and decay.

Exploring Alternative Perspectives on the Rapture

There are five views of the rapture. I addressed the pretribulational view in the previous chapter. The others are posttribulationism, midtribulationism, the pre-wrath view, and the partial-rapture view. Don't worry if you're not familiar with these terms. I'll make them crystal clear below.

Posttribulationism

Posttribulationism is the view that Christ will rapture the church at His second coming after the tribulation. This means that the church will have to endure the time of judgment prophesied in Revelation. However, proponents of this view say that believers will be "kept through" this time of wrath (see Revelation 3:10).

Pretribulationists reject the idea that Christians will be "kept through" these tribulations, especially those relating to the wrath of the antichrist. Numerous indiscriminate calamities will fall upon the world during the tribulation period. These include devastating earthquakes and the Wormwood asteroid that will strike the earth. How could believers be "kept through" such disasters? Furthermore, we are informed that the antichrist (the beast) will severely persecute Christians, and many will be martyred. Christians will hardly be "kept through" the wrath of the antichrist.

FAST FACTS ON THE ANTICHRIST OVERCOMING "THE SAINTS"

- Prophetic Scripture reveals that the antichrist will "make war on the saints" and "conquer them" (Revelation 13:7).
- The antichrist will make "war with the saints" and he will prevail "over them" (Daniel 7:21).

> • Clearly, the "saints" are not "kept through" the tribulation; instead, they are "conquered" and "prevailed over."

Posttribulationists claim the Bible says all Christians will endure tribulation. Acts 14:22 says, "Through many tribulations we must enter the kingdom of God." Romans 12:12 instructs believers to "be patient in tribulation." Therefore, the idea that Christians will experience tribulation is inherent in Scripture.

Pretribulationists counter that the term "tribulation" is used in the Bible in both technical and nontechnical ways. The nontechnical usage reflects the difficulties we all encounter in our daily lives. This is what Jesus was referring to when He said, "In the world you will have tribulation. But take heart; I have overcome the world" (John 16:33). This is different from the technical use of the term "tribulation," which refers to a seven-year period immediately preceding the second coming of Christ (Matthew 24:29). It is only from this period of tribulation that Christians will be delivered.

Posttribulationists observe that saints are mentioned as being on the earth during the tribulation. They say this proves that the rapture has not yet taken place. Pretribulationists concede that there will be saints living on earth during the tribulation (Revelation 6:9-11), but these individuals will become believers sometime after the rapture, during the tribulation.

> The 144,000 Jewish evangelists will lead many to Christ during the tribulation period (Revelation 7:1-8).

> The two prophetic witnesses who have the same powers as Moses and Elijah (Revelation 11:1-14) will also no doubt lead many to Christ.

Posttribulationists counter by pointing to Revelation 20:4-6, which, they say, proves that all believers will be resurrected *at the end* of the tribulation. By contrast, pretribulationists hold that only believers who die during the tribulation will be resurrected at that time (Revelation 20:4). Believers who die before the tribulation will be resurrected earlier at the pretrib rapture (1 Thessalonians 4:13-17).

Posttribs rebut that the resurrection that occurs after the tribulation period is called "the first resurrection" (Revelation 20:5), which rules out the possibility of a resurrection at a pretrib rapture (before the tribulation). Pretribulationists respond by noting that the term "first resurrection" is a *type* of resurrection—that is, it is a resurrection of believers, regardless of when it occurs (see John 5:29; Luke 14:14; Hebrews 11:35). The first resurrection includes the resurrection of believers both before and after the tribulation period. The second resurrection, by contrast, refers to the resurrection of unbelievers who will face Christ at the great white throne judgment.

Matthew 24:40 is a crucial proof text for posttribulationism. In a section of Scripture dealing with the second coming of Christ, it says: "Two men will be in the field; one will be taken and the other left." Posttribulationists believe this proves that the rapture will occur after the tribulation, at the second coming. However, pretribs maintain that the context of this verse shows that those who are taken are not taken in the rapture, but rather are taken for judgment and punishment. When the disciples asked Jesus where these people would be taken, He replied, "Where the corpse is, there will the vultures gather" (Luke 17:37). This is a Jewish expression for judgment and punishment.

A Notable Problem for Posttribulationism

- Here is a crucial question: What redeemed people will populate the millennial kingdom of Christ in their mortal bodies, as Scripture teaches?

- Prophetic Scripture says that these millennial believers will marry, have children, grow old, and die (see Isaiah 65:20; Matthew 25:31-46).

- If all believers are raptured at the second coming, after the tribulation period, no believers will be left to enter the millennium in their mortal bodies.

- This is not a problem for pretribulationism, which teaches that many will become believers after the rapture, during the tribulation period. These are the ones who will enter the millennium in their mortal bodies.

Midtribulationism

Midtribulationism is the view that Christ will rapture the church in the middle of the tribulation. According to this view, the second half of the tribulation will be far more severe than the first half.

In midtribulationism, the rapture will occur after the "beginning of sorrows" (Matthew 24:8 NKJV), which includes all seven seal judgments and the first six trumpet judgments of Revelation 6–9. All of which, it is claimed, occur before the "great tribulation" (verse 21 NKJV).

> In midtribulationism, the "beginning of sorrows" is the first half of the tribulation.

> The "great tribulation" is the second half.

> The church will go through the first half but will be spared from the second half.

Proponents of this view observe that the two witnesses of Revelation 11 ascend to heaven at the midpoint of the tribulation period. Midtribs view these two prophets as representing the church, so their ascension must allude to a midtrib rapture. Pretribs counter that there is virtually no indication in the context that these two Jewish witnesses represent the church. Midtribs seem to be practicing *eisegesis* (reading a meaning into the text) when they should be practicing *exegesis* (deriving meaning from the text).

Midtribs then argue that the church will be delivered from the wrath of God (1 Thessalonians 5:9), which they say will be in the second half of the tribulation. But the church will not be delivered from the general tribulation in the first half of the tribulation period, which will be characterized by human wrath. Pretribulationists counter that because the entire tribulation period is characterized by wrath (Zephaniah 1:15, 18; 1 Thessalonians 1:10; Revelation 6:17; 14:7, 10; 19:2), it makes more sense to say that the church will be delivered from the entire seven-year period (1 Thessalonians 1:9-10; 5:9; Revelation 3:10).

We do indeed witness examples of what might be called "human wrath" in the first half of the tribulation period. However, midtribs often forget that divine wrath can be expressed through human agency (and human wrath).

HISTORICAL INSIGHT
God Can Work Through Humans to Express His Wrath

> God showed His displeasure with Israel by sending the Jews into captivity in Babylon.

> The Assyrian captivity is another example.

> God employed pagan human beings as His whipping rod against Israel.

> Therefore, the fact that we see human wrath during the first half of the tribulation does not mean that God's wrath is not being manifested.

A classic midtribulationist argument is that since the rapture occurs at the last trumpet (1 Corinthians 15:52), and the seventh trumpet sounds in the middle of the tribulation period (Revelation 11:15-19), the rapture must occur in the middle of the tribulation period. Pretribulationists counter that the seventh trumpet sounds at the end of the tribulation, not in the middle of it (compare Matthew 24:21; Daniel 7:25; 12:7). Furthermore, the seventh trumpet in Revelation 11 has nothing to do with the rapture, but rather with judgment. This is different from the trumpet in 1 Corinthians 15, which refers to the rapture and glorification. These are two completely different contexts, and therefore the trumpets are unrelated.

In conclusion, a rapture at the midpoint of the tribulation period is nowhere mentioned or even hinted at in Scripture. It is simply not there. While the Bible does outline specific events that will take place at the midpoint of the tribulation period, Scripture is deafeningly silent about a rapture taking place at that time.

We conclude by noting that if the midtribulationist scenario is correct, then the doctrine of the imminent rapture must be rejected. Three-and-a-half years of signs must precede a midtribulational rapture. Because the tribulation begins when the antichrist makes a covenant with Israel (Daniel 9:27), the signing of this covenant would mark a three-and-a-half-year countdown to the day of the rapture. So in this scenario, the rapture could not occur "at any time," as the doctrine of imminence teaches.

CROSS-REFERENCES

Imminence

Coming of the Lord is at hand—James 5:8
Salvation nearer now than when we first believed—Romans 13:11-12
The Judge is standing at the door—James 5:9
The Lord is at hand—Philippians 4:5
The Lord is coming quickly—Revelation 3:11; 22:7, 12, 17, 20

The Lord is invited to come now—1 Corinthians 16:22
We await God's Son—1 Thessalonians 1:10
We await great God and Savior—Titus 2:13
We await mercy of the Lord Jesus Christ—Jude 21
We await revealing of the Lord—1 Corinthians 1:7
We await revelation of Jesus Christ—1 Peter 1:13
We await the Savior—Philippians 3:20
We eagerly await Him—Hebrews 9:28

The Partial-Rapture Theory

The partial-rapture theory holds that only believers who are faithful, watchful, and praying will be raptured. We can summarize this view with four theological points:

1. Only Christians who have "loved his appearing" (2 Timothy 4:8) and those "who are eagerly waiting for him" (Hebrews 9:28) will be caught up to meet the Lord in the air.

2. Unfaithful Christians, or professed Christians who are not true Christians, will be "left behind" to endure the tribulation.

3. Many people who expect to be raptured will not be raptured.

4. Unfaithful and unprepared Christians will be purged and refined by the fiery afflictions of the tribulation, so that when they become prepared, they too can be raptured to meet the Lord.

Partial rapturists claim that the parable of the ten virgins supports their view. In this parable, there are five prepared virgins and five unprepared virgins (Matthew 25:1-13). Only the prepared will meet the Lord at the rapture.

Pretribulationists counter that the parable of the ten virgins has nothing to do with the rapture. These unprepared virgins represent people who live during the tribulation period and are unprepared for Christ's second coming, which will take place seven years *after* the rapture.

YOU MAY BE INTERESTED TO KNOW...
Partial Rapture Is Like Purgatory

> Many critics of the partial-rapture theory see it as a Protestant version of purgatory.

> Christians must become prepared to meet the Lord by being purged during the tribulation period.

> This view seems to say that trusting in Christ alone is not enough (2 Corinthians 5:21; see also Romans 5:1; Colossians 2:13).

> Scripture says that if you are a believer, you are saved (John 3:16-17; Acts 16:31).

> This alone qualifies you to participate in the rapture (1 Corinthians 15:51-52).

The partial-rapture theory ultimately requires good works. Only those who qualify will be rewarded with the rapture. Only those who are worthy will be raptured.

The problem is, how do you know if you have "passed the test?" How do you know if you have been faithful enough? How do you know if you've prayed enough? How do you know if you've watched for the Lord's coming with enough fervency?

In this way of thinking, the rapture is no longer a "blessed hope" (Titus 2:13), because no one can know for sure whether they will participate in the event. It is more of a cross-your-fingers "blessed perhaps."

By contrast, Scripture affirms that *all* of salvation is by grace through faith (see Ephesians 2:8-9). Because this is the case, we can rest assured that *all* believers will be raptured.

It is particularly important to note that the baptism of the Holy Spirit incorporates *all* believers into the body of Christ (1 Corinthians 12:13). Therefore, all believers will be raptured (1 Thessalonians 4:16-17). The partial-rapture theory denies the perfect unity of the body of Christ (1 Corinthians 12:12-13).

> 1 Corinthians 15:51 says, "We shall *all* be changed."

> "We" includes even the carnal believers in the Corinthian church to whom Paul was writing.

> No Christian will be excluded.

> If you are a believer, you will "be changed" at the rapture.

The Pre-Wrath Theory

According to the pre-wrath theory, the rapture will occur near the end of the tribulation, before the great wrath of God is unleashed. This view holds that the church will endure the first part of Daniel's seventieth week (the tribulation, Daniel 9:24-27), but not the wrath of God (2 Thessalonians 1:5-10). Revelation does not mention "wrath" until after the sixth seal; pre-wrath proponents conclude this must mean God's wrath is not unleashed until then (Revelation 6:12–8:8). They suggest that the rapture must take place between the sixth and seventh seals. More specifically, the rapture will occur 21 months before the end of the seven-year tribulation.

Here's the backdrop: pre-wrath proponents divide the seventieth week of Daniel into three recognizable periods—the "Beginning of Sorrows," the "Great Tribulation," and the frequently predicted "Day of the Lord."

- The first three-and-a-half years are "the Beginning of Sorrows."
- The midpoint of the seventieth week of Daniel begins "the Great Tribulation" and lasts only 1 3/4 years (21 months).
- The final 21 months—the fourth quarter of the seven-year period— is "the Day of the Lord," in which alone falls the "wrath of God."
- The rapture occurs just before the day of the Lord.

The fundamental flaw in this view is that God's wrath is poured out on the earth long before the seventh seal (Zephaniah 1:15, 18; 1 Thessalonians 1:10; Revelation 6:17; 14:7, 10; 19:21). The seven seals are presented in the Bible as coming from the same ultimate source: God (Revelation 6; 8). This sequence contains divine judgments that intensify with each successive seal. During the first six seals, man and war are seen as instruments of God's wrath. Even the unsaved who experience this wrath recognize it as the "wrath of the Lamb" (Revelation 6:15-16), for it is the Lamb Himself who opens each seal, resulting in each respective judgment (see Revelation 6:1, 3, 5, 7, 9, 12; 8). This alone invalidates the pre-wrath theory.

Unity in Diversity

Although Christians may disagree about when the rapture will occur, there are some points of agreement. These agreements should serve as a basis for unity despite our differing perspectives:

- All agree that God is in charge of the exact timing of end-time events.

- All agree that there will be a rapture.

- All agree that there will be a physical second coming of Christ.[1]

- All agree that there will be a future resurrection from the dead.

- All agree that there will be a future judgment.

- All agree that there will be an eternal state where believers will live with God forever.

- All agree that a beneficial aspect of studying Bible prophecy is that it motivates us to holiness.

Given these facts, Christians should be able to *agree to disagree in an agreeable way* on the timing of the rapture.

19

Investigating Historical Claims About the Origin of the Rapture

C ritics of pretribulationism often point to church history to undermine this view. They typically claim that pretribulationism is a recent view, developed by John Darby in 1830. Others claim that Darby got it from the visions of Margaret MacDonald, a fifteen-year-old demon-possessed girl. Others claim that he stole it from the Irvingites. Still others claim that the doctrine of imminence, a central tenet of pretribulationism, is new and has no support in early Christianity.

In this chapter, I will briefly evaluate these arguments from church history.

Pretribulationism—A Recent View?

Critics often claim that the pretribulational view of the rapture is a recent doctrine formulated by John Nelson Darby in 1830. They say the idea had no support before that time.

Pretribulationists concede that Darby was a popularizer of the pretribulational rapture. However, history proves that this doctrine long preceded Darby's time, contrary to the false claims of the critics. The following are just a few examples from church history:

Dr. John Gill was one of the most famous Bible expositors of the eighteenth century. In 1748, this Calvinist theologian published his commentary on the New Testament. His exposition of 1 Thessalonians 4:15-17 is particularly important, for he says that Paul is teaching a doctrine that is "something new and extraordinary." He calls the translation of the saints "the rapture" and urges watchfulness because "it will be sudden, and unknown beforehand, and when least thought of and expected."[1]

In the multi-authored book *When the Trumpet Sounds* by general editors Thomas Ice and Timothy Demy, we learn that Gill's rapture doctrine has eight primary components[2]:

HISTORICAL INSIGHT
Dr. John Gill on the Rapture

1. The Lord will descend in the air.
2. The saints will be raptured in the air to meet him.
3. In the air, Christ will stop and will be visible to all.
4. He will not descend to earth because it is not fit to receive him.
5. He will take up [the saints] with Him into the third heaven until the general conflagration and burning of the world is over.
6. This will preserve them from that conflagration.
7. Then all the elect of God shall descend from heaven.
8. Then they shall be with Him, wherever he is.

Dr. John Gill taught a pretribulational rapture almost 100 years before Darby. Others who lived in the same general time frame as Gill also held to a pretribulational rapture. As scholar Paul Benware summarizes in his book *Understanding End Times Prophecy: A Comprehensive Approach*:

- Peter Jurieu, in his book *Approaching Deliverance of the Church* (1687), taught that Christ would come in the air to rapture the saints and return to heaven before His coming in glory.
- Philip Doddridge's commentary on the New Testament (1738) uses the term *rapture* and speaks of it as imminent.
- James Macknight (1763) and Thomas Scott (1792) both taught that the righteous would be carried to heaven, where they would be secure until the time of judgment was over.[3]

This historical data refutes the idea that the viewpoint of a pretribulational rapture did not occur before the time of John Darby in 1830. How much stronger the case for pretribulationism becomes when we consider even earlier historical evidence for the pretribulational rapture.

Irenaeus was a disciple of Polycarp, who was himself a disciple of the apostle John. He was born about AD 130 and died about AD 202. He says that "in the end," believers will be "suddenly caught up" before the "tribulation."[4]

The *Shepherd of Hermas* is an early Christian document from the second century. It speaks of a pretribulational rapture, although the event is considered to be for the faithful only. It speaks of "the great tribulation that is coming. If then ye prepare yourselves, and repent with all your heart, and turn to the Lord, it will be possible for you to escape it, if your heart be pure and spotless, and ye spend the rest of the days of your life in serving the Lord blamelessly."[5] Pretribs believe that this document errs in requiring merit. But the idea of a pretrib rapture is clear.

The *Apocalypse of Elijah* is a treatise on the end times written in the third century. According to Francis Gumerlock, professor of historical theology at Providence Theological Seminary in Denver, Colorado, this document indicates that the rapture will take place before judgment falls. The purpose of the rapture is "specifically removal from the wrath of the Antichrist and escape from the tribulation sent on the world by God in the last days."[6]

Ephraem of Nisibis, also known as Pseudo-Ephraem, was born in AD 306 and died in AD 373. He was a theologian in the early Eastern (Byzantine) Church. He believed in a pretribulational rapture of Christians: "Count us worthy, Lord, of the rapture of the righteous, when they meet you the Master in the clouds, that we might not be tried by the bitter and inexorable judgment." He also said: "Watch always, praying continually, that you may be worthy to escape the tribulation…If anyone has tears and compunction, let him pray the Lord that he might be delivered from the tribulation which is about to come upon the earth, that he might not see it all, nor the beast himself, nor even hear of its terrors." He further explains: "All the saints and elect of God are gathered together before the tribulation, which is to come, and are taken to the Lord, in order that they may not see at any time the confusion which overwhelms the world because of our sins."[7] Pseudo-Ephraem predates Darby by more than 1,000 years. So do Irenaeus, the *Shepherd of Hermas*, and the *Apocalypse of Elijah*.

Aspringius of Beja was a bishop in southern Portugal in the sixth century AD. He believed that Revelation 3:10 refers to the rapture and promises: "Because you have kept my word about patient endurance, I will keep you from the hour of trial that is coming on the whole world, to try those who dwell on the earth." Aspringius says that God "promises that he will preserve his church in the last times, when the demon, enemy of the human race, will come to tempt those who live on the earth."[8] This implies a pretrib rapture, since the church will be delivered from the antichrist during the tribulation period.

There are other examples I could provide. Interested readers may wish to consult my book *Bible Prophecy Under Siege* (Harvest House Publishers).

Who knows how many other historical documents refer to a pretribulational rapture that have not yet been discovered and analyzed? Current historical research is still in its infancy. Undoubtedly, many more discoveries are on the horizon.

Are Earlier Doctrines More Correct?

It is commonly claimed that the earlier a doctrine appears in church history, the more likely it is to be the correct view. The implication is that because pretribulationism appeared late in church history, it must be false.

Recent historical discoveries prove that pretribulationism is not a late development, as previously thought. In light of this, critics would be wise to dispose of this common argument against pretribulationism. Even if pretribulationism were late, would this necessarily mean that the doctrine is likely wrong? We can make the following observations:

With the development of doctrine over the centuries, it is logical that eschatology would become a central topic of discussion in later church history.

HISTORICAL INSIGHT
Doctrines and Church History

> The doctrine of the Trinity was not formally articulated until the fourth century.

> The doctrine of human depravity did not become a settled doctrine until the fifth century.

> The doctrines of the sufficiency of Scripture and the priesthood of the believer were not recognized until the Protestant Reformation.

> Doctrines related to eschatology came into heaviest emphasis later.

The late Christian apologist Norman Geisler suggested that the argument from church history involves the fallacy of "chronological snobbery"—wrongly claiming that time determines truth.[9]

"The fact that something was taught in the first century does not make it right (unless taught in the canonical Scriptures), and the fact that something was not taught until the nineteenth century does not make it wrong, unless, of course, it is unscriptural."

—Charles C. Ryrie[10]

"It is absurd to disregard a view because it was not thought of in the past. The claims of relativity physics were not thought of in the past, but that hardly disqualifies Einstein's assertions."

—Thomas Howe[11]

It is relevant to our discussion that some in the early church held to false doctrines, such as baptismal regeneration. This illustrates that just because a doctrine is early does not mean it is true. Conversely, just because a doctrine is late does not mean it is false.

> > During the Reformation, charges of "newness" and "novelty" were leveled against the Reformers.[12]
> > But what the Reformers taught was theologically correct.

Pretribulationism should not be rejected because of its alleged "newness." Pretribulationism is a biblical doctrine. It is found in Scripture. Besides, as I've already demonstrated, it turns out that it is not "new" after all. The historical evidence proves otherwise.

The Alleged Role of the Irvingites

Critics sometimes claim that John Darby secretly stole the doctrine of pretribulationism from the Irvingites and then tried to pass it off as his own discovery. Here is the big problem with this view:

1. Edward Irving and his movement *never* taught pretribulationism.
2. The Irvingites held to historicism, which views the entire church age as the tribulation.[13]
3. Irving believed that the second coming was synonymous with the rapture.
4. John Darby held Edward Irving in very low regard, claiming that he held to "heresies."
5. It is absurd to suggest that Darby got his eschatology from the Irvingites.

Pretribulationism—From a Demon-Possessed Girl?

Another common argument critics raise against pretribulationism is that the doctrine originated in the utterances of a 15-year-old demon-possessed girl named Margaret MacDonald. Such a view is untenable for the following reasons[14]:

1. No one has ever demonstrated from the facts of history that MacDonald influenced John Darby.

2. History reveals that John Darby held his pretribulational view by January, 1827. This is three years before Margaret MacDonald had her prophetic "vision."

3. Darby's understanding of pretribulationism resulted from his interaction with the text of Scripture, not from a young girl's vision. This interaction with Scripture took place years before MacDonald's vision. History proves this.

4. When Darby personally investigated Margaret MacDonald, he classified her utterances as "demonic." It is inconceivable that Darby would borrow from an utterance that came from a demon.

5. Perhaps most importantly, MacDonald's views bear no resemblance to a pretribulational rapture. Her view is best categorized as posttribulationism. (I have read the entire transcript of her remarks.) If Darby borrowed his ideas from MacDonald, he would be a posttribulationist.

In light of these verifiable facts, it is unfortunate (and dishonest) for critics to continue to claim that pretribulationism originated with Satan.

Did Darby Have a Cultic Mentality?

An anti-pretrib video produced in the United Kingdom and distributed in the United States claims that Darby had a cult-like mentality comparable to that of Charles Taze Russell, the founder of the Jehovah's Witnesses, and Joseph Smith, the founder of Mormonism. The video places a photo of Darby between those of Russell and Smith.

As the author of multiple books on the cults, including *The Challenge of the Cults and New Religions* (Zondervan), *Reasoning from the Scriptures with Jehovah's Witnesses* (Harvest House), and *Reasoning from the Scriptures with Mormons* (Harvest House), I can categorically state that this claim is absurd. The video is fiction masquerading as fact. Darby has been falsely accused. He does not have even the slightest connection to the cults. Nor does he exhibit a cultic mentality. He has sought to expose falsehoods, not propagate them. This video is a feeble attempt to use the tactic of "guilt by association" against pretribulationism. It does not merit further comment.

Imminence—A Recent Doctrine?

Critics of pretribulationism claim that the doctrine of imminence is a recent development in church history. They claim that no examples can be found among the early believers who held to imminence.

These critics have not done their homework. The following are just a few examples of early believers who held to imminence:

HISTORICAL INSIGHT
Imminence in the Early Church

> The Didache said: "Watch for your life's sake...Be ready, for ye know not the hour in which our Lord cometh" (16.1, about AD 120–150).

> Clement of Rome (about AD 35–101) said, "Speedily will He come, and not tarry."

> Ignatius of Antioch (d. AD 110) said of Christ's coming, "Be watchful, possessing a sleepless spirit."

> In the Epistle of Pseudo-Barnabas (about AD 70–130), we read, "The Day of the Lord is at hand...the Lord is near."

The church fathers frequently emphasized the need to be vigilant, patient, and prepared for the imminent return of the Lord.[15] J. Barton Payne, a posttribulationist, acknowledged that the early Christians believed in the imminent return of Christ: "Belief in the imminence of the return of Jesus was the uniform hope of the early church."[16]

"The central feature of pretribulationism, the doctrine of imminency, is...a prominent feature of the doctrine of the early church... The early church lived in constant expectation of the coming of the Lord for His church."

—John F. Walvoord[17]

Pretribulationists grant that there was some confusion among the church fathers. One example is how they often openly expressed belief in imminency while at the same time expressing the belief that the events of the tribulation period were impending. So as Walvoord explains it, "At best, the situation is confused."[18] Nevertheless, the claim that imminency is not found among the early Christians is simply false, and critics of the rapture should stop making this claim. This is especially so since the biblical writers themselves held to imminence:

"as you wait for the revealing of our Lord Jesus Christ."	1 Corinthians 1:7
"Our Lord, come!"	1 Corinthians 16:22
"Our citizenship is in heaven, and from it we await a Savior, the Lord Jesus Christ."	Philippians 3:20
"The Lord is at hand."	Philippians 4:5
"to wait for his Son from heaven."	1 Thessalonians 1:10
"waiting for our blessed hope, the appearing of the glory of our great God and Savior Jesus Christ."	Titus 2:13
"Christ...will appear a second time...to save those who are eagerly waiting for him."	Hebrews 9:28
"The coming of the Lord is at hand."	James 5:8
"The Judge is standing at the door."	James 5:9
"I am coming soon."	Revelation 3:11; 22:7, 12
"Surely I am coming soon."	Revelation 22:20

Frequently Asked Questions About the Rapture

Through my decades of speaking at prophecy conferences across the country, certain questions about the rapture come up time and time again. I also receive many questions about the rapture via email. This chapter will address some of the most important frequently asked questions about the rapture.

If the doctrine of the rapture is biblical, why is the word *rapture* not found in the Bible?

One might as well ask, "If the doctrine of the Trinity is a biblical doctrine, why is the word not found in the Bible?" No single verse explicitly teaches the doctrine of the Trinity. But when we compare various verses about God, it becomes clear that (1) there is one and only one God (Deuteronomy 6:4; Isaiah 44:6; John 5:44; 1 Corinthians 8:4; 1 Timothy 2:5; James 2:19), (2) the Father is God (John 6:27; Romans 1:7; Galatians 1:1; 1 Peter 1:2), (3) Jesus is God (Titus 2:13; Hebrews 1:8; Revelation 1:17), (4) the Holy Spirit is God (Genesis 1:2; Exodus 31:3; Ezekiel 11:24; Romans 8:9, 14; 1 John 4:2), and (5) the Father, Son, and Holy Spirit are distinct persons (Matthew 3:16-17; 2 Corinthians 13:14). Comparing these verses leads to the conclusion that there is one God, and that within the unity of this one God are three co-equal and co-eternal persons: the Father, the Son, and the Holy Spirit.

Similarly, when we consider all the prophetic data derived from 1 Thessalonians, the Gospel of John, 1 Corinthians, Titus, the book of Revelation, and other prophetic books, we logically infer that the rapture is a biblical doctrine, even though the term *rapture* is not found in the Bible.

A well-known passage on the rapture is 1 Thessalonians 4:16-17: "The dead in Christ will rise first. Then we who are alive, who are left, will be caught up together with them in the clouds to meet the Lord in the air, and so we will always be with the Lord." The phrase "caught up" in the Latin translation of the Bible is *rapio*. From this word, we get the English term "rapture," which refers to the catching up of Christians to meet Christ in the air. So even though the word rapture is not found in the English Bible, it is definitely a biblical concept.

Will babies and toddlers be raptured?

Individual Christians answer this question differently. Some believe that only infants and toddlers of believers will be raptured. They find support for their position from the days of Noah. They note that in Noah's day, infants and young children from the general population were not saved from the flood, only Noah and his family were spared.

Others believe that all babies and young children will be raptured, along with all Christians. (This is my view.) The same theological support that suggests that infants and young children who die go to heaven also supports the idea that they will be raptured. For example, in all the descriptions of hell found in the Bible, we never read of infants or young children going there. Nor do we read of infants and young children standing before the great white throne judgment, which is the judgment of the wicked dead and the precursor to the lake of fire (Revelation 20:11-15).

The lost will be judged on the basis of their actions on earth (Revelation 20:11-13). Because infants and young children are not responsible for their actions, they must be excluded from this judgment. Jesus also said that children have a special place in His kingdom and that adults must become like children to enter it (Matthew 18:1-14). King David certainly believed that he would see his dead son again (2 Samuel 12:22-23).

> It is not that babies and toddlers do not have a problem with sin. In fact, they do.

> However, the benefits of Christ's death are automatically applied to them at the moment of death, which is why they go to heaven at death.

> Because infants and young children go to heaven at death, it follows that they will also be raptured before the tribulation period.

> There is no reasonable justification for infants and children being targets of God's wrath during the tribulation.

Does the pretribulational rapture give people false hope, as posttribulationists claim?

Some posttribulationists say that if a person believes in pretribulationism and that view proves to be false, that person will be spiritually unprepared for what they will encounter in the tribulation period. Pretribulationism, therefore, creates false hope and sets Christians up for a fall. Posttribulationists claim that we should prepare Christians to survive the tribulation.

This allegation is invalid because:

1. The argument erroneously assumes that pretribulationism is false. As we see in this book, there is strong theological support for pretribulationism.

2. Our basis for spiritual truth is the Bible alone, not a fear-driven speculative scenario about Christians supposedly being unprepared for the tribulation period.

3. Scripture points to a "great multitude" of people who will become Christians during the tribulation period (Revelation 7:9-17). If these new believers can survive the tribulation period by trusting in Jesus, why should we doubt God's sufficiency to help the rest of us get through in the unlikely event that we are there?

4. Posttribulationists accuse pretribulationists of setting Christians up for a fall during the tribulation period, while they themselves do nothing to prepare people to survive the tribulation. *Is this fair?*

5. There are no instructions in the Bible on how Christians should prepare for the tribulation. This means two things: (1) Posttribulationists should not blame pretribulationists for not preparing people for the tribulation; and (2) the fact that the Bible does not instruct Christians to prepare for the tribulation suggests that the church will not be in the tribulation at all but will have been raptured beforehand.

How should we respond to critics who argue that we should not waste time discussing the rapture because it is such a divisive issue within the church?

We can answer that by asking another question: Does this mean that we should avoid virtually any doctrine on which Christians disagree about the proper interpretation? If so, we must ignore a considerable portion of the

Bible. The divided opinions of Christians on various doctrines have given rise to numerous books: *Three Views on the Rapture, Four Views on Heaven, Five Views on Biblical Inerrancy, Three Views on the New Testament Use of the Old Testament, Five Views on Apologetics, Four Views on the Book of Revelation, Three Views on the Millennium and Beyond, Five Views on Law and Gospel, Five Views on Sanctification, Four Views on Divine Providence, Four Views on Eternal Security, Four Views on Christian Spirituality, Four Views on the Role of Works at the Final Judgment*, and many more.

It is unreasonable to suggest that the rapture should not be studied because it is a potentially divisive topic. The fact that there are multiple perspectives on the rapture should encourage us to study the Bible to determine which perspective on the rapture is correct.

We can do this without dividing ourselves from other Christians who hold to different views.

WE CAN HAVE DIVERSITY WITHOUT DIVISION

> We can follow the age-old maxim, "In essentials, unity; in non-essentials, liberty; and in all things, charity."

> Christian theologians consider the timing of the rapture to be a nonessential doctrine, despite its importance. (It is not essential because an individual's salvation does not depend on it.)

> So we can agreeably disagree with our brothers and sisters who see things differently regarding the timing of the rapture.

There are at least two other reasons to spend time studying the rapture: (1) We are wise to follow the example of the apostle Paul, who taught "the whole counsel of God" (Acts 20:27), which certainly included Bible prophecy. (2) One-fourth of the Bible was prophetic when it was written—including many verses about the rapture. We should not ignore such a large portion of Scripture.

Are pretribulationists so heavenly minded that they ignore the pressing social issues that need to be resolved in our day?

Critics sometimes claim that pretribulationists are so *heavenly minded* that they are insensitive to *this-world* problems. But I do not think this claim is valid.

Speaking of Christians in general (and not specifically about pretribulationists), C.S. Lewis commented, "If you read history, you will find that the Christians who did most for the present world were just those who thought most of the next...It is since Christians have largely ceased to think of the other world that they have become so ineffective in this."[1] I think Lewis's words ring true for pretribulationists. I have attended pretribulationist churches for decades, and in each case the church not only cared about a variety of social issues in our immediate area, but took action addressing them as well.

Critics forget that pretribulationists believe that Christians will face the judgment seat of Christ immediately after the rapture. Christians will be judged on how they have spent their short time on earth. Pretribulationists recognize that the way they helped those in need will likely come up in that judgment.

People running out of money and not being able to buy food for their families is a common social problem. In such cases, the church provides financial assistance. In addition, churches support local inner-city missions that feed and house the destitute. Further, many churches assist the sick who cannot afford to pay all their medical expenses. These are just a few of the types of social issues in which pretribulational churches regularly provide assistance.

The fact that we are "heavenly minded" motivates our social behavior. J.I. Packer, who was not a pretribulationist, once said that the "lack of long, strong thinking about our promised hope of glory is a major cause of our plodding, lackluster lifestyle."[2] Packer points to the Puritans as a much-needed example for us, for they believed that "it is the heavenly Christian that is the lively Christian." The Puritans understood that we "run so slowly, and strive so lazily because we so little mind the prize...So let Christians animate themselves daily to run the race set before them by practicing heavenly meditation."[3] It is the lively Christian—Christians who spiritually "animate themselves"—who are actively involved in meeting the needs of society.

There are two things I want you to notice about my comments above:

1. Pretribulationists are not the only Christians who are heavenly minded. Great Christian leaders such as C.S. Lewis and J.I. Packer were also heavenly minded. If critics target pretribulationists for being heavenly minded, then to be consistent, shouldn't Lewis and Packer be targeted as well? Don't get me wrong. I do not want Lewis and Packer to be targeted. I am simply pointing out the unfairness of singling out pretribulationists when others hold the same view.

2. Those of us who are heavenly minded, whether we are pretribulationists or not, believe that this perspective is biblical. One of many passages that speak to this issue is Colossians 3:1-2: "Seek the things that are above...Set your minds on things that are above." The apostle Paul, who wrote these words, was undoubtedly "heavenly minded." Jesus Himself spoke of being heavenly minded when He urged His followers: "Lay up for yourselves treasures in heaven, where neither moth nor rust destroys and where thieves do not break in and steal. For where your treasure is, there your heart will be also" (Matthew 6:20-21).

CROSS-REFERENCES

Eternal Perspective

Apart from the body, at home with the Lord—2 Corinthians 5:8
Death has lost its sting—1 Corinthians 15:55
Desire to depart and be with Christ—Philippians 1:23
Our inheritance awaits us—1 Peter 1:4
Set your mind on things above—Colossians 3:2
Joyful expectation—Titus 2:13
Readiness—Matthew 24:44
The Lord's return is near—Romans 13:11-12; Philippians 4:5; James 5:8-9; 1 Peter 4:7
Eagerly await the Lord's return—1 Corinthians 1:7; Philippians 3:20; Titus 2:11-13
Encourage one another—Romans 8:23-25; 1 Thessalonians 4:13-15, 17-18
Long for the Lord's return—2 Timothy 4:8; 2 Peter 3:12; Revelation 22:20

Do pretribulationists cherry-pick passages that they believe support their position, while ignoring the numerous other passages that contradict it?

This is a common criticism. But I believe it to be false. Pretribulationists have always wrestled with verses that seem to challenge pretribulationism. I have wrestled with many of these verses in my various books on prophecy.

Allow me to give one example. In Matthew 24:40-41, Jesus said, "Two men will be in the field; one will be taken and one left. Two women will be grinding at the mill; one will be taken and one left." The context of these verses is the "coming of the Son of Man," or the second coming (verse 39). This is a challenging passage for pretribulationists. At first glance, it seems to support a rapture that occurs in conjunction with the second coming. The verse is often cited as supporting posttribulationism.

However, a parallel passage to Matthew 24:40-41 is Luke 17:34-37, in which Jesus demonstrates that those who are "taken" are not taken in the rapture, but in judgment. In this passage, Jesus tells His followers: "'I tell you, in that night there will be two in one bed. One will be taken and the other left. There will be two women grinding together. One will be taken and the other left.' And they said to him, 'Where, Lord?' He said to them, 'Where the corpse is, there the vultures will gather.'" So where will they be taken? They will be taken to a place where vultures feed on dead bodies. These people will be taken away in judgment.

This means that Matthew 24:37-40 does not support a posttribulational rapture. It merely supports the idea of a posttribulational judgment. The fact that pretribulationists address this challenging verse—among many others—proves that they are not cherry-picking, as they are accused of doing.

CROSS-REFERENCES
Rightly Divide the Truth
Do not distort the Word of God—2 Corinthians 4:2
Correctly explain the Word—2 Timothy 2:15
Do not add to, or subtract from, God's Word—Deuteronomy 4:2; 12:32; Revelation 22:18-19

Is the rapture a "secret coming" of Christ?

The Bible makes no mention of a "secret rapture" or a "secret coming" of Christ. However, two theological factors sometimes give rise to talk of a "secret rapture":

1. First Corinthians 15:52 tells us that the rapture will take place "in the twinkling of an eye."
2. Believers will be "caught up in the clouds to meet the Lord in the air" (1 Thessalonians 4:17).

So the rapture will be instantaneous, and it will be far up in the air.

Despite these theological facts, the rapture will be anything but secret. With millions of people departing from the planet in the blink of an eye, people everywhere will be looking for explanations. This is likely to make international headlines. Videos of people disappearing will almost certainly go viral on the internet.

Will the angels be present at the rapture?

I believe they will. The apostle Paul tells us that the rapture of the church will come with "a cry of command, with the voice of an archangel" (1 Thessalonians 4:16). Scholars debate what is meant by the phrase, "with the voice of an archangel." Some speculate that Jesus will cry out with a voice similar to that of an archangel. However, it seems more natural to the text to interpret this cry as coming from the voice of the archangel. Scripture reveals that at the second coming, the Lord Jesus will be "revealed from heaven with His mighty angels" (2 Thessalonians 1:7). If angels accompany Christ at His second coming, there is no reason to believe that they will not accompany Him at the rapture seven or more years earlier. In fact, angels are often portrayed as playing a significant role in end-time events (see Revelation 5:11; 7:1-2, 11; 8:2, 4, 6, 13; 9:14-15; 10:10; 12:7, 9; 14:10; 15:1, 6-8; 16:1; 17:1; 21:9, 12).

CROSS-REFERENCES
Angelic Activities in the End Times

Giving instructions—Revelation 7:2-3; 14:15
Making proclamations—Revelation 5:2; 14:6, 8-10
Facilitating God's judgments—Revelation 16

21

The Mysterious Withdrawal of "He Who Now Restrains"

The antichrist cannot appear on the scene until "he who now restrains" is taken out of the way. Christian theologians have debated the identity of "he who now restrains" since the first century. We read in 2 Thessalonians 2:7-8: "The mystery of lawlessness is already at work. He who now restrains will continue to do so until he is taken out of the way. And then the lawless one will be revealed."

What is the "mystery of lawlessness"?

> **6ᴥ UNDERSTANDING OUR TERMS:** *Mystery*
>
> A *mystery* in the biblical sense is typically something that was unknown in earlier times (such as Old Testament times) but is now revealed through divine revelation.

In 2 Thessalonians 2:7-8, the "mystery" is the divine revelation of a future climax of global lawlessness. As *The Bible Knowledge Commentary* puts it, "Then and now a movement against divine law directed by Satan was and is operative. But it is being restrained somewhat, and this restraining will continue until the time appointed for revealing the man of sin and the climax of lawlessness."[1]

FAST FACTS ON THE MAN OF SIN

- The antichrist is the "man of sin" (2 Thessalonians 2:7-8).
- He will embody and propagate sin in an unprecedented way.
- Everything about him will be rooted in sin.

- He will be the *ultimate* man of sin.
- Sin will be the natural outflow of his character.

Is Rome the Restrainer?

Some church fathers believed that the restraining power mentioned in 2 Thessalonians 2:7-8 was the Roman Empire. The restraining power was seen as embodied in the Roman emperor.

According to this view, the apostle Paul was intentionally ambiguous about the identity of the restrainer. If he explicitly named Rome as the restrainer and his letter fell into the hands of Roman authorities, his statement about Rome being "removed" could be construed as an act of sedition.

This understanding of the restrainer may have made sense to the people living at the time. But from our vantage point today, we can see several problems with it. First, the Roman Empire fell in the fifth century after Christ, and the antichrist has not yet been revealed. This means that whoever the restrainer of 2 Thessalonians 2:7-8 is, it cannot be the Roman Empire.

Another difficulty with this view is the recognition that the antichrist will be empowered by Satan (2 Thessalonians 2:9). This requires that the restrainer be powerful enough to stand against Satan. This rules out Rome as the restrainer, since no human government (made up of finite human beings) is powerful enough to hold back the work of Satan.

We can also observe that the antichrist will rule over a revived Roman Empire (Daniel 2:7). It hardly makes sense to say that the Roman Empire—itself a bastion of false religion—would prevent the coming of the antichrist, who will rule over the empire.

Is Human Government the Restrainer?

A similar view is that human government in general will restrain the antichrist. In this view, the government restrains lawlessness by applying the rule of law. It is believed that this will prevent the rise of the man of sin—the antichrist. However, the antichrist will one day overthrow all human governments to impose his lawless agenda on the world.

Once again, we must ask whether the people who make up human government are strong enough to resist the antichrist, whom Satan energizes. Indeed, Satan is more powerful than human beings by a considerable measure, and hence it seems impossible that any form of human government could restrain him.

We can also observe that not all human governments restrain sin; some encourage it. Therefore, it may be unrealistic to say that the restrainer is human government, especially during the future tribulation period when lawlessness will prevail worldwide.

The Holy Spirit Is the Restrainer

Many theologians believe that only one entity—God—is all-powerful and can restrain Satan, who empowers the antichrist. For this reason, they interpret the restrainer to be the Holy Spirit, who dwells in and works through the church. Numerous early church fathers, including Theodoret, Theodore of Mopsuestia, and Chrysostom, held to this view.

How do we know that the Holy Spirit indwells the church? First Corinthians 3:16 tells us, "Do you not know that you are God's temple and that God's Spirit dwells in you?" Additionally, 1 Corinthians 6:19 states, "Do you not know that your body is a temple of the Holy Spirit within you, whom you have from God?"

As for the power of the Holy Spirit in dealing with Satan, we recall 1 John 4:4, which tells us: "He who is in you is greater than he who is in the world." "He who is in" Christians is the Holy Spirit, who is more powerful than "he who is in the world"—that is, the devil.

The word *restrain* in the original Greek carries the idea "to hold back from action, to keep under control, to deprive of physical liberty, as by shackling."[2] This is what the Holy Spirit is doing in our day through the church to avert the emergence of the antichrist.

The Holy Spirit's restraint of the lawless one (the antichrist) is in keeping with His broader work of restraining sin in the world (Genesis 6:3). And while the Holy Spirit presently abides in the church in a special way to restrain sin, this work of the Holy Spirit will be removed at the rapture, and the antichrist will be revealed.

YOU MAY BE INTERESTED TO KNOW...
The Holy Spirit Also Restrains Sin in the Christian's Heart

> The Holy Spirit not only restrains evil in the world but also empowers us as Christians to overcome evil in our lives.

> In Galatians 5:16-17, the apostle Paul said, "Walk by the Spirit, and you will not gratify the desires of the flesh. For the desires of the flesh are against the Spirit, and the desires of the Spirit are against the flesh, for these are opposed to each other, to keep you from doing the things you want to do."

> *Walk* is a present-tense word in the Greek, indicating continuous action. We are to walk in the Spirit 24/7.

FREQUENTLY ASKED QUESTION
If the Holy Spirit is "taken out of the way" at the rapture, will He still be active on earth during the tribulation period?

I believe He will. Even though the Holy Spirit will be "out of the way" in restraining evil, He will continue to serve in two crucial capacities:

1. He will actively lead people to salvation during the tribulation period (Revelation 7:9-12; John 16:7-11).

2. He will also empower and embolden His witnesses during this time (Revelation 7:1-4; 11:1-14; see Mark 13:11; Acts 1:8; Philippians 4:3).

"The church age is a parenthesis in God's dealing with the world. The church, injected supernaturally into history at Pentecost and supernaturally maintained throughout the age by the baptizing, indwelling, and filling works of the Holy Spirit, will be supernaturally removed when this age is over. What is to be removed, then, is the Holy Spirit's mighty working through the church. Until that happens, Satan cannot bring his plans to a head...After the rapture of the church, the Holy Spirit will continue His work in bringing people to salvation, but He will no longer baptize them into the mystical body of Christ, the church, nor will He actively hinder Satan from bringing His schemes to fruition. Once Satan has achieved his centuries-long goal, Christ will return and demolish the whole thing!"

—John Phillips[3]

"There seems to be abundant evidence that the Holy Spirit will be active in the earth during the tribulation period. He will empower His witnesses (Mark 13:11). Evangelism will be more effective than it has ever been (Matt. 24:14; Rev. 7:9-14). It is reasonable to assume that as satanic activity increases, so will the activity of the Holy Spirit."

—Paul Feinberg[4]

So, yes, the Holy Spirit will still be active on earth during the tribulation period. But His work will not be identical to that of the present age.

The removal of the church and the Holy Spirit may help explain the enormous and sudden apostasy (falling away from the truth) that will come upon the world during the first part of the tribulation period. At the rapture, the Holy Spirit—elsewhere called the "spirit of truth" (John 14:17; 16:13)—will be removed from the earth, thus facilitating the rapid emergence of untruth (or apostasy).

👤 PERSONALITY PROFILE: *Satan*

Satan is a fallen angel who is opposed to God and His purposes, and he leads a vast company of fallen angels called demons who are also opposed to God and His purposes. *Satan is called...*

> The ruler of this world—John 12:31

> The god of this world—2 Corinthians 4:4

> The prince of the power of the air—Ephesians 2:2

> The accuser of the brethren—Revelation 12:10

> Our adversary—1 Peter 5:8

> Beelzebub—Matthew 12:24

> The devil—Matthew 4:1

> Our enemy—Matthew 13:39

> The evil one—1 John 5:19

> The father of lies—John 8:44

> A murderer—John 8:44

> The tempter—Matthew 4:3

> A serpent—Genesis 3:1; Revelation 12:9

Satan deceives the entire world (Revelation 12:9; 20:3). He has power in the governmental realm (Matthew 4:8-9; 2 Corinthians 4:4), the physical realm (Luke 13:11, 16; Acts 10:38), the angelic realm (Jude 9; Ephesians 6:11-12), and the ecclesiastical (church) realm (Revelation 2:9; 3:9). He will empower the antichrist (2 Thessalonians 2:9). This Satan-empowered antichrist will be restrained by the Holy Spirit until God's chosen time (2 Thessalonians 2:7-8).

YOU MAY BE INTERESTED TO KNOW...
God Places Restrictions on Satan

> The Holy Spirit restrains the antichrist, as well as Satan who empowers the antichrist—2 Thessalonians 2:7-8.

> God restricts what Satan may do to believers; Satan is "on a leash"—Job 1:6-12.

> Satan will be bound in the bottomless pit during the millennial kingdom, and he will be unable to deceive the nations—Revelation 20:1-3.

> Satan will be judged and once for all cast into the lake of fire—Matthew 25:46; Revelation 20:10.

In the eternal state, Satan *and* the antichrist will be eternally quarantined from the people of God (Revelation 20:10).

22

Christians Face the Judgment Seat of Christ in Heaven

Every believer will ultimately face the judgment seat of Christ, also called the Bema (Romans 14:8-10; 1 Corinthians 3:11-15; 9:24-27). The lives of believers will be judged on the basis of their actions during their time on earth, taking into account their personal motives and intentions.

The idea of a "Bema," or judgment seat, goes back to the athletic games of the apostle Paul's day. When the games were over, a dignitary would sit on an elevated throne in the arena. One by one, the victorious athletes came to the judgment seat to receive a reward—usually a wreath of leaves that represented a crown of victory. In the case of Christians, we will stand before Christ the Judge and receive (or forfeit) rewards.

This judgment will not be in a corporate setting—like a big class being praised or scolded by a teacher. Rather, the judgment will be individual and personal. "We will all stand before the judgment seat of God" (Romans 14:10). We will be judged individually.

YOU MAY BE INTERESTED TO KNOW...
The Judgment Seat of Christ Is Unrelated to Salvation

> The Christian's salvation is not at stake in this judgment.

> Those who have faith in Christ are saved and nothing can disturb that.

> The believer's salvation is eternally secure (John 10:28-30; Romans 8:29-39; Ephesians 1:13; 4:30; Hebrews 7:25).

> This judgment concerns only the earning or forfeiting of rewards.

The apostle Paul used the metaphor of building a structure to illustrate the judgment of Christians. We read in 1 Corinthians 3:12-15:

> If anyone builds on the foundation with gold, silver, precious stones, wood, hay, straw—each one's work will become manifest, for the Day will disclose it, because it will be revealed by fire, and the fire will test what sort of work each one has done. If the work that anyone has built on the foundation survives, he will receive a reward. If anyone's work is burned up, he will suffer loss, though he himself will be saved, but only as through fire.

In this passage, Paul discusses materials that vary in their combustibility. Hay and straw are highly flammable, followed by wood. Precious metals and stones are noncombustible. Some materials are suitable for construction while others are not. Imagine building a house out of hay or straw—it simply wouldn't withstand the test of time, as it could easily topple over or be consumed by flames. In contrast, a structure made from durable materials such as stones and metals will not only stand firm but also endure for generations to come.

Bible scholars have pondered the symbolism of these building materials. It's possible that gold, silver, and precious stones symbolize our achievements made possible by the Holy Spirit's guidance, reflecting our Christ-centered intentions and godly obedience. On the other hand, wood, hay, and straw represent impermanent elements, perhaps alluding to worldly thinking, corrupt motives, actions rooted in arrogance, and self-centered desires.

FAST FACTS ON FIRE

- In Scripture, fire often symbolizes God's holiness (Leviticus 1:8; Hebrews 12:29).
- There are also clear instances in the Bible where fire represents God's judgment on that which His holiness has condemned (Genesis 19:24; Mark 9:43-48).
- We can surmise that God will examine our works and test them against the fire of His holiness.
- Our works will stand if they are built with proper materials such as precious metals and stones.
- They will burn up if our works are built with less valuable materials such as wood, hay, or straw.

The figure suggests that the works done to honor God are the ones that will endure. Those that are done to glorify self, that are the result of our own efforts, will be destroyed.

FREQUENTLY ASKED QUESTIONS

Is it possible that some believers will experience shame at the judgment seat of Christ?

It is indeed possible! Some believers may suffer the loss of certain rewards that they would otherwise have received. This forfeiture is bound to cause them a considerable amount of shame. As 2 John 8 warns us, it is important to "watch yourselves, so that you may not lose what we have worked for, but may win a full reward" (1 John 2:28).

How can we be happy for eternity if we do not fare well at the judgment seat of Christ?

Although not everyone will fare equally well at the judgment seat of Christ (2 John 8), it is important to maintain a balanced perspective. The prospect of Christ's return at the rapture and the opportunity to spend eternity with Him should fill all our hearts with joy. And that joy will last forever. Consider the analogy of high school students: although some may do better academically than others, they all share in the joy of graduation and look forward to their promising futures.

My late friend Norman Geisler once told me that in heaven, "all of our 'cups' will be 'running over,' but some cups will be larger than others." Perhaps the most important thing to consider is that each of us will be able to "proclaim the excellencies of him who called you out of darkness into his marvelous light" (1 Peter 2:9).

SOMETHING TO THINK ABOUT:

> There will be "haves" and "have-nots" regarding rewards handed out at the judgment seat of Christ (1 Corinthians 3:15).

> Make changes in your life today, for we are constantly being "filmed" by God's "camera."

> While we cannot erase past footage, we can begin recording new footage today.

FAST FACTS ON THE SCOPE OF THE JUDGMENT

- *The Scope of the Judgment Will Include Actions*
  Many Scriptures reveal that our actions will be judged before the Lord. The psalmist said to the Lord, "You will render to a man according to his work" (Psalm 62:12; see also Matthew 16:27). In Ephesians 6:7-8, we read, that "whatever good anyone does, this he will receive back from the Lord." As for specifics, we will certainly be held accountable for how we have used our God-given talents and abilities (1 Corinthians 12:4-7; 2 Timothy 1:6; 1 Peter 4:10), how we have spent our time (Ephesians 5:15-16; Colossians 4:5; 1 Peter 1:17), how we have treated other people (Matthew 10:41-42; Hebrews 6:10), and our hospitality to strangers (Matthew 25:35-36; Luke 14:12-14). We will give an account of how we responded to mistreatment (Matthew 5:11-12; Mark 10:29-30; Luke 6:27-28, 35; Romans 8:18; 2 Corinthians 4:17; 1 Peter 4:12-13), our efforts to win souls for Christ (1 Thessalonians 2:19-20), and our attitude toward money (Matthew 6:1-4; 1 Timothy 6:17-19).

- *The Scope of the Judgment Will Include Thoughts*
  In Jeremiah 17:10, God said, "I the LORD search the heart and test the mind, to give every man according to his ways, according to the fruit of his deeds." The Lord "will bring to light the things now hidden in darkness and will disclose the purposes of the heart" (1 Corinthians 4:5). The Lord is the One "who searches mind and heart" (Revelation 2:23).

- *The Scope of the Judgment Will Include Words*
  Christ once said that "people will give account for every careless word they speak" (Matthew 12:35-37). This is an essential aspect of judgment, for tremendous damage can be done by the human tongue (see James 3:1-12).

FAST FACTS ON THE REWARDS

Scripture often describes the rewards that await Christians at the judgment seat of Christ as crowns that we will wear. Here are four that are specified in Scripture:

- Those who endure trials, especially those who suffer to the point of death, will receive the *crown of life* (James 1:12; Revelation 2:10).

- Those who selflessly minister God's Word to the flock will receive the *crown of glory* (1 Peter 5:4).

- Those who triumph in the race of personal restraint and self-control will receive the *incorruptible crown* (1 Corinthians 9:25).

- Those who eagerly await the return of Christ will receive the *crown of righteousness* (2 Timothy 4:8).

Revelation 4:10 paints a picture of believers humbly casting their crowns before God's throne in worship and adoration. This scene conveys a powerful message: that our crowns, given to us as rewards, are not for our own glory but for the glory of God. Scripture reminds us that as believers, we are redeemed to bring glory to God (1 Corinthians 6:20). By offering our crowns in worship before His throne, we illustrate this beautiful truth.

Here is something else to consider. The greater the reward or crown we receive, the greater our capability to bring glory to the Creator in the afterlife. The smaller the reward or crown we receive, the smaller our capability to bring glory to the Creator in the afterlife. Because of the different rewards that will be distributed at the judgment seat of Christ, believers will have different capabilities to glorify God.

FREQUENTLY ASKED QUESTIONS

When will the judgment of Christ take place?

Scripture does not specify when this judgment will take place. But we can theologically infer that the judgment will take place after the rapture of the church. I say this because many Bible scholars believe that the 24 elders in heaven (Revelation 4:1, 10) represent believers—and these believers are portrayed as having already received their crowns in heaven at the very beginning of the tribulation period (see 2 Timothy 4:8; James 1:12; 1 Peter 5:4; Revelation 2:10). If they have already received their crowns at the beginning of the tribulation period, this would seem to indicate that the judgment will take place immediately after the rapture.

Consistent with this, Scripture reveals that at the second coming of Christ, which follows the tribulation period, the Bride of Christ (the corporate body of Christians) will return with Him. They will be clothed in "fine linen, bright and pure" (Revelation 19:8). Such clothing indicates that believers have already passed through judgment.

AN ENCOURAGEMENT OR A WARNING?

> The judgment seat of Christ is probably intended to be both an encouragement and a warning.

> It is an *encouragement* to those who consistently serve Christ with good motives.

> It is a *warning* to those who have fallen into carnal living. God will render perfect justice in the end.

What should our attitude be about the judgment seat of Christ?

I believe that Jesus takes great pleasure in rewarding His people. He longs to shower His believers with blessings and holy gifts. I can only imagine the joy on His face when He presents us with rewards at the judgment seat. Such a wonderful salvation should inspire us all to serve and follow Him with genuine excitement and a sense of eagerness for all the amazing things to come.

CROSS-REFERENCES

Judgment Seat of Christ

Believers judged for things done in the body—2 Corinthians 5:10

Believers must "run" to win the prize—1 Corinthians 9:24-27

Believers stand before the judgment seat—Romans 14:8-10

Believers' works tested by fire—1 Corinthians 3:10-15

Christ's eyes discern all—Revelation 1:14

Incorruptible crown for those who win the race of self-control—
  1 Corinthians 9:25

Crown of glory for those who faithfully minister God's Word—1 Peter 5:4

Crown of life for those who persevere under trial—James 1:12; Revelation
  2:10

Crown of righteousness for those who long for the second coming—2 Timothy 4:8

Each person is rewarded according to works—Psalm 62:12; Ephesians 6:7-8

The Lord examines the mind, heart, and conduct—Jeremiah 17:10; Revelation 2:23

The Lord will bring motives to light—1 Corinthians 4:5

The Lord will judge words—Matthew 12:35-37

Some believers will be ashamed at Christ's coming—1 John 2:28

Some believers will lose rewards but will still be saved—1 Corinthians 3:15; 2 John 8

23

The Sacred Union: The Marriage of the Lamb

The relationship between Christ and the church is often portrayed as a beautiful marriage. Christ is the divine Bridegroom, and the church is His beloved bride. Jesus Christ, the Lamb, often referred to Himself as the Bridegroom in the New Testament (Matthew 9:15; 22:2-14; 25:1-13; Mark 2:19-20; Luke 5:34-35; 14:15-24; John 3:29). The church, as a pure and innocent bride, is eagerly awaiting the arrival of her heavenly Bridegroom (2 Corinthians 11:2). This long-awaited event will be the rapture, a time when Christ will return to take His bride home. In the meantime, the church is obligated to keep herself pure by staying away from worldly temptations.

A PRELIMINARY THOUGHT TO ANCHOR IN YOUR HEART

> The bond between believers and Christ in heaven is one of profound closeness.

> The depth and degree of intimacy in this relationship surpasses all others.

We read about the marriage of the Lamb in Revelation 19:7-9:

> Let us rejoice and exult and give him the glory, for the marriage of the Lamb has come, and his Bride has made herself ready; it was granted her to clothe herself with fine linen, bright and pure—for the fine linen is the righteous deeds of the saints. And the angel said to me, "Write this: Blessed are those who are invited to the marriage supper of the Lamb." And he said to me, "These are the true words of God."

To understand this passage, it is necessary to first understand the three primary aspects of Hebrew weddings:

1. To start, the marriage was legally consummated by the parents of the bride and groom. "The marriage contract was often consummated by the parents when the future spouses were still children."[1] Immediately afterward, the groom went to his father's house to prepare a place for them to live.

2. Next, the groom would come to retrieve his bride. The bride would not know when the bridegroom would come for her. She had a constant attitude of expectation because it could happen any day.

3. Finally, there was a marriage supper that could last several days. Guests would be invited, and it would be an unforgettable experience.

Notice the parallels between typical Hebrew marriages and Christ's marriage to the church:

1. When individuals living in the church age come to salvation under the loving and sovereign hand of the Father, they become part of the church—the bride of Christ—betrothed to Christ the Bridegroom. If you trust in Christ at any time during the church age, *you are in!* You automatically become part of the bride of Christ.

2. The Bridegroom, Jesus Christ, will come at an unannounced time to retrieve His beautiful bride. No one knows when this will happen, but when it does, the bride will be whisked away to heaven, where He has prepared a special place just for them to live in: "I go to prepare a place for you," and "if I go and prepare a place for you, I will come again and will take you to myself, that where I am you may be also" (John 14:1-3). This amazing "place" is the magnificent New Jerusalem, a breathtakingly beautiful city where the bride of Christ will dwell for all eternity (Revelation 21–22). The marriage of the Lamb will be celebrated in heaven after the rapture but before Christ's second coming, which is seven years later (19:11-16).

The marriage ceremony will apparently take place following the judgment seat of Christ:

"The marriage ceremony takes place in heaven and involves the church. That it must take place after the judgment seat of Messiah is evident from [Revelation 19:8], for the bride is viewed as being dressed in white linen, which is the righteous acts of the saints. This means that all the wood, hay, and stubble has been burned away and all the gold, silver, and precious stones have been purified. Thus, following the rapture of the church in which the Bridegroom brings the bride with Him to His home, and following the judgment seat of Messiah which results in the bride having the white linen garments, the wedding ceremony takes place."

—Arnold Fruchtenbaum[2]

A THOUGHT TO ANCHOR IN YOUR HEART

Let the thought of what awaits you in the afterlife fill you with excitement and joy, inspiring you to live each day with great anticipation.

The bride will be beautifully clothed in shining linen, bright and clean. As Bible expositor Thomas Constable notes, "God graciously enabled her to clothe herself in fine linen (cf. 6:4; 8:3; 9:5; 15:6; 18:12; 19:14; Gen. 41:42; Dan. 10:5; 12:6-7). 'Bright' indicates divine glory, and 'clean' reflects purity (cf. 21:18, 21). This is dress appropriate for God's presence."[3] John MacArthur adds, "Such dazzling garments were worn earlier in Revelation by angels (15:6), and will be the clothing of the armies of heaven (made up of both angels and the redeemed saints) that accompany Christ when He returns to earth (v. 14)."[4]

YOU MAY BE INTERESTED TO KNOW...
Christ Is the Primary Person of Honor at This Wedding

> ➤ At most weddings, the bride is the primary person of honor.
> ➤ Although the bride of Christ is truly beautiful, it is Christ Himself, the divine Bridegroom, who will undoubtedly be the main person of honor at this wedding.
> ➤ "Let us...give him the glory" (Revelation 19:7).

The wedding ceremony will be an occasion of unparalleled joy and wonder. As our text tells us in Revelation 19:7, "Let us rejoice and exult...the marriage of the Lamb has come." The original Greek of this passage conveys the idea that "the marriage of the Lamb has come *at last*." All the inhabitants of heaven are invited to join in the celebration of this momentous event. It is a wondrous occasion that fills everyone's hearts with inexhaustible delight.

3. Finally there will be a marriage supper of the Lamb that will take place after the tribulation period but before the millennial kingdom. Daniel 12:11 reveals that there will be a 75-day interim period between the end of the tribulation and the beginning of the millennial kingdom. It would seem that the marriage supper takes place during this 75-day interval.

The guests of honor at the marriage supper of the Lamb will truly be blessed beyond measure. It will be an extraordinary privilege and a momentous occasion for all who are fortunate enough to be invited. Among the distinguished guests in attendance will be believers who were saved before the day of Pentecost, when the church was born. Like the church (the bride of Christ), these believers will be given glorified resurrection bodies and participate in Christ's millennial rule. The guests will also include those who become believers during the tribulation period, although they won't yet be glorified. They will be ushered into Christ's millennial kingdom in their mortal bodies. (They will eventually die during the millennial kingdom and be resurrected at its conclusion.)

> This magnificent marriage supper symbolizes the breathtaking conclusion of the wedding ceremony. As we move forward, for all eternity and without limit, the church, as the beautiful bride of Christ, will remain the cherished and adored companion of her beloved Groom. *How marvelous it will be!*

FAST FACTS ON ADDITIONAL PARALLELS WITH HEBREW WEDDINGS

- Ancient Jewish grooms used to pay a purchase price in order to establish the marriage covenant. In much the same way, Jesus paid a purchase price for the church: Acts 20:28 refers to "the church of God which He purchased with His own blood." Believers are informed: "You were bought with a price" (1 Corinthians 6:20).

- The church, the bride of Christ, is declared to be sanctified and set apart for her groom, just as a Jewish bride would be. She is to be cleansed of all blemishes and presented to her groom without spot or wrinkle, as a holy and perfect bride (Ephesians 5:25-27). God's people are washed, sanctified, and justified in the name of the Lord Jesus Christ, and through the Spirit of our God (1 Corinthians 1:2; 6:11). All this was made possible by the offering of the body of Jesus Christ once and for all (Hebrews 10:10).

- The anticipation of a Jewish bride waiting for her groom is not unlike the church's anticipation for the arrival of Jesus the Bridegroom at the rapture—an event that could happen at any time. No prophecy needs to be fulfilled before this glorious event takes place. The excitement of the unknown adds to the thrill of the wait.

God's Words About the Marriage Are Trustworthy and True

- God's words about the marriage supper of the Lamb "are the true words of God" (Revelation 19:9).

- "Write this down, for these words are trustworthy and true" (21:5).

- Indeed, "these words are trustworthy and true" (22:6).

- This threefold repetition regarding the truth of God's Word settles the matter without dispute. God's prophetic revelation can be trusted!

PART 7

The Ezekiel Invasion

IN THIS SECTION

24 — The Emerging End-Times Military Coalition Against Israel—206

25 — The Timing of the Invasion—214

26 — The Epic Defeat of the Invaders—228

The Emerging End-Times Military Coalition Against Israel

More than 2,600 years ago, the prophet Ezekiel boldly prophesied that in the end times the Jews would be restored to the land of Israel, gathered from the far reaches of "many nations" (Ezekiel 36–37). But he later described a terrifying invasion that would be launched against Israel by a monumental northern invasion force, consisting of a coalition of Russia and a group of Muslim nations, including Iran, Sudan, Turkey, Libya, and others. Their ultimate intentions are twofold: to annihilate the Jewish people and to claim Israel's vast wealth—from its precious "silver and gold," to its abundant "livestock and goods," and "great spoil" (38:11-13). The odds of Israel surviving such an attack are slim to none, but God will intervene and supernaturally destroy the invaders (38–39).

It is truly remarkable that Ezekiel prophesied that these specific discontiguous nations would unite for an end-time invasion of Israel. It's even more incredible when you consider that these nations had never before joined together for any kind of invasion. And yet, more than 2,600 years ago, Ezekiel foresaw their inevitable alliance.

YOU MAY BE INTERESTED TO KNOW...

There is a Religious Unifying Factor for the Northern Alliance

> An alliance between the nations mentioned in Ezekiel 38–39 would have been far-fetched in Ezekiel's day because of their geographical distance from each other.

> Today, it makes perfect sense because the coalition is made up of predominantly Muslim nations. (Russia is the one exception.)

> Islam wasn't established until the seventh century AD, long after Ezekiel's time.

> The Islamic nations may have their differences, but their shared animosity toward Israel serves as a powerful unifying force.

It is eye-opening that the nations prophesied to come together in the end times are already doing so in our day. It appears that the stage is being set for the prophesied future invasion of Israel.

The invasion is described in Ezekiel 38:1-9, which is admittedly not the easiest passage to understand. But hang in there with me. Give it a quick read:

> The word of the LORD came to me saying, "Son of man, set your face toward Gog of the land of Magog, the prince of Rosh, Meshech and Tubal, and prophesy against him and say, 'Thus says the Lord GOD, "Behold, I am against you, O Gog, prince of Rosh, Meshech and Tubal. I will turn you about and put hooks into your jaws, and I will bring you out, and all your army, horses and horsemen, all of them splendidly attired, a great company with buckler and shield, all of them wielding swords; Persia, Ethiopia and Put with them, all of them with shield and helmet; Gomer with all its troops; Beth-Togarmah from the remote parts of the north with all its troops—many peoples with you..."

> "After many days you will be summoned; in the latter years you will come into the land that is restored from the sword, whose inhabitants have been gathered from many nations to the mountains of Israel which had been a continual waste; but its people were brought out from the nations, and they are living securely, all of them. You will go up, you will come like a storm; you will be like a cloud covering the land, you and all your troops, and many peoples with you"'" (NASB 1995).

👤 PERSONALITY PROFILE: *Gog*

> The enigmatic figure of "Gog" is the powerful leader of the end-time northern military coalition that is foretold to launch an invasion against Israel.

> Gog is "the chief prince of Meshech and Tubal" (Ezekiel 38:2).

> > He is mentioned eleven times in Ezekiel 38–39, indicating that he plays a significant role in this end-time invasion.
>
> > The term *Gog* literally means "high," "supreme," "a height," or "a high mountain."
>
> > The term may therefore refer to a king-like role—such as pharaoh, caesar, czar, or president.
>
> > This czar-like leader will embody great stature and command great respect.

Gog must not be mistaken as just another reference to the antichrist. If we were to erroneously conflate the two, our understanding of prophecy would be thrown into chaos. It's essential to keep in mind that the antichrist leads a revived Roman Empire (Daniel 2; 7) while Gog commands an army from Russia and a number of Muslim nations (Ezekiel 38:1-6). In addition, Gog's invasion of Israel is in direct opposition to the antichrist's covenant with Israel (Daniel 9:27). Furthermore, Gog's time in the spotlight is short-lived, as God immediately defeats the invading army in Ezekiel 39. In contrast, the antichrist is in power throughout the tribulation period.

Ezekiel 38:1-6 reveals that Gog leads a formidable coalition that includes Magog, Rosh, Meshech and Tubal, Persia, Ethiopia, Put, Gomer, and Beth-Togarmah. But what are we to make of these ancient names and places? Let's dig in and find out.

📖 GEOGRAPHY IN THE END TIMES: *The Identity of Magog*

The ancient region of Magog is believed by many scholars to encompass the mountainous area near the Black and Caspian Seas that was formerly ruled by the Scythians. This area now includes modern Kazakhstan, Kyrgyzstan, Uzbekistan, Turkmenistan, Tajikistan, and possibly even parts of northern Afghanistan. This entire Muslim-dominated area has a strong religious motivation to act against Israel.

📖 GEOGRAPHY IN THE END TIMES: *The Identity of Rosh*

Rosh is modern Russia. This is something that respected Hebrew scholars believe to be true, and there is ample historical evidence to support it. Not only do numerous ancient sources refer to a place called Rosh—

sometimes spelled Rus, Ros, or Rox—in the same region as modern Russia, but there is also evidence of a people called Rosh or Rashu in Assyrian sources dating back to the ninth to seventh centuries BC, well before the time of Ezekiel. So we have quite early evidence of a "Ros" people who were geographically located in what is now Russia. Egypt also has inscriptions referring to a place called Rash, dating as far back as 2600 BC. An inscription from 1500 BC refers to a land called Reshu, located north of Egypt (as in modern Russia). Finally, in Ezekiel 39:2, Rosh is said to be in "the uttermost parts of the north." The term "north" is to be understood in reference to Israel. If you draw a line from Israel and go straight north, you end up in Russia.

FREQUENTLY ASKED QUESTION

Why does the term "Rosh" not appear in the ESV, NIV, NET, HCSB, and NLT translations except as a marginal note?

The meaning of "Rosh" has been hotly debated by Bible scholars, with a particular focus on whether the Hebrew word in this verse refers to a geographical location or a description of a leader. Some interpreters suggest that Rosh is a noun and refers to a place name (called "Rosh"). Others argue that the word is an adjective, and is better translated as "chief," qualifying the title of "prince," so that it reads "*chief* prince."

Hebrew scholars C.F. Keil and Wilhelm Gesenius are convinced that Rosh is a geographical place. The translation of Rosh as an adjective, meaning "chief prince," seems to have come from the Latin Vulgate, which was translated by Jerome. Jerome admitted that he did not base his translation on any grammatical considerations. He struggled to translate Rosh as a proper noun simply because he could find no reference to it as a geographical place elsewhere in Scripture. Even today, many modern English translations reflect Jerome's approach to this verse.

Taking Rosh as a geographical place is the most natural rendering of the original Hebrew. The NASB 1995 translation agrees with this. I don't see any valid reason for interpreting it as an adjective.

📖 GEOGRAPHY IN THE END TIMES: *The Identity of Meshech and Tubal*

Meshech and Tubal, two names often mentioned together in the Bible, refer to the area located south of the Black and Caspian Seas in Ezekiel's day. This region is now known as Turkey, although there may be some overlap with neighboring countries. Meshech and Tubal are believed to be the same as the Mushki and Tabal of the Assyrians and the Moschi and Tibareni of the Greeks. These ancient tribes are known to have inhabited the same region that is now modern Turkey. This is confirmed by the ancient historian Herodotus.

📖 GEOGRAPHY IN THE END TIMES: *The Identity of Persia*

The land of ancient Persia, now known as Iran, has a rich history. Its name has changed over time, from Persia to Iran in 1935 and, after the Iranian Revolution in 1979, to the Islamic Republic of Iran. From a prophetic perspective, it is no coincidence that the third largest buyer of Russian arms is Iran—a country known for its venomous hatred of Israel. It seems that the alliance between Rosh and Persia (Russia and Iran) and other Muslim nations is coming together in our own day. Iran's 25-year military modernization program for its air defense, naval warfare capabilities, and land combat capabilities is entirely dependent on Russian technology and weapons. Moreover, with Russia's assistance in Iran's nuclear program, the stakes have never been higher.

📖 GEOGRAPHY IN THE END TIMES: *The Identity of Ethiopia*

South of Egypt on the Nile River is a territory known today as Sudan (see Ezekiel 38:5). Sudan (Ethiopia) is a hardline Islamic state that shares a kindred spirit with Iran in its vicious hatred of Israel. It would not be unexpected for these two close allies to take a common stance against Israel. Sudan is notorious for its ties to terrorism and for harboring Osama bin Laden from 1991 to 1996.

📖 GEOGRAPHY IN THE END TIMES: *The Identity of Put*

Put, a land west of Egypt, is modern Libya (Ezekiel 38:5). However, ancient Libya is larger than modern Libya. Therefore, the boundaries of Put referred to in Ezekiel 38–39 may extend beyond modern Libya, perhaps including parts of Algeria and Tunisia.

▥ GEOGRAPHY IN THE END TIMES: *The Identity of Gomer*

Gomer is modern Turkey (see Ezekiel 38:6). The ancient historian Josephus said that Gomer founded those whom the Greeks called the Galatians. The Galatians of New Testament times lived near central Turkey. Therefore, there is a direct connection between ancient Gomer and modern Turkey. Many claim that Gomer may be a reference to the ancient Cimmerians or Kimmerioi. History shows that the Cimmerians occupied the geographical area of modern Turkey from about 700 BC.

▥ GEOGRAPHY IN THE END TIMES: *The Identity of Beth-Togarmah*

Beth-Togarmah is a compound word, with Beth meaning "house" in Hebrew. Beth-Togarmah means "the house of Togarmah." Ezekiel 38:6 refers to Beth-Togarmah as being from the remote parts of the north— that is, to the north *of Israel*. Some commentators believe that Beth-Togarmah is yet another reference to modern Turkey, far north of Israel. This view is consistent with the geography of Ezekiel's time, for at that time there was a city in Cappadocia (modern Turkey) known as Tegarma, Tagarma, Tilgarimmu, and Takarama. If this identification is correct, it confirms that Turkey will be one of the nations in the northern military coalition that will invade Israel in the end times (Ezekiel 38:1-6).

FREQUENTLY ASKED QUESTION
Will Iraq be a part of the invading force?

One may wonder why the Islamic nation of Iraq has not been included in this invading Islamic coalition. Undoubtedly, today's Iraq would fervently desire the destruction of Israel. Therefore, the absence of any mention of Iraq raises questions.

It is not beyond the realm of possibility that Iraq will indeed be part of this invading coalition. In addition to the specific nations mentioned in Ezekiel 38, we find the phrase "and many nations with you" (Ezekiel 38:6, 9, 15, 22).

Could Iraq be one of these "many nations"? It is impossible to say for sure, but this phrase opens the door to the possibility.

In an alternative scenario, the Islamic coalition invading force may exclude Iraq because the antichrist will establish his base in Babylon (or "New Babylon"), the rebuilt capital of Iraq, during the tribulation period (Revelation 17–18). The antichrist will sign a seven-year peace covenant with Israel, marking the beginning of the tribulation period (Daniel 9:27). If the Ezekiel invasion occurs in the first half of the tribulation, Iraq could not possibly be a part of the invading force simply because Iraq, with its capital in New Babylon, will be controlled by the antichrist, who has signed the peace treaty with Israel.

YOU MAY BE INTERESTED TO KNOW...
God Is Sovereign and Will Summon the Ezekiel Invaders

> - Psalm 50:1 identifies God as the Mighty One who "speaks and summons the earth from the rising of the sun to its setting."
> - Psalm 66:7 affirms that He "rules by his might forever."
> - Psalm 93:1 assures us that "the Lord reigns."
> - God asserts, "My counsel shall stand, and I will accomplish all my purpose" (Isaiah 46:10).
> - God assures us, "As I have planned, so shall it be, and as I have purposed, so shall it stand" (Isaiah 14:24).
> - Proverbs 16:9 says, "The heart of man plans his way, but the Lord establishes his steps."
> - Proverbs 19:21 says, "Many are the plans in the mind of a man, but it is the purpose of the Lord that will stand."
> - In light of verses like these, it is not surprising that God is also portrayed in Scripture as sovereign over the nations of the earth.
> - God says to the Ezekiel invaders: "I will turn you about and put hooks into your jaws, and I will bring you out" (Ezekiel 38:4).
> - God also says, "You will be summoned" (38:8 NASB 1995).
> - God says: "I shall bring you against my land" (38:16).
> - Such words indicate that it is God who is sovereignly orchestrating the events that are unfolding on earth.

Those interested in a detailed study of the Ezekiel invasion are invited to consult my book Northern Storm Rising: Russia, Iran, and the Emerging End-Times Military Coalition Against Israel *(Harvest House Publishers).*

The Timing of the Invasion

There's a lot of debate about when the Ezekiel invasion of Israel will take place:

> Will it be before the tribulation period, during the tribulation period, or perhaps toward the end of the tribulation period?

> Could it even be after the tribulation period or during the millennial kingdom?

> Let's explore these possibilities together.

Preliminary Considerations on the Timing of the Invasion

1. The "Latter Years" or "Last Days"

The prophet Ezekiel stated that the fulfillment of his prophecy of an invasion of Israel by a northern military coalition would occur "in the latter years" (Ezekiel 38:3) and "the last days" (verse 16).

> 🔎 **UNDERSTANDING OUR TERMS:** *Latter Years / Last Days*
>
> > The terms "latter years" and "last days" in the New Testament can refer to the present church age (Hebrews 1:1-2; 1 Peter 1:20).
>
> > However, in the Old Testament these terms refer specifically to the tribulation period (Deuteronomy 4:27-30; Daniel 2:28; 8:19, 23; 10:14) and the subsequent millennial kingdom (Isaiah 2:24; Micah 4:1-7). This is the intended meaning of the word in Ezekiel 36–37.

2. No Invasion on the Scale of Ezekiel 38–39 Has Ever Occurred in Israel's History

Israel has seen countless battles and invasions in its history. But there has never been an invasion in which:

1. A massive alliance consisting of Russia, Iran, Turkey, Sudan, Libya, and other Muslim nations attacked Israel.

2. The alliance was catastrophically destroyed by God with a massive earthquake, infighting among the troops, the outbreak of disease, and fire and brimstone from heaven, as will be the case with the Ezekiel invasion.

3. There were so many casualties that it took seven months to bury all the bodies in a large valley, as will be the case with the Ezekiel invasion.

We conclude that if the invasion has not happened yet, it will happen in the future. More to the point, the invasion did not take place in Ezekiel's day, as some have tried to argue, but will take place in the last days.

3. A Precondition: Israel Must Be Restored to the Land

A prerequisite for the invasion of Israel by a northern coalition is that Israel must first be restored to the land. Ezekiel 38:8 refers to the Holy Land "whose inhabitants have been gathered from many nations to the mountains of Israel" (see also Ezekiel 36–37). Because Israel was reborn in 1948 after a long and worldwide dispersion of Jews to many countries worldwide, a crucial piece of the puzzle has now fallen into place, paving the way for the future invasion of Israel by the northern military coalition (38–39).

4. Israel Must Be Living in Security and At Rest

Israel must live in security and be at rest as a prerequisite for the northern military invasion. The Jews in the land must be "living securely, all of them" (Ezekiel 38:8). This sense of security will mean that there won't be a need for walls or gates around the villages in Israel.

> Some Christians today believe that Israel is already secure because of its well-equipped army, top-notch air force, effective missile defense system, strong economy, and solid relationship with the United States.

> Others believe that Israel will not be safe until a covenant is signed with the antichrist guaranteeing Israel's protection (Daniel 9:27).

5. Certain National Developments Are to Be Expected

A final precondition for the invasion of Israel by the northern military coalition is that one would expect certain national developments to occur in connection with the emergence of this coalition. More specifically, one would expect certain nations to be in power and for alliances to develop between them prior to the invasion. We might also expect some indication among these nations of a motivation to invade Israel.

We can make the following observations:

> Expansionist Russia already has alliances with several Muslim nations.

> Russia has previously collaborated with Muslim nations in joint hostilities against Israel, such as the 1973 attack on Israel, where the Russians cooperated with Egypt, Syria, and other Islamic countries.

> The Muslim nations, in particular, hate Israel. Some have expressed a desire to "push Israel into the sea" and "wipe Israel off the map."

Prophetic Scenarios on the Timing of the Ezekiel Invasion

BEFORE THE TRIBULATION, BEFORE THE RAPTURE

Some Christians believe that the northern military coalition could possibly invade Israel before both the tribulation and the rapture. This perspective is presented in popular works such as the *Left Behind* series by Tim LaHaye and Jerry Jenkins, as well as Joel Rosenberg's novel *The Ezekiel Option*. Among the reasons given for this view are:

• If the Ezekiel invasion occurs before the rapture and the seven-year tribulation, the seven-year burning of the invaders' weapons (Ezekiel 39:9) can begin immediately after the tribulation begins.

- Israel's ability to build its new temple may be best explained by this view, considering that if Muslims were in power during the early part of the tribulation period, it would be difficult for Israel (whom the Muslims hate) to build its temple on the Temple Mount in Jerusalem. However, if God incapacitates the Muslim armies before the tribulation period begins, then this significant obstacle to Israel's rebuilding of the temple will be removed, with much less Muslim opposition.

Despite the arguments in favor of this position, there are also significant problems associated with it:

- The idea that the invasion will take place before the rapture seems to contradict Ezekiel's explicit statement that it will take place in the "last days" or "latter years" (Ezekiel 38:8, 16). These terms usually refer to the tribulation period and the subsequent millennial kingdom in Old Testament prophecies. However, pretribulationist Arnold Fruchtenbaum does not think this is a problem. He believes that "these terms simply apply to the whole period of the end times when prophecy is again being fulfilled, and so it can easily apply to the closing days of the Church Age as well."[1]

- Some pretribulationists believe that the idea of the invasion taking place before the rapture contradicts Ezekiel's prophecy that the invasion would take place when Israel is living in security and at rest (Ezekiel 38:11). According to these interpreters, Israel will not have this strong sense of security and rest until the leader of the revived Roman Empire (the antichrist) signs a peace pact, guaranteeing Israel's protection (Daniel 9:27). Until the covenant is signed, Israel will remain on high alert for the possibility of an attack.

- According to the New Testament, the rapture could happen at any time without other prophetic events having to occur first (Philippians 3:20; 4:5; 1 Thessalonians 1:10; Titus 2:13; James 5:8-9). Therefore, it is not accurate to say that a specific invasion must take place before the rapture. In fairness, however, many who believe that the invasion may occur before the rapture "carefully avoid saying that it *must* occur before the rapture."[2] They remain committed to the doctrine of imminence.

- According to 2 Thessalonians 2:6-8, the antichrist (also called the "lawless one") cannot appear until "he who now restrains" is removed. Many believe that the Holy Spirit is the Restrainer, and that the Holy Spirit will be "taken out of the way" at the rapture of the church. This is because the church is the temple of the Holy Spirit (1 Corinthians 3:16). Considering this, one could feasibly argue that (1) Israel will not experience security until the antichrist signs a peace pact with Israel, which begins the tribulation. But (2) the antichrist cannot appear on the scene until after the rapture, because that is when the Restrainer—the Holy Spirit—will be removed. Therefore, (3) Israel will not experience security until *after* the rapture. This means that (4) the invasion of the northern military coalition cannot take place until after the rapture.

AFTER THE RAPTURE, BEFORE THE TRIBULATION

Other Christians believe that the Ezekiel invasion will occur after the rapture but before the tribulation. There may be an interval between these two events. Several arguments are given to support this view:

- After the rapture, the world will be in chaos. Because of the large number of Christians in the United States, this country will suffer more than other countries. As a result, Russia and its Muslim allies may seize the moment and see this as an opportune time to launch a massive attack on Israel. (Israel has historically been protected by the United States.)

- After God destroys Russia and the Muslim invaders before the tribulation, this will likely pave the way for the rise of the antichrist as the political leader of a revived Roman Empire—a European superstate. Russia's expansionism would thus be thwarted. And any hope of a worldwide Islamic caliphate would be dashed. This would make the rise of the antichrist on the world stage easier and faster.

- With the Muslim invaders already destroyed before the tribulation begins, it may be easier for the antichrist to make a covenant with Israel (as prophesied in Daniel 9:27) and ensure Israel's protection. This is because Israel will be more defensible in the absence of Muslim forces.

- This scenario, like the previous one, could explain why Israel will be able to build the Jewish Temple on the Temple Mount in Jerusalem. With the destruction of Muslim forces, Muslim resistance will be minimal to nonexistent.

Among the common objections to this scenario are:

- Some interpreters object to the idea that the northern invasion occurs before the tribulation period because it seems to contradict the fact that the invasion is to occur in the "last days" or "latter years" (Ezekiel 38:8, 16). As noted above, many pretribulationists believe that these phrases, when used in reference to Israel, refer to the future tribulation period and the subsequent millennial kingdom. (However, other pretribs, such as Arnold Fruchtenbaum, say that the "last days" could also include some prophetic events prior to the tribulation period.)

- Some pretribulationists argue that the concept of the invasion occurring after the rapture but before the tribulation contradicts Ezekiel's prophecy that the invasion will take place only when Israel is living in security and at rest (Ezekiel 38:11). According to this view, Israel will not experience that security and rest until the leader of the revived Roman Empire (the antichrist) signs a covenant guaranteeing Israel's protection (Daniel 9:27). Other pretribs counter that Israel already lives in relative security because of its well-equipped army, first-rate air force, effective missile defense system, strong economy, and firm relationship with the United States.

FIRST HALF OF THE TRIBULATION OR MIDDLE OF THE TRIBULATION

A third position held by many is that the invasion of Israel by the northern military coalition could occur during the first half or even the middle of the tribulation. This position is supported by arguments such as:

- It easily meets the requirement that Israel be secure and at rest before the invasion. This state of security and rest will be based on Israel signing the peace pact with the leader of the revived Roman Empire—the antichrist.

- Those who believe in this theory claim that when God destroys the northern coalition in the first half of the tribulation, it will create a power vacuum that will allow the antichrist to quickly rise to power. Without the presence of Russia and the Muslims, the antichrist will have a much easier time achieving global dominance (Revelation 13).

- The destruction of the Muslim forces during the first half of the tribulation clears the way for the emergence of a one-world religion. Because the Christians will already have been raptured and the Muslim forces will also be out of the way, the emergence of a one-world religion will be much easier in this religious void.

As with the other scenarios, this view has some weaknesses:

- If the invasion occurs during the first half or midpoint of the tribulation period, the seven-year burning of enemy weapons would extend into the millennium. A midtrib invasion, for example, would require the burning of the invaders' weapons to continue for three-and-a-half years into the millennium.

- It's puzzling why God would dispose of the northern intruders during the middle of the tribulation to protect Israel only to then allow the horrific events of the second half to severely damage Israel. A more plausible option would be to place the invasion a few years before the tribulation.

END OF THE TRIBULATION (ARMAGEDDON)

Another view is that the invasion takes place toward the end of the tribulation and is synonymous with Armageddon. A number of suggested reasons underscore this perspective:

- Because Armageddon takes place during the tribulation, and because Ezekiel's invasion is said to take place in the "last days" and "latter years" (terms indicating the tribulation), these events must be equated.

- Not only will birds and predatory animals feast on the dead bodies left after God's destruction of the northern coalition (Ezekiel 39:4, 17-20), but they will also feast on the remains after Armageddon

(Revelation 19:17-18). This further solidifies the connection between these two events.

- Zechariah 12:10 tells us that many Jews will turn to the Lord at the end of the tribulation (in conjunction with Armageddon). At the Ezekiel invasion, God affirms that "the house of Israel will know that I am the Lord their God from that day onward" (Ezekiel 39:22). Ezekiel 39:29 also quotes God as saying, "I will have poured out My Spirit on the house of Israel." Therefore, the time of salvation seems to be the same in both cases.

Despite such arguments, there are also notable problems with this view:

- Armageddon is a conflict involving all the nations of the earth (Joel 3:2; Zephaniah 3:8; Zechariah 12:3; 14:4). In contrast, the northern military coalition that attacks Israel will involve only Russia, Iran, Sudan, Turkey, Libya, and some other Muslim nations (Ezekiel 38:1-6).

- At Armageddon, the destruction takes place on the "Mount of Megiddo," about 60 miles north of Jerusalem. However, in the Ezekiel invasion the devastation takes place on the mountains of Israel. The locations are different.

- The Armageddon casualties result from the personal appearance of Jesus Christ at the second coming (Revelation 19:15). The casualties of the northern military coalition are caused by a great earthquake, infighting among the troops, the outbreak of disease, and torrential rain coupled with fire and brimstone raining down on the troops (Ezekiel 38:20-22).

- At the end of the tribulation (at Armageddon), the Jews will face great persecution at the hands of the antichrist, depriving them of any possible security and peace. As noted above, security and peace are prerequisites for the Ezekiel invasion.

- In Ezekiel 38:13, some nations lamely protest the Ezekiel invasion against Israel. In the Armageddon campaign, however, the absence of protest is conspicuous because all nations are involved in the conflict.

- If we consider the Ezekiel invasion to be the same as Armageddon (toward the end of the tribulation period), the enemy's weapons will be burned for seven years, well into the millennial kingdom.

- In the epic battle of Armageddon, the beast (antichrist) reigns as the commander of the invasion campaign (Revelation 19:19), while Ezekiel's prophecy sees Gog as the head of the invading force (Ezekiel 38:7).

- The armies assembled at Armageddon are arrayed against Jesus Christ (Revelation 19:19), which is not the case with the Ezekiel invasion.

BETWEEN THE END OF THE TRIBULATION AND THE BEGINNING OF THE MILLENNIUM

A sparse number of interpreters place the Ezekiel invasion between the end of the tribulation and the beginning of the millennium. Allegedly, there will be an interlude during which Ezekiel 38–39 will be fulfilled.

To support this position, some claim that if it is possible for there to be an interlude between the rapture and the beginning of the tribulation, then, to be consistent, there could be an interlude between the end of the tribulation and the beginning of the millennial kingdom. An interlude of sufficient time would allow for the burial of the dead for seven months.

It is also suggested that after the second coming, Israel will truly live in security and rest. Therefore, the invasion must take place at that time.

The big problem with this view is not that there will be an interlude of some length between the end of the tribulation and the beginning of the millennial kingdom, but that there will be an interlude of sufficient time to accommodate all the details of Ezekiel 38–39. Many commentators grant that there will be an interlude of 75 days between the end of the tribulation period and the beginning of the millennial kingdom (see Daniel 12:11-12). (I hold to this view.) However, the interlude would have to be at least seven years to accommodate the burning of enemy weapons as prophesied in Ezekiel 39:9. There is no evidence in Scripture for such a long interlude.

BEGINNING OF THE MILLENNIUM

Another interpretation suggests that the invasion could take place at the beginning of the millennial kingdom. This view is supported by the belief that Israel will experience absolute peace and rest under the rule of Christ during

His reign, making it logical for the northern invasion to occur in the early stages of that kingdom.

There are significant problems with this view:

- Isaiah 2:4 specifically tells us that there will be no war in Christ's millennial kingdom. This would eliminate any possibility of an invasion of Israel by a northern military coalition. The only war that breaks out is when Satan is released after the millennium (Revelation 20:7-9).

- Such an invasion of Israel at the beginning of the millennium would be virtually impossible, because after Christ's return there will be a judgment of the nations in which all unbelievers will be put to death (Matthew 25:31-46). Jeremiah 25:32-33 clearly states that the Lord will destroy all the wicked of the earth at His return. This is reiterated in Revelation 19:15-18. *Only believers enter Christ's millennial kingdom.* And believers would never launch an invasion of Israel!

- Ezekiel 39:12 tells us that after the Ezekiel invasion, the land will be defiled for seven months until all the dead bodies are buried. It is difficult to believe that the land will be defiled for seven months during the inauguration period of Christ's millennial kingdom.

- Because Isaiah 9:4-5 tells us that all weapons of war will be destroyed after the beginning of Christ's millennial kingdom, where will the northern military coalition get its weapons?

- Many today consider the Muslim hatred of the Jewish people to be satanically inspired. However, at the beginning of the millennium, Satan will be bound until after the millennium (Revelation 20:1-3). Therefore, Satan will not be on earth during the early part of the millennium to stir up hatred against Jewish believers.

- It is inconceivable that any nation would attempt to attack Israel in a kingdom where Christ Himself reigns. It would be the height of madness.

END OF THE MILLENNIUM

Still other interpreters believe that the Ezekiel invasion will occur at the end of the millennial kingdom. This view is dominant among nonevangelicals. Arguments for this view include:

- At the end of the millennium, Revelation 20:7-10 tells us: "When the thousand years are completed, Satan will be released from his prison, and will come out to deceive the nations which are in the four corners of the earth, Gog and Magog, to gather them together for the war; the number of them is like the sand of the seashore. And they came up on the broad plain of the earth and surrounded the camp of the saints and the beloved city, and fire came down from heaven and devoured them. And the devil who deceived them was thrown into the lake of fire and brimstone, where the beast and the false prophet are also; and they will be tormented day and night forever and ever." Because Revelation 20:7-10 alludes to Gog and Magog, some argue that this invasion is the same as that described in Ezekiel 38–39. Therefore, the Ezekiel invasion takes place at the end of the millennial kingdom.

- In both cases, numerous soldiers are mentioned. In the Ezekiel invasion, we find phrases such as "a great company" (Ezekiel 38:4), "many peoples with you" (Ezekiel 38:6), and "a great assembly" (Ezekiel 38:15). Similarly, the invasion force described in Revelation is colossal, "the number of whom is as the sand of the sea" (Revelation 20:8).

- This view best explains the tremendous prosperity of Israel when this invasion occurs (Ezekiel 38:12). This prosperity is the fulfillment of God's promise of millennial blessings to Israel.

- In both cases, God defeats the invaders (Ezekiel 39:3-6; Revelation 20:9).

Among the problems with this interpretation are:

- The chronology is all wrong. The invasion described in Ezekiel 38–39 is part of a larger section of Ezekiel's book dealing with the restoration of Israel after a long and worldwide dispersion (chapters 33–39). These chapters are not in a millennial context.

- The invasion prophesied by Ezekiel is followed by the establishment of the millennial kingdom (Ezekiel 40–48). In contrast, the invasion prophesied in Revelation 20:7-10 leads to the establishment of the eternal state (Revelation 21–22).

- The seven months required to bury the dead makes little sense in an end-of-millennium scenario. Think about it. In this scenario, the Israelites spend seven hard months burying the wicked dead who invaded them. Immediately thereafter, according to Revelation, these wicked dead are resurrected to participate in the great white throne judgment and cast into the lake of fire. This makes little sense. Besides, Revelation 20:9 tells us that "fire came down from God out of heaven, and devoured them." There will be no bodies left to bury because they will all be incinerated.

- The next event in the book of Revelation after the great white throne judgment is the beginning of the eternal state (Revelation 21). This, of course, brings up the problem of the burning of the weapons for seven years. If this invasion occurs at the end of the millennial kingdom, then the burning of the weapons would have to extend beyond the millennial kingdom into the eternal state, which makes no sense.

- In the Ezekiel invasion, a coalition of localized nations (Russia and several Muslim nations) invades from the north. In the end-of-millennium invasion, an international army—"the nations which are in the four quarters of the earth"—participates in the battle (Revelation 20:8).

- The invasion mentioned in Revelation 20:9 is "up on the broad plain" and against "the camp of the saints." The invasion prophesied by Ezekiel takes place on the mountains of Israel (Ezekiel 39:2; 38:16).

- The invasion prophesied by Ezekiel takes place relatively soon after the rebirth of Israel and the gathering of the Jewish people from around the world (Ezekiel 36–37). The invasion mentioned in Revelation 20:7-10 occurs after Israel has enjoyed the fulfillment of God's covenant promises for a thousand years.

- It is likely that the apostle John used the terms *Gog and Magog* in Revelation 20:9 as a shorthand metaphor, just as we do today. For example, the word *Wall Street* in English has come to refer metaphorically to the stock market. Likewise, in New Testament times, terms such as *Corinthian* and *Nazarene* came to refer metaphorically to people with less than desirable characteristics. Whether among modern people or New Testament people, those who hear such words immediately make the proper connection and understand what is meant by the use of such terms. Likewise, when John used the terms *Gog and Magog* in Revelation 20:7-10, his readers undoubtedly immediately made the proper connection and understood that this invasion at the end of the millennium would be like what Ezekiel described in that a league of nations would attack Israel but not succeed. It would be a Gog/Magog-like invasion.

My Assessment

Here is my assessment of the matter:

1. I cannot consider either of the millennial views to be correct. The problems with these positions are far too substantial for them to be viable.

2. I also cannot agree that the invasion will take place between the end of the tribulation and the beginning of the millennium. I see virtually no evidence for such a view in the pages of Scripture.

3. The views that the invasion occurs either in the middle of the tribulation or at the end of the tribulation are difficult to reconcile with what the larger body of Bible prophecy reveals about the tribulation period. Therefore, I reject these views.

4. The two positions that I believe have the highest probability of being correct are as follows: (1) the invasion occurs after the rapture but before the tribulation; and (2) the invasion occurs at the beginning of the tribulation. If the invasion occurs before the tribulation, it makes good sense to place it at least three-and-a-half years before the tribulation. This view resolves one of the major puzzles: the burning of the weapons for seven years prior to Israel's flight from Jerusalem at the midpoint of the tribulation, after which the Jews will be severely persecuted by the antichrist.

CROSS-REFERENCES
The Ezekiel Invasion

Coalition of nations invades Israel—Ezekiel 38:1-6

Ancient weaponry—Ezekiel 38:4

Animals feast on the bodies of enemies—Ezekiel 39:17-20

Burial of enemy bodies will take seven months—Ezekiel 39:11-12, 14-16

Conversion of multitudes—Ezekiel 39:21-29

Enemies devise an evil plan—Ezekiel 38:10-11

Enemies covet Israel's wealth—Ezekiel 38:11-12

Enemy weapons gathered and burned—Ezekiel 39:9-10

God causes infighting and disease among enemy troops—Ezekiel 38:21-22

God destroys invaders—Ezekiel 38:17–39:8

God exalts Himself in His enemies' destruction—Ezekiel 38:23

God sends the rain, hailstones, fire, and burning sulfur on enemy troops—Ezekiel 38:22

God causes earthquake against enemies—Ezekiel 38:19-20

God watches over Israel—Psalm 121:4

Israel will live in security before the invasion—Ezekiel 38:11

Jews will be gathered from many nations—Ezekiel 36–37; 38:8, 12

No weapon against Israel prospers—Isaiah 54:17

Occurs in the "latter years" and "last days"—Ezekiel 38:8, 16

Pray for the peace of Jerusalem (Psalm 122:6).

26

The Epic Defeat of the Invaders

Israel will find itself alone, without allies, facing a formidable northern military coalition consisting of Russia and a group of Muslim nations. From a purely human standpoint, Israel's chances of survival seem virtually nonexistent, as it will be vastly and hopelessly outnumbered. With such an imbalance of power, one might assume that the outcome of this battle is easily predictable. Yet, in the looming shadow of this Goliath-like adversary, God stands strong!

God possesses unfathomable power (Jeremiah 32:17), capable of accomplishing all that He desires and wills. Throughout Scripture, He is referred to as almighty no less than 56 times (such as in Revelation 19:6). With an abundance of power (Psalm 147:5) and unparalleled might (2 Chronicles 20:6; Ephesians 1:19-21), no one can restrain God's actions (Daniel 4:35) or reverse His decisions (Isaiah 43:13). No one can hinder His divine plans (Isaiah 14:27). With Him, all things are possible (Matthew 19:26; Mark 10:27; Luke 1:37), and no challenge is insurmountable (Genesis 18:14; Jeremiah 32:17, 27). Indeed, the Almighty reigns supreme (Revelation 19:6).

YOU MAY BE INTERESTED TO KNOW...
The Invaders Will Seek to...

- Acquire Israel's territory (Ezekiel 38:8)
- Plunder Israel's wealth (38:12-13)
- Vanquish the people of Israel (38:16)

HISTORICAL INSIGHT

There Have Historically Been Two Views on the Invaders' "Swords" and "Horses"—Ezekiel 38:15, 21

1. *Literal View*—The invaders charge into Israel on horseback, wielding shining swords, intending to emulate the infamous prophet Muhammad. Known as the "Prophet of the Sword," Muhammad once commanded a formidable force of more than 10,000 mounted warriors who seized control of Mecca, forcing submission throughout the city. The Ezekiel invasion seems to draw inspiration from this legendary conquest, echoing a chilling historical parallel.

2. *Metaphorical View*—The "swords" and "horses" are symbolic terms chosen by Ezekiel to describe a modern invasion using transportation and weapons for which he had no words. Ezekiel may have been speaking in the language of his day to describe an otherwise indescribable invasion.

> "The Bible describes the use of primitive weapons—horses and horsemen clothed in full armor. Some believe these were the best words available to the prophet to describe modern technological warfare depending largely on tanks and armor."
>
> —John F. Walvoord[1]

> "How else could an ancient writer have described warfare? He knew nothing of planes and guns."
>
> —Charles Feinberg[2]

> "Ezekiel, inspired by the Holy Spirit, spoke in language that the people of that day could understand. If he had spoken of planes, missiles, tanks, and rifles, this text would have been nonsensical to everyone until the twentieth century."
>
> —Mark Hitchcock[3]

A key verse in our discussion, Psalm 121:4, powerfully conveys that "He who keeps Israel will neither slumber nor sleep." This means that God is unceasingly vigilant in overseeing Israel's affairs. Adversaries may be under the illusion of assured victory, but God's all-seeing presence ensures that their plans are futile in the face of Israel's divine protection. In earlier times, God reassured His people with the words, "No weapon that is formed against you will prosper" (Isaiah 54:17). Throughout the Old Testament, we see instances of the Almighty confronting Israel's enemies (Exodus 15:3; Psalm 24:8). Not infrequently, God is portrayed in warrior-like terms—such as the "Lord of Hosts" (2 Samuel 6:2, 18).

As we delve into the prophetic texts describing the Ezekiel invasion, we uncover God's sentiments towards the invaders—*fury, anger, zeal,* and *wrath* (Ezekiel 38:18-19). These words reveal the unbridled intensity of God's retribution against those who dare to harm His people. Unexpectedly, those who initiate the attack will come face to face with the searing wrath of God.

FAST FACTS ON GOD'S JUSTICE AND JUDGMENT

- The God described in the Bible is a God of justice.
- God's judgment fell upon Adam and Eve, driving them from the Garden of Eden (Genesis 3).
- In Noah's day, God purged the wicked world with a catastrophic flood (Genesis 6–8).
- Sodom and Gomorrah faced the wrath of God's judgment (Genesis 18–19).
- The Egyptians suffered ten devastating plagues as a form of divine retribution (Exodus 7–12).
- God punished the Israelites for worshiping the golden calf (Exodus 32:26-35).
- Ananias and Sapphira faced judgment for lying to God (Acts 5).
- God condemned Herod for his overwhelming arrogance (Acts 12:21).
- Irreverent Corinthian Christians received harsh consequences, including serious illness and death, after they dishonored the Lord's Supper (1 Corinthians 11:29-32; see also 1 John 5:16).
- Christians will one day stand before the judgment seat of Christ (1 Corinthians 3:12-15; 2 Corinthians 5:10).

- Unbelievers will face the great white throne judgment (Revelation 20:11-15).

- This very same God will judge the northern military coalition as it descends upon Israel.

God will use four mighty forces to destroy the mighty northern alliance. The cumulative effect of this quadruple judgment will result in lifeless corpses scattered across the landscape as far as the eye can see.

1. A Massive Earthquake—Ezekiel 38:19-20

Throughout the prophetic Scriptures, we learn that the tribulation period will usher in an increase in both the frequency and intensity of earthquakes (Matthew 24:7). The catastrophic earthquake foretold by Ezekiel, where "the mountains shall be thrown down, and the cliffs shall fall, and every wall shall tumble to the ground," will result in the death of countless soldiers. As transportation routes are shattered, the armies of the multinational forces will be thrown into utter chaos. The magnitude of this earthquake will be such that every living creature on earth will feel its powerful impact: "The fish of the sea and the birds of the heavens and the beasts of the field and all creeping things that creep on the ground, and all the people who are on the face of the earth, shall quake at my presence" (Ezekiel 38:20).

CROSS-REFERENCES
Earthquakes in Prophecy

Ezekiel Invasion—Ezekiel 38:19-20
Earthquakes in many parts of the world—Matthew 24:7; Mark 13:8
Greatest earthquake in human history—Revelation 16:18
Mount of Olives will split apart—Zechariah 14:4
Sixth seal judgment—Revelation 6:12

2. Infighting Among the Invading Troops—Ezekiel 38:21

In a breathtaking display of divine power, God will effortlessly cause the armies of the various invading nations to turn against one another. As a result, a colossal wave of "friendly fire" will sweep across the battlefield. This unprecedented chaos may stem from the confusion and disorder caused by the devastating earthquake. As John F. Walvoord puts it, "In the pandemonium, communication between the invading armies will break down and they will begin attacking each other. Every man's sword will be against his brother (Ezek. 38:21). Fear and panic will sweep through the forces, so each army will shoot indiscriminately at the others."[4]

Adding to the chaos, the armies of the various nations face language barriers as they speak Russian, Farsi, Arabic, and Turkic. Effective communication becomes a formidable challenge. As a result, the troops adopt a ruthless approach: "Shoot first, ask questions later."

> ➤ It is possible that the Russians and the Muslim nations will turn on each other.

> ➤ As chaos ensues, mistrust and suspicion of betrayal could lead them to unleash their firepower against each other.

> ➤ This could result in a staggering number of casualties on both sides.

3. The Outbreak of Disease—Ezekiel 38:22a

A devastating outbreak of disease will also sweep through the multitude of soldiers. It is easy to imagine the scene: In the aftermath of a massive earthquake, countless lifeless bodies will be scattered across the land. With transportation networks crippled, it will be increasingly difficult, if not impossible, to evacuate the injured or deliver essential supplies such as food and medicine. Meanwhile, flocks of birds and packs of predatory animals will voraciously consume the unburied remains. These circumstances create a fertile breeding ground for a virulent pandemic—a plague that, as foretold by Ezekiel, will mercilessly claim countless lives.

Skeptics of the devastating effects of disease should consider the worldwide devastation unleashed by COVID-19. The northern invaders who survive the outbreak of disease (and God's other judgments) will be utterly demoralized, and things will soon get even worse.

CROSS-REFERENCES
Disease

> Caused by an evil spirit—Luke 13:10-16
> Caused by Satan—Job 2:6-7
> Caused by sin—Leviticus 26:14-16; John 5:14
> Disobedience brings—Deuteronomy 28:21-22
> Divine discipline—Psalm 51:8
> Famine and disease—Jeremiah 29:17; Ezekiel 5:17
> Plagues that destroy—Leviticus 26:25

4. Torrential Rain, Hailstones, Fire, and Burning Sulfur—Ezekiel 38:22b

The culmination of God's divine judgment upon the invading forces will be marked by a storm of torrential rain causing severe flooding, coupled with hailstones, fire, and a deluge of burning sulfur. The cataclysmic earthquake may trigger volcanic eruptions in the region, unleashing a deadly shower of molten rock and sulfuric ash upon the unsuspecting enemy soldiers, leading to their ultimate destruction. The horrific fate of Sodom and Gomorrah serves as a stark reminder of just how devastating this retribution will be for the hapless northern alliance. In the aftermath of God's swift and decisive judgments, not a soul will be left standing.

Witness the astonishing twist of fate that unfolds: Invading armies arrive with the intent to slay, only to be slain by God. Convinced of their superior might, they instead find themselves outmatched by the divine power of God. Intent on conquering a new land, Israel, they ultimately meet their doom and become a permanent part of the very soil they sought to claim.

Fire Will Fall Upon Magog

As if this display of God's awesome power wasn't clear enough, He promises further: "I will send fire on Magog and on those who dwell securely in the coastlands" (Ezekiel 39:6). The term *Magog* most likely refers to the former southern Soviet republics of Kazakhstan, Kyrgyzstan, Uzbekistan, Turkmenistan, Tajikistan, and perhaps even the northern regions of present-day Afghanistan. This prophetic verse foretells a divine firestorm raining down on this corner of the globe, as well as on Magog's allies "who dwell securely in the coastlands," testifying to God's power and might.

> *"Targets throughout Russia and the former Soviet Union, as well as Russia's allies, will be supernaturally struck on this day of judgment and partially or completely consumed. These could be limited to nuclear missile silos, military bases, radar installations, defense ministries, intelligence headquarters, and other government buildings of various kinds. But such targets could very well also include religious centers, such as mosques, madrassas, Islamic schools and universities, and other facilities that preach hatred against Jews and Christians and call for the destruction of Israel. Either way, we will have to expect extensive collateral damage, and many civilians will be at severe risk."*
>
> —Joel Rosenberg[5]

The all-encompassing judgment of God will effectively put an end to any retaliation or future incursions. These vile forces will no longer stand a chance at launching any further assaults on Israel!

God's Purpose in Destroying the Coalition

At the heart of it all, God's primary goal is to protect Israel from harm. As the divine guardian of Israel, this is an expression of the enduring covenant God made with His dear friend Abraham. In Genesis 12:3, God assured Abraham, "I will bless those who bless you, and him who dishonors you I will curse." Unquestionably, the invading Islamic force—comprising countless Muslims—will seek to dismantle Israel, inevitably dishonoring it. Consequently, God's fierce wrath will be unleashed upon the invaders in the form of a devastating judgment.

However, the divine plan goes far beyond simply protecting Israel. In fact, by destroying the invading adversaries, God will powerfully and gloriously display His might for the entire world to witness:

> - God affirms: "I will show my greatness and my holiness and make myself known in the eyes of many nations. Then they will know that I am the Lord" (Ezekiel 38:23).
>
> - Of the invaders, God says: "They shall know that I am the Lord" (39:6).
>
> - God affirms: "The nations shall know that I am the Lord, the Holy One in Israel" (39:7).

> Of the Israelites, God says: "Then they shall know that I am the LORD their God" (39:28).

This vividly recalls the divine deliverance of the Israelites from the clutches of the Egyptians, a civilization that worshiped countless false deities, believing them to be more powerful than the God of any other nation. Their arrogance was soon shattered, however, as they were brought to their knees by the devastating effects of ten catastrophic plagues from the one true God.

Consider the powerful dual purpose behind God's unforgettable ten plagues unleashed upon the Egyptians:

> *To the Jews:* "You shall know that I am the LORD your God, who has brought you out from under the burdens of the Egyptians" (Exodus 6:7).

> *To the Egyptians:* You "shall know that I am the LORD" (7:17); "that you may know that I am the LORD in the midst of the earth" (8:22); "that you may know that there is none like me in all the earth" (9:14); "that you may know that the earth is the LORD's" (9:29); "that you may know that the earth is the LORD's" (14:4); "the Egyptians shall know that I am the LORD" (14:18).

The Almighty wanted unmistakable clarity regarding His divine purposes! He wanted all to understand that there is only one true God in all the cosmos. This very truth will also become undeniable when the formidable northern military alliance marches on Israel. It is then that the one true God—His name is Yahweh—will triumph over the primarily Islamic adversary, exposing the weakness of the counterfeit deity, Allah.

Imagine the scene unfolding before your eyes. A vast and formidable invading force sweeps across the terrain like a dark, ominous cloud, with the Muslim invaders chanting loudly, "Allahu-Akbar," which translates to "Allah is the greatest." However, in a breathtaking turn of events, after Yahweh's divine intervention and mighty judgment upon these invaders, not a single soul is found to be shouting Allahu-Akbar. This glorious moment serves as an unshakeable testament to the one true God.

PART 8

The First Half of the Tribulation Period

IN THIS SECTION

27 — The Rise of a Revived Roman Empire—238

28 — Menacing Features of the Tribulation Period—245

29 — The Stranglehold of Religious New Babylon on the World—253

30 — The 144,000 Courageous Jewish Evangelists—260

31 — God's Two Miracle-Working Prophetic Witnesses—267

32 — The Cataclysmic Unleashing of the Seal Judgments—274

The Rise of a Revived Roman Empire

A mighty revived Roman Empire will emerge in the end times, and it will be led by the antichrist. The prophetic book of Daniel in the Old Testament provides the historical context for the emergence of this end-times empire.

> *"After the regathering of Israel to her land, the most significant sign of the end times is the reuniting of the Roman Empire...The Bible predicts that when Jesus returns, the ruling power on earth will be a ten-kingdom confederation of nations reunited from the old Roman Empire and ruled over by the Antichrist. It will be 'Rome II.'"*
> —Mark Hitchcock[1]

In Daniel 7:3, we see four great beasts rise up out of the sea, each one unique and symbolic of a kingdom of great importance in Bible prophecy. These beasts provide us with insight into prophetic chronology, helping us to better understand the intricacies of God's plan for the future.

The first, Daniel says, was "like a lion and had eagles' wings," but "its wings were plucked off" (Daniel 7:4). The imagery represents Babylon, with its lion-like characteristics indicating power and dominance. The gates of Babylon's royal palaces were guarded by winged lions (see Jeremiah 4:7, 13). The wings represent swift mobility, whereas the removal of the wings represents a loss of mobility—possibly a reference to Nebuchadnezzar's insanity or Babylon's decline after his death.

Daniel continued in verse 5 by referring to "another beast, a second one, like a bear, an animal of great strength. It was raised up on one side. It had three ribs in its mouth between its teeth; and it was told, 'Arise, devour much flesh.'" This kingdom is Medo-Persia. With a fearsome reputation on the battlefield, Medo-Persia's prowess is legendary. Its might is symbolized by the "ribs"—possibly representing defeated enemies such as Lydia, Babylon, and Egypt (see Isaiah 13:17-18).

Daniel then referred to a third beast, "like a leopard, with four wings of a bird on its back. And the beast had four heads, and dominion was given to it" (Daniel 7:6). The leopard, a symbol of speed, cunning, and agility, perfectly symbolizes Greece under the rule of the mighty Alexander the Great. The "four heads" symbolize the quartet of generals who seized control of the empire after Alexander's death, governing Macedonia, Asia Minor, Syria, and Egypt with a firm grip.

FAST FACTS ON SYMBOLISM AND APOCALYPTIC LITERATURE

- The book of Daniel is classified as apocalyptic literature.
- Apocalyptic literature is a compelling genre that arose among Jews and Christians, unraveling mysteries about heaven and earth.
- Visions are characteristic of this genre of writing, and the book of Daniel is full of them.
- This form of literature makes extensive use of symbols, and the book of Daniel is no exception. For example, the four kingdoms are symbolically represented as different beasts:
  - the lion with eagle's wings is Babylon;
  - the strong bear-like creature is Medo-Persia;
  - the leopard with the four wings of a bird is Greece;
  - Rome is a hybrid beast composed of parts of a lion, bear, and leopard.

The fourth hybrid beast is more terrifying and powerful than the previous three beasts:

> Behold, a fourth beast, terrifying and dreadful and exceedingly strong. It had great iron teeth; it devoured and broke in pieces and stamped what was left with its feet. It was different from all the beasts that were before it, and it had ten horns. I considered the horns, and behold, there came up among them another horn, a little one, before which three of the first horns were plucked up by the roots. And behold, in this horn were eyes

like the eyes of a man, and a mouth speaking great things (Daniel 7:7-8).

At first glance, you might find yourself puzzled by such peculiar phrases. But it's not as complex as it seems! The fantastical imagery presented here is actually referring to the mighty Roman Empire.

> ## 📖 GEOGRAPHY IN THE END TIMES: *The Revived Roman Empire*
>
> > Rome had its glory days in antiquity, but fell in the fifth century AD.
> > It is prophesied to rise again in the end times as a confederation of ten nations ruled by ten kings (the infamous "ten horns").
> > In the midst of this confederation, an eleventh horn springs forth—also known as the antichrist. Initially inconspicuous, this figure gains immense power, eventually overthrowing three of the existing rulers (or horns).
> > Ultimately, the antichrist rises to power and reigns supreme over the entire revived Roman Empire.

We can observe that Rome has never experienced a ten-nation alliance with ten joint rulers. If it hasn't happened yet, this prophecy must refer to a future empire.

HISTORICAL INSIGHT
Horns

> The horn of an animal was used as a weapon (see Genesis 22:13; Psalm 69:31).
> Over time, the horn became a symbol of power and might.
> As an extension of this symbol, horns in biblical times eventually became emblems of dominion, representing kingdoms and kings.
> This is the case in the books of Daniel and Revelation (see Daniel 7–8; Revelation 12:13; 13:1, 11; 17:3-16).

> **PERSONALITY PROFILE:** *Nebuchadnezzar*
>
> > Nebuchadnezzar's name means "Nabu has protected my inheritance."
> > Of all the Babylonian monarchs, Nebuchadnezzar stood out as the most formidable and influential ruler.
> > He is famous for taking multitudes of Jews captive from 605 to 597 BC, including Daniel and his companions (Jeremiah 27:19; 40:1; Daniel 1:1-7).
> > After God's amazing rescue of Daniel's friends from the fiery furnace (Daniel 3), the king was stricken with a bizarre mental illness as divine retribution for his arrogance and vanity.
> > He was eventually restored.

In Daniel 2, we read of Nebuchadnezzar's prophetic dream. This end-time Roman Empire was described in the dream as a mixture of iron and clay (see verses 41-43). Daniel, the great dream interpreter, took this to mean that just as iron is strong, so too would the Roman Empire of the latter days be strong. However, just as iron and clay do not naturally mix, this empire would have some internal divisions. The constituent nations of the empire would not be fully integrated.

Many contemporary Bible scholars view today's European Union as a prime candidate for the fulfillment of this prophecy. The creation of a common currency paves the way for an eventual unified political entity. Could it be that the stage is being set for the fulfillment of Daniel's prophecies? *I believe so!*

FREQUENTLY ASKED QUESTIONS

Does the metaphor of clay and iron in Daniel 2 apply to the European Union today?

Yes, in several ways. The clay and iron mentioned in Daniel 2 represent both unity and diversity, both strength and weakness. The European Union today has great economic and political power, but its constituent nations are culturally, linguistically, and politically diverse, and therefore not perfectly united. Currently, the European Union has its own parliament, a rotating presidency, a supreme court, a common currency used by many member nations, allows open travel between member nations, and is working toward a unified

military. It may be, then, that the stage is now being set for the ultimate fulfillment of Daniel 2:40-43. What is happening in Europe today may be a precursor to Daniel's prophecy of a revived Roman Empire!

> *"Europe is moving to become the economic, political center of
> the world. It will also develop great military strength. One Europe,
> under one flag, will perhaps be the superpower that will challenge
> the world of the twenty-first century."*
>
> —"Birth of a Superstate" documentary[2]

With a common currency, a European Central Bank, and a growing political union, the stage is set for the complete fulfillment of the final prophecies
of Daniel 2 and 7.[3]

Will the balance of power shift from the United States to Europe during the tribulation period?

I believe it will. In the end times, the political and economic powerhouse
of the globe will be a revived Roman Empire, or what we might call the
"United States" of Europe. This is addressed prophetically in the book of Daniel (Daniel 7:3-8). The antichrist will eventually gain absolute authority and
rule over this revived Roman Empire (see 2 Thessalonians 2:3-10 and Revelation 13:1-10).

Does the revival of the Roman Empire foreshadow the decline of the United States in the end times?

It is not only possible, but highly probable. The United States may decline
due to a moral implosion, an economic collapse, a nuclear attack, an electromagnetic pulse (EMP) attack, the rapture of the church, or a combination of
these events. I address this in detail in chapter 16.

The Little Horn

As noted previously, Daniel's prophecy of the revived Roman Empire
speaks of ten horns representing ten nations. But there's another horn—a little one, seemingly insignificant at first, that is destined to become a force to
be reckoned with. This horn, the antichrist, will uproot three of the existing
horns through his cunning and diplomatic skills, leaving the political world
in awe. Rising from the shadows, the antichrist will soon become a household

name, his brilliant statesmanship and charisma propelling him to the pinnacle of worldwide power. With a global domain and all other leaders as his pawns, he will reign supreme, unchallenged in his political power.

The notorious "little horn" known as the antichrist will have a silver tongue and will utter grandiose proclamations (refer to Daniel 7:8). His eloquence will be unsurpassed, as indicated by the metaphorical comparison of his speech to a "lion's mouth" (Revelation 13:2). Many totalitarian leaders throughout history have relied on the persuasive power of their oratory skills to rally the masses around their political objectives. The antichrist will surpass them all by captivating the world with his powerful words.

Most Bible interpreters believe that the "great things" spoken by the antichrist will include self-aggrandizing statements. Revelation 13:5 tells us, "The beast [antichrist] was given a mouth uttering haughty and blasphemous words." Indeed, "it opened its mouth to utter blasphemies against God, blaspheming his name and his dwelling, that is, those who dwell in heaven" (verse 6). The antichrist's blasphemous words are in keeping with his blasphemous nature (see 2 Thessalonians 2:3-11). Both the Greek and Hebrew words for blasphemy imply a damaging of another's reputation, ranging from a lack of respect for God to outright contempt for Him (Leviticus 24:16; Matthew 26:65; Mark 2:7). Making claims of divinity—as the antichrist will—is also a form of blasphemy (Mark 14:64; John 10:33).

This individual, fueled by a burning desire for godhood, shall reign supreme over the revived Roman Empire.

> - The revived Roman Empire will be a mere stepping stone for the antichrist.

> - He will eventually gain world dominion (see Revelation 13).

QUESTIONS TO PONDER

With the world's problems spiraling out of control today, do you think the world is yearning for a powerful leader who can restore the world to sanity? Do you think the stage is being set for his appearance?

"I am not looking for the Antichrist today. I am looking for Jesus Christ. I am not even looking for the undertaker. I am looking for the upper-taker—the Lord, who is coming to call us home to be with Him. But once the rapture occurs, the center of world power will shift, and the Roman Empire—predominantly represented today by the European Union—will suddenly dominate the Western world."

—Ed Hindson[4]

THE REVIVED ROMAN EMPIRE

The antichrist will rule over this empire	Daniel 2; 7
It will consist of ten nations	Daniel 7:7, 20
The antichrist will start out insignificant, but eventually will gain control over the entire empire	Daniel 7:7-8, 24; 2 Thessalonians 2:3-10; Revelation 13:1-10
The empire will be fearsome and powerful	Daniel 2:40; 7:7
The empire will not be fully integrated	Daniel 2:41-43

"This final form of the Roman Empire will evidently begin as some form of democracy and then progress to a dictatorship—just like the historical Roman Empire began as a republic and eventually became a dictatorship ruled by Caesar."

—Mark Hitchcock[5]

The antichrist will be the supreme dictator!

28

Menacing Features of the Tribulation Period

Now we will explore the defining characteristics of the seven-year tribulation period.

> ### 👓 UNDERSTANDING OUR TERMS: *Tribulation*
>
> › The Greek word for "tribulation" (*thlipsis*) carries the idea "to press" (as grapes), "to press together," "to press hard upon."
> › It refers to times of oppression, affliction, and distress.
> › The word is variously translated as "tribulation," "affliction," "anguish," "persecution," "trouble," and "burden."

This Greek word for tribulation is used in Scripture in reference to:

1. Those hard-pressed by the calamities of war (Matthew 24:21);

2. A woman in childbirth (John 16:21);

3. The afflictions of Christ (Colossians 1:24);

4. Those who suffer from poverty and lack (Philippians 4:14);

5. Great anxiety and burden of the heart (2 Corinthians 2:4); and

6. An end-time period of unprecedented tribulation (Revelation 7:14).

There is a difference between general tribulation and the specific period of tribulation in the end times. It's a fact that all Christians will experience some degree of tribulation in their lives. Jesus Himself warned His disciples, "In the world you will have tribulation" (John 16:33). Paul and Barnabas also warned that "through many tribulations we must enter the kingdom of God" (Acts 14:22).

However, Scripture also points to a unique "tribulation period" in the end times:

1. Scripture refers to a specific period at the end of the age (Matthew 24:29-35).
2. The intensity of this unprecedented tribulation period will exceed anything that has ever occurred or will ever occur in history (Matthew 24:21).
3. God sovereignly puts a time limit on it for the sake of His people (Matthew 24:22), because otherwise no one could survive it.
4. The tribulation specifically lasts seven years (Daniel 9:24, 27).
5. It will be so bad that people will want to hide and even die (Revelation 6:16).

THIS CALAMITOUS PERIOD IS CHARACTERIZED BY:

> Wrath—Zephaniah 1:15, 18

> Judgment—Revelation 14:7

> Indignation—Isaiah 26:20-21

> Trial—Revelation 3:10

> Trouble—Jeremiah 30:7

> Destruction—Joel 1:15

> Darkness—Amos 5:18

> Desolation—Daniel 9:27

> Overturning—Isaiah 24:1-4

> Punishment—Isaiah 24:20-21

This tribulation period will afflict the entire world. Revelation 3:10 describes this period as "the hour of trial that is coming on the entire world, to try those who dwell on the earth." Isaiah likewise speaks of the tribulation: "Behold, the LORD will empty the earth and make it desolate, and he will twist its surface and scatter its inhabitants" (Isaiah 24:1). He then says, "Terror and the pit and the snare are upon you, O inhabitant of the earth" (Isaiah 24:17).

In the midst of this terrible time, the inhabitants of the earth will experience the full force of God's wrath and anger. The tribulation is a "day of the wrath of the LORD" (Zephaniah 1:18). The earth will experience "the wrath of the Lamb" (Revelation 6:16-17).

There will also be satanic wrath: "Then the dragon [Satan] became furious with the woman [Israel] and went off to make war on the rest of her offspring, on those who keep the commandments of God and hold to the testimony of Jesus" (Revelation 12:17, inserts added for clarity).

The tribulation period has three purposes:

1. The tribulation period will put an end to "the times of the Gentiles" (Luke 21:24). This phrase refers to the period of Gentile rule over Jerusalem. This period began with the Babylonian captivity in 605 BC. The time of the Gentiles was well established by AD 70, when Titus and his Roman warriors overran Jerusalem and destroyed the Jewish temple. This "time" will continue through the future seven-year tribulation period (Revelation 11:2) and will not end until the second coming of Christ (Luke 21:24). When Christ comes, He will overthrow all the Gentile powers that have stood against Jerusalem.

2. The tribulation will bring judgment upon the Christ-rejecting Gentiles of the world. Isaiah 26:21 tells us, "The LORD is coming out from his place to punish the inhabitants of the earth for their iniquity." The punishment will be so severe that people will try to hide from God's wrath: "The kings of the earth and the great ones and the generals and the rich and the powerful, and everyone, slave and free, hid themselves in the caves and among the rocks of the mountains, calling to the mountains and rocks, 'Fall on us and hide us from the face of him who is seated on the throne, and from the wrath of the Lamb, for the great day of their wrath has come, and who can stand?'" (Revelation 6:15-17). At the end of the tribulation period, the number of wicked people on earth will be greatly reduced. "This violent reduction of the world's unbelieving population will result from the divine judgments unleashed throughout the Tribulation (Rev. 6–18), climaxing with the battles of Armageddon under King Messiah (Rev. 19)."[1]

3. The tribulation will be a judgment upon Israel. As Jeremiah 30:7 puts it, "That day is so great there is none like it; it is a time of distress for Jacob." ("Jacob" is a reference to Israel.) Daniel 12:1 says that in the tribulation period Israel will experience "a time of trouble, such as never has been since there was a nation till that time."

The judgment of the Jews will be a time of purging that will prepare Israel for the restoration and regathering that will take place for the millennial reign of Christ after the second coming (see Isaiah 6:9-13; 24:1-6; Zechariah 13:7-9; Ezekiel 20:34, 37-38; John 12:37-41; Romans 11:26-27). A remnant of Jews will be saved (Romans 9–11)!

There are three major sets of judgment that will be unleashed during the tribulation period—the seal judgments, the trumpet judgments, and the bowl judgments. The following charts provide a brief summary of these judgments. I will explore them in much greater detail later in the book.

THE SEAL JUDGMENTS

First seal judgment	Antichrist emerges, seeks to conquer	Revelation 6:1-2
Second seal judgment	No peace, people slay one another	Revelation 6:3-4
Third seal judgment	Widespread famine	Revelation 6:5-6
Fourth seal judgment	Massive deaths, famine, pestilence	Revelation 6:7-8
Fifth seal judgment	Many martyrs	Revelation 6:9-11
Sixth seal judgment	Earthquake, cosmic disturbances	Revelation 6:12-17
Seventh seal judgment	The trumpet judgments are unleashed	Revelation 8

Parallels Between Jesus' Olivet Discourse and the Seal Judgments

- Jesus speaks of the rise of false Christs (Matthew 24:4-5), just as the first seal judgment speaks of the rise of the antichrist (Revelation 6:1-2).
- Jesus speaks of wars and rumors of wars (Matthew 24:6), just as the second seal judgment involves wars in which nations rise up against one another (Revelation 6:3-4).

- Jesus speaks of famines (Matthew 24:7), just as the third seal judgment does (Revelation 6:5-6).
- Jesus speaks of earthquakes (Matthew 24:7), just as the sixth seal judgment involves an earthquake (Revelation 6:12-14).

THE TRUMPET JUDGMENTS

First trumpet judgment	Hail, fire, earth burned	Revelation 8:7
Second trumpet judgment	Fiery mountain hurls into the sea; sea turns bloody; one-third of sea creatures die	Revelation 8:8
Third trumpet judgment	Star falls from heaven, poisons water	Revelation 8:10-11
Fourth trumpet judgment	Severe cosmic disturbances	Revelation 8:12-13
Fifth trumpet judgment	Demons released from bottomless pit, torment human beings	Revelation 9:1-12
Sixth trumpet judgment	Angels bound at the Euphrates released, killing one-third of humankind	Revelation 9:13-21
Seventh trumpet judgment	The bowl judgments are unleashed	Revelation 11:15-19

THE BOWL JUDGMENTS

First bowl judgment	Painful sores on human beings	Revelation 16:2
Second bowl judgment	Sea becomes blood; all sea creatures die	Revelation 16:3
Third bowl judgment	Rivers and springs of water become blood	Revelation 16:4-7
Fourth bowl judgment	People scorched by the sun	Revelation 16:8-9

Fifth bowl judgment	Darkness everywhere	Revelation 16:10-11
Sixth bowl judgment	Euphrates River dries up	Revelation 16:12-16
Seventh bowl judgment	Devastating earthquake with widespread destruction	Revelation 16:17-21

Armageddon

As the tribulation period unfolds, the suffering of humanity will steadily escalate. First are the seal judgments, followed by the trumpet and bowl judgments. When it seems like things can't possibly get any worse, humankind will be thrust into a series of catastrophic battles known as Armageddon (Daniel 11:40-45; Joel 3:9-17; Zechariah 14:1-3; Revelation 16:14-16).

Ꮾ᎐ UNDERSTANDING OUR TERMS: *Armageddon*

- ➤ Armageddon literally means "Mount of Megiddo" and refers to a location about 60 miles north of Jerusalem.
- ➤ This is the site of Barak's battle with the Canaanites (Judges 4) and Gideon's battle with the Midianites (Judges 7).
- ➤ This will be the site of humankind's final terrible battles just before the second coming (Revelation 16:16).

HISTORICAL INSIGHT

Napoleon

Napoleon, the legendary conqueror, once said that this place was the most important battlefield he had ever seen. But even Napoleon's battles pale in comparison to the apocalyptic Armageddon. So horrible will Armageddon be that no one would survive if it were not for Christ coming again (Matthew 24:22).

FREQUENTLY ASKED QUESTION

Why is the second half of the tribulation period called the "great tribulation"?

The antichrist will abruptly terminate animal sacrifices in the rebuilt Jewish temple. He will do this because of his desire to be the sole object of worship. He will take his seat in the Jewish temple, proclaim that he is God, and demand that his subjects worship him alone (see Daniel 7:8, 11, 20, 25; 11:36-37; 2 Thessalonians 2:3-4; Revelation 13:4, 8, 11-17; 19:20; 20:4). Jesus tells us what will happen next: "Then there will be great tribulation, such as has not been from the beginning of the world until now, no, and never will be" (Matthew 24:21). As bad as the first half of the tribulation may be, the second half will be exponentially more catastrophic.

CROSS-REFERENCES

The Tribulation Period

Antichrist will demand worship—2 Thessalonians 2:4
Cosmic disturbances—Luke 21:25-26; Revelation 8:12
Day of alarm—Zephaniah 1:16
Day of calamity—Deuteronomy 32:35; Obadiah 12-14
Day of gloom—Joel 2:2; Amos 5:18, 20; Zephaniah 1:15
Day of Lord's anger—Zephaniah 2:2-3
Day of ruin—Joel 1:15
Day of thick darkness—Joel 2:2; Zephaniah 1:15; Amos 5:18
Day of vengeance—Isaiah 34:8; 35:4; 61:2; 63:4
Day of waste—Zephaniah 1:15
Demons torment those on earth—Revelation 9:3
Desolation—Daniel 9:27
Destruction—Joel 1:15
Dominion of Antichrist—Revelation 13
Great and terrible day—Malachi 4:5
Great tribulation—Matthew 24:21
Hour of judgment—Revelation 14:7
Hour of trial—Revelation 3:10
Indignation—Isaiah 26:20-21
Judgments of tribulation—Isaiah 24:1-23; Revelation 14:7
Overturning—Isaiah 24:1-4

People will faint with fear—Luke 21:25-26
People will long for death—Revelation 9:6
Punishment—Isaiah 24:20-21
Scourge—Isaiah 28:15, 18
Seven years long—Daniel 9:27
Sun becomes black, full moon like blood—Revelation 6:12
Time of distress—Daniel 12:1
Time of Jacob's distress—Jeremiah 30:7
Trial—Revelation 3:10
Trouble—Jeremiah 30:7
Worldwide—Revelation 3:10
Wrath—Zephaniah 1:15, 18
Wrath of Lamb—Revelation 6:16-17
Wrath of God—Revelation 14:10, 19; 15:1, 7; 16:1
Wrath to come—1 Thessalonians 1:10

29

The Stranglehold of Religious New Babylon on the World

Babylon, a city deeply rooted in Old Testament history, is far from being just a relic of the past. It is destined for an astonishing resurgence, as "New Babylon" emerges in the end times. We read about it in Revelation 17–18.

HISTORICAL INSIGHT
Babylon Has Historically Been a Center of False Religion

> You may be curious as to why the term *Babylon* symbolizes false religion.

> In Babylon, each city had its own patron deity and temple.

> Numerous smaller shrines were also scattered throughout the countryside, where crowds often gathered to worship a variety of gods.

> Anu, the primary god of the Babylonians, was seen as the king of heaven, while Marduk served as Babylon's patron god.

> The Babylonians were well known for their practice of divination.

> Astrology can be traced back to Babylon around 3000 BC. The ancient Babylonians marveled at how methodically and rhythmically the planets moved across the sky, so they regarded them as night gods endowed with divine powers and attributes. These heavenly beings were believed to control the destinies of people on earth on a grand scale—even the future of nations (see Daniel 1:20; 2:2, 10, 27; 4:7; 5:7, 11, 15). As a result, the Babylonian priests pursued an understanding of these planetary movements, hoping to use such knowledge for the benefit of their nation.

YOU MAY BE INTERESTED TO KNOW...
Babylon Is a Literal City in the End Times

> We know this because other geographical locations in Revelation are literal, including the cities of the seven churches in Revelation 2 and 3.

> New Babylon is mentioned as being along the Euphrates River, indicating that it is a literal city (Revelation 9:14; 16:12).

> There is a close connection between the books of Revelation and Daniel. In Daniel, Babylon is invariably a literal city.

> Revelation 17–18 also draws heavily on Jeremiah 50–51. Because Jeremiah undeniably spoke of a literal Babylon, we can conclude that John was speaking of a literal Babylon in Revelation.

YOU MAY BE INTERESTED TO KNOW...
New Babylon Has Two Roles in Tribulation Period

> Scripture reveals that New Babylon plays two distinct roles during the first and second halves of the tribulation period.

> *Religious New Babylon* will dominate during the first half of the tribulation period and will then meet its demise (Revelation 17).

> *Commercial New Babylon* will be in power during the second half of the tribulation period (Revelation 18). (I will address commercial New Babylon in a separate chapter.)

Revelation 17:1-7 describes religious New Babylon, while verses 8-18 provide an interpretation of this description. Brimming with eye-opening symbolism, religious New Babylon is described as a "great prostitute" or "whore," symbolizing her unfaithfulness to God and her inclination toward idolatry and apostasy (Jeremiah 3:6-9; Ezekiel 20:30; Hosea 4:15; 5:3; 6:10; 9:1). During the first half of the tribulation period, this deceptive religion will cast its powerful spell over countless nations around the world (Revelation 17:1).

The prostitute is described as sitting on "many waters," meaning that she influences a wide range of people, multitudes, nations, and languages from around the world (Revelation 17:1). The kings of the earth are drawn into an adulterous relationship with this seductress and are lured into the false religious system she exemplifies (14:8). It appears that this deceptive religious force will wield immense power and operate in close cooperation with the political system or kings of the earth during the end times.

> Prostitution is often a graphic metaphor in Scripture that symbolizes unfaithfulness to God—see Jeremiah 3:6-9; Ezekiel 20:30; Hosea 4:15; 5:3; 6:10; 9:1.

Revelation 17:9 speaks of the "seven mountains on which the woman [the prostitute] is seated" (insert added). The seven mountains represent seven kingdoms and their respective monarchs (Revelation 10:1). The Bible often uses *mountains* as a metaphor for kingdoms (Psalm 30:7; Jeremiah 51:25; Daniel 2:44-45). These seven kingdoms are the seven major world empires: Egypt, Assyria, Babylon, Medo-Persia, Greece, Rome, and the antichrist's future kingdom.

Five of these kingdoms have fallen, one still stands (in the apostle John's day), and one is waiting to rise (Revelation 17:10). This means that in ancient history, the Egyptian, Assyrian, Babylonian, Medo-Persian, and Greek empires crumbled to dust. At the time John recorded these divine revelations, Rome continued to exist. But the dark kingdom of the antichrist is yet to be seen. Interestingly, every single empire—past, present, and future—has been or will be tainted by the deceitful and pagan influence of false religion. This is what is meant by the woman who sat on these seven mountains (or kingdoms).

THREE THINGS TO KEEP IN MIND:

1. This apostate religious system will wield powerful political influence (Revelation 17:12-13).
2. It will appear outwardly glorious while being inwardly corrupt (verse 4).
3. It will persecute all true believers (verse 6).

During the tribulation period, this false religious system will become intoxicated with the slaughter of the saints (Revelation 17:6). It will mercilessly slay countless Christian martyrs (Matthew 24:21). This includes all who resist the mark of the beast (Revelation 13:15).

This false religion will even temporarily control the antichrist: The great "prostitute" will sit on (and thus control) the "scarlet beast," who is the antichrist (Revelation 17:3). Because both are unfaithful to God and both are idolatrous, there is an initial close connection between the false religious system and the antichrist.

FAST FACTS ON BABYLON'S PREVALENCE

- The book of Revelation contains 404 verses.
- Of these, 44 deal with Babylon.
- This means that more than 10 percent of Revelation deals with Babylon.

Jerusalem and Babylon Contrasted

JERUSALEM	BABYLON
Jerusalem is God's city (Revelation 21:2-3).	Babylon is a demonic city (Revelation 18:2).
The New Jerusalem is described as a chaste bride (Revelation 21:9-10).	New Babylon is called a great prostitute (Revelation 17:1, 3).
The New Jerusalem is an eternal city (Revelation 21:1-4).	New Babylon is a temporal city that God will destroy (Revelation 18:8).

The City of New Babylon: The Epicenter of End Times False Religion

> New Babylon, a literal city on the Euphrates River, will symbolize as well as emanate a false religious system with global influence.

> To illustrate, Wall Street is a literal street in New York City, but it also symbolizes the stock market.

> The White House is a literal building in Washington DC, but it also symbolizes the presidency of the United States.

> Similarly, New Babylon will be a real city, but it will also symbolize and emanate a false religion (Revelation 17).

FREQUENTLY ASKED QUESTIONS

Is it possible that religious New Babylon in Revelation 17 is the Roman Catholic Church?

Many believe this today. This view became popular during the Protestant Reformation. This theory is based on the prostitute motif (Revelation 17:1). Just as a prostitute is sexually unfaithful, it is claimed that the Roman Catholic Church has long been unfaithful to God. Proponents of this view also note how the great prostitute is adorned: "The woman was arrayed in purple and scarlet, and adorned with gold and jewels and pearls" (Revelation 17:4). This seems comparable to the colors of the papal and cardinal vestments.

This idea is certainly plausible. I have long been critical of key Roman Catholic doctrines (see my book *Reasoning from the Scriptures with Catholics*). But there is a glaring problem with identifying Roman Catholicism as the prostitute of Revelation 17. Students of prophecy who make this identification also claim that the beast of Revelation represents Roman Catholicism. Thus, both the prostitute *and* the beast are said to embody Roman Catholicism. This becomes quite a conundrum because the book of Revelation distinguishes between the prostitute and the beast. In fact, at the end of Revelation 17, we witness the beast destroying the prostitute—which would imply that Roman Catholicism will destroy itself. So this doesn't make much sense contextually.

Some critics suggest that proponents of this view may be inadvertently injecting their own historical experiences into the interpretation of Scripture. This perspective gained traction during the Reformation, when influential figures such as John Calvin and Martin Luther fiercely opposed Roman Catholicism. It is easy to see how Roman Catholicism could be "read" into the harlot or beast of Revelation.

There is another problem. Revelation 17:9-10 reveals that the prostitute (false religion) has played an influential role in shaping the seven mighty empires of the world—Egypt, Assyria, Babylon, Medo-Persia, Greece, Rome, and even the future kingdom of the antichrist. Now, it's quite a stretch to say that Roman Catholicism had any influence over Egypt, Assyria, Babylon,

Medo-Persia, or Greece before the time of Christ. After all, Roman Catholicism didn't even exist at that time.

Is it possible that religious New Babylon is apostate Christianity?

It is possible. This theory is deeply rooted in the imagery of the prostitute motif found in Revelation 17:1. Just as a prostitute is unfaithful in her relationships, apostate Christianity betrays both God and true Christianity. Some even liken it to adultery, where once there was faithfulness, but now only infidelity remains. In this viewpoint, a vast number of people left behind after the rapture will belong to this corrupted form of Christianity. These would-be "Christians" denigrate the Bible, redefine God into a different God, redefine Jesus into another Jesus, and redefine the gospel that saves.

Is it possible that religious New Babylon is a general and broad form of paganism?

It is possible. As noted above, the prostitute (or false religion) is said to sit on "seven mountains"—a metaphorical reference to seven kingdoms: Egypt, Assyria, Babylon, Medo-Persia, Greece, Rome, and that of the antichrist. Five kingdoms have fallen, one still exists, and one is yet to come (Revelation 17:10). Whatever this false religion is, it has affected (or will affect) all of these kingdoms. Paganism was historically the religious backbone of Egypt, Assyria, Babylon, Medo-Persia, Greece, and Rome. Therefore, it is reasonable to assume that some form of paganism will be central to the false religion of New Babylon.

MY PERSONAL ASSESSMENT

> The false religion will likely be a hybrid—*a religious amalgam*—mixing Roman Catholicism, Eastern Orthodoxy, Liberal Protestantism, all forms of apostate Christianity, and will be brimming with pagan elements.

> These may well coalesce into an ecclesiastical superchurch.

> It is probably "a kind of religious amalgamation or world church that will pull together people of various religious backgrounds into one great ecclesiastical alliance after the disappearance of the true church at the rapture. And this world church will be centered in the rebuilt city of Babylon."
>
> —Mark Hitchcock[1]

How does religious New Babylon become commercial New Babylon?

The antichrist and his ten powerful subcommanders will bring an end to the false world religion (Revelation 17:16-18). This game-changing event is likely to transpire at the midpoint of the tribulation period. Seizing both political and religious power on a global scale, the antichrist will boldly demand worship as if he were God himself (Daniel 11:36-38; 2 Thessalonians 2:4; Revelation 13:8, 15). No competing religions will be permitted.

To be clear, the antichrist will demolish *only the religion*, leaving the actual city of New Babylon untouched. When the tribulation period reaches its halfway point, New Babylon will seamlessly transition into a thriving commercial hub for the world. (More on all this later in the book.)

CROSS-REFERENCES
Religious New Babylon

Description of—Revelation 17:1-7

Interpretation of—Revelation 17:8-18

Controls nations—Revelation 17:9

Outwardly glorious, inwardly corrupt—Revelation 17:4

Persecutes true believers—Revelation 17:6

Powerful political clout—Revelation 17:12-13

Unfaithful to the truth—Revelation 17:1, 5, 15, 16

Worldwide in impact—Revelation 17:15

Worship of Antichrist—1 Timothy 4:1-4; 2 Timothy 3:1-5; 4:1-4; 2 Peter 2:1; 1 John 2:18-19; Jude 4; Revelation 17:1-6

Violently overthrown—Revelation 17:16

30

The 144,000 Courageous
Jewish Evangelists

Behold the amazing grace of God! Even in humanity's darkest hour—the tribulation period—He will continue to shine His light on the world. In His prophetic Olivet Discourse, Jesus foretold that the "gospel of the kingdom shall be preached in all the world for a witness unto all nations" (Matthew 24:14). The book of Revelation reveals the heralds of this gospel— an assembly of 144,000 redeemed Jews, consisting of 12,000 from each of the twelve tribes of Israel (Revelation 7; 14).

HISTORICAL INSIGHT
God's Jewish Witnesses

> God originally chose the Jews to be His special witnesses, tasking them with spreading the incredible news about Him to all other people around the world (Isaiah 42:6; 43:10).

> The Jews were to be divine ambassadors for God among the Gentile nations.

> However, looking back at biblical history, it's clear that they failed to fulfill this mission, especially because they didn't even recognize Jesus as the true Messiah.

> Fast-forward to the future tribulation period, where these 144,000 Jews—who will become believers sometime after the rapture—will finally accept and fulfill God's long-standing mandate to serve as His witnesses worldwide.

> These dedicated individuals will passionately spread the good news of God's kingdom far and wide, ultimately reaping a bountiful harvest of souls (Revelation 7:9-14).

God has "got the backs" of His witnesses. These chosen 144,000 Jewish witnesses will each receive a divine "seal" for their protection. In biblical times, seals symbolized both ownership and protection. These faithful Jewish believers will be under God's wing as His property, and He'll use His almighty power to protect them as they carry out their duties during the tribulation period (Revelation 14:1, 3-4; see also 13:16-18).

▦ **NUMBERS IN PROPHECY:** *The 144,000 Jewish Witnesses*

> - Some modern Christians interpret the 144,000 as a metaphorical reference to the church.
> - Others take a similar view, suggesting that the number 144,000 is symbolic of all God's servants in the tribulation.
> - However, the context specifically mentions 144,000 Jewish men, with 12,000 from each tribe (Revelation 14:4).
> - The fact that specific tribes are mentioned in this context, along with specific numbers for those tribes (12), removes any possibility that this is a figure of speech.
> - Nowhere else in the Bible does a reference to the 12 tribes of Israel mean anything other than the 12 tribes of Israel.
> - In fact, the word "tribe" is never used in Scripture to refer to anything other than a literal ethnic group.

An Interpretive Challenge
The Tribes of Dan and Ephraim

- Some have wondered why the Old Testament tribes of Dan and Ephraim are not included in this list of Jewish tribes.
- The Old Testament has about 20 different lists of tribes.
- Therefore, no two lists of the 12 tribes of Israel are identical.
- Most scholars today agree that the tribe of Dan was omitted because it was often guilty of idolatry and was largely wiped out (Leviticus 24:11; Judges 18:1, 30; see also 1 Kings 12:28-29).
- The tribe of Ephraim was also involved in pagan worship (Judges 17; Hosea 4:17).

- Therefore, both tribes were left out of Revelation 7.

An Interpretive Challenge
The Tribe of Levi

- Others have wondered why the tribe of Levi was included in this list of Jewish tribes rather than retaining its unique status as a priestly tribe under the Mosaic Law.

- The priestly functions of the tribe of Levi ceased with the coming of Christ, the ultimate High Priest (Hebrews 7–10).

- Because there was no longer a need for the priestly services of the tribe of Levi, there was no longer a reason to keep this tribe separate from the others.

- Therefore, they were properly included in the list of tribes in Revelation.

👤 PERSONALITY PROFILE: *The 144,000 Jewish Evangelists*

- > There will be 144,000 Jewish evangelists (Revelation 14:1-5).
- > They will have the name of the Lamb and the name of the Father written on their foreheads (verse 1).
- > They will be among the redeemed (verse 3).
- > They will sing a new song (verse 3).
- > They will be sealed from every tribe (verse 4).
- > They will live in purity (verse 4).
- > They will be obedient to Jesus (verse 4).
- > They will be honest and blameless (verse 5).
- > They will preach the gospel of the kingdom during the tribulation period (Matthew 24:14).

The primary message of these 144,000 Jewish men will revolve around the kingdom of God. Like John the Baptist and Jesus, who frequently proclaimed the nearness of the kingdom of God, these 144,000 chosen witnesses will echo the same message during the tumultuous tribulation period. Presenting Jesus

Christ as the heavenly Messiah and sovereign King, they will proclaim His rule in the rapidly approaching millennial kingdom.

> *"The gospel of the kingdom is the good news that Christ is coming to set up his kingdom on earth, and that those who receive him by faith during the Tribulation will enjoy the blessings of his Millennial Reign."*
>
> —William Macdonald and Arthur L. Farstad[1]

The book of Revelation reveals that many people will respond to the gospel of the kingdom. There will be "a great multitude that no one could number, from every nation, from all tribes and peoples and languages, standing before the throne and before the Lamb, clothed in white robes, with palm branches in their hands, and crying out with a loud voice, 'Salvation belongs to our God who sits on the throne, and to the Lamb!'" (Revelation 7:9-10).

In the end, it all comes down to a crucial choice: During the tribulation period, those who seek refuge in the King will be granted access to Christ's magnificent 1,000-year millennial kingdom. Those who refuse to turn to Christ will be denied entry. After Christ's return, there will be a judgment in which He will separate people "as a shepherd separates the sheep from the goats" (Matthew 25:32). The faithful sheep will be welcomed into Christ's glorious kingdom, while the disbelieving goats will face a dire punishment (see Matthew 25:31-46). Let's dig a little deeper into the details.

Immediately after the second coming, Jesus will engage in the judgment of the "nations" (which is a judgment of *the Gentiles*). In His Olivet Discourse, Jesus spoke the following prophetic words to His followers about this judgment:

> When the son of Man comes in his glory, and all the angels with him, then he will sit on his glorious throne. Before him will be gathered all the nations, and he will separate people one from another as a shepherd separates the sheep from the goats. And he will place the sheep on his right, but the goats on the left. Then the King will say to those on his right, "Come, you who are blessed by my Father, inherit the kingdom prepared for you from the foundation of the world. For I was hungry and you gave me food, I was thirsty and you gave me drink, I was a stranger and you welcomed me, I was naked and you clothed me, I was sick and you visited me, I was in prison and you came to me." Then the righteous will answer him, saying,

"Lord, when did we see you hungry and feed you, or thirsty and give you drink? And when did we see you a stranger and welcome you, or naked and clothe you? And when did we see you sick or in prison and visit you?" And the King will answer them, "Truly, I say to you, as you did it to one of the least of these my brothers, you did it to me."

"Then he will say to those on his left, depart from me, you cursed, into the eternal fire prepared for the devil and his angels. For I was hungry and you gave me no food, I was thirsty and you gave me no drink, I was a stranger and you did not welcome me, naked and you did not clothe me, sick and in prison and you did not visit me." Then they also will answer, saying, "Lord, when did we see you hungry or thirsty or a stranger or naked or sick or in prison, and did not minister to you?" Then he will answer them, saying, "Truly, I say to you, as you did not do it to one of the least of these, you did not do it to me." And these will go away into eternal punishment, but the righteous into eternal life (Matthew 25:31-46).

The question that naturally arises is this: *Who are Christ's brothers?* To answer this question, let us recall that during the tribulation period, those who have not received the mark of the beast will not be able to buy or sell (Revelation 13:16-17). Christians will have to act sacrificially toward those who have not received this mark, including the "brothers" of Christ.

A comparison of Christ's discourse in Matthew 25:31-46 with the details of the tribulation as recorded in Revelation 6–19 suggests that the term "brothers" refers to the 144,000 men mentioned in Revelation 7—Christ's Jewish brethren who will bear witness to Him during the seven-year tribulation. They will be His worldwide witnesses, and their work will yield a mighty harvest of souls (see Revelation 7:9-14).

FREQUENTLY ASKED QUESTION

How do all these Jewish men suddenly become believers in Jesus Christ?

These Jews will probably become believers in Jesus in a manner similar to that of the apostle Paul, himself a Jew, who had a Damascus Road encounter with the risen Christ (see Acts 9:1-9). Curiously, in 1 Corinthians 15:8,

Paul describes his conversion to Christianity as being "one untimely born" or "born at the wrong time" (NLT). Some Bible scholars suggest that Paul might be alluding to his kinship with the 144,000 Jewish believers during the tribulation who would undergo a spiritual rebirth similar to his own—only that Paul's awakening occurred much earlier.

Many of today's finest Bible expositors agree that the 144,000 of Revelation 7 are the "brothers" of Matthew 24, and they are redeemed Jews:

> *"It seems best to say that 'brothers of Mine' is a designation of the godly remnant of Israel that will proclaim the gospel of the kingdom unto every nation of the world."*
>
> —Stanley Toussaint[2]

> *"During the tribulation period, God will sovereignly call and save 144,000 Jews...So glorious and wonderful will be the ministry of the 144,000 saved Jews and so faithful will be their powerful testimony, the King on his throne of glory will not be ashamed to call them 'My brothers.' More than that, he will consider himself so intimately united to them that what was done or not done to them is the same as being actually done or not done to himself...That the Lord's brothers endured hunger, thirst, homelessness, nakedness, sickness, and imprisonment suggests their fidelity to their newfound savior and Lord. They proved their willingness to suffer for him amid the terrible persecutions and trials of the tribulation through which they passed. They proved their loyalty to their King. He attests his identity with them."*
>
> —Merrill F. Unger[3]

> *"That phrase [my brothers] may refer to...the 144,000 of Revelation 7, who will bear witness of him during the Tribulation. Such ones will be under a death sentence by the beast [or antichrist]. They will refuse to carry the beast's mark, and so they will not be able to buy and sell. Consequently, they will have to depend on those to whom they minister for hospitality, food, and support. Only those who receive the message will jeopardize their lives by extending hospitality to the messengers. Therefore what is done for them will be an evidence of their faith in Christ, that is, what is done for them will be done for Christ."*
>
> —J. Dwight Pentecost[4]

"The expression 'these brothers' must refer to a third group that is neither sheep nor goats. The only possible group would be Jews, physical brothers of the Lord. In view of the distress in the Tribulation period, it is clear that any believing Jew will have a difficult time surviving (cf. 24:15-21). The forces of the world dictator [the antichrist] will be doing everything possible to exterminate all Jews (cf. Rev. 12:17). A Gentile going out of his way to assist a Jew in the Tribulation will mean that Gentile has become a believer in Jesus Christ during the Tribulation. By such a stand and action, a believing Gentile will put his life in jeopardy. His works will not save him; but his works will reveal that he is redeemed."

—*The Bible Knowledge Commentary*[5]

In the early stages of the tribulation period, sometime after the rapture, this group of 144,000 Jewish evangelists will make their dramatic entrance. Eagerly seizing the opportunity, they will begin their evangelistic mission immediately. As a result, many of their listeners will embrace the truth about Jesus and some of them will eventually become the martyrs mentioned in Revelation 6:9-11. All of this takes place during the first half of the tribulation.

The Twofold Outcome of the Judgment

- > The righteous (sheep) will enter Christ's 1,000-year millennial kingdom; the unrighteous (goats) will be thrown into the lake of fire.

- > The righteous demonstrate that they are true believers in God by rendering aid to the 144,000 Jews.

- > The wicked show that they are not true believers in God by their indifference to the 144,000.

ANTICIPATING THE FUTURE

Because the 144,000 are among the redeemed, you and I will one day get to meet them and fellowship with them in heaven. We'll have lots of new friends!

31

God's Two Miracle-Working Prophetic Witnesses

D uring the tribulation period, two powerful prophetic witnesses will arise and boldly testify of the one true God, displaying incredible power much like the Old Testament luminaries Elijah (1 Kings 17; Malachi 4:5) and Moses (Exodus 7–11).

▦ NUMBERS IN PROPHECY: *Two Prophetic Witnesses*

> The Old Testament requires two witnesses to confirm a testimony (Deuteronomy 17:6; 19:15; Matthew 18:16; John 8:17; Hebrews 10:28).

> These two prophets will testify about God and Messiah Jesus during the tribulation period, and the truth they share will be confirmed by mighty miracles.

In Revelation 11:3-6, we read God's promise concerning these two witnesses:

> I will grant authority to my two witnesses, and they will prophesy for 1,260 days, clothed in sackcloth. These are the two olive trees and the two lampstands that stand before the Lord of the earth. And if anyone would harm them, fire pours from their mouth and consumes their foes. If anyone would harm them, this is how he is doomed to be killed. They have the power to shut the sky, that no rain may fall during the days of their prophesying, and they have power over the waters to turn them into blood and to strike the earth with every kind of plague, as often as they desire.

The clothing of the two witnesses, made of goat or camel hair, holds deep symbolism (Revelation 11:3). These garments express mourning over the wretched state of the world and its lack of repentance.

> *Sackcloth and Mourning*—Genesis 37:34; 2 Samuel 3:31; 2 Kings 6:30; 19:1; Esther 4:1; Isaiah 22:12; Jeremiah 6:26; Matthew 11:21.

The symbolism of the olive trees and lampstands represents the radiant light of spiritual revival during the impending darkness of the tribulation period (Revelation 11:4). This "light of spiritual revival" is undoubtedly one reason why so many come to faith during the tribulation period (7:9-17).

These two chosen messengers will proclaim God's truth with unwavering perseverance for exactly 1,260 days—equivalent to three-and-a-half years, or 42 months, or a time and times and half a time (Revelation 12:14). (A "time" denotes a year, "times" is two years, and "half a time" is six months—totaling three-and-a-half years.)

If anyone dares to harm the two witnesses, they will be consumed by flames (Revelation 11:5). It's important to note that God's supernatural protection sustains these two witnesses during their years of ministry. The same was true of Jesus, who was providentially protected during His ministry. Despite His enemies' attempts to kill Him, Jesus continued to affirm that His time had not yet come (John 7:6, 8).

Only when the ministry of these two powerful witnesses is fulfilled will they meet their death at the hands of the treacherous antichrist. As was true of Jesus, these two witnesses will not meet their end until their purpose in this world is accomplished.

FAST FACTS ON AUTHORITY

- God will give authority to His two prophetic witnesses (Revelation 8:3).
- The term *authority* appears frequently in Revelation.
- Jesus received authority from the Father (2:27).
- Jesus will give authority to the "overcomers" in the millennial kingdom (2:26).

- Death and Hades will be given authority over one-fourth of the earth (6:8).
- Revelation 12:10 speaks of the authority of Christ.
- Satan the dragon gives authority to the antichrist (13:2, 4).
- The antichrist exercises authority for three-and-a-half years (13:5).
- He is given authority over "every tribe and people and language and nation" (13:7).
- The false prophet is also given authority (13:12).
- Angels have authority during the time of tribulation (14:18; 18:1).
- The kings of the earth have authority for a short time (17:12).

Scholars have long debated the timing of the ministry of the two witnesses during the tribulation period. While some argue for the latter half, the majority opinion is that they complete their work during the first three-and-a-half years. The antichrist's execution of them seems to coincide with other notable events that will take place in the middle of the tribulation, such as the antichrist's bold self-exaltation to godhood and his rebellion against the one true God. Furthermore, the resurrection of the two witnesses would have a greater impact on the world at the midpoint of the tribulation than it would just before the second coming of Christ.

When the two witnesses complete their ministry, God withdraws His providential protection from them. At that point, the antichrist will kill them, something that many have already lost their lives trying to do. The witnesses will not die prematurely. Everything will happen according to God's divine timing—that is, when the prophets "have finished their testimony" (Revelation 11:7).

YOU MAY BE INTERESTED TO KNOW...
God's Work Will Be "Finished"

> The word "finished" in Revelation 11:7 is the same word Jesus used on the cross when He said, "It is finished" (John 19:30).

> Christ died after completing His work of redemption.

> The two witnesses will die only after completing their work of ministry.

The bodies of the prophets will be left unburied in Jerusalem. Jerusalem is figuratively called "Sodom and Egypt" (verse 8) because of the apostasy and rejection of God by its inhabitants. The description of Jerusalem as being no better than Sodom and Egypt shows that the once holy city was now no better than places known for their hatred of the true God and His Word.

Apparently, through television and the internet, "the peoples and tribes and languages and nations will gaze at their dead bodies" for three days (Revelation 11:9). Only modern technology can explain how the inhabitants of the entire world can see this.

In biblical times, refusing to bury a corpse was a way of showing contempt (Deuteronomy 21:22-23; Psalm 79:2-3; Acts 14:19). Thus, by leaving the bodies in the streets, the people of the world give the greatest insult to God's spokesmen, and thus to God Himself. It is tantamount to the people of the world collectively spitting on the corpses in the face of God.

HISTORICAL INSIGHT
Burial Customs in Biblical Days

> ➤ In biblical times, burials were done quickly.

> ➤ This was because the hot climate would quickly cause decomposition and stench.

> ➤ Traditionally, when a person died, they were immediately bathed and then wrapped in strips of linen.

> ➤ Sometimes a gummy combination of spices was applied to the body's wrappings.

> ➤ It was then carried on a stretcher to the burial site, whether in the ground or in a cave.

> ➤ Sometimes entire families were buried in a single large cave.

> ➤ In some areas, due to lack of cave space, bones were often removed from a cave and placed in a wooden or stone box.

The people of the world will have a satanic "Christmas" celebration—exchanging gifts—after the antichrist executes the witnesses. The biblical text tells us: "Those who dwell on the earth will rejoice over them and make merry and exchange presents" (Revelation 11:10). "Those who dwell on the earth" is a term often used in Revelation to refer to unbelievers. The phrase carries the idea of *earth-dwellers*, or *worldlings*, who are characterized by this anti-God world system.

These worldlings will have their "Christmas" party because they are relieved that the two prophetic witnesses are no longer among them. Bible history shows that the only prophets that people love are the dead ones.

After three-and-a-half days of lying lifeless on the road, "a breath of life from God" will enter them (verse 11; cf. Genesis 2:7).

FAST FACTS ON "BREATH" AND NEW LIFE

- The term "breath" recalls an ancient prophecy about the rebirth of the nation of Israel.

- According to the prophecy of the dry bones, God "will cause breath to enter you, and you shall live" (Ezekiel 37:5), language that refers to the rebirth of the nation of Israel. This was fulfilled in 1948.

- Similarly, regarding the two witnesses, "a breath of life from God" will enter them (Revelation 11:11), and they will resurrect from the dead.

- God is a master at giving new life!

As the world revels in Christmas-like festivities, an astonishing event sends shockwaves across the globe. The corpses of the two prophets, once lying still, will suddenly rise from the dead in full view of live television and internet feeds. Clips of this event are sure to go viral. The two witnesses will then ascend into heaven. The resurrection and ascension of the two witnesses will serve as a giant exclamation point to their prophetic words throughout their three-and-a-half-year ministry. In my mind's eye, I can picture them resurrecting from the dead and then asking, "Any questions?"

👤 PERSONALITY PROFILE: *The Two Prophetic Witnesses*

- ➢ The two witnesses will prophesy for 1,260 days (Revelation 11:3).
- ➢ Fire will consume anyone who tries to kill them (verse 5).
- ➢ They will have miraculous power (verse 6).
- ➢ After their ministry is over, the antichrist will kill them (verse 7).
- ➢ Their dead bodies will lie unburied in the streets (verse 8).

> ➤ People all over the world will celebrate their deaths (verses 9-10).
>
> ➤ They will rise from the dead (verse 11).
>
> ➤ They will ascend to heaven (verse 12).

FREQUENTLY ASKED QUESTIONS

Are the Two Witnesses Moses and Elijah?

It is possible, for the following reasons:

1. The tribulation (the seventieth week of Daniel) is a time when God deals with the Jews—just as He did in the first 69 weeks of Daniel. Moses and Elijah are undoubtedly the two most influential figures in Jewish history. So it would make sense that they would be on the scene during the tribulation period.

2. The Old Testament and Jewish tradition expect Moses (Deuteronomy 18:15, 18) and Elijah (Malachi 4:5) to return in the future.

3. Moses and Elijah appeared with Jesus on the Mount of Transfiguration. This shows their centrality. Therefore, it would be appropriate for them to be on the scene during the future tribulation period.

4. The miracles described in Revelation 11 are similar to those previously performed by Moses and Elijah in Old Testament times (see Exodus 7–11; 1 Kings 17; Malachi 4:5).

5. Both Moses and Elijah left the earth in unusual ways. Elijah never died but was transported to heaven in a fiery chariot (2 Kings 2:11-12). God supernaturally buried the body of Moses in a place unknown to man (Deuteronomy 34:5-6; Jude 9).

Given these factors, some Bible interpreters speculate that God will send two of His mightiest servants during the tribulation period: Moses, the great deliverer and spiritual legislator of Israel, and Elijah, a prince among the Old Testament prophets. During Old Testament times, these individuals rescued Israel from bondage and idolatry. They may reappear during the tribulation period to warn Israel against succumbing to the false religion of the antichrist and the false prophet. However, it's also quite possible that the two prophets will not be Moses and Elijah.

Alternatively, is it possible that the two prophetic witnesses will be Enoch and Elijah?

Some Bible interpreters think so. Enoch and Elijah were righteous men who were raptured to heaven (see Genesis 5:24; Hebrews 11:5; 2 Kings 2:11). Neither experienced death. Both were prophets—one a Gentile (Enoch) and the other a Jew (Elijah). For the first 300 years of church history, the church fathers unanimously held that the two prophets of Revelation 11 would be Enoch and Elijah. So perhaps God will ordain one witness to speak to the Jews and the other to speak to the Gentiles during the tribulation period.

Is it possible that the two prophetic witnesses might be two entirely new prophets?

It is indeed possible! Those who hold this view reason that the biblical text would surely identify famous Old Testament figures if they were to return. Because they are not identified, the two witnesses could be new prophets whom God will raise up especially for ministry during the tribulation period.

AN INTERESTING THOUGHT

Because the two prophets are among the redeemed, you and I will one day have the opportunity to meet and fellowship with them in heaven.

32

The Cataclysmic Unleashing
of the Seal Judgments

The tribulation period is a time of immense upheaval and despair, where the weight of God's judgment bears down relentlessly on the world. The word *tribulation* literally means to be squeezed and pressed, and that's exactly what this time will feel like. The inhabitants of the earth will be crushed under the weight of tribulation and distress as the judgments of the tribulation period rain down upon them.

The book of Revelation vividly portrays the escalating human suffering during the tribulation period, beginning with the unleashing of the seal judgments. We will now consider the horror of these judgments and the calamity they bring upon the earth.

🔲 NUMBERS IN PROPHECY: *Seven*

> *Seven* is often associated with completion, fulfillment, and perfection (for example, see Genesis 2:2; Exodus 20:10; Leviticus 14:7; Acts 6:3).

> *Seven* occurs frequently in the book of Revelation.

> There are seven churches (1:4), seven lampstands (1:12), seven stars (1:16), seven torches before the throne (4:5), seven seals on the scroll (5:1), seven horns and eyes of the Lamb (5:6), seven spirits of God (4:5; 5:6), seven angels and trumpets (8:2), seven thunders (10:3), seven heads of the dragon (12:3), seven heads of the beast (13:1), seven golden bowls (15:7), and seven kings (17:10).

> The fact that there are seven of each of the seal, trumpet, and bowl judgments indicates a perfect and complete judgment upon humankind.

THE FIRST SEAL JUDGMENT

Scripture describes the first seal judgment this way: "Behold, a white horse! And its rider had a bow, and a crown was given to him, and he came out conquering, and to conquer" (Revelation 6:2).

> ### 🔍 UNDERSTANDING OUR TERMS: *Horses*
>
> > Horses are sometimes used in Scripture to symbolize God's activity on earth, representing the mighty forces He uses to accomplish His sovereign purposes.
>
> > It's as if these majestic creatures gallop into action at His command, bringing about the fulfillment of His plan with power (see Zechariah 1:7-17).

Some readers may wonder if the rider on the white horse in Revelation 6 is Jesus Christ, since He is also pictured on a white horse in Revelation 19:11. However, the contexts of these passages are very different. In Revelation 19, Christ returns as a triumphant conqueror on a horse at the end of the tribulation. But in Revelation 6, the rider on the white horse appears at the beginning of the tribulation, along with three other horses and their riders, all representing various judgments that will fall on the earth. The prevailing view among Bible interpreters is that the rider on the white horse in Revelation 6:2 is the antichrist (see Daniel 9:26).

In the book of Revelation, this rider has a bow and has been given a crown. The crown indicates that the horseman is a ruler. The fact that the crown was *given* to the horseman may indicate that the inhabitants of the world will voluntarily submit to his leadership.

Perhaps the absence of an arrow with the bow indicates that the antichrist's world domination will initially be achieved without a military confrontation. (The removal of peace from the earth does not occur until the second seal is opened—Revelation 6:3.) Speculatively, the antichrist may rely on the peace treaty with Israel, the covenant that signals the beginning of the tribulation period (Daniel 9:24-27).

The antichrist's government will begin with a time of peace, but it will be short-lived, for destruction will soon follow. This seems to parallel Paul's words about the end times in 1 Thessalonians 5:3: "While people are saying, 'There is peace and security,' then sudden destruction will come upon them as labor pains come upon a pregnant woman, and they will not escape."

The prophetic text informs us that the antichrist "came out conquering, and to conquer" (Revelation 6:2). The ultimate goal of the antichrist is nothing less than world domination (Revelation 13). He will stop at nothing until he achieves it.

THE SECOND SEAL JUDGMENT

Revelation 6:3-4 tells us: "When he opened the second seal, I heard the second living creature say, 'Come!' And out came another horse, bright red. Its rider was permitted to take peace from the earth so that people should slay one another, and he was given a great sword."

The horse mentioned in this passage is of a striking red color, symbolizing bloodshed, the wielding of swords in battle, and war—as Jesus prophesied in Matthew 24:6-7. It's worth noting that the rider is wielding a "great" sword. Many will fall in battle.

The rider of this horse "was permitted to take peace from the earth" (Revelation 6:4). Despite the many efforts of world leaders to promote peace, their efforts will be ineffective; peace eludes them. Sadly, this will only be the beginning of an even more devastating time to come upon the earth (Matthew 24:8; Mark 13:7-8; Luke 21:9). It is no secret that economic instability and food shortages inevitably develop during times of war. From this point forward, challenging circumstances will dramatically escalate for earth's inhabitants.

THE THIRD SEAL JUDGMENT

Revelation 6:5-6 tells us: "When he opened the third seal, I heard the third living creature say, 'Come!' And I looked, and behold, a black horse! And its rider had a pair of scales in his hand. And I heard what seemed to be a voice in the midst of the four living creatures, saying, 'A quart of wheat for a denarius, and three quarts of barley for a denarius, and do not harm the oil and wine!'"

The earth will now experience black days of famine. The color black represents the deep sorrow and mourning that comes with extreme deprivation. Lamentations 4:8-9 illustrates this: "Now their face is blacker than soot; they are not recognized in the streets; their skin has shriveled on their bones; it has become as dry as wood. Happier were the victims of the sword than the victims of hunger, who wasted away, pierced by lack of the fruits of the field."

The imagery in Revelation 6:5-6 is powerful—the horseman holds a pair of scales, which in biblical times were used to price food. However, here the scales serve as a symbol of famine and death, as the price of food skyrockets (see Lamentations 5:8-10). It's not hard to imagine famine following a world war.

Jesus also prophesied in His Olivet Discourse that the tribulation period would bring war and famine (Matthew 24:5-7). While much of the famine at this point in the tribulation will be due to the outbreak of war, those who refuse to receive the mark of the beast will experience further starvation because they will be unable to buy or sell (Revelation 13:18).

The skyrocketing cost of food is evident in the statement, "a quart of wheat for a denarius, and three quarts of barley for a denarius, and do not harm the oil and wine" (Revelation 6:6). In ancient times, a Roman denarius was the daily wage of a laborer. This verse indicates that during the tribulation period, prices will rise to such unprecedented levels that a person would have to work an entire day just to afford one quart of wheat or three quarts of barley.

Buying this amount of wheat would make a good meal. Buying the barley would provide three meals, but there would be nothing left for oil or wine. Foods that are considered "necessities" will become luxuries on that future day of judgment. Many people will understandably die of starvation during the tribulation period.

FAST FACTS ON FAMINES IN BIBLE TIMES

- In biblical times, there were always threats to the food supply—even in the Holy Land, the land of "milk and honey" (Exodus 13:5).
- Famines almost always follow wars and major war campaigns.
- An enemy could invade and destroy all the crops.
- Locusts could come out of nowhere and consume all the crops in less than an hour.
- Because of such factors, famines were common in biblical times.

THE FOURTH SEAL JUDGMENT

Revelation 6:7-8 tells us: "When he opened the fourth seal, I heard the voice of the fourth living creature say, 'Come!' And I looked, and behold, a pale horse! And its rider's name was Death, and Hades followed him. And they were given authority over a fourth of the earth, to kill with sword and with famine and with pestilence and by wild beasts of the earth."

The horse in this passage is called *pale*—a word that literally means, "yellowish-green." This is the sickening color of a corpse. It symbolizes death.

Even the rider's name was Death, and "Hades followed him" (Revelation 6:8). This daunting picture represents the natural aftermath of harsh judgment. Due to the ravages of war and famine, multitudes will meet their end. This, in turn, ignites a swarm of diseases (pestilences) worldwide leaving no corner untouched. Death reigns undeterred. Prowling beasts will feast upon the remains, acting as silent carriers in the spread of disease.

🖾 LEXICAL NUGGET: *Hades*

> Hades is a biblical term for the place of the dead—a New Testament equivalent of the Old Testament *Sheol.*

> The word is appropriate in Revelation 6 because of the prevalence of death from the judgments of God.

> Death and Hades are companions: Death claims a person's *body* while Hades claims his *soul.*

The death toll will be catastrophic. A quarter of the world's population will die. In today's terms, that means around 1.7 billion people will die.

THE FIFTH SEAL JUDGMENT

Revelation 6:9-11 tells us: "When he opened the fifth seal, I saw under the altar the souls of those who had been slain for the word of God and for the witness they had borne. They cried out with a loud voice, 'O Sovereign Lord, holy and true, how long before you will judge and avenge our blood on those who dwell on the earth?' Then they were each given a white robe and told to rest a little longer, until the number of their fellow servants and their brothers should be complete, who were to be killed as they themselves had been."

The forces of the antichrist will execute believers during the tribulation for the same reason that John was exiled to Patmos: "for the word of God and for the witness they had borne" (Revelation 6:9; compare with 1:9). Under the antichrist's regime, it appears that sharing the gospel of Jesus will be punishable by death.

FAST FACTS ON THE INTERMEDIATE STATE

- The souls of these martyred believers were in heaven while their dead bodies were still on earth.
- The state of existence between physical death and the future resurrection is called the "intermediate state."
- It is a disembodied state.
- While one's physical body is in the grave, one's spirit or soul is in heaven with Christ or in a place of great suffering apart from Christ (see 2 Corinthians 5:8; Philippians 1:21-23; Luke 16:19-31).
- One's destiny depends wholly on whether one has trusted Christ for salvation (Acts 16:31).

FAST FACTS ON THE DUAL NATURE OF HUMAN BEINGS

- Humans have both a material and immaterial component.
- The material component is the body.
- The immaterial component is the soul or spirit (these terms are used interchangeably in the Bible).
- The soul or spirit departs or separates from the physical body at the moment of death (Genesis 35:18; Ecclesiastes 12:7; Luke 23:46; Acts 7:59).
- This is what happened to the martyrs of Revelation 6:9-11.
- Eventually, the spirits of all believers will be reunited with a glorious new body that will never perish (1 Thessalonians 4:13-17).

These tribulation saints who have been martyred cry out to God: "How long before you will judge and avenge our blood on those who dwell on the earth?" (Revelation 6:10). This verse proves that people remain conscious even after death. Unbelievers exist in conscious agony (Luke 16:22-23; Mark 9:43-48; Revelation 19:20), while believers exist in conscious ecstasy (2 Corinthians 5:8; Philippians 1:23).

The fact that these souls ask about time in the afterlife suggests that there is still a sense of time beyond our earthly existence. And heaven seems to have its own unique markers of time—Scripture says that God's people serve Him *day and night* in His temple (Revelation 7:15) and that the tree of life bears fruit *every month* (Revelation 22:2).

How Long, O Lord?—Psalms 74:9-10; 79:5; 94:3-4; Habakkuk 1:2.

👓 UNDERSTANDING OUR TERMS: *Tribulation Saints*

> ➤ Church saints (or church believers) will be raptured before the tribulation period (1 Thessalonians 1:10; 4:13-17; 5:9; Revelation 3:10).

> ➤ Others, however, will become believers during the tribulation period (Revelation 7:9-17; see also Matthew 25:31-46).

> ➤ We call these "tribulation saints."

> ➤ Some of them will be martyred during the tribulation period, like the souls in Revelation 6:9-11.

The white robe of the overcomer is given to each of the martyrs (Revelation 3:5). Some interpret the robes as symbolic because souls (or spirits) cannot wear physical robes. Others suggest that perhaps believers are given temporary bodies in heaven until the future day of resurrection, when they will receive their resurrection bodies (Revelation 20:4).

God then assures the martyrs that their murderers will not escape retribution. God elsewhere affirms, "Vengeance is mine," and in His perfect time, those who have shed innocent blood will face the wrath of the Almighty (Deuteronomy 32:35; Romans 12:19).

The martyrs are then instructed to wait a little longer and rest (Revelation 6:11). Some commentators suggest that God instructs them to rest from their thirst for vengeance. Others suggest that God wants them to simply relax in quiet serenity (see Revelation 14:13). Perhaps both senses are intended.

They are instructed to rest "until the number of their fellow servants and their brothers should be complete, who were to be killed as they themselves had been" (Revelation 6:11). God, in His sovereignty, has predetermined a precise number of martyrs before moving to destroy those who are killing His children (see Revelation 11:7; 12:11; 14:13; 20:4-5).

FAST FACTS ON GOD'S SOVEREIGNTY OVER DEATH

- God is sovereign over life and death.
- Job 14:5 says of human beings: "His days are determined, and the number of his months is with you, and you have appointed his limits that he cannot pass." (See Acts 17:26.)
- David said to God, "In your book were written, every one of them, the days that were formed for me, when as yet there was none of them" (Psalm 139:16).

THE SIXTH SEAL JUDGMENT

Revelation 6:12-14 tells us: "When he opened the sixth seal, I looked, and behold, there was a great earthquake, and the sun became black as sackcloth, the full moon became like blood, and the stars of the sky fell to the earth as the fig tree sheds its winter fruit when shaken by a gale. The sky vanished like a scroll that is being rolled up, and every mountain and island was removed from its place."

Scripture reveals that there will be an increase in earthquakes in the end times. Jesus affirmed that "nation will rise against nation, and kingdom against kingdom, and there will be famines and earthquakes in various places" (Matthew 24:7; see also Mark 13:8; Luke 21:11). However, the earthquake associated with the sixth seal will be so severe that all the earth's fault lines will rupture simultaneously, with devastating worldwide effects.

There will likely be numerous volcanic eruptions, releasing vast amounts of ash and debris into the atmosphere as a result of these cataclysmic forces shaking the planet to its core. As a result, the sun will become darker, and the moon's light will appear red (see Zechariah 14:6-7).

It is also conceivable that nuclear explosions could cause the sun and moon to darken and turn red. According to Revelation 8:7, one-third of the earth, one-third of the trees, and all of the grass will be consumed by fire. Revelation 16:2 tells us that people worldwide will develop hideous sores, possibly due to radiation contamination. Some believe that Jesus was alluding to nuclear weapons when He spoke of "men fainting from fear and the expectation of the things which are coming upon the world; for the powers of the heavens will be shaken" (Luke 21:26). If nuclear weapons are detonated during the tribulation, the atmosphere will be filled with so much dust and debris that the light of the sun and moon will be dimmed.

There will be many cosmic disturbances during this time, perhaps the most terrifying of which is that "the sky vanished like a scroll that is being rolled up" (Revelation 6:14). The earth's atmosphere will be catastrophically affected by all these judgments (compare with Isaiah 34:4). Perhaps the terminology means that people will simply not be able to see the sky (with all the dust and debris), causing great fear on the earth.

Another result of the global earthquake—with all the earth's faults fracturing simultaneously—will be that mountains and islands will move, apparently due to the shifting of the earth's tectonic plates. The very landscape of the earth will change.

Things will be so terrible that people will seek to hide from the wrath of the Lamb. Those who dwell on the earth will realize with sobering clarity that what they are experiencing is the result of the wrath of the sovereign Lord Jesus (Revelation 6:16).

Thankful for the Rapture

- The seal judgments—like the trumpet judgments and the bowl judgments—express God's wrath.

- At the rapture, which takes place before the tribulation period, Jesus "delivers us from the wrath to come" (1 Thessalonians 1:10).

- "God has not destined us for wrath, but to obtain salvation through our Lord Jesus Christ" (5:9).

- Jesus promised, "I will keep you from the hour of trial that is coming on the entire world, to try those who dwell on the earth" (Revelation 3:10).

THE SEVENTH SEAL JUDGMENT

The seventh seal judgment will unleash a new set of trumpet judgments—which are even more catastrophic (Revelation 8).

Things will go from bad to worse during the tribulation period.

PART 9

The Antichrist and the False Prophet

IN THIS SECTION

33 — The Antichrist's Ascent to Global Power—286

34 — The Emergence of the Insidious False Prophet—295

33

The Antichrist's Ascent to Global Power

n our day, speculation about the person of the antichrist is a common topic of conversation and debate. Many different worldly influences and misconceptions contribute to individuals' understanding of this end-times ruler, and, in turn, views on him vary widely. In this chapter, we will look at the emergence of the antichrist from the only reliable point of view, our Lord's, through the revelation of Scripture.

👤 PERSONALITY PROFILE: *The Antichrist*

- > The apostle Paul warns us of a "man of lawlessness," referring to the antichrist (2 Thessalonians 2:3, 8-9).
- > The apostle John calls this anti-God individual "the beast" (Revelation 13:1-10).
- > He will be empowered by Satan and will rise to power during the tribulation period (2 Thessalonians 2:9).
- > He will lead a revived Roman Empire and make a peace covenant with Israel (Daniel 9:27).
- > Soon after, he will rise to global dominion and demand to be worshiped as God (2 Thessalonians 2:4; Revelation 13).

📖 LEXICAL NUGGET: *Antichrist*

- > "Antichrist" is a compound word made up of two Greek words—*anti* and *christos*.
- > *Anti* can mean "instead of," "against," or "opposed to."

> › *Christos* means "Christ."
>
> › So antichrist can mean:
>
>   » "instead of Christ"
>
>   » "against Christ"
>
>   » "opposed to Christ"
>
>   » or all three at the same time

CROSS-REFERENCES
Titles of the Antichrist

Beast—Revelation 11:7
Contemptable person—Daniel 11:21
Lawless one—2 Thessalonians 2:8
Little Horn—Daniel 7:8
Man of lawlessness—2 Thessalonians 2:3
One who makes desolate—Daniel 9:27
Prince who is to come—Daniel 9:26
Son of destruction—2 Thessalonians 2:3

The antichrist "shall make a strong covenant with many for one week, and for half of the week he shall put an end to sacrifice and offering" (Daniel 9:27). The signing of this strong covenant marks the beginning of the tribulation period.

Strong covenant can also be translated as "firm covenant" (NASB 1995) or "binding and irrevocable covenant" (AMP). The antichrist will solve the Middle East crisis and force all parties—Jews and Muslims—to live in harmony. It will be a covenant backed by the military might of the revived Roman Empire, over which the antichrist will rule. The idea is: *Comply with the agreement or suffer the consequences.*

The antichrist, a being of tremendous intellect (Daniel 8:23), will be a commanding presence in the areas of commerce (Daniel 11:43; Revelation 13:16-17), war (Revelation 6:2; 13:2), speech (Daniel 11:36), and politics (Revelation 17:11-12). Satan—the unholy spirit—will empower him for all his work (2 Thessalonians 2:9). The antichrist will also perform counterfeit signs and wonders and deceive many people during the tribulation (2 Thessalonians 2:9-10).

At the midpoint of the tribulation, the antichrist will double-cross and seek to destroy the Jews, persecute believers in Jesus, and set up his own kingdom on earth (Revelation 13). He will speak arrogant and boastful words to glorify himself and blaspheme God (2 Thessalonians 2:4). He will be characterized by perpetual self-exaltation.

FAST FACTS ON THE ANTICHRIST'S MIMICKING OF CHRIST

- Just as Christ amazed people with miracles, signs, and wonders (Matthew 9:32-33; Mark 6:2), the antichrist will deceive people with counterfeit miracles, signs, and wonders (Matthew 24:24; 2 Thessalonians 2:9).

- While Christ will manifest Himself in the millennial temple (Ezekiel 43:6-7), the antichrist will boldly enthrone himself in the tribulation temple (2 Thessalonians 2:4).

- While Jesus is truly God (John 1:1-2; 10:36), the antichrist will claim to be God (2 Thessalonians 2:4).

- While Jesus causes people to worship God (Revelation 1:6), the antichrist will cause people to worship Satan and himself (Revelation 13:3-4).

- Jesus' dedicated followers—the 144,000 Jewish evangelists—will have a seal on their foreheads (Revelation 7:4; 14:1), while followers of the antichrist will have a mark on their foreheads or right hands (Revelation 13:16-18).

- Jesus has a name worthy of awe and reverence (Revelation 19:16), compared to the blasphemous names of the antichrist (Revelation 13:1).

- Jesus is to be married to His virtuous bride—the church (Revelation 19:7-9); the antichrist will be associated with a repulsive "prostitute," a symbol of false religion (Revelation 17:3-5).

- While Jesus is adorned with many crowns as a symbol of His supreme divine authority (Revelation 19:12), the antichrist will wear ten crowns illustrating his ill-gotten power (Revelation 13:1).

- Jesus is rightfully called the King of kings (Revelation 19:16); the antichrist will be called "the king" (Daniel 11:36).

- Jesus' triumphant resurrection (Matthew 28:6) stands in stark contrast to the antichrist's apparent or bogus resurrection (Revelation 13:3, 14).

- Unlike Jesus, who will have a glorious, 1,000-year kingdom spanning across the world (Revelation 20:1-6), the antichrist's global reign will only last for three-and-a-half years (Revelation 13:5-8).
- Jesus is part of the Holy Trinity—Father, Son, and Holy Spirit (2 Corinthians 13:14), while the antichrist forms a sinister triad with Satan and the false prophet (Revelation 13).

FAST FACTS ON OBVIOUS DISSIMILARITIES BETWEEN CHRIST AND THE ANTICHRIST

- One is Christ (Matthew 16:16); the other will be the antichrist (1 John 4:3).
- Christ is the man of sorrows (Isaiah 53:3); the antichrist will be the man of sin (2 Thessalonians 2:3 KJV).
- Christ is the Son of God (John 1:34); the antichrist will be the son of perdition (2 Thessalonians 2:3 KJV).
- Christ is the Holy One (Mark 1:24); the antichrist will be the wicked one (2 Thessalonians 2:8 KJV).
- Christ came to do the Father's will (John 6:38); the antichrist will do his own will (Daniel 11:36).
- Christ humbled Himself (Philippians 2:8); the antichrist will exalt himself (Daniel 11:37 NIV).
- Christ cleansed the temple (John 2:14-16); the antichrist will defile the temple (Matthew 24:15).
- Christ was received up into heaven (Luke 24:51); the antichrist will go down into the lake of fire (Revelation 19:20).

The sinister figure known as the false prophet will serve as the antichrist's chief ally, right hand man, and top lieutenant. I'll take a closer look at this intriguing character in the next chapter. For now, I will simply emphasize that this devious individual will seek to motivate the entire world to worship the antichrist (Revelation 13:11-12). The world's population will be forced to accept the mark of the beast as a prerequisite for buying or selling anything, thus giving the antichrist complete control over the world's economy (Revelation

13:16-17). (I will discuss the mark of the beast in detail in chapter 36.) Ultimately, the antichrist will take control of every corner of the world (Revelation 13:7), paving the way for political, economic, and religious globalism.

At present, the Holy Spirit is actively restraining both the antichrist and his lawlessness. However, after the rapture—when Christians filled with the Holy Spirit are taken away from earth and the Holy Spirit is subsequently "out of the way" (2 Thessalonians 2:7)—the antichrist will quickly rise to power on a global scale.

Christ Himself will defeat the antichrist and the false prophet at His second coming. Destined for eternal torment in the lake of fire, Revelation 19:20 recounts their fate: "The beast was seized, and with him the false prophet who performed the signs in his presence, by which he deceived those who had received the mark of the beast and those who worshiped his image; these two were thrown alive into the lake of fire which burns with brimstone." As for Satan, his final destruction awaits the end of the millennium: "The devil who deceived them was thrown into the lake of fire and brimstone, where the beast and the False Prophet are also; and they will be tormented day and night forever and ever" (20:10). This will mark the final defeat of the evil triumvirate.

FAST FACTS ON THE LAMB VERSUS THE BEAST

- Jesus is the "Lamb"; the antichrist is the "beast."
- This contrast paints a vivid picture, with the "Lamb" emphasizing the tender nature of Christ and the "beast" showing the fierce character of the antichrist.
- We see love and kindness embodied by the Lamb (Hebrews 7:26), while heartlessness and cruelty consume the beast.
- When Jesus received the Holy Spirit during His baptism, it took on the serene form of a gentle dove. In stark contrast, Satan—the unholy spirit—will empower and energize the vicious beast, or antichrist (2 Thessalonians 2:9; Revelation 12:9).
- While the Lamb is the Savior of sinners, the beast persecutes and executes the saints.

FREQUENTLY ASKED QUESTIONS

Will the antichrist have a supernatural birth?

Nowhere in Scripture is there any mention of a supernatural birth with regard to the antichrist. Instead, the antichrist is portrayed as a mere mortal, albeit one heavily influenced or even possessed by Satan. Referred to as "the man of lawlessness" in 2 Thessalonians 2:3, we learn that his very being is driven by the power of Satan, accompanied by false miracles and wonders (verse 9). Thus, although he is a man, the antichrist gains the ability to perform seemingly supernatural acts through the empowerment of Satan. Revelation 13:4 also informs us that the dragon (Satan) gives his authority to the beast, the antichrist.

Will the antichrist know that he is the antichrist as he grows up as a child?

I am not aware of a single verse in Scripture that even remotely addresses this question. However, based on my general knowledge of Bible prophecy, my answer to this question is no.

Because Satan is not omniscient like God, he does not know God's sovereign timing of end-time events with pinpoint accuracy. He must guess at the timing of end-time events—including the timing of the initial appearance of a full-grown adult antichrist.

Satan's inability to pinpoint prophetic events even a few decades into the future would seem to make the idea of a child growing up knowing that he is the antichrist impossible. It is difficult to imagine how a child could know that he is the antichrist, and then three or four decades later emerge as an adult political leader in perfect synchronization with God's overall prophetic plan—a plan that first requires the rapture (1 Thessalonians 4:13-17), followed by the emergence of a revived Roman Empire (Daniel 2:7), with its leader (the antichrist) signing a covenant with Israel (Daniel 9:26-27). All of this is highly speculative.

How old will the antichrist be when he comes to power?

Jesus was about thirty years old when He began His public ministry. Some might argue that if the antichrist is a true counterfeit of Jesus, then perhaps he too will be at least 30 years old when he comes to power. But this is mere speculation. Scripture is silent on the subject.

We observe that most of the world's political leaders are older—from their mid-forties and up. It seems reasonable to assume that the antichrist will appear on the world scene at about this general age.

Is it possible for Christians to know the exact identity of the antichrist before the rapture?

I do not think so. I say this because the starting point of the tribulation period is when the antichrist signs a covenant agreement with Israel, as mentioned in Daniel 9:27. Now, because the rapture takes place before this signing, there's simply no way for Christians to determine the identity of the antichrist. Speaking tongue-in-cheek, if you have managed to identify the antichrist based on the criteria of Daniel 9:27, you have been "left behind."

Is the antichrist alive today?

I believe that Satan has had a man ready to play the role of the antichrist in every generation. Satan does not know God's sovereign and providential timing of the end times with divine precision, so he must always have a man ready, waiting in the wings.

The prophetic signs of the times are now casting their shadows before them. We are even now experiencing the foreshocks of some of these prophetic signs. The stage is now being set for the future seven-year tribulation period! Consequently, we can logically infer that the antichrist may be alive somewhere in the world today, waiting in the wings to take center stage to rule the world. Has he actually been born? Is he a youth, a teenager, a twenty-something, or a thirty-something? We do not know—indeed, we cannot know—but it is quite possible that he is alive in our day.

Will the antichrist be a Jew?

I don't think so. In Revelation 13:1 and 17:15, the antichrist is described as coming up out of the "sea"—a term the Bible often associates with Gentile nations. Likewise, Daniel 11 describes Antiochus Epiphanes, a paganized Gentile, as foreshadowing the future antichrist. It is therefore unlikely that the antichrist will be Jewish. The antichrist is not described as a Jew, but as the greatest persecutor of the Jews during the tribulation (Jeremiah 30:7; Matthew 24:15-21; Revelation 12:6, 13). Why would a Jew persecute his own people?

Will the antichrist be a Muslim?

I highly doubt it. Daniel 11:36 describes the antichrist as one who "shall exalt himself and magnify himself above every god." In addition, the antichrist "opposes and exalts himself against every so-called god or object of worship so that he takes his seat in the temple of God, proclaiming himself to be God" (2 Thessalonians 2:4). It's inconceivable that a devout Muslim would claim equality with Allah. Any Muslim who follows the Qur'an would probably call for the beheading of such a person.

Furthermore, Muslims claim that "God can have no partners." Therefore, it is inconceivable that a Muslim would elevate himself to divine status, as the Scriptures foretell of the antichrist. In addition, Muslims believe that Allah is completely separate from earthly realities and cannot be described in earthly terms. How then, could a mortal Muslim declare himself to be God and accept being portrayed in earthly terms like the antichrist?

Perhaps most importantly, it's highly unlikely that a Muslim antichrist would make a deal to protect Israel (Daniel 9:24-27). In modern times, numerous radical Muslims seek to destroy Israel. It's unlikely that Islamic followers in various Muslim countries would accept a Muslim leader who made such a pact with Israel. Based on a long historical precedent, Muslims would likely react strongly against such an alliance by a Muslim leader.

Likewise, Jews—who are acutely aware of Muslim hostility and contempt for them—would never entrust their survival and security to a Muslim. This perspective stretches credulity.

CROSS-REFERENCES
The Antichrist
> Beast, the—Revelation 13:1-10
> Commercial genius—Daniel 11:43; Revelation 13:16-17
> Counterfeit signs and wonders—2 Thessalonians 2:9-10
> Destiny is the lake of fire—Revelation 19:20
> Dominion of, during tribulation—Revelation 13
> Energized by Satan—2 Thessalonians 2:9
> False prophet will seek to make the world worship him—Revelation 13:11-12
> Headquarters in Rome—Daniel 2; 7; Revelation 17:8-9
> Inhabitants of the earth will worship—Revelation 13:8
> Intellectual genius—Daniel 8:23
> Is now restrained—2 Thessalonians 2:6
> Makes covenant with Israel—Daniel 9:27

Man of lawlessness—2 Thessalonians 2:1-10

Military genius—Revelation 6:2; 13:2

Oratorical genius—Daniel 11:36

Political genius—Revelation 17:11-12

Rises up out of the "sea" (Gentile nations)—Revelation 13:1; 17:15

Seeks to establish his own kingdom—Revelation 13

Son of perdition—2 Thessalonians 2:3

Speaks arrogant, boastful words—2 Thessalonians 2:4

Will be defeated by Jesus at second coming—2 Thessalonians 2:8; Revelation 19:11-16

Will deceive many—Revelation 19:20

Will eventually rule the entire world—Revelation 13:7

Will persecute Christians—Revelation 13:7

World will follow—Revelation 13:3

34

The Emergence of the Insidious False Prophet

As we move deeper into the end times, a variety of deceptive figures will continue to appear on the religious landscape, functioning as false prophets (Matthew 24:24). Spreading the sinister teachings of demons, these prophets serve as puppets of Satan himself (1 Timothy 4:1). However, the tribulation period will unveil an unparalleled false prophet, one who stands by the side of the antichrist as his loyal accomplice (Revelation 13). While the antichrist's strengths lie in military and political dominance, his right-hand man will excel in religious leadership.

PERSONALITY PROFILE: *The False Prophet*

- > The false prophet will be the right-hand man—the first lieutenant—of the antichrist (Revelation 13:11).

- > His purpose will be to lead the entire world to worship the antichrist (verse 12).

- > To this end, he will perform an endless series of "great signs" (verse 13).

- > He will somehow animate an idolatrous image of the antichrist in the Jewish temple (verse 15).

- > He will cause people worldwide to receive the mark of the beast (verses 16-18).

So the antichrist is not weaving his devious web alone; he is accompanied by a wily first lieutenant. Through the lens of Scripture, especially the book of Revelation, we learn more about this cunning and deceptive false prophet.

The apostle John introduces him to us in Revelation 13:11: "I saw another beast rising out of the earth. It had two horns like a lamb and it spoke like a dragon." This false prophet is not just any beast but "another beast," revealing that both he and the antichrist share a similar beastly nature.

📖 LEXICAL NUGGET: *"Another" Beast*

> The Greek word for "another" (in the phrase "another beast") is *allos.*

> It means "another of the same kind."

> This beastly duo will ravage the earth for seven years.

This second beast rises "out of the earth." Some commentators argue that while the antichrist is a Gentile who emerges out of the "sea" of Gentile nations (Revelation 13:1), the false prophet will be a Jew.

"This individual is evidently a Jew, since he arises out of the earth, or land, that is Palestine (13:11)."

—J. Dwight Pentecost[1]

"Just as the sea is used symbolically in prophecy to refer to the Gentile nations, the land (or earth) is used to refer to Israel. This does not mean the False Prophet will be an Orthodox Jew. It only means that he will be of Jewish heritage. Religiously, he will be an apostate Jew who will head up the One World Religion of the Antichrist."

—David Reagan[2]

Other Bible scholars believe that the term "earth" does not indicate the ethnic identity of the false prophet.

"While the first beast was a Gentile, since he came from the entire human race as symbolized by 'the sea' (v. 1), the second beast was a creature of the earth. Some have taken this as a specific reference to the Promised Land and have argued that he was therefore a Jew. There is no support for this in the context as the word for 'earth' is the general [Greek] word referring to the entire world... Actually, his nationality and geographic origin are not indicated."

—John F. Walvoord[3]

This false prophet is said to have "two horns like a lamb and it spoke like a dragon" (Revelation 13:11). Recall that the Bible describes the antichrist as having "ten horns" (13:1). Because horns indicate power and authority, we can infer from the false prophet's two horns that he has less power and authority than the antichrist. The false prophet will be meeker and gentler in his dealings with others, like a lamb. But he speaks like a dragon because his words are inspired by Satan, the dragon. In the same way that the Holy Spirit inspires genuine prophets, Satan will inspire this false prophet.

> *"He looks religious, but he talks like the devil."*
>
> —Ed Hindson[4]

> *"He will speak winsome, deceiving words of praise about the Antichrist, luring the world to worship that vile, satanic dictator."*
>
> —John MacArthur[5]

The false prophet will be a gifted communicator, adept at inspiring loyalty to the false world religion and the antichrist. Bible expositor John Phillips explains:

> The role of the False Prophet will be to make the new religion appealing and palatable to men. No doubt it will combine all the features of the religious systems of men, will appeal to man's total personality, and will take full advantage of his carnal appetite. The dynamic appeal of the False Prophet will lie in his skill in combining political expediency with religious passion, self-interest with benevolent philanthropy, lofty sentiment with blatant sophistry, moral platitude with unbridled self-indulgence. His arguments will be subtle, convincing, and appealing. His oratory will be hypnotic, for he will be able to move the masses to tears or whip them into a frenzy. He will control the communication media of the world and will skillfully organize mass publicity to promote his ends. He will be the master of every promotional device and public relations gimmick. He will manage the truth with guile beyond words, bending it, twisting it, and distorting it. Public opinion will be his to command. He will mold world thought and shape human opinion like so much potter's clay. His deadly appeal will lie in the

fact that what he says will sound so right, so sensible, so exactly what unregenerate men have always wanted to hear.[6]

FAST FACTS ON THE AUTHORITY OF THE FALSE PROPHET

- The false prophet "exercises all the authority of the first beast in its presence and makes the earth and its inhabitants worship the first beast" (Revelation 13:12).
- This indicates that the false prophet's authority is delegated; he speaks on behalf of the antichrist (the first beast).
- He employs his delegated authority to convince the world to worship the antichrist.

The Miraculous Works of the False Prophet

Revelation 13:13-15 informs us that the false prophet "performs great signs, even making fire come down from heaven to earth in front of people, and by the signs that it is allowed to work in the beast's [antichrist's] presence it deceives those who dwell on earth, telling them to make an image for the beast [antichrist] that was wounded by the sword and yet lived. And it was allowed to give breath to the image of the beast, so that the image of the beast might even speak and might cause those who would not worship the image of the beast to be slain" (inserts added for clarification).

FAST FACTS ON "SIGNS"

- The Greek word for "sign" is *semeion* and carries the idea of a miracle that attests to something.
- Jesus' signs (miracles) attested that He was who He claimed to be (John 2:11; 4:54; 6:2; 12:18).
- The apostles' signs (miracles) attested that they were genuine messengers of God (Hebrews 2:3-4).
- The unspoken assumption is that where there are miracles, there is God.
- The signs of the false prophet are therefore highly deceptive.

> » They seem to support the antichrist's claim to deity.
>
> » However, these are "false signs and wonders" (2 Thessalonians 2:9).

FAST FACTS ON SATAN'S LIMITED POWER

- Satan does not have the ability to perform Grade-A miracles like God, but he can perform Grade-B miracles, which he empowers the false prophet to do (see Exodus 7:11; 2 Timothy 3:8).

- He does this so that people will worship the antichrist, Satan's substitute for Christ (see Daniel 9:27; 11:31; 12:11; Matthew 24:15).

Notice that in the original Greek, the phrase "performs great signs" uses a present tense verb. This indicates an ongoing action. Thus, the false prophet will perform successive miraculous signs. His miracles will be continuous, and people will be in awe.

These miracles are described as being "great." This means they will be impressive.

LEXICAL NUGGET: *"Great" Miracles*

- > The word "great" comes from the Greek word *megas.*
- > It literally means "large."
- > This Greek word is typically used for that which is "great" in the sense of outstanding, significant, important, or prominent.
- > From this we can infer that the signs performed by the false prophet will not be "the run-of-the-mill miracles that one hears about with pseudo-healers or the paranormal events of today."[7] The signs performed by the false prophet will seem impressive (1 Kings 18:38), even though they fall far short of God's Grade-A miracles.

This means that some pretty incredible deception will occur during the tribulation period. The enchanting wonders of the false prophet are designed to entice and deceive people (Revelation 13:14).

FAST FACTS ON THE SUSCEPTIBILITY OF CHRISTIANS TO BE DECEIVED

- According to Revelation 13:14, those who dwell on the earth will be deceived. The Bible affirms that even God's people are susceptible to deception.
- Ezekiel 34:1-7 affirms that wicked shepherds can lead God's sheep astray.
- Jesus warned His followers to beware of false prophets who may appear to be good on the outside but are extremely dangerous on the inside (Matthew 7:15-16).
- Paul warned Christians against being "led astray from a sincere and pure devotion to Christ" (2 Corinthians 11:3).
- Paul also warned the elders of the church in Ephesus of "ferocious wolves" who would not spare "the flock" and would "draw away the disciples after them" (Acts 20:28-30).
- Paul warned the Ephesians that Christians could be "tossed to and fro by the waves and carried about by every wind of doctrine" (Ephesians 4:14).

Christians living in the tribulation period must exercise great discernment, for the deceptive wonders of the false prophet will surely deceive many.

The Animating of the Antichrist's Image

The false prophet performs an amazing miracle by animating an image of the beast in the Jewish temple. The apostle Paul had previously foretold that the antichrist would sit enthroned in God's temple, receiving worship that rightfully belongs to God alone (2 Thessalonians 2:4). Some contend that when the antichrist is absent from the sanctuary, an image of him will be set up there to serve as an object of worship (Revelation 13:14-15; 14:9, 11; 15:2; 16:2; 19:20; 20:4).

The false prophet "gives breath" to the image of the beast, allowing it to "speak." Bible interpreters differ on what this means. Some believe that the image of the beast can give the impression of breathing and speaking mechanically, like today's computerized talking robots using AI (artificial intelligence). Perhaps a holographic deception could be used. Remember that Satan possesses a high level of intelligence, including scientific intelligence, and probably has the skills necessary to accomplish all of this.

Other interpreters see something more supernatural going on here, although it does not involve the miracle of the image actually coming to life. Only God has the ability to give life.

> "We are told that the false prophet is able to give breath to the image. This gives it the appearance of life. However, it isn't real life but only breath. Since breath or breathing is one of the signs of life, men think the image lives, but John is careful not to say that he gives life to the image. Only God can do that. It is something miraculous, but also deceptive and false...Then we are told the image of the beast, through this imparted breath, speaks. This is to be a further confirmation of the miraculous nature of the beast's image. Some might see this as the result of some product of our modern electronic robot-type of technology. But such would hardly convince people of anything spectacular. Evidently, it will go far beyond that."
>
> —J. Hampton Keathley[8]

While Christian scholars may have differing opinions on the matter, the image's apparent animation distinguishes it from typical Old Testament idols. As we read in Psalm 135:15-16, "The idols of the nations are silver and gold, the work of human hands. They have mouths, but do not speak; they have eyes, but do not see." Likewise, Habakkuk 2:19 says, "Woe to him who says to a wooden thing, Awake; to a silent stone, Arise! Can this teach? Behold, it is overlaid with gold and silver, and there is no breath at all in it." In contrast to such "dead" idols, this antichrist idol will *appear* to be alive. Perhaps the false prophet, utilizing Satan's power, causes all of this to occur in order to give the impression that the antichrist, unlike a dead idol, is God.

The False Prophet's Goal

The aim of the false prophet will be to persuade people worldwide to worship the antichrist. Remember that *antichrist* means "instead of Christ" or "in place of Christ." The antichrist places himself "in place of Christ" as the object of worship (for example, see Matthew 2:11; 8:2; 9:18; 15:25; 28:9, 17; John 9:38; 20:28).

According to Revelation 13:16-18, the false prophet will compel all humans on earth to receive the mark of the beast. This "mark" will be addressed in a separate chapter. Here, it is sufficient to observe that the false prophet will bring about global economic bondage so that no one will be able to buy or sell anywhere on earth without receiving a mark that demonstrates allegiance to, submission to, and the worship of, the antichrist.

> ***Exodus 34:14*** *instructs us: "You shall worship no other god, for the* LORD, *whose name is Jealous, is a jealous God." By demanding worship, the antichrist assumes the position of deity.*

PART 10

The "Great Tribulation"

IN THIS SECTION

35 — The Wounding and "Resurrection" of the Antichrist—304

36 — 666 and the Mark of the Beast—310

37 — Religious New Babylon Falls, Commercial New Babylon Rises—316

38 — The Terrifying Trumpet Judgments Are Unleashed—322

39 — Darkness Descends: The Antichrist Is Worshiped—329

40 — The Onset of the "Great Tribulation"—335

41 — The Catastrophic Unleashing of the Bowl Judgments—341

42 — Armageddon Ignites—349

43 — The Collapse of Commercial New Babylon—355

44 — Jerusalem Is Besieged, the Jewish Remnant Is Imperiled—363

The Wounding and "Resurrection" of the Antichrist

The midpoint of the tribulation period has now arrived. The antichrist intends to seize both political and religious dominion over the entire world. However, he cannot do this as long as there are competing religious systems. The rapture of Christians has already taken place. When God judged the Ezekiel invaders who moved against Israel, countless Muslims perished. The antichrist now seeks to eliminate all remaining religious resistance in the world. The first order of business is to destroy religious New Babylon. Then he will execute the two prophetic witnesses of God who speak forth Christian truths. Finally, he will violate his covenant with Israel and abolish the Jewish sacrificial system. He will even enthrone himself in the Jewish temple. (More on all of this in subsequent chapters.)

For his strategy to succeed, he cannot simply eliminate rival religious systems. He must also accomplish something spectacular—something that will inspire the world to worship him. What better way to accomplish this than to die and resurrect from the dead, like Jesus did. At the very least, he needs to *persuade* the world that he has resurrected, regardless of whether he actually has or not (see Revelation 13:3, 14).

YOU MAY BE INTERESTED TO KNOW...
Who or What Will Be Resurrected?

> Some have suggested that Revelation 13:3 may refer to the revival (resurrection) of the Roman Empire, and that when it occurs, people will be amazed.

> Prophecy scholar Arnold Fruchtenbaum responds, "A revived Roman Empire would not cause man to worship it as God any more than the revival of Poland or Israel did. This kind of thinking

is purely imaginary. It is the resurrection of the man Antichrist which creates this worship."[1]

> According to some, a historical figure from the past—Nero, Judas Iscariot, Mussolini, Hitler, and Stalin are common candidates—will reappear in the end times to play the role of the antichrist.

> This hypothesis seems to be based more on eisegesis (reading a meaning into the text) than exegesis (deriving the meaning out of the text). There is no indication in Scripture that this will happen.

> A literal interpretation of the biblical text indicates that in the end times, a new and distinct individual will emerge as the antichrist who will be crueler and more destructive than Nero, Judas Iscariot, Mussolini, Hitler, Stalin, or any other historical figure.

Most Bible commentators interpret Revelation 13 as referring to the antichrist. However, there is great debate as to whether this passage means that the antichrist will actually rise from the dead. Some prophecy scholars say it will be a false or bogus resurrection. Others say it will be real. Let us briefly consider each view.

The Bogus Resurrection View

In the first scenario, the antichrist suffers some kind of head wound, usually fatal, but in this case, it is healed by Satan so that the antichrist does not die but lives on. This is consistent with the biblical statement that the antichrist "*seemed* to have a mortal wound" (Revelation 13:3; emphasis added), or "*appeared* to be fatally wounded" (csb; emphasis added), or it was "*as if* it had been fatally wounded" (nasb; emphasis added). Perhaps the antichrist will seem to or appear to be killed when he is not. Perhaps Satan will perform a "Grade-B" miracle in healing him, making it appear to the world that he has risen from the dead.

"The final world ruler receives a wound which would normally be fatal but is miraculously healed by Satan. While the resurrection of a dead person seems to be beyond Satan's power, the healing of a wound would be possible for Satan, and this may be the explanation. The important point is that the final world ruler comes into power obviously supported by a supernatural and miraculous deliverance by Satan himself."

—John F. Walvoord[2]

FAST FACTS ON SATAN'S ABILITY TO BLIND MINDS

- Second Corinthians 4:4 tells us that "the god of this world [Satan] has blinded the minds of the unbelievers, to keep them from seeing the light of the gospel of the glory of Christ, who is the image of God."
- This passage shows that Satan has the ability to inhibit the unbeliever's ability to think or reason properly in spiritual matters.
- Could we infer from this that if Satan were to perform some kind of counterfeit resurrection—a "Grade-B" healing of a wound or some satanic trick—that Satan would be able to blind the minds of the people on earth in such a way that they would accept it as a genuine resurrection and subsequently worship the antichrist?
- There is good reason to believe so.

The Resurrection View

Other prophecy enthusiasts believe that the antichrist will suffer a fatal head wound that will kill him, and that Satan will resurrect him.

> "We believe that the Beast really is killed, for John twice says that he 'ascends out of the bottomless pit' (11:7; 17:8); we believe this means that the Beast is killed, descends to the pit, and ascends from there to the earth when he is resurrected."
>
> —Tim LaHaye and Jerry Jenkins[3]

One problem with this view is that only God is infinite in power (omnipotent); the devil is finite and limited (see "Frequently Asked Question" below). In addition, this view does not reflect the biblical teaching that the antichrist only *appeared to* or *seemed to* have been killed.

Regardless of which view is correct, the biblical text reveals that people during the tribulation period will believe that the antichrist has been resurrected. As a result, they will worship him.

FREQUENTLY ASKED QUESTION

Does Satan have the ability to resurrect someone from the dead?

The Scriptures make it clear that there is a significant difference between Satan and God. Satan is a creature, while God is the Creator. Satan does not have the divine attributes that belong to God alone, such as omnipresence (being everywhere present), omnipotence (being all-powerful), and omniscience (being all-knowing). Satan is limited in his abilities, as he can only be in one place at a time, has limited strength, and has limited knowledge. Only God can create life (Genesis 1:1, 21; Deuteronomy 32:39); the devil cannot (see Exodus 8:19). Only God can truly raise the dead (John 10:18; Revelation 1:18).

This raises the question: If the devil can resurrect people from the dead, why didn't he resurrect dead Roman emperors who were so effective in killing Christians, or the founders of the various cults and false religions to give them credibility? If the devil *could*, he *would*.

How Do We Explain the Abyss?

Assuming that the antichrist does not die, how do we explain his emergence from the abyss? Bible scholar Walter Price offers a viable explanation:

> *"The apostle Paul...was stoned in Lystra, and the citizens 'dragged him out of the city, supposing that he was dead' (Acts 14:19). While in an unconscious state, Paul 'was caught up into Paradise, and heard unspeakable words, which it is not lawful for a man to utter' (2 Cor. 12:4). Paul had received what seemed like a death stroke. While he was thought to be dead, his spirit was caught up into the third heaven and there received a profound revelation from God. This same thing, in reverse, will happen to the antichrist. The antichrist...will be no more dead than was the apostle Paul. But just as the citizens of Lystra thought Paul was dead, so the antichrist will be thought dead."*

> —Walter Price[4]

This is an intriguing theory. In the same way that Paul's spirit left his body and was taken to God's domain, the third heaven, where he received additional revelations, so the antichrist's spirit may depart his body (appearing to be deceased) and be taken into the abyss. Satan will then offer him the kingdoms of the world.

> *"Just as Satan took Jesus up into a high mountain and showed him all the kingdoms of the world, and offered them to him, if he would fall down and worship him; so Satan will take the antichrist into the depths of the Abyss and show him all the kingdoms of the world... Jesus refused to bow down to Satan. The antichrist will not refuse."*

> —Walter Price[5]

If this hypothesis is correct, the antichrist's spirit will come forth from the abyss (Revelation 11:7), reenter what appears to be a dead body—giving the appearance of a resurrection from the dead—and continue on his satanically inspired mission.

> *While in the abyss, the "antichrist probably receives his orders and strategy from Satan, literally selling his soul to the devil, and then comes back to earth with hellish ferocity to establish his world dominion over a completely awestruck earth."*
>
> —Mark Hitchcock[6]

FREQUENTLY ASKED QUESTION

Why do theologians say Satan is a master counterfeiter?

Augustine said Satan is the ape of God. He "copycats" God in many ways:

> - The antichrist has his own congregation called the "synagogue of Satan" (Revelation 2:9).

> - He has his own ministers who preach false sermons (2 Corinthians 11:45).

> - He has developed his own theological system, which the Bible refers to as "teachings of demons" (1 Timothy 4:1; see also Revelation 2:24).

> - His ministers preach a false gospel, "a gospel contrary to the one we preached to you" (Galatians 1:7-8).

> - Satan has his own throne (Revelation 13:2) and his own worshipers (13:4).

> - He inspires counterfeit christs and self-proclaimed messiahs (Matthew 24:4-5).

> - He employs false teachers who bring in "destructive heresies" (2 Peter 2:1).

> - He dispatches false prophets (Matthew 24:11) and false apostles who imitate the genuine (2 Corinthians 11:13).

> - As it pertains to the antichrist, a resurrection—or what *appears* to be a resurrection—would be consistent with Satan's deceptive nature as a counterfeiter.

FAST FACTS ON SATAN—THE MASTER TRICKSTER

- Satan has extensive experience in deceiving and bringing down people.
- Because of his longevity, Satan has amassed a wealth of knowledge that far exceeds that of human beings.
- He has personally observed people in every conceivable situation, allowing him to accurately anticipate how they will respond to various circumstances.
- Therefore, although Satan is not omniscient, his vast experience has given him knowledge superior to that of any human being.
- He is a skilled magician and an exceptional scientist.
- As a result of his extensive experience, Satan has acquired a vast arsenal of deceptive techniques.
- He may use some of his deceitful tricks in the "resurrection" of the antichrist.
- Therefore, Christians are warned to be cautious (1 Peter 5:8; 2 Corinthians 2:1).

SOMETHING TO THINK ABOUT:

> If talented Las Vegas magicians can deceive large crowds of people with sleight of hand, how much more will Satan, the master deceiver with thousands of years of experience, be able to deceive large numbers of people with the apparent resurrection of the antichrist!

> These are deceptive times (John 8:44; 1 Thessalonians 2:3; see also 1 Timothy 4:1; 2 Timothy 4:4).

36

666 and the Mark of the Beast

One of the most disturbing prophecies in Revelation 13 is that the antichrist and the false prophet will subjugate the entire world so that no one will be able to buy or sell unless he receives the mark of the beast. The false prophet "causes all, both small and great, both rich and poor, both free and slave, to be marked on the right hand or the forehead, so that no one can buy or sell unless he has the mark, that is, the name of the beast or the number of its name" (verses 16-17). We are then informed, "This calls for wisdom: let the one who has understanding calculate the number of the beast, for it is the number of a man, and his number is 666" (verse 18).

The false prophet will attempt to force people to worship the antichrist, the man of sin. This "squeeze play" will compel people to either receive the mark of the beast and worship the antichrist or starve for lack of purchasing power.

YOU MAY BE INTERESTED TO KNOW...
The Mark of the Beast—A Parody of God's Sealing

> - Revelation 7:4 states that God will *seal* 144,000 Jewish servants.

> - Revelation 14:1 indicates that they have the "Father's name written on their foreheads."

> - The "mark" of the beast on the right hand or the forehead parodies God's sealing of 144,000 witnesses in Revelation 7 and 14.

"God's seal of His witnesses most likely is invisible and for the purpose of protection from the antichrist. On the other hand, the antichrist offers protection from the wrath of God—a promise he cannot deliver—and his mark is visible and external...For the only time in history, an outward indication will identify those who reject Christ and His gospel of forgiveness of sins."

—Thomas Ice and Timothy Demy[1]

Revelation 14:9-10 warns of the utter folly of receiving the mark of the beast: "If anyone worships the beast and its image and receives a mark on his forehead or on his hand, he also will drink the wine of God's wrath, poured full strength into the cup of his anger, and he will be tormented with fire and sulfur in the presence of the holy angels and in the presence of the Lamb." We are also told in Revelation 16:2: "The first angel went and poured out his bowl on the earth, and harmful and painful sores came upon the people who bore the mark of the beast and worshiped its image."

These words give pause to the thoughtful person. Whoever declares allegiance to the antichrist and his cause will incur the wrath of our holy and righteous God. How terrible it will be for these individuals to experience the full force of God's divine wrath and unbridled vengeance (see Psalm 75:8; Isaiah 51:17; and Jeremiah 25:15-16)!

Believers in Jesus who reject the mark of the beast have a blessed future, despite the possibility of temporary suffering at the hands of the antichrist—*or even martyrdom*: "I saw the souls of those who had been beheaded for the testimony of Jesus and for the word of God, and who had not worshiped the beast or its image and had not received its mark on their foreheads or their hands. They came to life and reigned with Christ for a thousand years" (Revelation 20:4).

▦ NUMBERS IN PROPHECY: 666

> The meaning of 666 has been interpreted in numerous ways by Bible scholars.

> Some Bible expositors suggest that seven is the number of perfection. The number 777 may therefore represent the Trinity in its perfection. Perhaps 666 indicates a being that aspires to complete divinity (like the Trinity) but never achieves it. The antichrist, Satan, and the false prophet comprise the satanic triumvirate.

> Others speculate that the number may refer to a specific individual, such as the Roman emperor, Nero. The numerical value of the letters in the Hebrew translation of Nero's name is 666. So it is possible that the deceiver will resemble ancient Nero.

> All of this is speculation.

> Scripture does not define what is meant by 666.

> The number 666 will play a crucial role in identifying the antichrist in ways we do not yet know.

It may be that the meaning of 666 is intended to remain a mystery—*an enigma*—until the antichrist appears on the world stage during the tribulation period (see Revelation 13:18; 17:9; see also Daniel 9:22; 12:10). The church, of course, will be raptured prior to this time.

Receiving the mark of the beast indicates tacit acceptance of the antichrist as a leader and agreement with his mission. No one will receive this mark by accident. One must make a voluntary choice, armed with all relevant information. It will be a conscious decision with eternal consequences. Those who choose to receive the mark will do so with full awareness of their actions.

This squeeze play employed by the false prophet will result in extreme polarization. There is no room for compromise when it comes to receiving the mark of the beast. One is either for or against the antichrist. One is either for God or against God. At present, people believe they can avoid God and His demands on their lives by professing neutrality. However, during the tribulation, neutrality will be impossible. If one follows the antichrist, one may eat well for a while, but in the end, one will pay with eternal consequences. If one follows God, one may go hungry for a time and may even die, but eternal life awaits.

"The mark will serve as a passport for business (v. 17a). They will be able to neither buy nor sell anything unless they have the mark... Only those who have this number will be permitted to work, to buy, to sell, or simply to make a living."

—Arnold Fruchtenbaum[2]

HISTORICAL INSIGHT
Identifying Marks

> Identifying "marks" were often used in a variety of contexts during ancient times.

> Soldiers were marked by their commanders.

> Slaves were marked by their owners.

> Religious devotees of pagan deities were marked.

"The mark must be some sort of branding similar to those given to soldiers, slaves, and temple devotees in John's day. In Asia Minor, devotees of pagan religions delighted in displaying such a tattoo as an emblem of ownership by a certain god. In Egypt, Ptolemy Philopator I branded Jews, who submitted to registration, with an ivy leaf in recognition of their Dionysian worship (cf. 3 Mace. 2:29). This meaning resembles the long-time practice of carrying signs to advertise religious loyalties (cf. Isa. 44:5) and follows the habit of branding slaves with the name or special mark of their owners (cf. Gal. 6:17). Charagma *("mark") was a [Greek] term for the images or names of emperors on Roman coins, so it fittingly could apply to the beast's emblem put on people."*

—Robert Thomas[3]

In the Roman Empire, a mark "was a normal identifying symbol, or brand, that slaves and soldiers bore on their bodies. Some of the ancient mystical cults delighted in such tattoos, which identified members with a form of worship. Antichrist will have a similar requirement, one that will need to be visible on the hand or forehead."

—John MacArthur[4]

FAST FACTS ON THE MARK OF THE BEAST LINKING THE ECONOMY WITH RELIGION

* The false prophet will be primarily a religious leader.
* However, during the future tribulation, religion and economics will merge, making one dependent on the other.
* The mark of the beast will bind them together.
* Although receiving the mark is primarily a spiritual decision, it will have life-or-death economic consequences.

"The mark will allow the Antichrist's followers to buy and sell because it identifies them as religiously orthodox—submissive followers of the Beast and worshipers of his image. Those without the mark are forbidden to buy because they are identified as traitors."

—David Jeremiah[5]

FREQUENTLY ASKED QUESTIONS

How does modern technology relate to the mark of the beast?

The mark of the beast will be a visible symbol on the skin, such as a tattoo, indicating allegiance to the antichrist. Revelation 13:16 specifies that the mark will be "on" the right hand or head, and not "in" or "under" the right hand or head, or beneath the skin.

The antichrist and false prophet will be able to use modern technology to enforce the global economic system associated with the mark of the beast.

"There is no doubt that with today's technology, a totalitarian world leader would be able to keep a constantly updated census of all living people and know day-by-day precisely who had pledged allegiance to him and received the mark and who had not."

—John F. Walvoord[6]

Others assert that chip implants, scanning technology, and biometrics will be used to enforce the policy that prohibits buying and selling without the mark of the beast.

Does the mark of the beast hinge on a cashless world?

It is very likely. Certain aspects of our society have already shifted to cashless transactions. According to economists, the amount of cash used today is less than half of what it was in the 1970s. Why is that? Because more and more people are using cashless payment methods such as credit cards, debit cards, digital wallet platforms, and others.

Today, more than 70 percent of consumer payments are made electronically.[7] According to economists, currency may soon become obsolete. Bills and coins will be consigned to the annals of history. Attempts to use cash in retail establishments may soon be accompanied by additional fees.

A cashless system, possibly involving a global cryptocurrency, would make it simple for the antichrist to regulate who can purchase and sell during the tribulation. With the current global trend toward cashlessness, the stage is being set for the mark of the beast.

Does receiving the mark of the beast have eternal consequences?

Yes, it does. Receiving the mark of the beast—in conjunction with worshiping the beast—is an unforgivable sin. Revelation 14:9-10 states, "If anyone worships the beast and its image and receives a mark on his forehead or on his hand, he also will drink the wine of God's wrath, poured full strength into the cup of his anger, and he will be tormented with fire and sulfur in the presence of the holy angels and in the presence of the Lamb." Thus, anyone who expresses loyalty to the antichrist and his cause will suffer the wrath of God (Psalm 75:8; Isaiah 51:17; Jeremiah 25:15-16).

Unlike those who receive the mark of the beast during the tribulation period, you and I have the mark of the Holy Spirit, also known as the "seal" of the Holy Spirit (Ephesians 1:13; 4:30). A seal indicates ownership and security. God "possesses" believers as His offspring and will see to it that they enter heaven safely. Praise God!

CROSS-REFERENCES

Mark of the Beast

Contrasts with the seal of living God—Revelation 7:2
Invokes God's fury—Revelation 14:9-10
False prophet forces it on people—Revelation 13:16
No one can buy or sell without it—Revelation 13:17
The alternative is persecution or death—Revelation 13:7, 10, 15, 17

Religious New Babylon Falls, Commercial New Babylon Rises

I n a dramatic turn of events, the once-dominant religious New Babylon will suddenly be destroyed. Revelation 17:16-18 reveals that the antichrist, along with his ten powerful subcommanders, will put an end to the deceptive world church—the treacherous "prostitute" of the end times. We read: "The ten horns that you saw, they and the beast will hate the prostitute. They will make her desolate and naked, and devour her flesh and burn her up with fire, for God has put it into their hearts to carry out his purpose by being of one mind and handing over their royal power to the beast, until the words of God are fulfilled."

Although the prophetic text doesn't explicitly reveal when this event will take place, weaving together clues from the book of Revelation and other prophetic books suggests that it will occur in the middle of the tribulation period. At the same time, the antichrist will seize the opportunity to declare himself a global dictator (Daniel 9:27; Matthew 24:15). Consequently, from this point onward, the antichrist holds both political and religious control over the world, even claiming to be God and demanding worship from the world's inhabitants.

> The antichrist "opposes and exalts himself against every so-called god or object of worship, so that he takes his seat in the temple of God, proclaiming himself to be God."
>
> —2 Thessalonians 2:4

> "He shall exalt himself and magnify himself above every god, and shall speak astonishing things against the God of gods."
>
> —Daniel 11:36

"The beast and his allies will eventually throw off the harlot and thoroughly destroy her...This will probably occur in the middle of the Tribulation when the Antichrist breaks his covenant with Israel and demands that everyone on earth worship him or die (Dan. 9:27; 11:26-38; Matt. 24:15; 2 Thess. 2:4; Rev. 13:8, 15)."

—Thomas Constable[1]

The antichrist operates on a sinister principle: "Exploit it, then eliminate it." Revelation 17:16 unveils how the antichrist cunningly uses the deceptive religious system—the "prostitute"—to unite the diverse peoples of the world. Once his mission is accomplished, however, he has no further use for her. Driven by contempt for the religion and a feverish desire for self-aggrandizement and godhood, he and his ten loyal subcommanders ruthlessly cast the religion aside.

"Throughout history, political systems have 'used' religious bodies to further their political causes...When dictators are friendly with religion, it is usually a sign that they want to make use of religion's influence and then destroy it."

—Warren Wiersbe[2]

YOU MAY BE INTERESTED TO KNOW...
God Is Sovereign Over the Antichrist

> The antichrist and his ten subcommanders will destroy the false religious system.

> However, God will be working *through* them to accomplish His sovereign purposes (Revelation 17:17). He will put the motivation in their hearts to destroy the religion.

> All of human history, including the most minute details, is merely the outworking of God's eternal purposes.

> What has happened in the past, what is happening in the present, and what will happen in the prophetic future are all indications of the unfolding of a plan designed by the awesome personal God of the Bible (Ephesians 3:11; 2 Timothy 1:9).

> In relation to the antichrist, God will motivate the destruction of the false world religion and grant the antichrist world dominance for a brief period of time.

As the dust settles from the collapse of religious New Babylon, the vibrant, *commercial* New Babylon springs to life in its place! The very same city—but with a whole new electrifying purpose: *The center of commerce on planet earth.*

It is essential to understand that when the antichrist and his ten subcommanders bring down the false religion, they do not demolish the city of New Babylon itself. The city is left untouched, and instead, they repurpose New Babylon into a global commercial hub, eradicating only the religious aspect.

Revelation 18 informs us of the essential features of commercial New Babylon:

1. Across the globe, political leaders will support and promote New Babylon. As Revelation 18:3 states, "The kings of the world have committed adultery with her." This isn't alluding to actual sexual promiscuity, but rather a deep and entwined connection between global rulers and this commercial powerhouse. The support of politicians around the world solidifies New Babylon's international presence. Eventually, this anti-God commercial system will influence every person on earth.

World leaders will favor commercial New Babylon because it brings each of them great luxury (Revelation 18:9).

2. Entrepreneurs from every corner of the globe will be irresistibly drawn to New Babylon because this thriving business center holds the key to unlocking unimaginable wealth and success. Revelation 18:3 affirms, "Because of her desires for extravagant luxury, the merchants of the world have grown rich." Businesspeople from around the world will amass incredible wealth by offering their products to the thriving metropolis of New Babylon (verses 12-13).

3. New Babylon's bustling commercial scene will offer an eclectic assortment of products, handpicked from various corners of the globe. It will include such things as "gold, silver, jewels, and pearls; fine linen, purple, silk, and scarlet cloth; things made of fragrant thyine wood, ivory goods, and objects made of expensive wood; and bronze, iron, and marble…cinnamon, spice, incense, myrrh, frankincense, wine, olive oil, fine flour, wheat, cattle, sheep, horses, wagons, and bodies—that is, human slaves" (Revelation 18:12-13). No doubt this list only scratches the surface. Commercial New Babylon

will likely offer an unimaginable array of items, ensuring that all who trade in its goods will amass remarkable wealth.

4. All who are associated with commercial New Babylon will bask in opulence and grandeur. Influential leaders around the world will indulge in "her great luxury" (verse 9), while savvy business magnates will amass vast fortunes (verse 15). Even shipping tycoons won't be left behind—they'll rake in riches by moving her enormous wealth across the oceans (verse 19). *Can you see the recurring theme here?*

> Many people will love commercial New Babylon for one primary reason: ***They love money***.

5. As the bustling commercial center of New Babylon thrives, shipowners amass immense wealth. The vast array of products procured by this commercial powerhouse travels the oceans aboard merchant ships steered by captains and their crews. These individuals, including the shipowners, serve as the lifeline connecting a myriad of commercial goods to the vibrant shores of New Babylon (Revelation 18:17, 19). *And they all get rich in the process.*

6. New Babylon will be headed up by an economic genius—the Satan-inspired antichrist. At the midpoint of the tribulation period, the antichrist's religious capital will be Jerusalem, where he will set up an image of himself in the Jewish temple. His economic and public capital, however, will be the city of New Babylon, which will become the commercial center of the world.

As noted previously in the book, the antichrist—through the false prophet—will require "everyone—small and great, rich and poor, free and slave—to be given a mark on the right hand or the forehead. And no one [will] buy or sell anything without that mark, which [is] either the name of the beast or the number representing his name" (Revelation 13:16-17 NLT). We can infer from this that the items procured by New Babylon's commercial sector will come from merchants who have already been branded with the infamous mark of the beast.

The Feasibility of a Rebuilt Babylon

Some have questioned whether the expectation that Babylon will be rebuilt in the end times is realistic. Here are my thoughts on the matter:

1. In 1940, some questioned whether the expectation that Israel would be

restored as a nation was realistic. And yet, in 1948, Israel was reborn, just as Ezekiel 37 predicted. My point is that you can rely on Bible prophecy, even though some naysayers will invariably claim it is unrealistic.

2. When Saddam Hussein was in authority, he spent well over a billion dollars in oil money to enhance Babylon. In his case, a billion dollars accomplished the revitalization of the city relatively quickly. The antichrist will have considerably more money at his disposal.

3. When the antichrist assumes authority during the tribulation, he will have access to an unlimited budget and unlimited manpower. We could also say: *Whatever the antichrist desires, he will get!* He will make Hussein's efforts appear trivial.

4. It is conceivable that Iraqi oil will be the main source of funding for the reconstruction of Babylon. An oil-rich Iraq could be part of God's plan for the end times.

> *"It's no accident that Babylon is in Iraq, a nation with such stagger-ing oil reserves. God said that Babylon will be rebuilt as a great commercial center in the end times."*
>
> —Mark Hitchcock[3]

With access to staggering wealth—nearly two-thirds of the world's remaining oil—the antichrist would undoubtedly find New Babylon an ideal location for a bustling commercial hub. Remember, whoever controls the majority of the world's oil has tremendous leverage over the nations of the world.

It may be that world powers such as China will find it difficult to suppress their craving for this oil-rich territory. What if China—those kings of the east mentioned in Revelation 16:12—were to directly challenge the antichrist's authority while he sits enthroned in New Babylon, controlling the planet's Middle Eastern oil supply? With the reins on this precious resource, the antichrist could easily strangle any nation. Perhaps China will become desperate for fuel and have no choice but to take action against the Satan-inspired oil czar who rules New Babylon.

Regardless of how these events unfold, there's no denying that the antichrist will possess *the might* and *the means* to rapidly restore Babylon to its former glory. It is on the horizon.

CROSS-REFERENCES

New Babylon

Center of false religion—Revelation 17:4-5; 18:1-2

Center of world commerce—Revelation 18:9-19

38

The Terrifying Trumpet Judgments Are Unleashed

The tribulation period will be characterized by God's increasingly severe judgments. That's why it's called the "tribulation period," because turmoil, chaos, and suffering will reign supreme. The ominous seal judgments (found in Revelation 6) involve the rise of the antichrist, the shattering of world peace, widespread famine, catastrophic loss of life, the relentless persecution and martyrdom of Christians, and an earth-shattering earthquake that redefines devastation.

Then come the trumpet judgments, as described in Revelation 8. As if the seal judgments weren't terrifying enough, the trumpet judgments take it up a big notch. So intense are these judgments that even heaven itself will fall into a deafening 30-minute silence when its inhabitants catch wind of what's coming.

FIRST TRUMPET JUDGMENT

The trumpet judgments burst forth with a torrent of hail and fire mixed with blood falling upon the earth. This vivid scene recalls one of the divine plagues unleashed by Moses on the Egyptians (Exodus 9:18-26) and brings to mind Joel's prophecy of a devastating judgment of "blood and fire and columns of smoke" in the end times (Joel 2:30).

This cataclysmic event won't just be confined to a specific area but will have far-reaching consequences. Indeed, a staggering "third of the earth" will be set ablaze, incinerating "a third of the trees" and scorching "all green grass" that carpets our world (Revelation 8:7). These terrible fires could be ignited directly by God's hand, or they could even result from nuclear explosions. Such massive burning could also indicate the destruction of a significant portion of the earth's crops, exacerbating the crippling food shortages already plaguing the famine-stricken planet.

FREQUENTLY ASKED QUESTION

Are there any other references in Scripture that may allude to possible nuclear detonations in the end times?

It is hard not to suspect the use of nuclear weapons when we consider that vast portions of the earth will be scorched and consumed by fire. Revelation 16:2 goes a step further and describes the horrifying scene of people all over the world being afflicted with horrible, malignant sores. Could these sores be the result of radiation poisoning from the detonation of nuclear weapons? Some believe that Jesus may have been alluding to nuclear weapons when He spoke of "people fainting with fear and with foreboding of what is coming on the world. For *the powers of the heavens will be shaken*" (Luke 21:26; emphasis added).

SECOND TRUMPET JUDGMENT

This massive burning in the first trumpet judgment is followed by a "fiery mountain" plummeting into the sea. This "fiery mountain" has been variously interpreted. Some believe it could be a colossal island volcano that erupts explosively, seemingly throwing a burning mountain into the sea. Others suggest that this flaming mass could be a massive asteroid falling from the sky. Still others suggest it could be a nuclear missile plunging into the sea before detonating. Regardless of its true nature, this event turns one-third of the sea into crimson blood, resulting in the death of one-third of all sea creatures (Revelation 8:8). As global famine continues to plague humankind, this judgment will take a further toll on already dwindling food resources. There will be far fewer fish to eat.

We are informed that "a third of the ships" will be destroyed. Some speculate that if the "fiery mountain" were a giant asteroid crashing into the watery depths of the earth, it would likely create a massive tidal wave that would destroy one-third of the earth's ships. The same would be true if a nuclear missile exploded underwater. Currently, countless ships sail around the globe, transporting vital industrial goods across vast oceans. The moment this cataclysmic judgment hits earth, chaos will ensue in the shipping industry, as one-third of all ships will be immediately rendered useless. Not only will this disaster wreak havoc on international trade and economies, but it will also severely impact food supplies, assuming that many of the ships were carrying food.

THIRD TRUMPET JUDGMENT

Humanity will continue to face judgment when a "star" falls from heaven (Revelation 8:10-11). This "star" will likely be a colossal meteor or asteroid that collides with the earth, causing a near-apocalyptic event. As it hurtles toward our planet, it lights up the sky, becoming a blazing torch in its fiery descent through our atmosphere. This catastrophic event will contaminate one-third of the earth's water resources, making the water deadly to drink. With each passing day, leading scientists warn that this type of celestial catastrophe isn't just a possibility; it's an inevitable reality waiting to unfold. The mathematical odds confirm its certainty in the indefinite future.

FOURTH TRUMPET JUDGMENT

As if this were not bad enough, severe cosmic disturbances will now occur around the earth. We are told that "a third of the sun was struck, and a third of the moon, and a third of the stars, so that a third of their light might be darkened, and a third of the day might be kept from shining, and likewise a third of the night" (Revelation 8:12-13). It seems reasonable to conclude that the dimming of the light could be due to the massive dust thrown into the atmosphere when the giant meteor or asteroid associated with the third trumpet judgment strikes the earth. Of course, our text does not require that there be such a "natural" explanation for the dimming of the light from these heavenly bodies. It is possible that God Himself will supernaturally cause the luminosity of these heavenly bodies to diminish.

In any event, all of this will result in a decrease in global temperatures. With one-third of the trees already destroyed, there will be much less firewood to keep people warm. With less light, the growth of plant life will be hindered, further reducing the food supply. Things are now cascading out of control—going from bad to worse.

FIFTH TRUMPET JUDGMENT

Worse still, hideous demons will now be released from the bottomless pit to torment people for five months (Revelation 9:1-12). They will be given "power like the power of the scorpions of the earth" (verse 3). Victims of scorpion bites are usually in agony. They sometimes succumb to foaming at the mouth and grinding their teeth in pain. Prophetic Scripture tells us that during this time, people will have a desire to die, but they will not be able to escape their pain. They will long for death rather than repent before a holy God.

FAST FACTS ON THE BOTTOMLESS PIT

- The bottomless pit is "the abyss."
- The abyss is the dwelling place of imprisoned demons or disobedient spirits (Revelation 9:1-21).
- It is the place where Jesus sent demons when He cast them out of people—a place that they feared to go (Luke 8:31).
- The term is translated seven times as "the bottomless pit" (Revelation 9:1, 2, 11; 11:7; 17:8; 20:1, 3) and twice as "the deep" (Luke 8:31; Romans 10:7).

YOU MAY BE INTERESTED TO KNOW...
Demons Are "On a Leash"

- In the book of Revelation, God sets limits on what He allows demons to do (Revelation 9:4). They are "on a leash."
- Satan is also "on a leash." This is illustrated in the book of Job, for God set limits on what Satan could do to Job.
- Evil spirits cannot go beyond what God will allow them.

YOU MAY BE INTERESTED TO KNOW...
There Are Ranks Among Demons

- Scripture reveals that there are ranks among fallen angels (Ephesians 6:12).
- Their ranks include principalities, powers, rulers of the darkness of this world, and spiritual wickedness in high places.
- All fallen angels, regardless of rank, follow their malevolent commander-in-chief—Satan (Revelation 12:7).

SIXTH TRUMPET JUDGMENT

In recent years, our world endured the devastating effects of COVID-19, which claimed the lives of millions worldwide. Although this was a dark period in history, it pales in comparison to the chilling sixth trumpet judgment described in Revelation 9:13-21. According to this prophecy, angels confined at the Euphrates River will be set free and unleash deadly plagues that wipe out a staggering one-third of the human race. With a current world population of around 7 billion, this means that more than 2 billion people would perish.

But it doesn't end there. When you factor in the fourth seal judgment, which accounts for the annihilation of one-fourth of the world's population, the total death toll now reaches about 3.5 billion people, or about half of the earth's inhabitants.

> The angels bound at the Euphrates are fallen angels.

> We know this because no holy angel of God is ever bound as these angels are.

FREQUENTLY ASKED QUESTION
Why are some demons bound?

There are two major classes of demons:

- The first group roams freely, devoting their energy to warfare against God and His people (Ephesians 2:1-3).

- The second group is captive (Luke 8:31; 2 Peter 2:4; Jude 6; Revelation 9:1-3, 11).

- These captive fallen angels are being punished for transgressions other than their original rebellion against God (Ezekiel 28:11-19; Isaiah 14:12-17).

- Some theologians believe that these angels are guilty of the unnatural sin mentioned in Genesis 6:2-4.

👁 UNDERSTANDING OUR TERMS: *Plagues*

> Biblically, a plague is a disease or epidemic caused by God or allowed by God for judgment.

> > There will be a massive outbreak of plagues in the end times (see Revelation 6:8; 9:18, 20; 11:6; 15:1, 6, 8; 16:9, 21; 18:4, 8; 21:9; 22:18).

Astoundingly, the prophetic Scriptures tell us, "The rest of mankind, who were not killed by these plagues, did not repent of the works of their hands nor give up worshiping demons and idols of gold and silver and bronze and stone and wood, which cannot see or hear or walk, nor did they repent of their murders or their sorceries or their sexual immorality or their thefts" (verses 20-21). *The hearts of people during the tribulation period will be so calloused—so hardened against God—that they absolutely refuse repentance.*

YOU MAY BE INTERESTED TO KNOW...
There Is No Fear of God Among Many People in the Tribulation

> > It appears that most people during the tribulation period will have no fear of God. (The exception is people who become Christians during this time—Revelation 7:9-17.)

> > It is wise to live in reverent fear of God (1 Samuel 12:14, 24; 2 Chronicles 19:9; Acts 10:35; 1 Peter 1:17; 2:17).

> > It is unwise to ignore the fear of God (Genesis 20:11; 2 Kings 17:25; Psalm 36:1; Ecclesiastes 8:13; Romans 3:18).

> > The fear of God:

>> » Motivates obedience (Deuteronomy 5:29; Ecclesiastes 12:13).

>> » Encourages the avoidance of evil (Proverbs 3:7; 8:13; 16:6).

>> » Brings God's blessing (Psalm 115:13).

SEVENTH TRUMPET JUDGMENT

The climactic seventh trumpet judgment will trigger a fresh wave of divine retribution—*the bowl judgments*—packing an even greater punch than previous judgments (see Revelation 16). It's going to be a harrowing time for the inhabitants of the earth. Plagued by the disastrous trumpet judgments, people will be convinced they've hit rock bottom. Things will soon get even worse with God's increasingly severe bowl judgments.

FAST FACTS ON THE CAUSE-AND-EFFECT RELATIONSHIP OF GOD'S JUDGMENTS

A perusal of God's various judgments reveals the intriguing cause-and-effect connections that often exist between them. One judgment seems to trigger another, creating a fascinating chain of events:

- The first seal judgment introduces the antichrist, who goes out to wage war (Revelation 6:1-2). This leads directly to the second seal judgment, where peace is taken from the earth and people turn against one another (Revelation 6:3-4). The cause-and-effect relationship here is clear.

- Moving on to the third seal judgment, famine afflicts the entire world (Revelation 6:5-6). War (in this case resulting from the first and second seal judgments) always tends to disrupt the transportation and distribution of supplies, including food. Also, when people kill each other (first and second seal judgments), there are fewer hands available to produce and distribute food worldwide. Once again, we see the cause-and-effect dynamic between these judgments.

- As we reach the fourth seal judgment, massive casualties result from the widespread famine caused by the previous judgment (Revelation 6:7-8). Cause and effect strikes again!

- Another example relates to the third trumpet judgment in which a meteor or asteroid strikes the earth (Revelation 8:12-13). The fourth trumpet judgment immediately follows with a great reduction in sunlight, moonlight, and starlight. This is likely a result of the dust that fills the atmosphere following the catastrophic impact of the meteor or asteroid. Cause and effect!

When exploring prophetic Scripture, it is always wise to keep an eye out for cause-and-effect relationships woven throughout the divine judgments.

Lord, thank You for rapturing the church prior to the beginning of the tribulation period.

39

Darkness Descends: The Antichrist Is Worshiped

The antichrist will engage in gross self-exaltation at the midpoint of the tribulation period. He will demand to be worshiped as God. Prophetic Scripture reveals the various ways in which his self-exaltation will be manifested.

I have touched on the self-exaltation of the antichrist previously in this book. My purpose in this chapter is to provide further insight into how the antichrist's self-exaltation is (1) rooted in the work of Satan, (2) directly related to the abomination of desolation, and (3) directly related to the antichrist's blasphemy against the one true God.

Energized by Satan

Second Thessalonians 2:9 reveals that the antichrist operates "by the activity of Satan." Various translations highlight this intriguing connection. The Amplified Bible phrases it "through the activity and working of Satan." The CSB translation renders it "based on Satan's working." The NIV puts it "in accordance with how Satan works." These different translations show that Satan will be the driving force behind the antichrist's thoughts and actions.

Why does this matter? Well, it shows that the antichrist will take on the persona of none other than Satan himself. And nowhere is this more evident than in their common quest to elevate themselves to a god-like status.

Ezekiel 28 and Isaiah 14 offer fascinating insights into the story of Lucifer's fall and his transformation into Satan. Scripture reveals that Lucifer was created in a flawless state (Ezekiel 28:12, 15) and maintained his flawless ways until wickedness emerged within him (verse 15b). What was the nature of that wickedness? Verse 17 tells us, "Your heart became proud on account of your beauty, and you corrupted your wisdom because of your splendor." Lucifer became enamored of his own beauty, intelligence, power, and status—so much so that he craved the recognition and majesty reserved for God alone. His downfall came in the form of self-generated pride.

This connects seamlessly with Isaiah 14:13-14, where we discover that Lucifer proclaimed within his heart: "I will ascend to heaven; above the stars of God I will set my throne on high; I will sit on the mount of assembly in the far reaches of the north; I will ascend above the heights of the clouds; I will make myself like the Most High." Let's take a moment to unpack each of these bold declarations and consider their implications:

- *"I will ascend to heaven."* Lucifer longed to reside in heaven and craved equal recognition alongside God Himself.

- *"I will raise my throne above the stars of God."* The "stars" probably refer to God's angels (see Job 38:7). Lucifer longed to rule the angelic realm with the same authority as God.

- *"I will sit enthroned on the mount of assembly, on the utmost heights of the sacred mountain."* Scripture elsewhere suggests that the "mount of assembly" denotes the center of God's kingdom rule (see Isaiah 2:2; Psalm 48:2). This phrase is sometimes associated with Messiah's future earthly rule in Jerusalem during the millennial kingdom. Perhaps Satan sought to rule over humanity in place of the Messiah.

- *"I will ascend above the tops of the clouds."* Clouds frequently symbolize God's glory in the Bible (Exodus 13:21; 40:28-34; Job 37:15-16; Matthew 26:64; Revelation 14:14). It seems that Lucifer pursued glory equal to that of God Himself.

- *"I will make myself like the Most High."* Scripture describes God as possessing heaven and earth (Genesis 14:18-19). Lucifer sought for himself the highest position in the universe. Satan wanted to exercise authority and control in this world that rightfully belongs only to God. His sin was a direct challenge to the power and authority of God.

The Almighty pronounced a righteous judgment on this powerful heavenly being, saying, "I threw you to the earth" (Ezekiel 28:18). Lucifer's terrible transgression led to his exile from living in heaven (Isaiah 14:12). His identity transformed from Lucifer, meaning "morning star," to Satan, the "adversary." His power became utterly perverted (Isaiah 14:12, 16-17). Following Christ's second coming, his destiny is to be bound in the bottomless pit during the

1,000-year millennial kingdom over which Christ will rule (Revelation 20:3) and eventually be thrown into the lake of fire forever (Matthew 25:41).

YOU MAY BE INTERESTED TO KNOW...
Satan Instills Boundless Conceit into the Heart of the Antichrist

- The antichrist, like Satan, will be arrogant, indulge in blatant self-exaltation, and attempt to replace Christ (God).

- First Timothy 3:6 informs us that Satan can "puff up" a human being with conceit in the heart so that he thinks more of himself than he ought.

- Satan will accomplish this in the antichrist to a measureless degree.

- The antichrist—as energized by Satan (2 Thessalonians 2:9)—will be the epitome of conceit.

Self-Exaltation and the Profaning of the Jewish Temple

I noted previously in the book that the antichrist will defile the rebuilt Jewish temple at the midpoint of the tribulation period. This sacrilege is widely referred to as "the abomination of desolation." The prophet Daniel described the antichrist this way: "On the wing of abominations shall come *one who makes desolate*" (Daniel 9:27, emphasis added).

It is important to remember that the temple is considered to be God's very own dwelling place among His people, and is a place to be revered:

- The temple is "the house of the Lord" (1 Kings 9:1).
- It is called the "house of God" (Ezra 5:13).
- It is called "the temple of the Lord" (Ezra 3:10).
- We are told that "the glory of the Lord filled the house" (2 Chronicles 7:1).

The antichrist's abominable move to usurp the holy sanctuary of "the house of the Lord," the "house of God," the "temple of the Lord," and the sacred abode of "the glory of the Lord," is nothing short of a monstrous display of sacrilege that can only leave one absolutely aghast.

Against this backdrop, the apostle Paul defines the antichrist as "the son of destruction, who opposes and exalts himself against every so-called god or object of worship, so that *he takes his seat in the temple of God, proclaiming himself to be God*" (2 Thessalonians 2:3-4, emphasis added). Absolutely astounding!

> "By the middle of the 70th week, [the antichrist] will turn against every form of established worship to clear the way for the worship of himself. He will magnify himself to the level of deity."
>
> —Renald Showers[1]

After enthroning himself as God in the Jewish temple, the antichrist will prohibit all further sacrifices and offerings in the Jewish temple (Daniel 9:27). The antichrist will not allow competing systems of worship. No one will be worshiped except him.

The Antichrist Will Blaspheme God

As the antichrist ascends to a self-proclaimed godlike status, fueled by Satan's perverted influence, he will then boldly defy and insult the one true God. He will engage in outright blasphemy.

> - Daniel 11:36 tells us that the antichrist "shall exalt himself and magnify himself above every god."

> - Revelation 13:5-6 tells us that "the beast was given a mouth uttering haughty and blasphemous words, and it was allowed to exercise authority for forty-two months. It opened its mouth to utter blasphemies against God, blaspheming his name and his dwelling, that is, those who dwell in heaven."

FAST FACTS ON A PERSON'S "NAME"

- In biblical times, a person's name represented everything that person was.
- It indicated his or her very nature.

- It included the very attributes of a person.
- For the antichrist to blaspheme God's name is to blaspheme God's very identity and nature.

The antichrist also blasphemes God's "dwelling, that is, those who dwell in heaven" (Revelation 13:6). The antichrist here targets not only the holy angels but also the glorified saints—believers who were raptured and then taken up to heaven before the beginning of the tribulation period. This will be the antichrist's way of saying to God, "I disdain everything about You and everyone who follows You."

SOMETHING TO THINK ABOUT:

> The antichrist will enthrone himself in the inner sanctum of the rebuilt Jewish temple—*a place reserved for God alone.*

> This is strikingly similar to Lucifer's transgression (Satan's sin) of seeking to "set my throne on high" (Isaiah 14:13-14).

> Mirroring Satan's desire to enthrone himself in the place of God, the antichrist—under Satan's influence—now seeks to enthrone himself in the place of God (in the Jewish temple).

LEXICAL NUGGET: *Blasphemy*

> The Greek word for *blasphemy* can range in meaning from simply showing a lack of reverence for God to having an extreme attitude of contempt for either God or something held sacred (Leviticus 24:16; Matthew 26:65; Mark 2:7).

> Blasphemy can involve speaking evil against God (Psalm 74:18; Isaiah 52:5; Romans 2:24; Revelation 13:1, 6; 16:9, 11, 21).

> Blasphemy may involve showing contempt for the true God by claiming divinity for oneself (see Mark 14:64; John 10:33).

> The antichrist will engage in all these aspects of blasphemy.

We can observe that people who live during the tribulation period who worship the antichrist as God will also engage in blasphemy. It is highly revealing to see that the language often used of God in Scripture will be used of the antichrist during the tribulation period. In Old Testament times, worshipful believers would say to God: "Who is like you, O LORD, among the gods? Who is like you, majestic in holiness, awesome in glorious deeds, doing wonders?" (Exodus 15:11). Similar words are used for worshiping the antichrist. People will say, "Who is like the beast?" (Revelation 13:4).

CROSS-REFERENCES

Blasphemy

Antichrist's names and words—Revelation 13:5-6; 17:3

Antichrist's nature—2 Thessalonians 2:3-11

Claiming divinity for oneself—Mark 14:64; John 10:33

Contempt or lack of reverence for God—Leviticus 24:16; Matthew 26:65; Mark 2:7

Speaking evil against God—Psalm 74:18; Isaiah 52:5; Romans 2:24; Revelation 13:1, 6; 16:9, 11, 21

40

The Onset of the "Great Tribulation"

The tribulation period is distinct from the "great tribulation." While the tribulation period encompasses the entire seven-year period of travail that will engulf the entire world, the great tribulation embraces *only* the last three-and-a-half years. It is critical to keep this distinction in mind.

Although some may argue against dividing the tribulation period into two segments, the books of Daniel and Revelation offer compelling evidence to make a clear distinction between the two halves. In the crucial prophecy found in Daniel 9:27, we learn about the antichrist's actions: "He shall make a strong covenant with many for one week, and for half of the week he shall put an end to sacrifice and offering." This week symbolizes a seven-year period. Animal sacrifices will be prohibited in the Jewish temple during the last three-and-a-half years of the seven-year tribulation period. This clearly sets the two halves of the tribulation apart.

In Revelation 11:2, God's two prophetic witnesses are said to minister on earth for a precise duration of 42 months, and they prophesy for 1,260 days (verse 3). The terms "42 months" and "1,260 days" signify a period of precisely three-and-a-half years—the first half of the tribulation period.

We are also informed that God's watchful eye remains on the Jewish remnant in the wilderness for "a time, and times, and half a time" (Revelation 12:14). In this context, "time" denotes a year, "times" refers to two years, and "half a time" signifies half a year. This verse tells us that God will protect the Jewish remnant throughout the latter three-and-a-half years of the tribulation period.

These scriptural factors clearly differentiate between the two halves of the tribulation period. Scripture also indicates that the second half of the tribulation will constitute the most horrific period of human suffering ever to hit planet earth.

Jesus' Olivet Discourse underscores these horrors, which begin at the midpoint of the tribulation: "Then there will be great tribulation, such as has not been from the beginning of the world until now, no, and never will be. And if those days had not been cut short, no human being would be saved. But for the sake of the elect those days will be cut short" (Matthew 24:21-22; compare with Revelation 7:14). Similarly, the prophet Daniel refers to the last half of the tribulation period as "a time of trouble, such as never has been since there was a nation till that time" (Daniel 12:1).

The severity of this time for Israel is vividly described in Jeremiah 30:7: "That day is so great there is none like it; it is a time of distress for Jacob." ("Jacob" means Israel.) The Amplified Bible translates the verse this way: "That day is great, there is none like it; It is the time of Jacob's [unequaled] trouble."

You may be wondering what makes the second half of the tribulation period so incredibly "great." Among other things, here's what's in store for the inhabitants of the earth during this time:

- The antichrist, fueled by Satan's influence, will relentlessly perse-cute and martyr the Jews with unimaginable fury (Revelation 12:13, 17).

- The antichrist will persecute and martyr Christians to such an extent that he'll not only *conquer* them but also *prevail over* them (Revelation 13:7-10; Daniel 7:21).

- The catastrophic bowl judgments will be unleashed—the most ter-rifying of God's judgments (Revelation 16). These include excru-ciating sores on people, bodies of water turning into blood, the extinction of all sea life, scorching heat from the sun, dried-up riv-ers, all-encompassing darkness over the land, massive earthquakes, widespread destruction, and more.

- Finally, Armageddon—a catastrophic war campaign—will be unleashed upon the earth (Revelation 16:16). This will be a pro-longed, escalating conflict, and the loss of life will be unimaginable.

Prophetic Scripture reveals that the intense period of the great tribulation commences at the midpoint of the tribulation, right after the abomination of desolation occurs. This is evident in Jesus' warning to the Jews to get out of Jerusalem when they witness this abomination:

When you see the abomination of desolation spoken of by the prophet Daniel, standing in the holy place (let the reader understand), then let those who are in Judea flee to the mountains. Let the one who is on the housetop not go down to take what is in his house, and let the one who is in the field not turn back to take his cloak. And alas for women who are pregnant and for those who are nursing infants in those days! Pray that your flight may not be in winter or on a Sabbath. For *then there will be great tribulation, such as has not been from the beginning of the world until now, no, and never will be* (Matthew 24:15-21, emphasis added).

A remnant of Jews will flee from Jerusalem. Revelation 12:14 tells us that God will supernaturally protect the remnant in the wilderness during the last three-and-a-half years of the tribulation period.

FAST FACTS ON GOD AS A PROTECTOR

- "You are a hiding place for me; you preserve me from trouble" (Psalm 32:7).
- "He will hide me in his shelter in the day of trouble; he will conceal me under the cover of his tent" (Psalm 27:5).
- "God is our refuge and strength, a very present help in trouble" (Psalm 46:1).
- "Hide me from the secret plots of the wicked, from the throng of evildoers" (Psalm 64:2).
- "When you pass through the waters, I will be with you; and through the rivers, they shall not overwhelm you; when you walk through fire you shall not be burned, and the flame shall not consume you" (Isaiah 43:2).

Although the existential threat against the Jewish remnant will never be greater, God will providentially watch over and protect the remnant. His plans for Israel will not be thwarted. God Himself declares, "I am God, and there is no other; I am God, and there is none like me, declaring the end from the beginning and from ancient times things not yet done, saying, 'My counsel shall stand, and I will accomplish all my purpose'" (Isaiah 46:9-10).

The Duration of the Great Tribulation

The duration of the great tribulation is three-and-a-half years. During this time, the antichrist exercises authority "for forty-two months" (Revelation 13:5). "Forty-two months" is three-and-a-half years. We are also told that the antichrist "shall wear out the saints of the Most High…and they shall be given into his hand for a time, times, and half a time" (Daniel 7:25). Again, this is exactly three-and-a-half years.

> *"When this Antichrist shall have devastated all things in this world, he will reign for three years and six months, and sit in the temple at Jerusalem; and then the Lord will come from heaven in the clouds, in the glory of the Father, sending this man and those who follow him into the lake of fire; but bringing in for the righteous the times of the kingdom."*
>
> —Irenaeus, *Against Heresies*, Book 5, Chapter 30

If the tribulation period lasts exactly three-and-a-half years, how are we to understand Jesus' intriguing words about the shortening of the great tribulation? "Then there will be great tribulation, such as has not been from the beginning of the world until now, no, and never will be. And if those days had not been cut short, no human being would be saved. But those days will be cut short for the sake of the elect" (Matthew 24:21-22). Was Jesus suggesting that the great tribulation would last less than three-and-a-half years? Or was He suggesting that the three-and-a-half-year period was already a shortened period?

The key to solving this mystery lies in Mark 13:20, a related verse: "And if the Lord had not cut short the days, no human being would be saved. But for the sake of the elect, whom he chose, he shortened the days." Greek scholars point out that the two verbs in this passage—"cut short" and "shortened"—imply actions taken by God in the past.

This means that God sovereignly decreed a limit to the length of the great tribulation in eternity past. What are God's sovereign decrees? Theologian Henry C. Thiessen says, "The decrees are God's eternal purpose. He does not make His plans or alter them as human history develops. He made them in eternity, and, because He is immutable, they remain unaltered (Ps. 33:11; James 1:17)."[1] (See also Isaiah 14:24-27; 46:9-11; Daniel 9:24, 26-27; 11:36; Luke 22:22; Acts 2:23; 4:27-28; Ephesians 1:11; 3:11.)

We can infer that Jesus was suggesting that God had previously intervened to shorten the great tribulation. This divine action was a result of God's sovereign decision to set a specific end point for the tribulation, rather than allowing it to continue indefinitely. In His omniscience, God knew that the great tribulation, if left unchecked, would eventually lead to the extinction of humankind. To prevent this from happening, God in eternity past "sovereignly fixed a specific time for the Great Tribulation to end when it had run its course for three-and-a-half years, 42 months, or 1,260 days. That fixed time cannot be changed."[2]

THE "BIG PICTURE" TO REMEMBER

> The prophetic books of Daniel and Revelation distinguish between the two halves of the tribulation period.

> The last three-and-a-half years are called the "great tribulation." It will be a time of unimaginable distress.

> Mercifully, God has set a time limit on the great tribulation. It will not last longer than three-and-a-half years.

FREQUENTLY ASKED QUESTION

How can a loving God allow the Jewish people to experience such a "great tribulation"?

God has a plan for national Israel. This plan includes allowing Israel to go through the great tribulation. During this time, God will purge Israel to motivate the nation to repent of its rejection of Jesus (Zechariah 13:8-9). At the very end of the tribulation period, a remnant of Jews will repent and turn to Jesus for salvation (Romans 9–11). After the second coming, these redeemed Jews will be invited into Christ's millennial kingdom (Ezekiel 20:34-38). God will then fulfill all the promises He has made to Israel. God will give Israel the land promised in the Abrahamic covenant (Genesis 12:1-3; 15:18-21; 17:21; 35:10-12). He will also fulfill the throne promise in the Davidic covenant, with Christ reigning on the throne of David throughout the millennial kingdom (2 Samuel 7:5-17).

I could sum it up this way: God loves His child Israel so much that He finds it necessary to discipline this rebellious child so that the child will learn to behave properly. Once good behavior has been achieved, the child will now be able to receive the magnificent blessings God has in store for her.

> - God has reasons for allowing His children to go through a "day of trouble."
> - God allows us to experience trials because they are beneficial to us.
> - First Peter 1:6-7 instructs us: "In this you rejoice, though now for a little while, if necessary, you have been grieved by various trials, so that the tested genuineness of your faith—more precious than gold that perishes though it is tested by fire may be found to result in praise and glory and honor at the revelation of Jesus Christ."
> - James 1:2-4 also tells us: "Count it all joy, my brothers, when you meet trials of various kinds, for you know that the testing of your faith produces steadfastness. And let steadfastness have its full effect, that you may be perfect and complete, lacking in nothing."

41

The Catastrophic Unleashing of the Bowl Judgments

Human suffering will steadily escalate throughout the tribulation period. First are the seal judgments, involving bloodshed, famine, death, economic upheaval, a great earthquake, and cosmic disturbances (Revelation 6). Then come the trumpet judgments, involving hail and fire mixed with blood, the sea turning to blood, water turning bitter, further cosmic disturbances, affliction by demonic scorpions, and the death of one-third of humankind (Revelation 8:6–9:21). Then come the increasingly worse bowl judgments.

The bowl judgments will unfold with the activity of angels, just like the seal and trumpet judgments: There will be "seven angels with seven plagues, which are the last, for with them the wrath of God is finished" (Revelation 15:1).

> "Bless the LORD, O you his angels, you mighty ones who do his word, obeying the voice of his word!"
>
> —Psalm 103:20

FAST FACTS ON ANGELS AND THE ELEMENTS OF NATURE

- Revelation 16:5 speaks of "the angel in charge of the waters."
- Revelation 7:1 tells us that four of God's angels restrain the four winds of the earth, which blow from the north, south, east, and west.
- Revelation 14:18 speaks of an angel with authority over fire.

The bowl judgments will be the most severe judgments that will fall on the world during the tribulation period. They will be unleashed near the end of the tribulation. Each new judgment is progressively worse than the previous one. The bowl judgments can be viewed as a crescendo of escalating horrors.

The bowl judgments are a powerful expression of God's wrath (Revelation 15:7). This wrath is appropriate for a world that has turned its back on God and stubbornly refuses to repent (Revelation 15:7). Woe to all who live on the earth at this time.

The first four bowl judgments are directed at individuals on earth and result in escalating misery. The last three judgments are more global and lead to Armageddon.

YOU MAY BE INTERESTED TO KNOW...
The Bowl Judgments Are Similar to the Egyptian Plagues

> The bowl judgments are strikingly similar to the plagues God inflicted on the Egyptians through Moses, highlighting the divine consequences of rebellion against the Almighty.

> Just as the ancient Egyptians faced the severe judgment of God, so will the godless inhabitants of the earth face the same fate. The Almighty will bring justice to all who defy His divine authority.

FIRST BOWL JUDGMENT

The first angel will empty his bowl, resulting in excruciating sores on all the followers of the antichrist (Revelation 16:3). The Greek word for "sores" conveys the idea of skin ulcers on the surface of the body. Some Bible scholars theorize that this could occur as a result of radiation contamination from the possible detonation of nuclear weapons. According to Revelation 8:7, one-third of the earth, one-third of the trees, and all of the grass will be consumed by fire. But it's also possible that God will inflict these painful sores directly.

The grievous wounds described in Revelation 16:1-2 are reminiscent of the Old Testament judgments of God. In the Exodus account, we read of "boils breaking out in sores on man and beast throughout all the land of Egypt" (Exodus 9:9). The Lord later warned His people of the dangers of disobedience: "The Lord will strike you with the boils of Egypt, and with tumors and scabs and itch, of which you cannot be healed" (Deuteronomy 28:27). Indeed, "the Lord will strike you on the knees and on the legs with grievous boils of which you cannot be healed, from the sole of your foot to the crown of your head" (Deuteronomy 28:35). The righteous Job suffered from such a malady at the hand of Satan: "Satan went out from the presence of the LORD and struck Job with loathsome sores from the sole of his foot to the crown of his head" (Job 2:7).

FAST FACTS ON GOD'S JUDGMENTS AND HIS JUSTICE

- God's justice is an underlying theme throughout Scripture.
- The foundation of God's throne is justice (Psalm 89:14).
- God's dealings with the earth are always just (Genesis 18:25).
- He always administers justice (Psalm 98:9).
- He opposes all forms of injustice (compare Job 34:12 and Deuteronomy 32:4).
- All of the bowl judgments are expressions of God's justice.
- The same is true of the seal and trumpet judgments.

SECOND BOWL JUDGMENT

The second angel will pour out his bowl, turning the sea into blood and destroying all marine life (Revelation 16:3). In contrast to the second trumpet judgment, in which the waters turned to blood and *one-third* of the sea creatures perished (Revelation 8:8-9), the present judgment results in the destruction of *virtually all* marine life. This is reminiscent of God's judgment against the Egyptians when the Nile turned to blood (Exodus 7:17-21).

THIRD BOWL JUDGMENT

The third angel will pour out his bowl. The rivers and springs of water become blood, as does the sea (Revelation 16:4). This is catastrophic because there will now be no sources of fresh water. The ancient Egyptians faced similar circumstances. The people "could not drink the water of the Nile" after God turned the Nile into blood (Exodus 7:24). Psalm 78:44 states, "He [God] turned their rivers to blood, so that they could not drink of their streams."

People can survive without food for a time, but they cannot survive for long without water.

FOURTH BOWL JUDGMENT

The fourth angel will pour out his bowl on the sun, causing the sun's heat to intensify to the point of scorching the inhabitants of the earth (Revelation 16:8; compare Isaiah 24:6; 42:25; Malachi 4:1). With all the other environmental judgments that will occur during the tribulation, it is conceivable that the ozone layer will become so depleted and thin that the sun's rays will become much more intense. The combination of a blazing sun and lack of drinking water will cause extreme suffering. People will refuse to repent as they curse the name of God (Revelation 16:9). As Pharaoh's heart hardened when the judgments came upon Egypt (Exodus 7:13-14, 22; 8:15, 19, 32; 9:7, 34-35; 13:15), so will the hearts of those who endure the tribulation (Psalm 95:8; Ephesians 4:18).

Although the earth was designed to be an ideal environment for humankind (Genesis 1), it will become a terrible place during the tribulation.

FIFTH BOWL JUDGMENT

The fifth angel will pour out his bowl on the throne of the beast, bringing God's judgment on the kingdom of the antichrist (Revelation 16:10). In fact, the antichrist's kingdom will be "plunged into darkness." Other places in the Bible associate darkness with God's judgment (see Isaiah 60:2; Joel 2:2; Mark 13:24-25). People will grind their teeth, blaspheme God, and refuse to repent (Revelation 16:10-11 NLT). They will maintain their allegiance to the antichrist instead of turning to the one true God of heaven who can provide salvation. The power of Satan will continue to blind people's minds (2 Corinthians 4:4).

SIXTH BOWL JUDGMENT

The sixth angel will pour his bowl into the Euphrates River (Revelation 16:12). This river is of strategic importance as the main body of water separating the Holy Land from Asia to the east. The supernatural drying up of the river will aid the Asian kings and their armies in their march to Armageddon. These Asian kings probably believe that the Israelite God is responsible for their torment. They may believe that attacking the Jews is tantamount to attacking God Himself. Revelation 16:13 indicates that demons will gather kings from around the world for Armageddon (Revelation 16:14).

▥ GEOGRAPHY IN THE END TIMES: *The Euphrates River*

> The Euphrates River, the longest river in western Asia (nearly 1,800 miles), begins in modern-day Turkey, flows toward the Mediterranean Sea, turns south, flows more than 1,000 miles to finally join with the Tigris River, and then empties into the Persian Gulf.

> Numerous ancient cities, including Ur and Babylon, are located at various points along the river.

THE SEVENTH BOWL JUDGMENT

There is an interval between the sixth and seventh bowl judgments. In fact, the seventh bowl judgment occurs immediately after the second coming of Jesus. Although I will discuss the second coming a little later in this book, I will summarize the seventh bowl judgment here for the sake of continuity.

Revelation 16:17 indicates that "the seventh angel poured out his bowl into the air." Then came a loud voice from the temple, undoubtedly God Himself speaking. No other heavenly being (except God) may enter the heavenly temple "until the seven plagues of the seven angels are finished" (Revelation 15:8).

The loud voice of God declares, "It is done." When this bowl judgment is unleashed, it will finally complete the wrath of God upon the world. The original Greek conveys the idea, "It is now done and will remain done." God's wrath will now truly be over.

There will then be lightning, thunder, and a catastrophic earthquake greater in effect than any previous earthquake (see Revelation 6:12; 8:5; 11:13, 19; Haggai 2:6; Hebrews 12:26-27). This final earthquake is like an exclamation point on the previous judgments that brought devastation to the earth and its environment.

The earthquake causes the "great city" to be divided into three parts (Revelation 16:19). Scholars debate whether the "great city" is Jerusalem or Babylon.

Some point out that Jerusalem is mentioned in Revelation 11:8 as "the great city that symbolically is called Sodom and Egypt, where their Lord was crucified." If the great city is Jerusalem, this verse would be consistent with Zechariah, who prophesied that an earthquake would change the topography of the city (see Zechariah 14:4).

Other scholars say that the context of Revelation 16:19 seems to indicate that the great city is Babylon. The last part of the verse singles out Babylon as the primary target of God's wrath. The debate continues!

The landscape will change dramatically toward the end of the tribulation (Revelation 16:20). This change in topography is apparently to prepare the earth for the millennial kingdom. As we read in Isaiah 40:4, "Every valley shall be lifted up, and every mountain and hill be made low; the uneven ground shall become level, and the rough places a plain."

Finally, great hailstones will rain down from heaven (Revelation 16:21). With each hailstone weighing around 100 pounds, the damage will be unimaginable. Very little will be left standing after the great earthquake and the apocalyptic hailstorm. Amazingly, despite the destruction, people will still refuse to repent.

YOU MAY BE INTERESTED TO KNOW...
"It Is Done" and "It Is Finished" Are Phrases that Mark the End of Major Biblical Events

- In Revelation 16:17, we read, "It is done," indicating that God's wrath against an unbelieving world is finally over.

- This reminds us of the wrath of God that was poured out on Jesus for our sins on the cross of Calvary.

- When Christ's saving work was complete, He uttered the famous words, "It is finished" (John 19:30), which can also be translated as "paid in full."

- Jesus took our individual "certificates of debt," listing all our sins, and nailed them to the cross.

- Our sins have been "paid in full," and hence we can be saved (see Colossians 2:14).

THE BOWL JUDGMENTS

First bowl judgment	Harmful sores
Second bowl judgment	Sea becomes like blood; death of all sea creatures
Third bowl judgment	Rivers and springs of water become blood; no remaining freshwater
Fourth bowl judgment	Sun's heat scorches people
Fifth bowl judgment	Antichrist's kingdom plunged into darkness
Sixth bowl judgment	Euphrates River dries up
Seventh bowl judgment	Results in the completion of God's wrath

FREQUENTLY ASKED QUESTION

How can people's minds become so twisted that they refuse to repent of sin so that things can get better for them?

A primary factor is that people are fallen in sin. They have an inclination toward evil. Every aspect of their being—including their minds—is fallen (see Genesis 6:5; Jeremiah 17:9; Romans 7:18).

To use an analogy, faulty software can cause a computer to crash. Likewise, faulty thinking—sinful thoughts in the mind—can cause people to "crash" in the sense of making wrong decisions.

This brings to mind Psalms 1 and 2. Psalm 1:2 tells us that the blessed person constantly meditates on God's law. This is in contrast to the ungodly imaginations of the unbeliever: "Why do...the people imagine a vain thing?" (Psalm 2:1 KJV). "Meditate" and "imagine" are translations of the same Hebrew word. While believers meditate on God and His Word, unbelievers meditate on sinful things—including reasons for refusing to repent in the face of God's judgments (Revelation 16:9, 11). *Their imaginations are truly vain!*

Like the Egyptian Pharaoh of old, their hearts are hardened against the things of God. Just as callouses on a hand make it insensitive to the pain of raking the lawn, so a calloused heart is insensitive to God and His moral demands.

A Warning to Christians

- The hearts of sinners will become increasingly hardened against God during the time of tribulation.
- Let us heed the biblical teaching that even Christians can develop hard or calloused hearts (Psalm 95:8; Hebrews 3:8, 15).
- The formula for avoiding a hard heart is simple: *Trust and obey* God (Hebrews 4).

42

Armageddon Ignites

There will be relentless waves of human suffering throughout the entire seven-year tribulation period:

First come the **seal judgments**, which include bloodshed, famine, death, economic upheaval, a great earthquake, and cosmic disturbances (Revelation 6).

Then come the **trumpet judgments**, which include hail and fire mixed with blood, the sea turning to blood, the water turning bitter, more cosmic upheaval, affliction by demonic scorpions, and the death of one-third of humankind (Revelation 8:6–9:21).

Then come the **bowl judgments**, which include painful sores on people, more water turned to blood, the death of all sea creatures, people scorched by the sun, total darkness covering the land, a devastating earthquake, and much more (Revelation 16).

Worse yet, the already-traumatized people of the earth will now face Armageddon, a catastrophic war campaign (see Daniel 11:40-45; Joel 3:9-17; Zechariah 14:1-3; Revelation 16:14-16). This military campaign will take place at the end of the tribulation period. Millions of people will perish in the deadliest escalation of conflict in the history of the planet.

The word *Armageddon* literally means "Mount of Megiddo."

▥ GEOGRAPHY IN THE END TIMES: *The Mount of Megiddo*

> The Mount of Megiddo is a site in northern Israel, approximately 20 miles southeast of Haifa and 60 miles north of Jerusalem.

> It was a famous battlefield in Old Testament times.

> This is the site of Barak's battle with the Canaanites (Judges 4) and Gideon's battle with the Midianites (Judges 7).

> This will be the site of humankind's final terrible battles just before the second coming (Revelation 16:16).

HISTORICAL INSIGHT
Napoleon and the Mount of Megiddo

> Napoleon is said to have remarked that this was the greatest battlefield he had ever seen.

> Of course, the battles Napoleon fought will pale in comparison to Armageddon.

> Armageddon will be so terrible that no one would survive if Christ did not return (Matthew 24:22).

I want to emphasize that it would be wrong to refer to the "battle" of Armageddon, as if it were a single event. Armageddon will involve a protracted, catastrophically escalating conflict.

The Antichrist's Allies Assemble for War

At the beginning of Armageddon, the allied armies of the antichrist will gather for the final extermination of the Jews. This gathering is described in Revelation 16:12-16. Demonic spirits are portrayed as going "abroad to the kings of the whole world, to assemble them for battle on the great day of God the Almighty…and they assembled them at the place that in Hebrew is called Armageddon" (verse 14).

Prophetic Scripture reveals that the bowl judgments are related to Armageddon. In fact, the initial gathering of the armies that will participate in Armageddon occurs when the sixth bowl judgment is released (Revelation 16:14). The sixth bowl judgment also causes the Euphrates River to be dried up, preparing the way for the coming of the armies of the east (verse 12).

A controversial question is: *Who are the kings of the east?* Bible scholars are divided on this point. A survey of 100 prophecy books reveals more than 50 interpretations of who they are. According to one imaginative theory, the kings of the east are the seven princes of Daniel 7 who have submitted to the authority of the antichrist.

A more literal approach seems preferable:

▦ GEOGRAPHY IN THE END TIMES: *Kings of the East*

"The simplest and best explanation…is that this refers to kings or rulers from the Orient or East who will participate in the final world war. In the light of the coming of Christ and the contemporary world situation in which the Orient today contains a large portion of the world's population with tremendous military potential, any interpretation other than a literal one does not make sense."

—John F. Walvoord[1]

This is why the Euphrates River is so important. As noted above, this river is the main body of water separating the Holy Land from Asia to the east. Theologian Charles Ryrie comments, "The armies of the nations of the Orient will be aided in their march toward Armageddon by the supernatural drying up of the Euphrates River."[2] The drying up of this river is foretold in Isaiah 11:15.

The goal of the eastern coalition will be to eradicate the Jewish people once and for all. Every member of the satanic trinity will be involved—Satan, the antichrist, and the false prophet. Demons will also summon the kings of the earth. As one Bible expositor put it, "The summons will be reinforced by demonic activity to ensure that the nations will indeed cooperate in assembling their armies. These demonic messengers will be empowered to perform signs in order to assure compliance and defeat any reluctance to fall into line on the part of the other kings."[3]

YOU MAY BE INTERESTED TO KNOW…

There are Eight Stages of Armageddon

There are eight stages that comprise the campaign of Armageddon:

1. The allies of the antichrist will gather for battle (Psalm 2:1-6; Joel 3:9-11; Revelation 16:12-16).

2. New Babylon will be destroyed (Isaiah 13–14; Jeremiah 50–51; Zechariah 5:5-11; Revelation 17–18).

3. Jerusalem will fall (Micah 4:11–5:1; Zechariah 12–14).

4. The armies of the antichrist will move against the Jewish remnant at Petra/Bozrah (Jeremiah 49:13-14).

5. The Jewish remnant will finally believe in Jesus (Psalm 79:1-13; Isaiah 64:1-12; Hosea 6:1-3; Joel 2:28-32; Zechariah 12:10; Romans 11:25-27).

6. Christ will return at His second coming (Isaiah 34:1-7; Micah 2:12-13; Habakkuk 3:3).

7. There will be a terrible battle spanning from Bozrah to the Valley of Jehoshaphat (Jeremiah 49:20-22; Joel 3:12-13; Zechariah 14:12-15).

8. Christ will ascend the Mount of Olives (Joel 3:14-17; Zechariah 14:3-5; Matthew 24:29-31; Revelation 16:17-21; 19:11-21).

These various stages confirm that Armageddon is not a single battle but rather an ongoing campaign. In subsequent chapters in this book, I will examine each of these phases of Armageddon in more detail.

Here I will simply point out that Armageddon, the epic battle between good and evil, will come to an anticlimactic end. The antichrist and his massive army will be ready to take on Christ and His two armies, one made up of angelic forces and the other of the redeemed saints of the church who were raptured seven years earlier. One would expect a brutal fight to the death, but that is not what will happen. The antichrist's army will be swiftly defeated by a "sword" from the mouth of Jesus Christ Himself, in an all-encompassing display of divine judgment. And just like that, Christ's enemies fall dead at His feet. In modern parlance, it is as if Christ says "drop dead" and His enemies obey. (More on all this later.)

YOU MAY BE INTERESTED TO KNOW...
Many Believe Psalm 2 Prophesies Armageddon

Many prophecy scholars relate Psalm 2 to the forces of the antichrist gathering against Christ at Armageddon. Psalm 2:1-6 tells us:

> Why are the nations in an uproar
> and the peoples devising a vain thing?
> The kings of the earth take their stand
> and the rulers take counsel together
> against the Lord and against His Anointed, saying,
> "Let us tear their fetters apart

and cast away their cords from us!"
He who sits in the heavens laughs,
the Lord scoffs at them.
Then He will speak to them in His anger
and terrify them in His fury, saying,
"But as for Me, I have installed My King
upon Zion, My holy mountain" (NASB 1995).

Thomas Ice observes, "The psalmist records God's response of laughter at the puny human plans to overthrow God Himself at Armageddon."[4] After Christ triumphs over the forces of the antichrist in the final battle, He will set up His millennial kingdom. The King of kings will reign from the throne of David in Jerusalem, fulfilling His promise to rule over all nations. As God the Father Himself said in Psalm 2:6, "I have installed My King upon Zion, My holy mountain" (NASB 1995).

FREQUENTLY ASKED QUESTION
Is the Gog-Magog invasion the same as Armageddon?

No. There are numerous discrepancies between the Gog-Magog invasion of Israel and the campaign of Armageddon.

> The Gog-Magog invasion occurs before or at the beginning of the tribulation period. Armageddon occurs at the end of the tribulation.

> During the Gog-Magog invasion, Russia and several Muslim nations will move against Israel (Ezekiel 38:2-6). Armageddon will involve every nation on earth (Joel 3:2; Zechariah 14:4).

> The Gog-Magog invasion will be an assault on Israel from the north (Ezekiel 38:6, 15; 39:9). Armageddon will be fought by armies from the north, south, east, and west (Daniel 11:40-45; Zechariah 14:2; Revelation 16:12-16).

> The purpose of the Gog-Magog invasion is to plunder Jerusalem (Ezekiel 38:12). Armageddon is intended to wipe out the Jews and then fight against Christ and His armies (Zechariah 12:2-3, 9; 14:2; Revelation 19:19).

> Gog leads the Gog-Magog invasion (Ezekiel 38:2). The commander of Armageddon will be the antichrist (Revelation 19:19).

> God destroys the Gog-Magog invaders with an earthquake, infighting among the troops, the spread of disease, and hail mixed with fire. God destroys the armies of Armageddon with the "sharp sword" that is the word of Christ (Revelation 19:15, 21).

> During the Gog-Magog invasion, Israel's adversaries will perish on the mountains of Israel (Ezekiel 39:4-5). At Armageddon, slain combatants will be strewn across the globe (Jeremiah 25:33).

> After the Gog-Magog invasion, the bodies of the enemy invaders will be buried (Ezekiel 39:12-15). The victims of Armageddon will be devoured by birds (Jeremiah 25:33; Revelation 19:17-18, 21).

Obviously, these are two different military conflicts.

CROSS-REFERENCES
Armageddon

Catastrophic series of battles—Daniel 11:40-45; Joel 3:9-17; Zechariah 14:1-3; Revelation 16:14-16

Devastating to humanity—Matthew 24:22

The final battle—Revelation 16:14, 16

Antichrist's allies are assembled—Psalm 2:1-6; Joel 3:9-11; Revelation 16:12-16

Battle from Bozrah to Valley of Jehoshaphat—Jeremiah 49:20-22; Joel 3:12-13; Zechariah 14:12-15

Babylon destroyed—Isaiah 13–14; Jeremiah 50–51; Zechariah 5:5-11; Revelation 17–18

Siege of Jerusalem—Zechariah 14:2

Jerusalem falls—Micah 4:11–5:1; Zechariah 12–14

War on the great day of God—Revelation 16:14

Climaxes with Christ's return—Isaiah 34:1-7; Micah 2:12-13; Habakkuk 3:3; Revelation 19:11-21

No one would survive if not for Christ's coming—Matthew 24:22

43

The Collapse of Commercial New Babylon

Areawakened Babylon will rise in the end times under the reign of the antichrist (Revelation 17–18). This powerful metropolis—*New* Babylon—will emerge as a global center for religion and commerce. During the first half of the tribulation, it will serve as the spiritual center of the false world religion. After the religion is destroyed by the antichrist at the midpoint of the tribulation, New Babylon will transform into a commercial powerhouse. New Babylon's commercial prowess will entangle the world in an octopus-like grip, enabling merchants worldwide to amass fortune upon fortune. As materialism with an anti-God sentiment pervades the earth, political and business leaders will find themselves consumed by their insatiable thirst for wealth.

I find it interesting to observe the antichrist's preferred centers of operation during the seven-year tribulation period. As a backdrop, it is not uncommon for citizens of the United States to have a somewhat insular view, believing that their nation will serve as the epicenter of power in every era. However, as mentioned earlier in this book, it is very likely that the United States will experience a decline in power and influence in the end times.

Prophetic Scripture reveals that the antichrist will maintain three power bases during the tribulation period:

- Politically, his stronghold will rest in the revived Roman Empire.
- Religiously, his epicenter will be in Jerusalem.
- Economically, his dominance will emanate from New Babylon.

Because of its immense economic influence, bolstering the economies of countries around the world, one might naturally assume that New Babylon would be virtually invincible. But in a stunning turn of events, one of the very first things to happen when Armageddon breaks out at the end of the tribulation period is the utter destruction of New Babylon. *See how the mighty fall!*

356   The Complete Reference Guide to Bible Prophecy

An Angelic Announcement

- Before the devastating downfall of New Babylon, a heavenly angel proclaims: "Fallen, fallen is Babylon the great" (Revelation 18:2).

- The repetition of "fallen" emphasizes both the woeful state of this mighty commercial empire and the inevitability of divine judgment (see Isaiah 21:9; Jeremiah 51:8).

- Notice how Revelation 18:2 articulates the collapse of New Babylon as if it has already happened. This is a proleptic statement, describing a future event as if it had already transpired.

- This literary device indicates the certainty of God's triumph over wicked New Babylon, even though its ultimate fulfillment is still in the future. The destruction of New Babylon is presented as a *fait accompli*, even though it will occur in the future.

The angel's proclamation soon becomes a reality. New Babylon will be obliterated in divine judgment. What an irony we have here! While Armageddon is underway and the antichrist is preparing his armies to attack Israel, God causes a military force to rise up and attack the antichrist's headquarters in Babylon. God turns the tables on the antichrist.

Several passages describe the total destruction of Babylon in connection with Armageddon. In Jeremiah 50:13-14, we read that because of God's wrath, Babylon will become "an utter desolation; everyone who passes by Babylon shall be appalled, and hiss because of all her wounds. Set yourselves in array against Babylon all around, all you who bend the bow; shoot at her, spare no arrows, for she has sinned against the Lord." Indeed, "How Babylon has become a horror among the nations! I set a snare for you and you were taken, O Babylon, and you did not know it; you were found and caught, because you opposed the Lord. The Lord has opened his armory and brought out the weapons of his wrath" (verses 23-25).

Isaiah 13:19 says that Babylon's destruction "will be like Sodom and Gomorrah when God overthrew them." Jeremiah 50:40 echoes this idea: "As when God overthrew Sodom and Gomorrah and their neighboring cities, declares the Lord, so no man shall dwell there, and no son of man shall sojourn in her."

The book of Revelation is quite graphic in its description of New Babylon's destruction:

Then a mighty angel took up a stone like a great millstone and threw it into the sea, saying, "So will Babylon the great city be thrown down with violence, and will be found no more; and the sound of harpists and musicians, of flute players and trumpeters, will be heard in you no more, and a craftsman of any craft will be found in you no more, and the sound of the mill will be heard in you no more, and the light of a lamp will shine in you no more, and the voice of bridegroom and bride will be heard in you no more, for your merchants were the great ones of the earth, and all nations were deceived by your sorcery. And in her was found the blood of prophets and of saints, and of all who have been slain on earth" (Revelation 18:21-24).

The swiftness of New Babylon's destruction is breathtaking. "Babylon...in a single hour your judgment has come" (Revelation 18:10). In just 60 minutes, mighty Babylon will fall. The world's leaders, witnessing this catastrophe from afar (possibly via live television and internet streams), will find themselves utterly powerless. With no time to react or take economic precautions, their nations will be left to suffer the consequences of this sudden calamity.

FREQUENTLY ASKED QUESTION
Who will be the attackers of New Babylon and the antichrist?

A formidable alliance of northern military forces will launch the attack. As foretold by God Himself in Jeremiah 50:

> For behold, I am stirring up and bringing against Babylon a gathering of great nations, from the north country. And they shall array themselves against her...Behold, a people comes from the north; a mighty nation and many kings are stirring from the farthest parts of the earth. They lay hold of bow and spear; they are cruel and have no mercy. The sound of them is like the roaring of the sea; they ride on horses, arrayed as a man for battle against you, O daughter of Babylon! (verses 9, 41-52).

Just as the Babylonians served as God's instrument of judgment against Israel in Old Testament days, so a powerful northern alliance now assumes the role of God's disciplinary instrument against New Babylon. As merciless as

Babylon was in its subjugation of Israel, so divine retribution shows no leniency toward New Babylon in return.

The antichrist will be absent from New Babylon when it meets its final end. Couriers will bring him news of New Babylon's utter destruction, as prophesied in Jeremiah 50:43 and 51:31-32.

Thomas Ice and Timothy Demy, in their book *Prophecy Watch,* note that some of the Jews will be able to make it out of New Babylon before judgment falls on the city: "The attack will be swift, but there will be some warning or opportunity for Jews who are living in Babylon to flee from the city (Jeremiah 50:6-8, 28; 51:5, 6). Even in these last days, God will preserve a remnant of His people. These refugees are to go to Jerusalem and tell them of the city's destruction and their escape (Jeremiah 51:10, 45, 50; Revelation 18:4, 5)."[1]

Speaking of God's judgment on New Babylon, a voice from heaven will declare: "Her sins are heaped high as heaven, and God has remembered her iniquities. Pay her back as she herself has paid back others, and repay her double for her deeds" (Revelation 18:5-6). New Babylon will face a staggering double punishment for her heinous transgressions against the Almighty.

YOU MAY BE INTERESTED TO KNOW...
God Does Not "Remember" the Sins of His People

> Revelation 18:5 makes it clear that God remembers the sins of wicked and unrepentant Babylon.

> In contrast, for those who have faith in Jesus Christ, we can find solace in the words of the new covenant from Jeremiah 31:34: "I will forgive their iniquity, and I will remember their sin no more."

> Similarly, Hebrews 8:12 conveys God's promise, stating, "I will be merciful toward their iniquities, and I will remember their sins no more."

> Psalm 103:12 demonstrates God's forgiveness by declaring, "As far as the east is from the west, so far does he remove our transgressions from us."

> *There's nothing better than experiencing God's forgiveness and knowing that He remembers our sins no more!*

Flee from Evil Babylon—Genesis 12:1; 19:12; Exodus 8:1; Numbers 16:26; Isaiah 48:20; 52:11; Jeremiah 50:8; 51:6-9, 45.

Materialism and Riches—Proverbs 15:27; Ecclesiastes 5:10; Jeremiah 17:11; Matthew 6:19-21; 1 Timothy 6:10; James 5:3.

A LESSON TO LEARN
Come Out and Be Separate

- Jews living in New Babylon are urged to flee before God's judgment falls. They are urged to separate themselves from this wicked city.

- Christians are urged to separate themselves from ungodly influences and pursue a path of righteousness.

- First Timothy 5:22 urges Christians not to "take part in the sins of others; keep yourself pure."

- Ephesians 5:11 admonishes us, "Take no part in the unfruitful works of darkness, but instead expose them."

- Second Corinthians 6:14-15 instructs, "Do not be unequally yoked with unbelievers. For what partnership has righteousness with lawlessness? Or what fellowship has light with darkness? What accord has Christ with Belial? Or what portion does a believer share with an unbeliever?"

FAST FACTS ON GOD'S DOUBLE-JUDGMENT

Here we find an echo of the *lex talionis*, the law of retaliation. As Matthew 7:2 says, "For with the judgment you pronounce you will be judged, and with the measure you use it will be measured to you." Galatians 6:7 assures us, "Whatever one sows, that will he also reap." New Babylon will face an intensified form of *lex talionis* by double reciprocation. Double repayment was a familiar element in the Old Testament legal system:

- "If the stolen beast is found alive in his possession, whether it is an ox or a donkey or a sheep, he shall pay double" (Exodus 22:4).

- "If a man gives to his neighbor money or goods to keep safe, and it is stolen from the man's house, then, if the thief is found, he shall pay double" (Exodus 22:7).

- "For every breach of trust, whether it is for an ox, for a donkey, for a sheep, for a cloak, or for any kind of lost thing, of which one says, 'This is it,' the case of both parties shall come before God. The one whom God condemns shall pay double to his neighbor" (Exodus 22:9).

- "Speak tenderly to Jerusalem, and cry to her that her warfare is ended, that her iniquity is pardoned, that she has received from the Lord's hand double for all her sins" (Isaiah 40:2).

- "I will doubly repay their iniquity and their sin, because they have polluted my land with the carcasses of their detestable idols, and have filled my inheritance with their abominations" (Jeremiah 16:18).

- "Bring upon them the day of disaster; destroy them with double destruction" (Jeremiah 17:18).

On the surface, such a severe punishment may seem excessive. However, consider that those involved in New Babylon's commercial empire have consistently plunged into an abyss of depravity, devoid of any signs of repentance. They have been perpetually devoted to the antichrist and his malicious intentions. Having irrevocably crossed the Rubicon, their judgment has become inevitable and inescapable.

> *Revelation 18:7 is worthy of deep reflection:* "As she glorified herself and lived in luxury, so give her a like measure of torment and mourning, since in her heart she says, I sit as a queen." The once proud New Babylon is now humbled to the core. The city that once basked in opulence and splendor is now drowning in anguish and sorrow. Pretending to be a majestic queen, New Babylon's illusion is shattered by the true King of kings. Once seemingly unrivaled, New Babylon's darkest moral shortcomings are now exposed and judged.

FREQUENTLY ASKED QUESTION
How will the world respond when New Babylon is destroyed?

"The kings of the earth...will weep and wail" (Revelation 18:9). The rulers of the earth, each with a deep stake in their nation's economic prosperity, will be consumed with utter anguish and despair as they witness the cataclysmic collapse of the very financial system that once provided them with such opulence. This downfall of New Babylon signals to world leaders that the lavish empire upon which the antichrist's power and fortune is built *is unequivocally doomed.* For them, this revelation brings unimaginable devastation as their own influence and wealth are irrevocably tied to the antichrist.

Revelation 18:11 reveals that the merchants of the earth will weep and mourn over New Babylon, for their cargo will henceforth find no buyers. Notice that we are first informed that the rulers and kings of the world will mourn the fall of New Babylon, and now we learn that the merchants will share in this grief. The close relationship between government and business is highlighted, showing the profound effect on one when the other is affected.

> *The irony here cannot be overlooked.* Previously, the economic system of the antichrist was designed so that no one could participate in buying or selling without receiving the mark of the beast. But now that very system is crumbling, leaving all those associated with it powerless to buy or sell in any way. "In a single hour all this wealth has been laid waste" (Revelation 18:17). The sudden fall of Babylon will be infinitely more devastating than the stock market crash of 1929. This cataclysmic event will wipe out the global economy and world trade with irreversible consequences.

As spectators witness the dramatic collapse of New Babylon, they will be moved to cast "dust on their heads" (Revelation 18:19). Following Old Testament custom, the act of scattering dust over one's head served as a poignant expression of immense grief. This powerful gesture was especially demonstrated by Job's companions as they witnessed his agonizing plight (see Job 2:12).

FAST FACTS ON THE SUDDENNESS OF DESTRUCTION

- The Bible often depicts the sudden and devastating downfall of the wicked.
- Proverbs 6:15 warns, "Therefore calamity will come upon him suddenly; in a moment he will be broken beyond healing."
- Proverbs 24:22 warns that disaster "will rise suddenly."
- Isaiah 47:11 warns, "Ruin shall come upon you suddenly, of which you know nothing."
- In Jeremiah 15:8, God affirms, "I have made anguish and terror fall upon them suddenly."
- In 1 Thessalonians 5:3, the apostle Paul warns: "While people are saying, 'There is peace and security,' then sudden destruction will come upon them as labor pains come upon a pregnant woman, and they will not escape."

FAST FACTS ON JOY IN HEAVEN OVER BABYLON'S FALL

- As sorrow overwhelms the earth, immeasurable joy fills heaven.
- In contrast to the heartache experienced by those on earth, the inhabitants of heaven rejoice with unbridled enthusiasm as New Babylon crumbles to her end.
- "Rejoice...God has given judgment...against her" (Revelation 18:20).

44

Jerusalem Is Besieged, the Jewish Remnant Is Imperiled

I n the aftermath of New Babylon's catastrophic downfall, the heart of the antichrist's economic empire lay in ruins. Remarkably, instead of losing focus and seeking vengeance against those who ravaged his once pristine city, the antichrist remains steadfast in his pursuit. His ultimate ambition—the annihilation of the Jewish people—consumes him as he relentlessly advances toward Jerusalem.

The prophet Zechariah describes how all nations will advance against Jerusalem under the leadership of the antichrist:

> Thus declares the LORD, who stretched out the heavens and founded the earth and formed the spirit of man within him: "Behold, I am about to make Jerusalem a cup of staggering to all the surrounding peoples. The siege of Jerusalem will also be against Judah. On that day I will make Jerusalem a heavy stone for all the peoples. All who lift it will surely hurt themselves. And all the nations of the earth will gather against it" (Zechariah 12:1-3).

> I will gather all the nations against Jerusalem to battle, and the city shall be taken and the houses plundered and the women raped. Half of the city shall go out into exile, but the rest of the people shall not be cut off from the city (Zechariah 14:2).

The fact that "all the nations" will gather against Jerusalem implies that the United States, or what is left of it, will be part of this alliance. This is hardly shocking when you consider that all pro-Israel Christians will have vanished from the earth at the rapture. It's quite plausible to imagine a Christian-free United States allied with the revived Roman Empire under the command of the antichrist.

364 The Complete Reference Guide to Bible Prophecy

Tragically, Jerusalem will fall and be ravaged in the face of this overwhelming attack force. The armies of the antichrist emerge victorious, but only for the time being. The tide will soon shift dramatically against the antichrist and his minions when Jesus makes His triumphant return at the second coming.

The Antichrist Moves South Against the Remnant

Earlier in this book, I noted that the antichrist would defile the Jewish temple in two shocking ways: first, by boldly positioning himself as God in the temple; and second, by setting up an idol of himself in the temple. This defiling of the temple is called the abomination of desolation. Jesus urged that when the Jews witness this terrible event, they must not waste a moment and flee Jerusalem to save their lives (Matthew 24:16-31). Many will flee to remote deserts and mountains, possibly seeking refuge in Bozrah/Petra, located about 80 miles south of Jerusalem.

This means that when the antichrist and his dark forces lay siege to Jerusalem, not every Jew will be in the city. A significant number will be with the rest of the Jewish remnant in the deserts and mountains south of Jerusalem.

This Jewish flight from Jerusalem is described in Revelation 12:6: "The woman [a metaphor referring to Israel] fled into the wilderness, where she has a place prepared by God, in which she is to be nourished for 1,260 days [three-and-a-half years]" (inserts added for clarity). Indeed, "the woman was given the two wings of the great eagle so that she might fly from the serpent into the wilderness, to the place where she is to be nourished for a time, and times, and half a time [three-and-a-half years]" (verse 14, insert added for clarity). Thus, by divine providence, a resilient band of Jewish survivors manages to escape the clutches of the antichrist in Jerusalem and find sanctuary in the wilderness, where God sovereignly oversees their protection. All of this unfolds during the harrowing final three-and-a-half years of the tribulation period.

Fast forward to the end of the tribulation period. The remnant of Jews in the wilderness now find themselves in the crosshairs of the antichrist. An air of impending doom hangs ominously over them as the threatening forces of the antichrist gather in the wilderness, ready to attack and destroy every trace of their existence. Vulnerable and without hope, they stand seemingly defenseless.

The Jewish Remnant Is Endangered and Experiences National Regeneration

From a worldly perspective, the situation for the Jewish remnant appears dire. The Jews are painfully aware that the forces of the antichrist are gathering to destroy them. They teeter on the brink of destruction, their very existence hanging by a thread.

In the face of such despair, the Jews finally repent and find redemption only by embracing the divine Messiah they have so long rejected. They can do this only because God has finally lifted the veil of spiritual blindness that was cast upon them as a divine judgment in the first century when they rejected Jesus. With their spiritual vision restored, they turn wholeheartedly to their Savior-Redeemer, Jesus Christ.

The Jewish leaders will call the entire remnant to heartfelt repentance—a profound and transforming process that will take place over three remarkable days: "Come, let us return to the LORD; for he has torn us, that he may heal us; he has struck us down, and he will bind us up. After two days he will revive us; on the third day he will raise us up, that we may live before him. Let us know; let us press on to know the LORD; his going out is sure as the dawn; he will come to us as the showers, as the spring rains that water the earth" (Hosea 6:1-3). Just as the Jewish leaders in the first century led the Jewish people to deny Jesus as their Messiah, they will now urge repentance and instruct everyone to accept Jesus as their Messiah. This, the remnant will do, and they will be saved.

For centuries, the words of the prophet Joel have echoed the promise of a remarkable spiritual awakening among a Jewish remnant (Joel 2:28-29). Now that prophecy is finally being fulfilled. Against the dramatic backdrop of Armageddon, Israel will experience a profound conversion to Christ (Zechariah 12:2–13:1). Israel's journey to restoration begins with the nation's confession of its sins (Leviticus 26:40-42; Jeremiah 3:11-18; Hosea 5:15), paving the way for its salvation as foretold by the apostle Paul in Romans 11:25-27.

With their very existence threatened at Armageddon, Israel will desperately cry out to their newly discovered Messiah for deliverance, mourning for Him as one mourns for an only son (Zechariah 12:10; Matthew 23:37-39; see also Isaiah 53:1-9). Soon they would witness the power of the King of kings and Lord of lords, and their deliverance would be a "guarantee" (Romans 10:13-14).

At long last, Israel's leaders will comprehend the reason for their tribulation—whether through the Holy Spirit's illumination of Scripture, or the powerful testimony of the 144,000 Jewish evangelists, or even the two prophetic witnesses. In my mind's eye, I can picture the Jewish leaders saying to themselves, "How could we have been so unwise all these years?!"

FAST FACTS ON ISRAEL'S "HARDENING"

- In Romans 11:25, the apostle Paul sheds light on the partial hardening of Israel.
- The Jews, reluctant to accept the grace-filled salvation offered by Jesus, found Him incompatible with their pre-existing notions of the Messiah (Matthew 12:14, 24).
- Consequently, they sought salvation by keeping the law—an impossible task for any mortal (Romans 9:31-33).
- As a judgment from God, Israel suffered a partial judicial blindness and hardness of heart.
- As a result, Israel lost its cherished status before God. Instead, the gospel was preached to the Gentiles. The goal was to provoke a sense of jealousy in the Jews, ultimately leading them to salvation (Romans 11:11).
- Israel's rejection and hardening are only temporary; this will change when the Jewish remnant faces imminent danger from the antichrist and his armies at the end of the tribulation period.

CROSS-REFERENCES
Israel's Blindness

Stumbled over "stumbling stone," Jesus Christ—Romans 9:31-33
Refused to believe in Christ—Matthew 12:14, 24
Hardened—Romans 11:25
Jealous of Gentiles—Romans 11:11
Remnant saved—Romans 11:25
End-times repentance—Isaiah 53:1-9; Zechariah 12:10; Matthew 23:37-39

ISRAEL'S CONVERSION

"I will make known my holy name among my people Israel...It is coming! It will surely take place, declares the Sovereign Lord. This is the day I have spoken of" (Ezekiel 39:7-8).

"I will pour out on the house of David and the inhabitants of

Jerusalem a spirit of grace and supplication. They will look on me, the one they have pierced, and they will mourn for him as one mourns for an only child, and grieve bitterly for him as one grieves for a firstborn son" (Zechariah 12:10).

"On that day a fountain will be opened to the house of David and the inhabitants of Jerusalem, to cleanse them from sin and impurity" (Zechariah 13:1).

"In this way all Israel will be saved, as it is written, 'The Deliverer will come from Zion, he will banish ungodliness from Jacob'; 'and this will be my covenant with them when I take away their sins'" (Romans 11:25-27).

FREQUENTLY ASKED QUESTION

Will many Jews lose their lives during the tribulation period?

Tragically, yes. As revealed in Zechariah 13:7-9, a staggering two-thirds of the Jewish population will meet their end during the tribulation period. Yet in the midst of this darkness there is a glimmer of hope—a remnant of one-third will persevere, seek refuge in Jesus, and find salvation (Isaiah 64:1-12). The tribulation period will be a time of intense purging of nonbelieving Israel. But it will pave the way for the remnant to embrace Jesus as their Messiah and attain redemption.

Later, in the millennial kingdom, the Jewish remnant will finally enjoy the full possession of their long-promised land (Genesis 12:1-3; 15:18-21; 17:8; 35:10-12) and witness the glorious restoration of the Davidic throne, with Christ Himself reigning on it (2 Samuel 7:5-17). This kingdom will be characterized by an abundance of physical and spiritual blessings, all deeply rooted in the transforming power of the new covenant (Jeremiah 31:31-34).

Spiritual Warfare in the End Times

- Just as the antichrist will target the Jewish remnant at the end of the tribulation period, so Satan—much more powerful—is now targeting Christians.

- Just as the Jewish remnant will find salvation only by calling on Jesus, so you and I can find salvation by calling on Jesus.

- It is good to remember that the sheep who are safest from the wolf are those who stay closest to the shepherd (Psalm 23; John 10:1-18).

👤 PERSONALITY PROFILE: *The Archangel Michael*

> The word *archangel* implies a rank first among angels.

> Apparently, Michael has authority over all the other angels (1 Thessalonians 4:16; Jude 9; Revelation 12:7).

> He is called the chief prince (Daniel 10:13) and "the great prince" (Daniel 12:1).

> His name means "Who is like God?"

> Michael seems to have a special relationship with Israel as her guardian, including watching over the Jewish remnant during the time of tribulation (Daniel 12:1; see also Psalm 91:11-12).

A LESSON TO LEARN
When Circumstances Threaten You:

- The besieged Jewish remnant will be gripped with despair, overwhelmed by the massive might of the antichrist.

- Have you ever felt completely powerless in the face of insurmountable challenges?

  · Never forget that God is "a stronghold to the needy in his distress" (Isaiah 25:4).

  · "The LORD is near to the brokenhearted and saves the crushed in spirit" (Psalm 34:18).

  · "God is our refuge and strength, a very present help in trouble" (Psalm 46:1).

PART 11

The Awe-Inspiring Second Coming of Christ

IN THIS SECTION

45 —— The Glorious Appearing—370

46 —— The Subsequent 75-Day Transition Period—380

45

The Glorious Appearing

The Jewish remnant is in grave danger as the menacing forces of the antichrist approach. Faced with a vast invading army composed of "all the nations," their chances of withstanding the onslaught seem bleak. Yet, transformed by their newfound faith in the Lord Jesus, they raise their voices and cry out to Jesus for deliverance from the invading army (Zechariah 12:10; Matthew 23:37-39; Romans 11:25-27).

Jesus will quickly respond to their pleas and make a triumphant return to save the remnant. As the King of kings and Lord of lords, Christ's arrival will be an unstoppable force (Revelation 19:11-16). The armies of the antichrist will crumble to dust in the presence of His Eternal Royal Majesty.

The second coming is vividly described in Revelation 19:11-16:

> I saw heaven opened, and behold, a white horse! The one sitting on it is called Faithful and True, and in righteousness he judges and makes war. His eyes are like a flame of fire, and on his head are many diadems, and he has a name written that no one knows but himself. He is clothed in a robe dipped in blood, and the name by which he is called is The Word of God. And the armies of heaven, arrayed in fine linen, white and pure, were following him on white horses. From his mouth comes a sharp sword with which to strike down the nations, and he will rule them with a rod of iron. He will tread the winepress of the fury of the wrath of God the Almighty. On his robe and on his thigh he has a name written, King of kings and Lord of lords.

HISTORICAL INSIGHT: *White Horses*

> In biblical times, generals of the Roman army rode gleaming white horses.

> ➤ Their presence contrasted sharply with the common soldiers astride their humble black or brown mounts.

> ➤ Christ, mounted on a majestic white steed, will lead the heavenly armies as their commander-in-chief. This vivid portrayal contrasts sharply with the humble colt He rode upon His first arrival on earth, as described in Zechariah 9:9.

In ancient times, names and titles had deep meaning, reflecting one's true nature. Perhaps Jesus is called "Faithful and True" in Revelation 19:11 because He will return to earth in glory *just as He promised* (Matthew 24:27-31).

NOTICE THE STRIKING DICHOTOMY BETWEEN CHRIST AND THE ANTICHRIST:

➤ While *Christ* is hailed as "Faithful," *the antichrist* epitomizes unfaithfulness, breaking his covenant with Israel.

➤ While *Christ* is hailed as "True," *the antichrist's* nature is steeped in falsehood, often resorting to deceptive actions.

Christ's eyes are said to be like a flame of fire. This refers not only to His absolute holiness, but also to His penetrating gaze, which sees all things as they really are (Revelation 1:14). At the second coming, no one will escape His omniscient gaze.

On Jesus' head are "many crowns" (Revelation 19:12). These crowns represent complete sovereignty and royal kingship. No one will challenge the royal authority of Christ. The "armies of heaven"—both angelic and previously raptured Christians—will accompany Christ back to earth.

Jesus is called King of kings and Lord of lords (Revelation 19:16) because He is supreme and sovereign over all earthly rulers and angelic powers (1 Timothy 6:15; see also Deuteronomy 10:17; Psalm 136:3). No one can challenge His rule.

Our text tells us, "From his mouth comes a sharp sword with which to strike down the nations" (Revelation 19:15). With the image of a sword coming out of His mouth, it becomes clear that Christ's triumph over His adversaries will be accomplished by the sheer power of His spoken word. Just as Christ spoke the universe into existence (Psalm 33:6; Colossians 1:16; John 1:3), so God's enemies will face their ultimate demise at the command of Christ's authoritative word.

Habakkuk 3:13 prophesies Christ's victory over the antichrist: "You went out for the salvation of your people, for the salvation of your anointed. You crushed the head of the house of the wicked, laying him bare from thigh to neck." In line with this, the apostle Paul speaks of the antichrist "whom the Lord Jesus will kill with the breath of his mouth and bring to nothing by the appearance of his coming" (2 Thessalonians 2:8).

The second coming will be a visible, bodily coming of the glorified Jesus. The New Testament often uses the Greek word *apokalupsis* to describe this event. This word means "revelation," "visible disclosure," "unveiling," and "removing the cover" from something that is hidden. We read in 1 Peter 4:13, "To the degree that you share the sufferings of Christ, keep on rejoicing; so that also at the *revelation of his glory*, you may rejoice with exultation" (emphasis added).

Another Greek word used in the New Testament for the second coming of Christ is *epiphaneia*, which has the basic meaning of "to appear" or "to shine forth." In Titus 2:13, Paul speaks of "looking for the blessed hope and *the appearing* of the glory of our great God and Savior, Christ Jesus" (emphasis added). In 1 Timothy 6:14, Paul urges Timothy to "keep the commandment without stain or reproach until *the appearing* of our Lord Jesus Christ" (emphasis added).

The second coming will be a universal experience in that "every eye" will witness the event. Revelation 1:7 says, "Look, he is coming with the clouds, and every eye will see him, even those who pierced him; and all the peoples of the earth will mourn because of him." "Then will appear in heaven the sign of the Son of Man, and then all the tribes of the earth will mourn, and they will see the Son of Man coming on the clouds of heaven with power and great glory" (Matthew 24:30). At the time of the second coming, there will also be great signs in the sky (Matthew 24:29-30).

Old Testament prophecy reveals that Jesus will first return to the rugged terrain of Bozrah, where the Jewish remnant faces imminent danger (Isaiah 34:1-7; 63:1-6; Habakkuk 3:3; Micah 2:12-13). They will not be in danger for long!

FAST FACTS ON JESUS' KINGSHIP

- Genesis 49:10 prophesied that the Messiah would come from the tribe of Judah and reign as a king.

- Psalm 2:6 records the divine proclamation of God the Father, establishing God the Son as the sovereign ruler in Jerusalem.

- Psalm 110 confirms that the Messiah will defeat His adversaries and exercise His dominion over them.

- Daniel 7:13-14 speaks of the Messiah-King's everlasting reign.

- Revelation 19:16 portrays Jesus as the incomparable "King of kings and Lord of lords."

- The Davidic covenant in 2 Samuel 7:16 promises a Messiah who will inherit a dynasty and rule over a people from an eternal throne, echoed in Luke 1:32-33.

- After His second coming, Jesus will reign on the throne of David during the millennial kingdom.

FREQUENTLY ASKED QUESTIONS

Do "armies" accompany Christ because He needs them to defeat the antichrist?

No. It is Christ alone—as the all-powerful God, the King of kings and Lord of lords, the eternal Potentate—who will fight against God's enemies. These armies accompany Christ to participate in the events that follow the second coming, including the establishment of Christ's millennial kingdom (Revelation 20:4; 1 Corinthians 6:2; 2 Timothy 2:12).

Why does it sometimes seem that the second coming is being delayed?

Second Peter 3:9 instructs us: "The Lord is not slow to fulfill his promise as some count slowness, but is patient toward you, not wishing that any should perish, but that all should reach repentance." God is patiently waiting for people to repent. Of course, time is running out. Once Jesus comes, there will be no more opportunity to repent and turn to Him.

This is consistent with God's established history of showing remarkable forbearance before calling people to face judgment (Joel 2:13; Luke 15:20; Romans 9:22). We should not be surprised that He continues this patience in the present age.

What is the sign of the Son of Man?

Jesus said in His Olivet Discourse, "Then will appear in heaven the sign of the Son of Man, and then all the tribes of the earth will mourn, and they will see the Son of Man coming on the clouds of heaven with power and great glory" (Matthew 24:30).

Bible scholars debate what might be meant by "the sign of the Son of Man."

- Some suggest that a cross symbol will appear in the sky, visible to all.
- Others suggest that it refers to the lightning that "flashes in the east and shines to the west" (Matthew 24:27 NLT).
- Others suggest that it may be the glory of Christ, which will be powerfully displayed at the second coming.
- Still others choose not to define the sign, affirming that the main thing is that Christ Himself will return visibly.
- Perhaps the Son of Man Himself is the sign (see Daniel 7:13; Acts 1:11; Revelation 19:11-21).

Why will "all the tribes of the earth" mourn when Christ comes in glory (Matthew 24:30)?

There may be several aspects to this mourning.

- On the one hand, just before the second coming, the Jewish remnant in the wilderness will finally recognize that Jesus is the divine Messiah, and these Jews will finally put their faith in Him for salvation. They will mourn for their foolish rejection of the Messiah in the past (Zechariah 12:10-12).
- On the other hand, people throughout the world who have lived in open defiance and rebellion against God throughout the tribulation period will mourn because they realize that the divine Judge has come, and it is time to face the consequences of their rebellion.

Was Jesus wrong when He said in the first century AD, "Behold, I am coming soon" (Revelation 22:7)?

Bible scholars have examined this question from several angles:

1. Some suggest that the word "soon" should be considered in light of God's timelessness and eternity. Oecumenius, in his sixth-century AD Greek commentary on the book of Revelation, noted that although he was writing more than 500 years after the time of Christ, the "soon" events of Revelation had not yet occurred.

2. Others take a similar view, suggesting that "soon" is a relative term. When someone waiting for his microwave popcorn says, "I'll be eating a big bowl of popcorn soon," he means in a few minutes. A pregnant woman in her third month who says, "I will give birth soon," means another six months. For a grieving husband at his wife's funeral, "soon" might refer to the rest of his life when he says, "My dear, I'll be joining you in heaven soon enough." Because "soon" is relative, its use in Revelation may not require events within the first century. Given God's timelessness and eternity, "soon" could encompass an extended period of time.

3. Some scholars contend that Revelation discusses a long series or long train of events, with "soon" referring only to their beginning. This series of events could span centuries or even millennia, beginning with the glorified appearance of Jesus in Revelation 1 and continuing with His involvement with the seven churches of Asia Minor (chapters 2–3). The timeline continues through history and into the future to the eternal state described in chapters 21–22. If "soon" refers only to the beginning of this long series of events, it means that most of the prophecies in Revelation do not have to occur "soon."

4. Perhaps the most compelling argument comes from a proper understanding of the Greek term for "soon." Renowned scholars William F. Arndt and F. Wilbur Gingrich, in their authoritative *A Greek-English Lexicon of the New Testament*, assert that this word can mean "quick," "swift," or "speedy."[1] Joseph Thayer agrees in his *Greek-English Lexicon of the New Testament*, noting that the word can mean "quickly" or "speedily."[2] The *Expository Dictionary of New Testament Words*, by W.E. Vine, also agrees that it can mean "swift," "quick," or "quickly."[3] Given this, it's not necessary to interpret the word to mean that the events described in Revelation would take place soon from John's first-century perspective. Rather,

it can be understood to mean that once these events begin, they will proceed with remarkable speed, unfolding rapidly and with great urgency. Thus, the words of Revelation do not convey a sense of events that are about to occur, but rather a series of events that will one day unfold with breathtaking speed.

Is it possible that Christ will be ashamed of me at the second coming?

Jesus issues a sober warning to His followers in Luke 9:26: "Whoever is ashamed of me and of my words, of him will the Son of Man be ashamed when he comes in his glory and the glory of the Father and of the holy angels" (compare with 1 John 2:28). Believers who are ashamed of their faith in Jesus will not lose their salvation, but they may indeed experience a sense of shame at the second coming. This is consistent with the truth that Christians who do not live fully committed lives may experience the forfeiture of certain rewards at the judgment seat of Christ (1 Corinthians 3:10-15; 2 Corinthians 5:10).

In what sense will Christ return "with the clouds" (Revelation 1:7)?

Clouds are often associated with the visible glory of God (Exodus 16:10; 40:34-35; 1 Kings 8:10-11; Matthew 17:5; 24:30; 26:64). Christ will return in the clouds of heaven, just as He was caught up in the clouds at His ascension (Matthew 24:30; 26:64; Mark 13:26; 14:62; Luke 21:32; Acts 1:9). Just as Jesus' departure was accompanied by a visible manifestation of the glory of God (clouds were present), so Christ's return will be accompanied by a visible manifestation of the glory of God (clouds will be present).

The Tribulation Period Ends

After His return, Jesus will victoriously ascend the Mount of Olives. We read about this in Zechariah 14:3-4: "On that day his feet shall stand on the Mount of Olives that lies before Jerusalem on the east, and the Mount of Olives shall be split in two from east to west by a very wide valley, so that one half of the Mount shall move northward, and the other half southward."

Immediately thereafter, in the gripping finale of the tribulation period, we reach the climactic moment when the seventh bowl judgment is poured out with unparalleled intensity:

The seventh angel poured out his bowl into the air, and a loud voice came out of the temple, from the throne, saying, "It is done!" And there were flashes of lightning, rumblings, peals of thunder, and a great earthquake such as there had never been since man was on the earth, so great was that earthquake. The great city was split into three parts, and the cities of the nations fell, and God remembered Babylon the great, to make her drain the cup of the wine of the fury of his wrath. And every island fled away, and no mountains were to be found. And great hailstones, about one hundred pounds each, fell from heaven on people; and they cursed God for the plague of the hail, because the plague was so severe (Revelation 16:17-21).

As these terrible events gradually subside, the tribulation period comes to its inevitable end. However, other judgments remain on the horizon—the judgment of the nations (Matthew 25) and the judgment of Israel (Ezekiel 20). Both judgments set the stage for the establishment of Christ's glorious millennial kingdom.

FAST FACTS ON THE FATE OF THE ANTICHRIST AND THE FALSE PROPHET

After the second coming, the antichrist and the false prophet will be thrown into the lake of fire:

- Scripture assures us that the lake of fire (hell) is a real place.
- But hell was not part of God's original creation, which He called "good" (Genesis 1).
- Hell was created later to accommodate the banishment of Satan and his fallen angels who rebelled against God (Matthew 25:41).
- People who reject Christ will join Satan and his fallen angels in this infernal place of suffering.

> • Scripture uses a variety of words to describe the horrors of hell, including fiery furnace (Matthew 13:42), unquenchable fire (Mark 9:47), fiery lake of burning sulfur (Revelation 19:20), lake of fire (Revelation 20:15), eternal fire (Matthew 18:8), eternal punishment (Matthew 25:46), destruction (Matthew 7:13), eternal destruction (2 Thessalonians 1:8-9), the place of weeping and gnashing of teeth (Matthew 13:42), and the second death (Revelation 20:14).

It is to this place that the antichrist and the false prophet will be eternally consigned.

TWO LESSONS TO LEARN

1. Jesus must reign on the throne of our hearts.

- Jesus is the sovereign "King of kings and Lord of lords" (Revelation 19:16).
- *Ask yourself:* Is Christ my King and Lord? Is Christ currently enthroned in my heart? Is there anything I am holding back from Him?
- The place of blessing in the Christian life is the place of complete surrender and submission.

2. God is always greater than our problems.

- The international forces of the antichrist will all but guarantee the Jewish remnant's destruction, but God will rescue them.
- Let us learn a lesson: God is always greater than our problems, no matter how immense those problems may seem.
- God can come through for us against all odds.

CROSS-REFERENCES

Second Coming of Christ

Anticipated—Psalm 110:1; Isaiah 2:2-4; 42:4; Daniel 7:13-14; Joel 2:30-32; Zechariah 14:34; Malachi 3:1; Hebrews 9:28

Be blameless until He comes—1 Thessalonians 5:23; 1 Timothy 6:13-15

Be faithful until He returns—1 Timothy 6:11-16

Be patient awaiting Lord's return—James 5:7

Coming as Lord, King—Hebrews 9:24-28

Coming from heaven—1 Thessalonians 1:10

Coming in clouds—Revelation 1:7

Coming like a thief—1 Thessalonians 5:1-3; Revelation 16:15

Coming soon—Philippians 4:5; Hebrews 10:37; James 5:7-8; Revelation 3:11; 22:12, 20

Coming visibly—Acts 1:9-11

Crown of righteousness for those longing for His coming—2 Timothy 4:8

Every eye will see Him—Zechariah 12:10; Revelation 1:7

Israel will welcome her coming King—Zechariah 9:9-17

Judgment of the nations will follow—Matthew 25:31-46

Last days conduct—2 Timothy 3:1-5

Messiah of Israel will come in triumph—Zechariah 14:1-8

No one knows hour—Matthew 24:42, 44, 46-50; Mark 13:32-37; Luke 21:34-36

Prepared for second coming—1 Thessalonians 3:13

Promise of Christ's coming reaffirmed—Revelation 22:12

Remnant of Israel rescued at Christ's return—Isaiah 64:1-12

Return of Lord Jesus—1 Corinthians 1:7-8; Hebrews 9:28

Scoffers in last days—2 Peter 3:4

Signs in sun, moon, stars—Luke 21:25, 27

Those not ready punished—Matthew 24:45-51; Mark 13:34-37; Luke 22:34-36

Vision of Christ's coming—Daniel 7:9-14

Watch for Lord to come—Luke 12:35-40

We eagerly wait—Philippians 3:20; Titus 2:13

We will be like Him—1 John 3:2

Will come back on clouds of heaven—Matthew 26:64

Will come in glory—Matthew 16:27; 25:31; Mark 8:38; Luke 9:26

Yearning for Messiah—Isaiah 64:1

46

The Subsequent 75-Day Transition Period

There will be a 75-day interim between the end of the tribulation period and the onset of the millennial kingdom. We can infer this interim period from the following biblical facts:

- Daniel 12:12 says, "Blessed is he who waits and arrives at the 1,335 days."
- The second half of the tribulation period is three-and-a-half years, or 1,260 days.
- This means that Daniel's 1,335 days extend 75 days beyond the end of the tribulation period.
- The math is simple: 1,335 minus 1,260 equals 75.

Because the millennial kingdom has not yet begun, we conclude that there is a 75-day interval between the end of the tribulation period and the beginning of the millennial kingdom. Eight primary prophetic events will take place during this interim period:

1. The Judgment of the Nations

I addressed the judgment of the nations earlier in this book. Here, for the sake of continuity, I will highlight only the pertinent points:

> Believers and unbelievers from among the Gentile nations are pictured as sheep and goats (Matthew 25:31-46).

> Once the 75-day interim begins, the sheep and goats are pictured as being intermingled and require separation by a special judgment.

> The sheep (believers) will enter Christ's 1,000-year millennial kingdom.

> The goats (unbelievers) will go into eternal punishment.

> Christ will judge the Gentiles based on how they treated His "brothers" during the tribulation period.

> The "brothers" are the 144,000 Jewish evangelists mentioned in Revelation 7 and 14. These are Christ's Jewish brothers who faithfully bear witness to Him during the tribulation.

> In Christ's reckoning, treating His brothers kindly is the same as treating Him kindly, while treating His brothers with contempt is the same as treating Him with contempt.

> The redeemed Gentiles (the sheep) will enter the millennial kingdom in their earthly, mortal bodies and continue to marry and have children throughout the millennium.

> The redeemed Gentiles will not yet receive glorified/resurrected bodies. Although longevity will characterize the millennial kingdom, mortal Gentiles will continue to age and die (Isaiah 65:20). They will be resurrected after the millennial kingdom (Revelation 20:4-5).

FREQUENTLY ASKED QUESTION

What does Scripture say about the close connection between Jesus Christ and His followers?

In Matthew 25:31-46, we see the profound truth that when we show kindness to Christ's followers, we are essentially extending that kindness to Him. Likewise, to treat His followers with contempt is to show contempt for Christ Himself.

Other Bible passages underscore the deep intimacy between Jesus and His followers. We remember that Saul was a persecutor of Christ's followers. When Jesus appeared to Saul on the road to Damascus, He asked him, "Saul, Saul, why are you persecuting me?" (Acts 9:4).

Jesus also told His followers, "Whoever receives you receives me, and whoever receives me receives him who sent me" (Matthew 10:40). He further said, "The one who hears you hears me, and the one who rejects you rejects me, and the one who rejects me rejects him who sent me" (Luke 10:16). The apostle Paul instructed the Corinthian Christians, "Sinning against your brothers and wounding their conscience when it is weak, you sin against Christ" (1 Corinthians 8:12).

Christ thus viewed His followers as being intimately connected to Him.

A LESSON TO LEARN

> Given what you have learned about the close connection between Christ and His followers (Matthew 10:40; 25:31-46; Luke 10:16; Acts 9:4), does this change the way you want to treat your brothers and sisters in Christ?

> Are there any relationships that need to be restored?

2. The Judgment of the Jews

The judgment of the Jews is described in Ezekiel 20:34-38. God affirms:

I will bring you out from the peoples and gather you out of the countries where you are scattered, with a mighty hand and an outstretched arm, and with wrath poured out. And I will bring you into the wilderness of the peoples, and there I will enter into judgment with you face to face. As I entered into judgment with your fathers in the wilderness of the land of Egypt, so I will enter into judgment with you, declares the Lord God. I will make you pass under the rod, and I will bring you into the bond of the covenant. I will purge out the rebels from among you, and those who transgress against me. I will bring them out of the land where they sojourn, but they shall not enter the land of Israel. Then you will know that I am the Lord. (See also Matthew 25:1-30.)

Here are the essential facts about this judgment:

- It will take place during the 75-day interim after the Lord has gathered the Israelites from all over the world to the Holy Land.
- Christ will wipe out the rebels—those who have refused to turn to Him for salvation.
- Believers from among the Jews will enter Christ's millennial kingdom to enjoy the blessings of the new covenant (verse 37; see also Jeremiah 31:31; Matthew 25:1-30).
- These redeemed Jews will not yet receive glorified bodies. They will

enter the kingdom in their earthly, mortal bodies and continue to have children throughout the millennium (as will their Gentile counterparts—Matthew 25:46). Although longevity will characterize the millennial kingdom, both mortal Jews and Gentiles will continue to age and die (Isaiah 65:20). They will be resurrected at the end of the millennium (Revelation 20:4).

3. The Antichrist and the False Prophet Will Be Cast into the Lake of Fire

The judgments of the 75-day interim continue as the antichrist and the false prophet are cast into the lake of fire: "The beast was captured, and with it the false prophet who in its presence had done the signs by which he deceived those who had received the mark of the beast and those who worshiped its image. These two were thrown alive into the lake of fire that burns with sulfur" (Revelation 19:20).

4. Satan Will Be Bound

Satan will also be bound at this time: "Then I saw an angel coming down from heaven, holding in his hand the key to the bottomless pit and a great chain. And he seized the dragon, that ancient serpent, who is the devil and Satan, and bound him for a thousand years, and threw him into the pit, and shut it and sealed it over him, so that he might not deceive the nations any longer" (Revelation 20:1-3).

5. Old Testament Saints Will Be Resurrected

The 75-day interim is not just about judgment. It's also about resurrection. The Old Testament saints will now be raised from the dead: "Your dead shall live; their bodies shall rise. You who dwell in the dust, awake and sing for joy! For your dew is a dew of light, and the earth will give birth to the dead" (Isaiah 26:19; see also Daniel 12:2).

6. Tribulation Saints Who Have Died Will Be Resurrected

The dead saints of the tribulation period will also be resurrected from the dead at this time: "I saw the souls of those who had been beheaded for the testimony of Jesus and for the word of God, and those who had not worshiped the beast or its image and had not received its mark on their foreheads or their hands. They came to life and reigned with Christ for a thousand years" (Revelation 20:4). So preliminary to their reigning with Christ during the millennial kingdom, they will be resurrected during the 75-day interim.

7. The Marriage Feast of the Lamb Will Be Celebrated

Scripture often refers to the relationship between Christ and the church using a marriage motif—Christ being the Bridegroom, the church being the bride (Matthew 9:15; 22:2-14; 25:1-13; Mark 2:19-20; Luke 5:34-35; 14:15-24; John 3:29). The church is even now seen as a virgin bride awaiting the arrival of her heavenly Bridegroom at the rapture (2 Corinthians 11:2). While she waits, she keeps herself pure, unspotted by the world.

Traditional Hebrew weddings always concluded with a marriage feast. Jesus and the church will already have had a marriage ceremony in heaven (Revelation 19:7-16). After the second coming, the marriage feast will be celebrated on earth as the crowning event of the 75-day interim.

We read in Revelation 19:7-9:

> Let us rejoice and exult and give him the glory, for the marriage of the Lamb has come, and his Bride has made herself ready; it was granted her to clothe herself with fine linen, bright and pure—for the fine linen is the righteous deeds of the saints. And the angel told me, "Write this: Blessed are those who are invited to the marriage supper of the Lamb." And he said to me, "These are the true words of God."

It will be an incredible spectacle—the climax of the two-and-a-half-month interim. It is wondrous to ponder that the bride will reign alongside the Bridegroom during the millennial kingdom (Revelation 20:6).

FAST FACTS ON METAPHORS FOR THE CHURCH

The Church Is...

- The bride of Christ (Revelation 21:2).
- The body of Christ (Colossians 1:18).
- The temple of the Holy Spirit (1 Corinthians 3:16).
- God's household (Ephesians 2:19-20; 1 Timothy 3:14-15).

FAST FACTS ABOUT REIGNING WITH CHRIST

- Believers are a kingdom of priests and will reign with Christ—Revelation 5:10; 20:6.
- If we endure, we will reign with Christ—2 Timothy 2:12.
- Christ's martyrs will reign with Christ—Revelation 20:4.
- Overcoming Christians will sit on the throne with Christ—Revelation 3:21.
- Christ's servants will reign forever—Revelation 22:5.

8. Millennial Appointments Will Be Made

The governmental structure of the coming millennial kingdom will almost certainly be set up during this 75-day interim. Scripture reveals that the saints will reign with Christ in varying capacities during the millennial kingdom (2 Timothy 2:12; Revelation 20:4-6). Hence, millennial appointments must now be made.

> *"After the saints and unbelievers have been separated and the unbelievers are removed in judgment, it will take time to appoint saints to different government positions and inform them of their various responsibilities."*
>
> —Renald Showers[1]

Once the 75-day interval is over, Christ will finally set up His long-anticipated millennial kingdom (Isaiah 2:2-4; Ezekiel 37:1-13; 40-48; Micah 4:1-7; Revelation 20). There will be unimaginable physical and spiritual blessings for God's people in this kingdom. I'll address this in the next chapter.

PART 12

The Millennial Kingdom

IN THIS SECTION

47——Bountiful Spiritual and Material Blessings in the Millennial Kingdom—388

48——Satan's Dramatic Final Act: The Climactic Uprising—396

Bountiful Spiritual and Material Blessings in the Millennial Kingdom

J esus will set up His kingdom on earth after His second coming and the 75-day interim period. Theologians call this "the millennial kingdom" (Revelation 20:2-7).

The word *millennium* is derived from two Latin words: *mille*, meaning "thousand," and *annum*, meaning "year." The millennial kingdom will last for 1,000 years.

Only redeemed Jews and Gentiles will enter the millennial kingdom. The Gentiles will face Christ at the judgment of the nations (Matthew 25:31-46), while the Jews will face Christ at a separate judgment (Ezekiel 20:34-38). Both judgments take place during the 75-day interim period. Only those in both groups who are found to be believers will be invited into the millennial kingdom in their mortal bodies (Matthew 25:34, 46).

FREQUENTLY ASKED QUESTIONS

How do we know that only believers will enter the millennial kingdom?

Daniel says that only the saints will enter the kingdom: "The saints of the Most High shall receive the kingdom and possess the kingdom...The time came when the saints possessed the kingdom" (Daniel 7:18, 22).

The word "saint" in Daniel comes from an Aramaic word derived from a Hebrew root, *Oilp*. This word has the connotation of a divine claim and ownership of the person. It refers to that which is distinct from the common or profane. Thus, only those who are God's people—those who are "owned" by God—enter the kingdom.

It is inconceivable that both the wicked and the saints could inherit a kingdom universally characterized by righteousness (Isaiah 61:11), peace (Isaiah 2:4), holiness (Isaiah 4:34), and justice (Isaiah 9:7). The parables of the wheat and tares (Matthew 13:30) and the good and bad fish (Matthew 13:49-50) confirm that only the saved will enter the kingdom.

> Both Jewish and Gentile married couples will continue to have offspring throughout the millennium. And while people will live much longer in the millennium than they do today, mortal Jews and Gentiles will continue to age and die (Isaiah 65:20). They will be resurrected at the end of the millennium (Revelation 20:4).

Will all the children of the believers who enter the millennial kingdom also become believers?

No. Although only saints will enter the kingdom, some of their children, grandchildren, and great-grandchildren will not believe. Some will reach adulthood while rejecting the Savior-King in their hearts, despite their outward submission to His rule in the kingdom. Eventually, some of these individuals will participate in the final rebellion against God at the close of the millennial kingdom. Satan will be released from the abyss and will lead a host of rebellious people in this final revolt against God (Revelation 20:7-8).

The good news for the Jewish people is that after thousands of years of waiting, God's unbreakable covenants with Israel will finally be fulfilled during the millennial kingdom. God will fulfill the land promises of the Abrahamic covenant (Genesis 15:18-21; 26:3-4; 28:13-14) and the throne promises of the Davidic covenant, which will entail the Lord Jesus ruling on the throne of David (2 Samuel 7:12-16). The promise of Israel's regeneration and spiritual empowerment in the new covenant will also be fulfilled (Jeremiah 31:31-34).

A new temple will be built in the millennial kingdom (Ezekiel 40–48). It will be significantly larger than any other temple in the history of Israel. This magnificent temple will symbolize God's unwavering presence among His people during the millennium (Ezekiel 37:26-27) and will serve as the center for worshiping the Savior, Jesus Christ. Redeemed Gentiles will also gather within its walls to worship the Savior (Isaiah 60:6; Zephaniah 3:10; Zechariah 2:11).

FREQUENTLY ASKED QUESTION

Why will there be animal sacrifices in the millennial kingdom?

Sacrifices in the millennial temple will play a critical role in removing ceremonial impurities and preventing temple defilement, thereby ensuring the purity of the temple environment. As Yahweh dwells among sinful mortal people, such ceremonial cleansing of the temple becomes necessary to maintain its purity. (Remember, these people survive the tribulation period and enter the millennial kingdom in their mortal bodies—still retaining their sinful natures, even though redeemed by Christ as believers.) The sacrifices will thus remove all ceremonial impurity in the temple.

These sacrifices *are not* a return to the Mosaic Law. Through Jesus Christ, the law has been abolished for all time (Romans 6:14-15; 7:16; 1 Corinthians 9:20-21; 2 Corinthians 3:7-11; Galatians 4:17; 5:18; Hebrews 8:13; 10:16). Since fallen, though redeemed, human beings remain on earth during the millennium, the sacrifices are for the sole purpose of cleansing the temple of ritual impurities.

The Physical Blessings of the Millennium

Redeemed Jews and Gentiles in the millennial kingdom will enjoy an abundance of physical blessings. The environment will be improved and enhanced. The desert will blossom richly with vegetation, and the terrain will be unimaginably beautiful—a sight to behold that will take one's breath away (Isaiah 35:1-2). The rain will nourish the soil, and the food for animals will be abundant (30:23-24; 35:7). Everything will be perfect.

Animals and humans will coexist in a peaceful and harmonious environment. The innate predatory and carnivorous instincts of animals will be a thing of the past, as they live in harmony with each other and with humanity (Isaiah 11:6-7).

Human life expectancy will be greatly increased: "No more shall there be in it an infant who lives but a few days, or an old man who does not fill out his days, for the young man shall die a hundred years old" (Isaiah 65:20).

The healthcare industry will become obsolete because physical infirmities and diseases will be removed: "In that day the deaf shall hear the words of a book, and out of their gloom and darkness the eyes of the blind shall see" (Isaiah 29:18). "And no inhabitant will say, 'I am sick'" (Isaiah 33:24).

The world will be filled with prosperity, bringing about immense joy and happiness everywhere:

> They shall be radiant over the goodness of the Lord, over the grain, the wine, and the oil, and over the young of the flock and the herd; their life shall be like a watered garden, and they shall languish no more. Then shall the young women rejoice in the dance, and the young men and the old shall be merry. I will turn their mourning into joy; I will comfort them, and give them gladness for sorrow…My people shall be satisfied with my goodness, declares the Lord (Jeremiah 31:12-14).

The millennial kingdom will overflow with an abundance of physical blessings. How overwhelmingly wonderful it will be!

PHYSICAL BLESSINGS IN THE KINGDOM

Enhanced environment	Isaiah 35:1-2
Plenty of rain, plenty of food for animals	Isaiah 30:23-24
Animals living in harmony	Isaiah 11:6-7
Human longevity increased	Isaiah 65:20
Diseases removed	Isaiah 29:18
Prosperity will prevail	Jeremiah 31:12-14

A Perfect Government

The millennial government will be global (Psalm 2:6-9; Daniel 7:14) and centered in Jerusalem (Isaiah 2:1-3; Jeremiah 3:17; Ezekiel 48:30-35; Joel 3:16-17; Micah 4:1, 6-8; Zechariah 8:2-3). It will be led by Jesus Himself, who will reign on the throne of David (Jeremiah 23:5-6). It will be a government that is both effective and perfect (Isaiah 9:6-7), and it will bring lasting world peace (Micah 4:3-4). In short, Christ's government will create an ideal environment for life on earth, succeeding where all previous human governments have failed!

The saints will be privileged to reign with Christ. In 2 Timothy 2:12, the apostle Paul tells us: "If we endure, we will also reign with him." Revelation 5:10 reveals that believers have been made "a kingdom and priests to our God, and they shall reign on the earth." Revelation 20:6 affirms: "Blessed and holy is the one who shares in the first resurrection! Over such the second death has no power, but they will be priests of God and of Christ, and they will reign with him for a thousand years."

Spiritual Blessings in the Millennium

The millennial kingdom will feature unfathomable spiritual blessings and an unparalleled spiritual joy. The richness of these blessings will be magnified by the very presence of Christ Himself among His people on earth.

The prophet Isaiah proclaims that "the earth shall be full of the knowledge of the Lord as the waters cover the sea" (Isaiah 11:9). The depth of spiritual blessing that will prevail on earth during the millennial kingdom, coupled with the binding of Satan (Revelation 20:1-3), is unimaginable.

The new covenant will result in vibrant spiritual prosperity for the people (Jeremiah 31:31-34). As a result of this wondrous covenant, the earth will be showered with abundant spiritual blessings. The Holy Spirit will be present and indwell all believers (Ezekiel 36:27; 37:14). Righteousness (Isaiah 46:13; 51:5; 60:21), obedience to the Lord (Psalm 22:27; Jeremiah 31:33), holiness (Isaiah 35:8-10; Joel 3:17), and unified worship of the Messiah (Zephaniah 3:9; Zechariah 8:23; Malachi 1:1) will prevail worldwide. God's presence will be gloriously manifested throughout the entire earth (Ezekiel 37:27-28; Zechariah 2:10-13).

SPIRITUAL BLESSINGS IN THE KINGDOM	
Everyone will know the Lord.	Isaiah 11:9
Satan will be quarantined.	Revelation 20:1-3
The Holy Spirit will be present everywhere.	Ezekiel 36:27; 37:14
Righteousness will prevail.	Isaiah 46:13; 51:5; 60:21
Obedience to the Lord will prevail.	Psalm 22:27; Jeremiah 31:33
Holiness will prevail.	Isaiah 35:8-10; Joel 3:17
Faithfulness will prevail.	Psalm 85:10-11; Zechariah 8:3
The entire world will worship the Messiah.	Malachi 1:11; Zephaniah 3:9; Zechariah 8:23
God's presence will be made manifest.	Ezekiel 37:27-28; Zechariah 2:10-13

FREQUENTLY ASKED QUESTIONS

If Satan is incarcerated during the millennial kingdom, what about demons?

John specifies in Revelation 20:1-3 that Satan will be imprisoned in the abyss during the millennial kingdom so that he cannot "deceive the nations any longer." Although this prophetic text mentions only Satan, it is likely that demons will also be imprisoned during this time. Several biblical truths support this position.

We know that the fallen angels are subject to Satan and serve his purposes. This is illustrated in Revelation 12:7 where we read of "the dragon and his angels" (compare with Matthew 12:41). The "messenger of Satan" who plagued Paul is an illustration of a demon carrying out Satan's commands (2 Corinthians 12:7). Here is why this is important: If Satan were imprisoned during the millennium, but demons were still free, they could carry out his orders on earth. I do not believe God would permit that.

Satan is not the "Lone Ranger" of deception. Fallen angels also deceive. First Timothy 4:1 warns us of "teachings of demons." We are thus instructed to "test the spirits" (1 John 4:1). These verses demonstrate that people on earth are deceived not only by Satan but also by fallen angels who do Satan's bidding.

Satan will be imprisoned during the 1,000-year kingdom so that he can no longer "deceive the nations" (Revelation 20:3). If Satan's angels (demons) were still at large, the nations would undoubtedly continue to be susceptible to deception. Therefore, we can infer that Satan's fallen angels will also be imprisoned to prevent deception.

We also know that the millennial kingdom will be characterized by tremendous spiritual blessings—global righteousness, obedience to the Lord, holiness, faithfulness, and unified worship. With fallen angels still at large, it is difficult to imagine all of this taking place on earth.

What are the implications of the absence of Satan and demons during the millennial kingdom?

Satan will no longer condemn the consciences of believers for their moral failures (Revelation 12:10). He will no longer take an adversarial position against them (1 Peter 5:8) or spread deception as the father of lies (John 8:44).

Satan will no longer influence the world as the "god of this age" (2 Corinthians 4:4) or as "the prince of this world" (John 12:31). He will no longer be a "roaring lion" seeking to devour believers (1 Peter 5:8-9), nor will he persuade them to do evil (Matthew 4:3; Acts 5:3; 1 Corinthians 7:5; Ephesians 2:13; 1 Thessalonians 3:5).

Satan will no longer hinder the work of believers (1 Thessalonians 2:18), wage war against them (Ephesians 6:11-12), sow weeds among them (Matthew 13:38-39), incite persecution against them (Revelation 2:10), or sow doubt in their minds (Genesis 3:15). He will no longer plant spiritual pride in their hearts (1 Timothy 3:6) or lead them away from "the simplicity and purity of devotion to Christ" (2 Corinthians 11:3). Demons will no longer prevent believers' prayers from being answered (Daniel 10:12-20) or incite jealousy and dissension among them (James 3:13-16).

Digging Deeper: There Are Three Theological Views of the Millennial Kingdom

1. *Amillennialism* holds that there is no future literal millennial kingdom. Rather, Christ simply reigns from heaven over the church.

2. *Postmillennialism* holds that the world will be "Christianized" by the progressive influence of the church before Christ returns. The kingdom of God is supposedly now being extended in the world through the preaching of the gospel.

3. *Premillennialism* (the view I hold to) teaches that after the second coming, Christ will establish a kingdom of perfect peace and righteousness that will last for 1,000 years. This view naturally follows from a literal approach to prophecy and best explains the unconditional covenants God made with Israel.

THREE LESSONS TO LEARN
1. Christ must reign over our lives.

> Christ's millennial reign is still in the future.

> But Christ's heart-rule over our lives is present tense. It is a reality now.

> Let us redouble our efforts to be completely submissive to King Jesus (John 8:31; 14:23-24; 15:10-15).

> Hold nothing back!

2. The Holy Spirit empowers us.

> The Holy Spirit will pour out great spiritual blessings on the inhabitants of the millennial kingdom (Ezekiel 36:27; 37:14).

> But we do not have to wait until the millennial kingdom to be blessed by the Holy Spirit.

> Even now, we can walk in dependence on the Holy Spirit and gain victory over sin (Galatians 5:16-21).

> We can enjoy and manifest the fruit of the Holy Spirit (Galatians 5:22-25) and minister to others through the spiritual gift(s) the Holy Spirit gives us (Romans 12:6-8; 1 Corinthians 12:7-10, 28-30).

3. Obedience brings many blessings.

> Obedience to God will prevail during the millennial kingdom (Psalm 22:27; Jeremiah 31:33).

> But we do not have to wait until the millennial kingdom to enjoy the benefits of obedience to God, which brings...

  » long life (1 Kings 3:14; John 8:51),

  » happiness (Psalm 112:1; 119:56),

  » peace (Proverbs 1:33),

  » and a state of well-being (Jeremiah 7:23).

> *I want these blessings, don't you?*

48

Satan's Dramatic Final Act: The Climactic Uprising

The millennial kingdom will provide an ideal living environment for the redeemed. The devil and, most likely, the fallen angels who serve him will be imprisoned in the bottomless pit for the duration of the kingdom (Revelation 20:1-3). This quarantine will effectively eliminate a powerful destructive and deceptive force in all areas of human life and thought.

> *The Work of Satan*—Genesis 3:1-5; John 8:44; Acts 5:3; 1 Corinthians 7:5; 2 Corinthians 11:14; 1 Timothy 3:6; 1 Peter 5:8; James 3:13-16; Revelation 12:10.

📖 UNDERSTANDING OUR TERMS: *The Bottomless Pit*

The bottomless pit is the *abyss*—a place of imprisonment for some demonic spirits (Luke 8:31; 2 Peter 2:4).

At the end of Christ's millennial kingdom, Satan will be released from the abyss and he will stage the ultimate uprising against the Almighty: "When the thousand years are ended, Satan will be released from his prison and will come out to deceive the nations that are at the four corners of the earth, Gog and Magog, to gather them for battle; their number is like the sand of the sea" (Revelation 20:7-8).*

The target city of the satanic revolt is none other than Jerusalem. The

---

* Because of the reference to Gog and Magog in this passage, some prophecy students wonder if this is the same as the Ezekiel invasion on Israel (Ezekiel 36–39). See chapter 25 for a full discussion of why this cannot be the case.

significance of this lies in the fact that Christ will establish His headquarters in the millennial kingdom in Jerusalem (Isaiah 2:1-5). Thus, any attack on Jerusalem becomes an attack on Christ Himself, making it a truly strategic target.

The attack will be real, but it has no chance of success. It is like a canoe attacking a battleship. Scripture affirms that fire will immediately come down upon the invaders (Revelation 20:9).

FREQUENTLY ASKED QUESTION

Who will side with Satan in this final revolt?

After the tribulation, only believers will be invited into Christ's millennial kingdom (Matthew 25:31-46). But these redeemed people—still in their mortal bodies—will give birth to babies and raise children, some of whom will not follow Jesus.

When Satan is released at the end of the millennium, he will cause many of these unbelieving children—as well as grandchildren and great-grandchildren—to rebel against Christ. "Their number is like the sand of the sea" (Revelation 20:8). This rebellion will represent Satan's "last stand."

FAST FACTS ON IMPRISONED ANGELS

- Satan is incarcerated during the millennial kingdom.
- Within the realm of fallen angels, there are two distinct groups—those who are imprisoned and those who are free.
- The imprisoned angels, destined for the judgment to come, await their fate in eternal chains under a veil of darkness, as described in Jude 6.
- Second Peter 2:4 affirms that God did not spare the angels who sinned, but "committed them to chains of gloomy darkness to be kept until the judgment."
- Many believe that these fallen angels are the "sons of God" referred to in Genesis 6, guilty of committing heinous acts of sexual sin with human women.
- Other demonic spirits remain free to continue their attacks on people, especially believers in Christ (Matthew 12:43; Mark 1:23, 26; 3:28-30; 5:2, 8; 7:25; 9:25; Luke 4:33; 8:29; 9:42; 11:24; John 13:2, 27).
- Satan will be released from incarceration in the abyss following the millennium. True to character, he then leads a revolt against God.

FAST FACTS ON SATAN THE DECEIVER

- Revelation 20:7-8 paints a grim picture of Satan's release from prison—he will come forth to deceive the nations in the four corners of the earth.
- Deception has always been at the heart of Satan's malicious activities.
- Through a lie, he brought spiritual and physical death to humankind (Genesis 3:4, 13; 1 John 3:8, 10-15).
- John 8:44 speaks clearly of Satan's true nature: "He was a murderer from the beginning, and does not stand in the truth, because there is no truth in him. He speaks out of his character when he lies, for he is a liar and the father of lies."
- When Satan engages in deception, he is simply being true to his own character.

SATAN'S INSIDIOUS ACTIVITIES

Rebelled against God before the creation of humankind	Isaiah 14:12-15
Disguises himself as an angel of light	2 Corinthians 11:14
Deceives the entire world	Revelation 12:9
Is a liar and murderer	John 8:44
Gathers the armies of the world at Armageddon	Revelation 16:13-16
Gathers rebels against God after the millennium	Revelation 20:7-10

YOU MAY BE INTERESTED TO KNOW...

God Often Uses Fire in Judgment

Throughout biblical history, fire has been a powerful form of God's judgment on those who commit serious offenses:

- "The LORD rained on Sodom and Gomorrah sulfur and fire from the LORD out of heaven" (Genesis 19:24).

- Nadab and Abihu committed a serious offense, and "fire came out from before the LORD and consumed them" (Leviticus 10:1-2).

- When the people rose up in complaint against the Lord, "the fire of the LORD burned among them and consumed some outlying parts of the camp" (Numbers 11:1).

- Anyone who tries to harm God's two prophetic witnesses during the tribulation period will experience a fiery response: "If anyone would harm them, fire pours from their mouth and consumes their foes" (Revelation 11:5).

After God's fiery wrath is unleashed on the Satan-motivated rebel invaders, the devil himself will be cast into the fiery depths of the lake of sulfur, where the antichrist and the false prophet have already been tormented for 1,000 years. It is a fate that all three members of the satanic trinity will share. While the antichrist and false prophet will have already endured the flames for 1,000 years, Satan will finally join them, and the three will continue to suffer for all eternity. Justice will be served, and their punishment will be commensurate with their wicked deeds.

The fallen angels, or demons, who have faithfully served Satan for eons, will not escape judgment. As stated in Matthew 25:41, "the eternal fire prepared for the devil and his angels" awaits them. Their torment of humanity throughout history will finally meet a just and fiery reckoning.

SATAN AND DEMONS ARE ON A LEASH

God will not allow Satan to succeed in his revolt. Scripture consistently portrays God as placing limits on Satan and his fallen angels, limiting their destructive power. Satan is not free to wreak havoc as he pleases, for God's divine hand restricts his every move (as seen in Job 1:12 and 2:6). This is a remarkable testimony to God's protective care, as expressed in Psalm 91:1-12.

THE SIX JUDGMENTS OF SATAN

There are six distinct judgments of Satan in Scripture:

1. It begins with his being cast out of heaven after his fall (Ezekiel 28:16).

2. He was later judged in the Garden of Eden (Genesis 3:14-15).

3. He was judged again at the cross (John 12:31; Colossians 2:15; Hebrews 2:14).

4. He will be cast out of heaven at the midpoint of the tribulation (Revelation 12:13).

5. He will be incarcerated in the abyss during the millennial kingdom (Revelation 20:2).

6. He will meet his end by being cast into the lake of fire after the millennial kingdom (Revelation 20:10; Matthew 25:41).

FREQUENTLY ASKED QUESTION

What is God's purpose in releasing Satan from the abyss after the millennial kingdom?

God's ultimate purpose seems to be to demonstrate conclusively that the heart of every human being is desperately wicked (Jeremiah 17:9). Even in the best of environments—Christ's millennial kingdom, which will be bountifully filled with physical and spiritual blessings—the fallen human heart will still have a strong inclination to sin and will be easily susceptible to Satan's evil temptations (Revelation 20:8-9).

FAST FACTS ON THE DEPTHS OF HUMAN SIN

- At the end of Christ's millennial kingdom, which provides a perfect living environment, there will be a massive human rebellion instigated by Satan.

- This reveals the profound effects of human sin.

- Throughout His teachings, Jesus used metaphors to illustrate the devastation that sin can cause.

- He described sin as blindness (Matthew 23:16-26), sickness (Matthew 9:12), being enslaved in bondage (John 8:34), and living in darkness (John 8:12; 12:35-46).

- He affirmed that both internal thoughts and external actions make a person guilty (Matthew 5:28; Mark 7:21-23).
- At the end of the millennial kingdom, unbelievers will succumb to their sinful natures without restraint and revolt against God.

"While we don't know all the reasons God will allow Satan a brief reprieve from his life sentence, I believe that it will prove once and for all, beyond any doubt, that man's heart is black as midnight and that only the grace of God can save us. Revelation 20:7-10 says that when Satan is released, he will gather many people willing to battle against the Lord. This will be the final rebellion. These people who were born and raised during the millennium, living under the righteous reign of the King of kings with Edenic conditions restored, will turn on Him the first time they get an opportunity. This sounds unbelievable, but it's true. Man will quickly fall prey to the archdeceiver."

—Mark Hitchcock[1]

"One of the most amazing commentaries on the fallen human nature to be found in all the Word of God is right here in this passage. After one thousand years of a perfect environment, with an abundance of material possessions and spiritual instruction for everyone, no crime, no war, no external temptation to sin, with the personal presence of all the resurrected saints and even Christ Himself, and with Satan and all his demons bound in the abyss, there are still a multitude of unsaved men and women on earth who are ready to rebel against the Lord the first time they get a chance."

—Henry Morris[2]

A LESSON TO LEARN

The human heart is capable of great wickedness and rebellion. Even Christians retain a sinful nature that makes them vulnerable to rebellion against God (Romans 7:15-20). Here's a three-part strategy for keeping rebellion in check:

1. Begin each day feasting upon Scripture with a firm resolve to obey (Psalm 119).

2. Stay seamlessly connected to Jesus every minute of the day (John 15:1-11).

3. Walk in constant dependence on the Holy Spirit (Galatians 5:16-25).

PART 13

The Great White Throne Judgment and the Lake of Fire

IN THIS SECTION

49 — The Divine Reckoning: The Wicked Face the Great White Throne Judgment—404

50 — The Divine Retribution: The Lake of Fire Is Populated—410

The Divine Reckoning: The Wicked Face the Great White Throne Judgment

The moment we die, we enter the "intermediate state." The intermediate state refers to our existence between physical death and the future resurrection. We might call it an *in-between* state—it is the state of our existence between the time our mortal bodies die and the time we receive resurrection bodies in the future.

This means that the intermediate state is a disembodied state. The body remains in the grave while the spirit or soul enters an intermediate state, either basking in the glory of heaven with Christ or enduring a place of great suffering without Him. One's destiny in the intermediate state depends entirely on whether one has placed faith in Christ during one's earthly life.

In the intermediate state, believers enjoy pure, unadulterated bliss and joy (2 Corinthians 5:8; Philippians 1:21-23). The intermediate state of unbelievers, however, is nothing short of agonizing. Upon their death, they are transported as disembodied spirits to a place of temporary suffering (Luke 16:19-31), where they remain until their eventual resurrection and judgment, which leads them to their fateful incarceration in the lake of fire (Revelation 20:11-15).

Second Peter 2:9 highlights the fate of the wicked dead by portraying them as condemned prisoners: "The Lord knows how to...keep the unrighteous under punishment until the day of judgment." The word "keep" in this verse is a present tense, indicating that the wicked (unbelievers) are being held captive and punished *continuously*. Peter portrays them as condemned prisoners, closely guarded in a spiritual prison, awaiting future sentencing and final judgment.

Jesus' parable of the rich man and Lazarus (Luke 16:19-31) gives us some sobering insights into the intermediate state of the wicked dead. Here's what we learn:

- The wicked dead are condemned to suffer in excruciating torment, with no consolation to be found in the afterlife.
- There is no possibility of escape.
- The wicked dead bear the full weight of responsibility for ignoring the warnings of Scripture while on earth.

The unbeliever's worst agony will be the eternal knowledge of the missed opportunity to trust in Christ for salvation and escape punishment. Throughout the endless vastness of time, the realization that a heavenly destiny was within their grasp, missed only because they chose to reject Christ, will relentlessly haunt the unbeliever's soul.

GOD'S JUDGMENT OF HUMAN BEINGS

After death comes judgment	Hebrews 9:27
Based on truth	Psalm 96:13; Romans 2:1-2
Believers will be judged by Christ	1 Corinthians 3:10-15; 2 Corinthians 5:10
Day of judgment is coming	2 Peter 3:7
Every deed will be judged	Ecclesiastes 12:14
Great white throne judgment	Revelation 20:12
Inevitability of judgment	Jeremiah 44:15-28
Judgment awaits all	Matthew 12:36; Romans 14:10, 12
Motivates holiness	2 Corinthians 5:9-10; 2 Peter 3:11, 14
Motivates repentance	Acts 17:30-31
Nations judged at the second coming	Joel 3:2; Matthew 25:31-46
Nothing is hidden from God	Hebrews 4:13

The intermediate state is temporary. Nonbelievers will soon face the great white throne judgment—a terrifying event in which all unbelievers will be cast into the fiery depths of the lake of fire as described in Revelation 20:11-15. Jesus presides as the Judge because the Father has entrusted all judgment to Him, as described in Matthew 19:28, John 5:22-30, Acts 10:42, and 17:31.

This throne is "great" because the One who sits upon it is our "great God and Savior," Jesus Christ (Titus 2:13-14). Its pristine white color symbolizes the purity, holiness, and righteousness of the divine Judge who sits upon it (see Psalm 97:2; Daniel 7:9).

The judgment takes place *after* the millennial kingdom. We know this because after Revelation 20 describes the millennium, it clearly states: "*Then* I saw a great white throne and him who was seated on it" (verse 11, emphasis added). (The word "then" implies that the great white throne judgment occurs sequentially after the millennium.)

Those who stand before the great white throne judgment have already sealed their fate by choosing to reject Christ's salvation. They are referred to as "the dead," as opposed to "the dead in Christ" (that is, dead believers).

To be clear, this judgment will not separate believers from unbelievers, for all who experience it will have already chosen to reject Christ during their lifetime. That people come to this judgment is grievous because they have no chance of salvation. They are there because they are unsaved and about to be cast into the lake of fire. I cannot begin to imagine the fearful dread that will permeate the minds of those who will be there.

Those who participate in the great white throne judgment will be resurrected to face the divine Judge, Jesus Christ. During His earthly ministry, Jesus soberly proclaimed that "an hour is coming when all who are in the tombs will hear his voice and come out, those who have done good to the resurrection of life, and those who have done evil to the resurrection of judgment" (John 5:28-29). Virtually every location on earth will give up the bodies of the unrighteous dead, and they will be resurrected (Revelation 20:13-14).

SOMETHING TO THINK ABOUT:

> - The resurrected bodies of the unsaved will be imperishable and immortal.
> - This means that although they will suffer the flames of torment, they will not be consumed but will endure for all eternity in an environment of suffering.
> - How terrible are the eternal consequences of rejecting Christ!

Revelation 20:12 tells us that "books" will be opened at the great white throne judgment. These books will detail the lives of the unsaved. Every action, word, and thought will be recorded. These books will provide evidence to support the divine verdict of a destiny in the lake of fire. The works that will be judged will include the actions of unbelievers (Matthew 16:27), their words (Matthew 12:37), and even their thoughts and motives (Luke 8:17; Romans 2:16).

We also read of another book—the book of life. The idea of a divine record of names goes back to Moses' encounter with God on Mount Sinai (Exodus 32:32-33). The apostle Paul speaks of his fellow workers as those "whose names are in the book of life" (Philippians 4:3). In the book of Revelation, the "book of life" is mentioned six times (3:5; 13:8; 17:8; 20:12, 15; and 21:27), and it contains the names of all those who belong to God. In Revelation 13:8 and 21:27, the book of life is specifically said to belong to the Lamb of God, Jesus Christ.

When Christ opens the book of life at the judgment before the vast white throne, none of the wicked are found in it. Their names are not written in the book of life because they have shunned Jesus Christ, the source of life. Because of their rejection of the source of life, they will be cast into the lake of fire, which represents the "second death" and eternal separation from God.

At the great white throne judgment, the punishment meted out to each individual person by our Savior and Judge, Jesus Christ, will vary according to the extent of their sins. There will be varying degrees of punishment among the unsaved.

> *All* those who are judged at the great white throne judgment will experience weeping and gnashing of teeth (Matthew 13:41-42), condemnation (Matthew 12:36-37), destruction (Philippians 1:28), eternal punishment (Matthew 25:46), separation from God's presence (2 Thessalonians 1:8-9), and trouble and distress (Romans 2:9).

FAST FACTS ON DEGREES OF PUNISHMENT AT THE GREAT WHITE THRONE JUDGMENT

- The great white throne judgment awaits all the wicked.
- There will be degrees of punishment, the severity of which will be directly proportional to one's sins.

- Jesus Himself spoke of things being more tolerable for some than others on the day of judgment (Matthew 11:20-24).
- Jesus spoke of the possibility of receiving only a light beating as opposed to a severe one (Luke 12:47-48).
- Jesus also indicated that there are greater and lesser sins that result in greater and lesser guilt (John 19:11; see also Matthew 10:15; 16:27; Revelation 20:12-13; 22:12).

YOU MAY BE INTERESTED TO KNOW...
God Is Perfectly Fair

> At the judgment seat of Christ, believers will face a reckoning for the lives they have lived.
> Some of them will receive rewards for living in accordance with Christ's teachings, while others will suffer the loss of rewards for falling short.
> This judgment will be conducted with perfect fairness, as Christ recognizes the deeds of each individual without prejudice or favoritism.
> Similarly, at the great white throne judgment, Christ will judge the wickedness of each unbeliever as an individual, considering their deeds on earth. Christ will be fair in recognizing that some unbelievers are more wicked than others.
> Hitler, for example, will be judged much more severely than a non-Christian moralist.
> Jesus' judgment of the unsaved will reflect their degree of wickedness.

Just as believers differ in their response to God's law and, therefore, in their reward in heaven, so unbelievers differ in their response to God's law and, therefore, in their punishment in hell. Just as there are degrees of reward in heaven, so there are degrees of punishment in hell.

FREQUENTLY ASKED QUESTION
Does God really condemn people to hell?

Yes, He does. But let me hasten to say that God is "not wishing that any should perish, but that all should reach repentance" (2 Peter 3:9). God specifically sent Jesus into the world to pay the penalty for our sins by dying on the cross (John 3:16-17). He *wants* everyone to be saved!

Unfortunately, not all people will admit that they sin and will not trust Christ for forgiveness. They do not accept the payment of Jesus' death for them. Therefore, God allows them to experience the severe consequences of their decision (Luke 16:19-31).

> ➤ C.S. Lewis once said that in the end there will be two groups of people.
> ➤ One group of people says to God, "Thy will be done." They have put their faith in Jesus Christ and will live forever with God in heaven.
> ➤ The second group of people are those to whom God sadly says, "Thy will be done!" These people have rejected Jesus Christ and will spend eternity apart from Him.[1]

CROSS-REFERENCES
Great White Throne Judgment
Condemnation—Matthew 12:36-37
Degrees of punishment—Matthew 10:15; 16:27; Luke 12:47-48; Revelation 20:12-13; 22:12
Destruction—Philippians 1:28
Eternal punishment—Matthew 25:46
Judgment of unbelievers—Revelation 20:11-15
Judgment based on works—Revelation 20:12-13; see also 2:23; 11:18; 14:13; 18:16; 22:12
Participants are resurrected unto judgment—John 5:28-29
Separation from God's presence—2 Thessalonians 1:8-9
Trouble and distress—Romans 2:9
Weeping and gnashing of teeth—Matthew 13:41-42

50

The Divine Retribution: The Lake of Fire Is Populated

The lake of fire is a place of unimaginable suffering where Satan, the antichrist, the false prophet, and unbelievers of all ages will spend eternity (Revelation 19:20; 20:10-15). All inhabitants of the lake of fire will be tormented forever.

In describing the eternal destiny of unbelievers, Jesus often spoke of the "eternal fire." A vivid example of this is His comment to the "goats" (nonbelievers): "Depart from me, you cursed, into the eternal fire prepared for the devil and his angels" (Matthew 25:41). This eternal fire is a stark reminder of the consequences of rejecting God's offer of salvation through Christ.

The lake of fire is another name for hell. Scripture assures us that hell is a real place. But hell was not part of God's original creation, which He called "good" (Genesis 1:31). Hell was created later to accommodate the banishment of Satan and his fallen angels who rebelled against God (Matthew 25:41). People who reject Christ will join Satan and his fallen angels in this infernal place of suffering.

BIBLICAL DESCRIPTIONS OF THE HORROR OF HELL	
"The fire is not quenched"	Mark 9:48
"Eternal punishment"	Matthew 25:46
"Destruction"	Matthew 7:13
"Eternal destruction"	2 Thessalonians 1:8-9
The place of "weeping and gnashing of teeth"	Matthew 13:42
The "second death"	Revelation 20:14

FREQUENTLY ASKED QUESTIONS
What exactly is the "fire" of hell?

Some believe that the fire of hell is literal. And it may well be. Others believe that the "fire" is a metaphorical way of expressing the great wrath of God. Scripture tells us:

- "The LORD your God is a consuming fire, a jealous God" (Deuteronomy 4:24).
- "Our God is a consuming fire" (Hebrews 12:29).
- "His wrath is poured out like fire" (Nahum 1:6).
- "Who can stand when he appears? For he will be like a refiner's fire" (Malachi 3:2).
- God's wrath will "go forth like fire, and burn with none to quench it" (Jeremiah 4:4).

Whether the fire of hell is literal or figurative, it will bring terrible suffering to those who are there. It may well be that the fire of hell is both literal *and* metaphorical.

What does "weeping and gnashing of teeth" mean?

Weeping and gnashing of teeth are a common experience in hell (Matthew 13:42; Luke 13:28). "Weeping" carries the idea of wailing. Weeping will be caused by the environment, the company, the remorse and guilt, and the shame that is part and parcel of hell.

People "gnash their teeth" when they are angry. They will be angry at the sin that brought them to hell, angry at what they have become, angry at Satan and demons for tempting them to do evil while on earth, and angry that they have rejected their ticket out of hell—salvation in Jesus Christ.

🔍 UNDERSTANDING OUR TERMS: *Gehenna*

> One of the most important New Testament words for hell is "Gehenna" (Matthew 10:28).

> For several generations in ancient Israel, unspeakable acts were committed in the Valley of Ben Hinnom, including the slaughter of children and human sacrifices (2 Kings 23:10; 2 Chronicles 28:3; 33:6; Jeremiah 32:35).

> These unfortunate victims were sacrificed to the false Moabite god Molech.

> The valley eventually became a public dumping ground for all the filth of Jerusalem. The bodies of dead animals and the corpses of criminals were also thrown into the pile.

> Everything in the garbage dump burned constantly.

> "Gehenna" eventually became a striking metaphor for the reality of hell.

> Jesus used the term eleven times to describe the eternal place of suffering for unsaved humanity.

Evaluating Annihilationism

Annihilationism has become popular in some theological circles today. This view holds that humans were created immortal, but those who continue to sin and reject Christ are stripped of their gift of immortality by God's intervention and are ultimately annihilated. They do not experience a conscious afterlife, and there is no eternal suffering in hell.

Annihilationism is an unscriptural doctrine. Matthew 25:46 clearly states that the unsaved will face *eternal* punishment. This punishment must include suffering, for punishment without suffering is not true punishment. Therefore, the idea of nonsuffering extinction of consciousness does not do justice to the Bible's references to "*eternal* punishment." Punishment requires consciousness.

One can exist without being punished, but one cannot be punished without existing. Annihilation refers to the eradication of existence and everything associated with it, including punishment. Annihilation *avoids* punishment rather than experiencing it.

Notice that Matthew 25:46 describes the punishment as "eternal." The adjective *aionion* in this verse means "everlasting, without end." In Romans 16:26, Hebrews 9:14, 13:8, and Revelation 4:9, the same adjective is used to describe God as the "eternal" God. The punishment of the wicked is just as eternal as our eternal God.

Notice also that there are no degrees of annihilation. Either you are annihilated or you are not. (Whether you are Hitler or a non-Christian moralist, you will be annihilated in the same way.) In contrast, Scripture teaches that there will be degrees of conscious punishment in hell (see Matthew 10:15; 11:21-24; 16:27; Luke 12:47-48; Hebrews 10:29; Revelation 20:11-15). These degrees of punishment will be proportional to one's degree of depravity. Such punishment is therefore completely just.

FREQUENTLY ASKED QUESTION

How can we be happy in heaven knowing that people are suffering in hell?

This is a difficult question. On this side of eternity, we lack the requisite knowledge and wisdom to give a comprehensive answer. However, a few scriptural considerations can help us keep perspective on this question.

First, God has promised to remove all sorrow and mourning in heaven (Revelation 21:4). He has it in hand. We can be confident that God has the power and ability to fulfill His promises. Heaven will be a happy place; that is a reality. God has guaranteed it.

Second, we will recognize the complete righteousness and justice of God's decisions. We will see that those in hell are there only because they refused God's only means of escape. These are the individuals to whom God ultimately declares, "Thy will be done."

Third, we will recognize that there are degrees of punishment in hell, just as there are degrees of reward in heaven. This ensures that the Hitlers of human history will suffer more than, say, a non-Christian moralist (Luke 12:47-48).

Finally, God can erase the memory of unbelieving loved ones from our consciousness. In Isaiah 65:17, God promises, "Behold, I create new heavens and a new earth, and the former things shall not be remembered or come into mind."

Let us never forget that God is perfectly wise and just. He knows what He is doing! You and I can rest with quiet assurance in God's wisdom and righteousness.

A Sense of Urgency in Delivering People from a Destiny in Hell

Hebrews 9:27 affirms: "It is appointed for man to die once, and after that comes judgment." Notice the order of events. The text does not say that a person dies, has a second chance to believe, and then faces judgment. Rather, it says that a person dies and then faces judgment.

The apostle Paul's sense of urgency in 2 Corinthians 6:2, is rooted in the sobering truth that we only die once and then face judgment. That's why he implores us: "Now is the favorable time; behold, now is the day of salvation."

There's simply no time to waste in responding to the gospel, because death could come at any moment. This fleeting life on earth is the only window we have to make our decision for or against Christ. Once we leave this world, there are no second chances to accept Jesus as our Savior. Let us not wait another day to secure our eternal salvation.

Ecclesiastes 9:12 warns us that death often comes unannounced, just as fish and birds are caught in a trap. This verse implies that we must always be ready, for death can ensnare us at any time, without giving us a second chance. Therefore, we must develop a sense of urgency and prepare for the inevitable moment.

Proverbs 27:1 admonishes, "Do not boast about tomorrow, for you do not know what a day may bring." Each new day brings the possibility of death. Therefore, it is only wise to turn to Christ for salvation while there is still time, lest we be lost forever in eternity.

Many people believe that they can wait until later in life to turn to the Lord, dismissing the importance of salvation now. But this view is misguided. In Luke 12:16-21, Jesus gives a powerful warning against such thinking:

> The land of a rich man produced plentifully, and he thought to himself, "What shall I do, for I have nowhere to store my crops?" And he said, "I will do this: I will tear down my barns and build larger ones, and there I will store all my grain and my goods. And I will say to my soul, 'Soul, you have ample goods laid up for many years; relax, eat, drink, be merry.'" But God said to him, "Fool! This night your soul is required of you, and the things you have prepared, whose will they be?" So is the one who lays up treasure for himself and is not rich toward God.

Many people today live as if they are entitled to a long life; one that extends even into their 80s, 90s, or beyond. They do not even consider the possibility of dying younger. This has led to unpreparedness when it comes to facing death. It is important to realize that death is unpredictable and comes without warning. Therefore, it is crucial to take the gospel of Jesus Christ seriously, even in one's youth. Today is the perfect time to embrace salvation.

Hell is as terrible as heaven is wonderful.

FREQUENTLY ASKED QUESTIONS
Doesn't 1 Peter 3:18-19 imply a second chance?

This passage says that after Christ died, "he went and proclaimed to the spirits in prison." This does not refer to the wicked dead hearing the gospel again. Many Bible scholars suggest that these spirits are the fallen angels referred to in Genesis 6:1-6 who defied God's authority and engaged in forbidden sexual relations with human women in the days of Noah.

In 1 Peter 3:18-19, the Greek word for "proclaimed" (*kerusso*) does not refer to the proclamation of the gospel, but to a proclamation of victory. This passage may imply that the powers of darkness thought they had destroyed Jesus at His crucifixion, but that God turned the tables on them by raising Him from the dead, and that Jesus Himself proclaimed their doom. If this interpretation is correct, the verse has nothing to do with the concept of a "second chance."

Another interpretation is that between His death and resurrection, Jesus went to the place of the dead and proclaimed a message to the wicked contemporaries of Noah (since the context includes mention of the "days of Noah"). However, the proclamation was not a gospel message but a declaration of victory.

Still another interpretation is that this passage portrays Christ making a proclamation through the person of Noah to those who, because they rejected his message, died in the flood, and are now (at the time of Peter's writing) spirits in prison (compare with 1 Peter 1:11; 2 Peter 2:5). These imprisoned spirits await final judgment.

Regardless of which of the above interpretations is correct, Bible scholars unanimously agree that this passage does not teach that people can hear and respond to the gospel in the next life (see 2 Corinthians 6:2; Hebrews 9:27).

Doesn't 1 Peter 4:6 imply a second chance?

First Peter 4:6 says, "For this is why the gospel was preached even to those who are dead, that though judged in the flesh the way people are, they might live in the spirit the way God does." Bible scholars suggest that perhaps the best way to interpret this problematic verse is that it refers to those who are *now* dead but who heard the gospel *while they were still alive*. This makes sense in light of the tenses used: the gospel "was" preached (*in the past*) to those who "are" dead (*in the present*). Seen in this light, the verse does not teach a second chance for the wicked dead.

CROSS-REFERENCES
Lake of Fire

Beast and False Prophet thrown in—Revelation 19:20

Death and Hades thrown in—Revelation 20:14

Devil thrown in—Revelation 20:10

Eternal fire—Matthew 18:8

Eternal punishment—Matthew 25:46

Everlasting destruction—2 Thessalonians 1:8-9

Fiery furnace—Matthew 13:42

Fiery lake of burning sulfur—Revelation 19:20

Gloomy dungeons—2 Peter 2:4

God's "wrath is poured out like fire"—Nahum 1:6; see Deuteronomy 4:24; Jeremiah 4:4

Lake of fire—Revelation 20:13-15

Not part of God's original creation—Matthew 25:41

Second death—Revelation 20:14

Sinners thrown in—Revelation 21:8

Those not in book of life thrown in—Revelation 20:15

Torment—Luke 16:23

Unquenchable fire—Mark 9:47

Weeping and gnashing of teeth—Matthew 13:42

PART 14

The Eternal State for Believers:
All Things Made New

IN THIS SECTION

51—The Majestic New Heavens—the Pristine New Earth—418

52—The Resplendently Glorious New Jerusalem—424

51

The Majestic New Heavens—
the Pristine New Earth

The earth in its current state is not fit for the eternal habitation of God's redeemed. We recall that after Adam and Eve sinned against God, God cursed the earth in judgment (Genesis 3:17-18). The universe was "subjected to futility" and is now in "bondage to corruption" (Romans 8:20-22).

Before the eternal kingdom can be established, God must deal with this cursed earth and universe. A related defilement is that Satan has long carried out his evil plans on earth (see Ephesians 2:2), and therefore the earth must be cleansed of all stains resulting from his prolonged presence here. No trace of his former presence must remain.

In short, the earth, along with the first and second heavens—that is, the earth's atmosphere (Job 35:5) and the starry universe (Genesis 1:17; Deuteronomy 17:3)—must be renewed. The old must give way to the new. The polluted must give way to the pure.

A RENEWED UNIVERSE—A TWO-STEP PROCESS:

> First, God must destroy the old.

> Second, He must create the new.

Scripture often speaks of the passing of the old heavens and earth. For example, Psalm 102:25-26 speaks of the earth and the starry universe: "Of old you [O God] laid the foundation of the earth, and the heavens are the work of your hands. They will perish, but you will remain; they will all wear out like a garment. You will change them like a robe, and they will pass away" (insert added for clarification).

God also tells us, "Lift up your eyes to the heavens, and look at the earth beneath; for the heavens vanish like smoke, the earth will wear out like a garment...but my salvation will be forever" (Isaiah 51:6). This reminds us of Jesus' words in Matthew 24:35: "Heaven and earth will pass away, but my words will not pass away."

Peter describes the passing away of the old heavens and earth in his second letter:

> The heavens and earth that now exist are stored up for fire, being kept until the day of judgment and destruction of the ungodly. But do not overlook this one fact, beloved, that with the Lord one day is as a thousand years, and a thousand years as one day. The Lord is not slow to fulfill his promise as some count slowness, but is patient toward you, not wishing that any should perish, but that all should reach repentance. But the day of the Lord will come like a thief, and then the heavens will pass away with a roar, and the heavenly bodies will be burned up and dissolved, and the earth and the works that are done on it will be exposed. Since all these things are thus to be dissolved, what sort of people ought you to be in lives of holiness and godliness, waiting for and hastening the coming of the day of God, because of which the heavens will be set on fire and dissolved, and the heavenly bodies will melt as they burn! But according to his promise we are waiting for new heavens and a new earth in which righteousness dwells (2 Peter 3:7-13).

Again, the old must pass away to make room for the new. That which is polluted and corrupt must give way to that which will be completely pure and eternal. *A new world is coming!*

God Creates a New Heaven and a New Earth

After God cleanses the universe with fire, He will create a new heaven and a new earth. All traces of the curse and Satan's presence will be completely and forever removed from all creation.

> *"The earth will be no more cursed, and will produce no more thorns and thistles; man will be no more compelled to earn his bread by the sweat of his brow; woman will be no more doomed to bear the sufferings which she does now; and the abodes of the blessed will be no more cursed by sickness, sorrow, tears, and death."*
>
> —Albert Barnes[1]

All things will be made new, and how blessed it will be!

Heaven Will Be Expanded

We can theologically infer that there will be a difference between the present heaven, where God now dwells and where believers go upon the moment of death (2 Corinthians 5:8; Philippians 1:21-23), and the future heaven, where believers will spend all eternity (2 Peter 3:13; Revelation 21:1). I say this because a renovation is coming that will expand the parameters of heaven.

> *"In the consummation of all things, God will renovate the heavens and the earth, merging His heaven with a new universe for a perfect dwelling-place that will be our home forever. In other words, heaven, the realm where God dwells, will expand to encompass the entire universe of creation, which will be fashioned into a perfect and glorious domain fit for the glory of heaven."*
>
> —John MacArthur[2]

This means that you and I can look forward to living eternally in a glorious kingdom where both heaven and earth are united in a glory that is beyond the imagination of the finite human brain. As wonderful as you can imagine heaven to be, *it will be even better*!

The prophecy of Isaiah 65:17 will be fulfilled as God promises: "Behold, I create new heavens and a new earth, and the former things shall not be remembered or come into mind."

The prophecy of Revelation 21:1, 5 will be fulfilled: "Then I saw a new heaven and a new earth, for the first heaven and the first earth had passed away, and the sea was no more...And he who was seated on the throne said, 'Behold, I am making all things new.' Also he said, 'Write this down, for these words are trustworthy and true.'"

The Universe Will Be Renewed

There will be continuity between the present universe and the heavenly universe. That is, the new heavens and new earth will be this *present* universe—only it will be cleansed of all evil, sin, suffering, and death. The Greek word used to describe the newness of the cosmos is not *neos*, but *kainos*. *Neos* means "new in time" or "new in origin." But *kainos* means "new in nature" or "new in quality." Therefore, the phrase "new heavens and a new earth" does not refer to a cosmos that is completely different from the present cosmos. Rather, the new cosmos will be in continuity with the present cosmos, but it will be completely renewed and renovated. *There is literally a new world (and a new cosmos) coming.*

> "It is the same heaven and earth, but gloriously rejuvenated, with no weeds, thorns, or thistles."
>
> —William Hendrickson[3]

> "The picture is of the universe transformed, perfected, purged of everything that is evil and that exalts itself against God. It is 'new,' not in the sense of being a new creation, but of being new in character—a worthy milieu for the residents of God's redeemed people."
>
> —J. Oswald Sanders[4]

This means that a resurrected people will live in a resurrected universe!

> "What happens to our bodies and what happens to the creation go together. And what happens to our bodies is not annihilation but redemption...Our bodies will be redeemed, restored, made new, not thrown away. And so it is with the heavens and the earth."
>
> —John Piper[5]

Matthew 19:28 therefore speaks of "the regeneration" (NASB; see also Isaiah 65:18-25; Ezekiel 28:25-26; 34:25-30). The phrase "the regeneration" is translated variously in different Bible translations. The NIV renders it "the renewal of all things." The NLT renders it to say that the "world is made new." The Amplified Bible refers to "the renewal [that is, the Messianic restoration and regeneration of all things]." *A new day is coming!*

The new heavens and earth, like our newness in Christ, will be regenerated, glorified, free from the curse of sin, and eternal. Our planet—indeed, the entire universe—will be put in the crucible, transformed, changed, and made new to last forever.

The new earth, as a renewed and eternal earth, will be adapted to the vast moral and physical changes that the eternal state requires. All things are new in the eternal state. Everything will be according to God's own glorious nature. The new heavens and the new earth will be brought into blessed conformity with all that God is—in a state of fixed bliss and absolute perfection.

FREQUENTLY ASKED QUESTIONS
What are the three heavens mentioned in Scripture?

The Scriptures speak of three heavens:

- The first heaven is the earth's atmosphere (Job 35:5).

- The second heaven is the starry universe (Genesis 1:17; Deuteronomy 17:3).

- The third heaven is the ineffable and glorious dwelling place of God in all His glory (2 Corinthians 12:2). This third heaven is elsewhere called the "highest heaven" (1 Kings 8:27; 2 Chronicles 2:6).

Which of the three heavens will be renewed?

Only the first and second heavens have been adversely affected by the fall of humankind. The entire physical universe is deteriorating, so it will be renewed. The perfect and glorious dwelling place of God, the third heaven, remains untouched by human sin. It needs no renewal. The only change that will occur is that heaven will be expanded to include the new heavens (earth's atmosphere and the starry universe) and the new earth.

SOMETHING TO THINK ABOUT:

Go outside on a clear night and look straight up. Are you impressed with the starry universe? Christ created it all (John 1:3; Colossians 1:16). He's a great designer, isn't He? But you haven't seen anything yet. Christ will one day create new heavens and a new earth—as well as the eternal city called the New Jerusalem (Revelation 21). All of this is part and parcel of "what no eye has seen, nor ear heard, nor the heart of man imagined, what God has prepared for those who love him" (1 Corinthians 2:9). It will be incredible!

CROSS-REFERENCES

New Heavens and New Earth

A "regeneration" is coming—Matthew 19:28

Believers will see God face to face—Revelation 22:4

Earth and heaven doomed to destruction—2 Peter 3:10-14

Earth now subject to futility—Romans 8:20

First heaven and earth pass away; new heaven and new earth—Revelation 21:1-4; see also Psalm 102:25-26; Isaiah 51:6; Matthew 5:18; 24:35; Hebrews 1:10-12; 2 Peter 3:7-13

God makes all things new—Revelation 21:5

God will wipe away every tear, abolish death—Revelation 21:3-4

New heavens, new earth—Isaiah 65:17; 66:22; Matthew 19:28; Acts 3:21; Romans 8:18-22; 1 Corinthians 15:22-28; Ephesians 1:9-10; 2 Peter 3:13; Revelation 21:1-8

New Jerusalem coming down out of heaven—Revelation 21:2

New Jerusalem indescribably beautiful—Revelation 21:9-11

No more curses—Revelation 22:3

No more death, crying, or pain—Revelation 21:1

Physical world to perish—Hebrews 1:10-12

Present earth/heaven fled away, destroyed—Revelation 20:11

Restoration of all things—Acts 3:21

Saints will see the face of God—Revelation 22:45

Satan and sinners quarantined—Revelation 20:10

Will reflect the glory of God—Isaiah 65:17-25

52

The Resplendently Glorious
New Jerusalem

Jesus told His followers that He would "prepare a place" for them in the Father's house in heaven (John 14:1-3). That "place" is the New Jerusalem. We find a detailed description of the New Jerusalem—the heavenly city—in Revelation 21:2-25:

> I saw the holy city, new Jerusalem, coming down out of heaven from God...And I heard a loud voice from the throne saying, "Behold, the dwelling place of God is with man. He will dwell with them, and they will be his people, and God himself will be with them as their God. He will wipe away every tear from their eyes, and death shall be no more, neither shall there be mourning, nor crying, nor pain anymore, for the former things have passed away."

> And he who was seated on the throne said, "Behold, I am making all things new." Also he said, "Write this down, for these words are trustworthy and true." And he said to me, "It is done! I am the Alpha and the Omega, the beginning and the end. To the thirsty I will give from the spring of the water of life without payment...

> Then came one of the seven angels who...spoke to me, saying, "Come, I will show you the Bride, the wife of the Lamb." And he carried me away in the Spirit to a great, high mountain, and showed me the holy city Jerusalem coming down out of heaven from God, having the glory of God, its radiance like a most rare jewel, like a jasper, clear as crystal. It had a great, high wall, with twelve gates, and at the gates twelve angels, and on the gates the names of the twelve tribes of the sons of Israel were

inscribed—on the east three gates, on the north three gates, on the south three gates, and on the west three gates. And the wall of the city had twelve foundations, and on them were the twelve names of the twelve apostles of the Lamb...

The city lies foursquare, its length the same as its width...12,000 stadia. Its length and width and height are equal...The wall was built of jasper, while the city was pure gold, like clear glass. The foundations of the wall of the city were adorned with every kind of jewel. The first was jasper, the second sapphire, the third agate, the fourth emerald, the fifth onyx, the sixth carnelian, the seventh chrysolite, the eighth beryl, the ninth topaz, the tenth chrysoprase, the eleventh jacinth, the twelfth amethyst. And the twelve gates were twelve pearls, each of the gates made of a single pearl, and the street of the city was pure gold, like transparent glass...

The city has no need of sun or moon to shine on it, for the glory of God gives it light, and its lamp is the Lamb...Its gates will never be shut by day—and there will be no night there... Nothing unclean will ever enter it, nor anyone who does what is detestable or false, but only those who are written in the Lamb's book of life.

This description is astonishing. A scene of such transcendent magnificence is presented to our astonished gaze in Revelation 21 that the human mind can scarcely comprehend it. It is a scene of ecstatic joy and fellowship between sinless angels and redeemed, glorified human beings. The voice of the One identified as the Alpha and the Omega, the beginning and the end, utters a climactic declaration: "Behold, I am making all things new" (Revelation 21:5).

Wonderful as this description of the New Jerusalem is, these words undoubtedly represent a human attempt to describe the utterly indescribable.

"The overall impression of the city as a gigantic brilliant jewel compared to jasper, clear as crystal, indicates its great beauty. John was trying to describe what he saw and to relate it to what might be familiar to his readers. However, it is evident that his revelation transcends anything that can be experienced."

—John F. Walvoord[1]

"Images suggesting immense size or brilliant light depict heaven as a place of unimaginable splendor, greatness, excellence, and beauty...It is likely that while John's vision employs as metaphors those items which we think of as being most valuable and beautiful, the actual splendor of heaven far exceeds anything that we have yet experienced."

—Millard Erickson[2]

"However wonderful it might be to imagine these things, earthly images are not really adequate...These biblical images...are 'very faint shadows' that represent the joys of heaven humans are intended to enjoy."

—Jonathan Edwards[3]

SOMETHING WONDERFUL

> Think of the glory of God in close proximity to the holy city.

> The mention of transparency in Revelation 21 reveals that the city is strategically designed to transmit the glory of God in the form of light without hindrance.

> The human imagination is simply incapable of fathoming the immeasurably brilliant glory of God that will be eternally manifested in the eternal city.

> This is especially true when you consider that all kinds of precious stones will be built into the eternal city.

The New Jerusalem Is Perfect in Every Way

You and I are at a disadvantage right now. We have a faulty perception. What I mean is that we are so accustomed to living in a fallen world marked by sin and corruption that it's hard for us to imagine a perfect heavenly habitat where there is no sin or fallenness. From birth to death, we are confronted with imperfection on every level. But in the eternal city, we will experience nothing but perfection.

> There shall be no more curse—*perfect restoration.*

> The throne of God and of the Lamb shall be in it—*perfect administration.*

> His servants shall serve him—*perfect subordination.*

> And they shall see his face—*perfect transformation.*

> And his name shall be on their foreheads—*perfect identification.*

> And there shall be no night there; and they need no candle, neither light of the sun; for the Lord giveth them light—*perfect illumination.*

> And they shall reign forever and ever—*perfect exultation.*

—A.T. Pierson[4]

The New Jerusalem Is Huge

The length and width and height of the New Jerusalem measure 12,000 stadia. This means that the heavenly city measures approximately 1,500 miles by 1,500 miles by 1,500 miles. Although some interpret these large numbers symbolically, ostensibly representing the idea that "saved people are never overcrowded," I believe the dimensions are meant to be interpreted literally. The eternal city is so large that it would measure approximately the distance from Canada to Mexico and from the Atlantic Ocean to the Rocky Mountains. This is an area of 2,250,000 square miles. For comparison, London is only 621 square miles. So the ground area of the eternal city will be 15,000 times the area of London.

The eternal city is so large that it would extend from the surface of the earth to about one-twentieth of the way to the moon. If the city has stories, each being twelve feet high, then the city would have 600,000 stories. *That is huge!*

Someone has calculated that if this structure is cube-shaped, it would allow for 20 billion residents, each having their own private 75-acre cube.[5] If each residence were smaller, there would be room for one-hundred-thousand-billion people. Even then, there is still plenty of room for parks, roads, and other things you would see in a normal city.

I know what you're thinking: *This city is so big, it might be hard to get around.* I don't think that will be a problem. It might be hard to get around in this city with your current earthly body, which is aging and wearing out, but it won't be a problem with your resurrected/glorified body. In fact, your resurrected/glorified body will have eternal youthful endurance that will never wear out.

FAST FACTS ON THE SHAPE OF THE NEW JERUSALEM

- The eternal city could be shaped as either a giant cube or a giant pyramid.
- There are good Christian scholars on both sides of this debate.
- Some prefer to see it as pyramid-shaped, because that would explain how the river of the water of life could flow down its sides, as described in Revelation 22:1-2.
- Others prefer to see it as a cube, for the Holy of Holies in Solomon's temple was cube-shaped (1 Kings 6:20), and thus a cubic shape of the New Jerusalem could be intended to convey that this eternal city could be compared to a Holy of Holies for all eternity.

The New Jerusalem Has High Walls and Open Gates

Revelation 21:12 tells us that the New Jerusalem has "a great, high wall, with twelve gates, and at the gates twelve angels, and on the gates the names of the twelve tribes of the sons of Israel were inscribed." Moreover, we are told, "the wall of the city had twelve foundations, and on them were the twelve names of the twelve apostles of the Lamb" (Revelation 21:14).

I CAN ONLY IMAGINE...

> Perhaps the angels are stationed at each of the 12 gates both as guardians and as ministering spirits to the heirs of salvation (Hebrews 1:14).

> Perhaps the names of the 12 tribes of Israel are inscribed on the gates as a reminder that "salvation is from the Jews" (John 4:22).

> Perhaps the names of the apostles appear on the foundations to remind us that the church was built on these men of God (Ephesians 2:20).

YOU MAY BE INTERESTED TO KNOW...
John's Name Was Written on the Foundation of the Eternal City

> ➤ John, the author of Revelation, was an apostle.

> ➤ This means that when he wrote Revelation 21:14, he would have realized that his own name was written on the foundation of the eternal city.

> ➤ He must have been thrilled beyond words, but also deeply humbled.

FAST FACTS ON OPEN GATES

- Our text says of the eternal city that "its gates will never be shut by day—and there will be no night there" (Revelation 21:25).
- In ancient times, it was necessary to lock the gates of cities at night, lest the city be overrun by evil invaders during the night.
- The gates were part of the city's security.
- In the eternal city, however, there will never be an outside threat to those who dwell therein.
- Satan, demons, and unbelievers will be in eternal quarantine in hell.
- Moreover, God Himself will dwell in the city. Who would dare to attack it?

Three Blessings in the New Jerusalem
1. The River of the Water of Life:

- In his vision, John witnessed "the river of the water of life, bright as crystal, flowing from the throne of God and of the Lamb through the middle of the street of the city" (Revelation 22:1).
- This pure river of life, though real and material, may also be symbolic of the abundance of spiritual life that will characterize those who live in the eternal city.

- The "flowing" river seems to symbolize the continual outpouring of spiritual blessings to all the redeemed of all ages, who now bask in the full glory of eternal life.

2. The Tree of Life:

- The last time we read about the tree of life was in Genesis 3, where Adam and Eve sinned in the Garden of Eden. Paradise was lost.
- Now, in the book of Revelation, paradise is restored, and we again witness the tree of life in the glorious eternal state (Revelation 22:2).

3. The Healing Leaves:

- The leaves of the tree are for the healing of the nations.
- The Greek word for "healing" is *therapeia*. We derive the English word *therapeutic* from this word.
- The word carries the idea of "health-giving."
- The leaves of the tree are spiritually health-giving.

FAST FACTS ON KEEPING THE LIGHTS ON IN THE ETERNAL CITY

- Revelation 21:23 tells us that "the city has no need of sun or moon to shine on it, for the glory of God gives it light, and its lamp is the Lamb."
- This is consistent with the prophecy of Isaiah 60:19: "The sun shall be no more your light by day, nor for brightness shall the moon give you light; but the LORD will be your everlasting light, and your God will be your glory."

> "In that city which Christ has prepared for His own there will be no created light, simply because Christ Himself, who is the uncreated light (John 8:12), will be there...The created lights of God and of men are as darkness when compared with our Blessed Lord. The light He defuses throughout eternity is the unclouded, undimmed glory of His own Holy presence. In consequence of the fullness of that light, there shall be no night."
>
> —Lehman Strauss[6]

FREQUENTLY ASKED QUESTIONS

How is the New Jerusalem different from earthly cities?

The New Jerusalem is better in every way:

- Earthly cities constantly need to be rebuilt or repaired, but the New Jerusalem will never need to be repaired.

- Believers and unbelievers live in earthly cities, but only believers will be in the eternal city.

- Many people go hungry and thirsty in earthly cities, but no one will go hungry or thirsty in the New Jerusalem.

- Earthly cities have crime, but the eternal city has perfect righteousness.

- Earthly cities often have outbreaks of rebellion, but there is no such rebellion in the heavenly city. All are in submission to the divine King, Jesus Christ.

- People in earthly cities have many broken relationships, but all relationships in the New Jerusalem are perfect and loving.

- Widespread sickness is common in earthly cities, but perfect health prevails in the New Jerusalem.

- Earthly cities have cemeteries, but the eternal city has none. (Death will be completely foreign to our experience in heaven.)

- Earthly cities go dark at night, but the eternal city is always illuminated.

Clearly, our existence in heaven will be completely different from our experience on earth. The eternal city, the New Jerusalem, will be absolutely wonderful, far more so than any human mind can fathom or even begin to imagine (1 Corinthians 2:9).

What kinds of things will never be found in the heavenly environment of the New Jerusalem?

In heaven we will have resurrection bodies with no sin nature. Satan and demons will be eternally quarantined away from our presence forever. And we will live in a perfectly holy environment. A natural consequence of this wondrous state of affairs is that there are many things that will be foreign to our heavenly experience. The following are just a few:

- We will never have to confess sin. (There is no sin to confess in heaven.)
- We will never feel guilt or shame for any action. (Again, there is no sin in heaven that would cause guilt.)
- We will never have to repair our houses or other things. (Nothing runs down in heaven.)
- We will never need to defend ourselves against others. (Relationships will be perfect in every way in heaven.)
- We will never have to apologize. (Again, all relationships will be perfect in heaven. Our actions will be focused on others, not on ourselves.)
- We will never feel isolated or alone. (There will be a perfect expression of love between all the redeemed in heaven.)
- We will never need rehabilitation. (We will remain whole and healthy for all eternity. There will never be addictions of any kind.)
- We will never be depressed or discouraged. (We will enjoy the abundant life of heaven forever.)
- We will never be tired or worn out in heaven. (Our resurrection bodies will be strong and never need rest.)
- There will never be any offense (given or received) in heaven. (All our words will be free from sin and full of grace.)

- We will never experience envy or jealousy in heaven. (Our love for others will be perfect, without unwholesome emotions.)

- We will never again lust after another person. (Our hearts will be pure, without any sin.)

- We will never have misunderstandings with other people. (No relationships will ever be broken in heaven.)

- We will never feel a sense of want. We will never have to earn money or worry about having enough money to survive. (We will have an abundance of everything we need in heaven.)

- There will be no wars or bloodshed in heaven. (The sinful attitudes that cause wars will not exist in heaven.)

CROSS-REFERENCES

New Jerusalem

Christ is building—John 14:1-3
Is always illuminated—Revelation 22:5
Measures 1,500 by 1,500 by 1,500 miles—Revelation 21:16
River of water of life flowing down sides—Revelation 22:1-2
Twelve foundations with the names of 12 apostles—Revelation 21:14
Twelve gates, with 12 angels at the gates—Revelation 21:12

PART 15

Living in the Light of Bible Prophecy

IN THIS SECTION

53——Living Expectantly—436

54——Living Righteously—444

55——Living with an Eternal Perspective—452

53

Living Expectantly

God doesn't give us prophecy just to give us a glimpse of the future. He also gives us prophecy because it can shape the way we live. Based on decades of studying prophecy, I have identified three key areas where prophecy can have a significant impact on our lives:

1. Prophecy inspires us to live with a sense of hopeful anticipation.
2. Prophecy inspires us to walk in the way of righteousness.
3. Prophecy inspires us to live daily with an eternal perspective.

Living with a Sense of Hopeful Anticipation

Here's the "big picture" of our future hope:

> The rapture is an event that could happen at any moment—it is imminent.

> After the rapture or after the moment of our death, whichever comes first, we will find ourselves in the direct presence of Christ in heaven.

> Our resurrected bodies will be extraordinary—free from sickness, aging, and death.

Let's delve deeper into these awe-inspiring revelations.

1. The Rapture Is an Imminent Event

As mentioned earlier in this book, the term *imminent* signifies "ready to occur" or "impending." The apostle Paul tells us that our "salvation is nearer to us now than when we first believed" because the rapture is imminent (Romans 13:11-12). It could happen at any time. Every day that passes brings Christians one step closer to this glorious event.

This inspired Paul to declare that we eagerly "wait for the revealing of our

Lord Jesus Christ" (1 Corinthians 1:7; Philippians 3:20; see also Hebrews 9:28). Indeed, "the Lord is at hand" (Philippians 4:5). We "wait for his Son from heaven…who delivers us from the wrath to come" (1 Thessalonians 1:10). Our lives are filled with the eager anticipation of the rapture.

Remember, the rapture is a signless event. There are no prophecies that must be fulfilled before it takes place. In stark contrast, Christ's second coming is heralded by a seven-year sequence of prophetic signs during the tribulation period (Revelation 4–18).

Embrace each day with the exhilarating thought that the rapture could happen at any moment.

THE RAPTURE IS IMMINENT

The coming of the Lord is at hand	James 5:8
The Judge is standing at the door	James 5:9
The Lord is at hand	Philippians 4:5
The Lord is coming quickly	Revelation 3:11; 22:7, 12, 17, 20
Salvation is nearer now than when we first believed	Romans 13:11-12
We await God's Son	1 Thessalonians 1:10
We await our great God and Savior	Titus 2:13
We await the mercy of the Lord Jesus Christ	Jude 21
We await the revealing of the Lord	1 Corinthians 1:7
We await the revelation of Jesus Christ	1 Peter 1:13
We await the Savior	Philippians 3:20
We eagerly await Him	Hebrews 9:28

2. Following the Rapture—or Death, if It Comes First— We Will Be with Christ in Heaven

There is a duality of being in every human being—a tangible, material side, and an intangible, immaterial side. The material part of a human being is the body (Genesis 2:7; 3:19). The immaterial part is the soul or the spirit. The words "soul" and "spirit" are interchangeable in Scripture. I say this because Scripture refers to the entire immaterial part of a person as "soul" in 1 Peter 2:11 and as "spirit" in James 2:26. We can theologically infer that these terms both refer to the immaterial nature of a person.

At the moment of one's last breath, the human spirit or soul effortlessly separates from the physical body, much like a hand slipping out of a glove (Genesis 35:18; 2 Corinthians 5:8; Philippians 1:21-23). When this happens, the "clothing" of the body is no longer on the spirit, resulting in a feeling of "nakedness" (2 Corinthians 5:1-4). This clothing of the body is left on earth as the Christian's spirit or soul ascends to heaven. (Do not be concerned: This feeling of "nakedness" is only temporary; we will receive resurrection bodies in the future. More on this shortly.)

Numerous scriptures describe the departure of the soul from the body at the moment of death, with Ecclesiastes 12:7 being a prime example. This verse teaches us that at death, "the spirit returns to God who gave it." A clear illustration of this can be found in the crucifixion of Jesus. As He faced His final moments on the cross, He uttered this prayer to His heavenly Father: "Father, into your hands I commit my spirit" (Luke 23:46). Jesus knew that His physical body was about to die. And He knew that when that happened, His spirit would leave the body. He entrusted that spirit to the care of the Father.

We find another example in Stephen, who was a firm believer in the Lord Jesus. In the face of hostile Jewish opponents, Stephen courageously refused to abandon his commitment to Jesus, despite the deadly rain of stones that threatened his life. As the end approached, he uttered a simple prayer: "Lord Jesus, receive my spirit" (Acts 7:59). Stephen knew that his physical body was dying. But he also knew that his spirit would survive death and leave his body at that very moment. He committed his spirit to the care of Jesus.

Paul affirmed that he had no fear of death because the spirit leaves the body and goes directly to be with Jesus at the moment of death: "We are of good courage, and we would rather be away from the body and at home with the Lord" (2 Corinthians 5:8).

Paul also rejoiced: "My desire is to depart and be with Christ, for that is far better" (Philippians 1:23). In the original Greek, the word *depart* has the sense of being released from bondage. During our time on earth, we often find ourselves bound by the cares and challenges of life. However, at the point of death, these bonds are broken, allowing us to experience true emancipation as we enter the heavenly realm. When our spirit separates from the mortal body at the final moment of earthly life, it is immediately welcomed into the divine presence of the Lord, and we are free from bondage.

The idea of death often instills a sense of fear and dread in many people. For Christians, however, death serves as a mere passageway to paradise or heaven. As we look back at the apostle Paul's ministry, we witness his extraordinary experience of being "caught up to the third heaven," referred to as "paradise" (2 Corinthians 12:2-3). He was given a glimpse of what awaits him in the afterlife. With this knowledge, Paul faced death confidently and without fear, for he knew exactly where his journey would take him!

What an incredible experience Paul must have had in heaven. The Bible says that while he was there, Paul "heard things that cannot be told, which man may not utter" (2 Corinthians 12:4). This paradise of God is apparently so resplendently glorious, so wondrous, that God forbade Paul to say anything about it to living people still in the earthly realm. This makes me wonder what exactly Paul saw and heard in heaven that was so amazing. Perhaps this explains why Paul was so anxious to get back there (Philippians 1:21-23). And maybe it explains why Paul affirmed that "no eye has seen, nor ear heard, nor the heart of man imagined, what God has prepared for those who love him" (1 Corinthians 2:9). Paul was a firsthand eyewitness to heaven. He saw with his own eyes that paradise is indescribably glorious. This means that we can live with a strong sense of expectation. We can look forward to what God has in store for us in heaven.

Death is not to be feared. To be absent from the body is to be at home with the Lord.

DESCRIPTIONS OF OUR HEAVENLY HABITAT

Description	Meaning	Scripture
Heavenly Country	A country full of light, glory, splendor, and love.	Hebrews 11:13-15
Holy City	A city of purity, without sin.	Revelation 21:1-2
Home of Righteousness	A perfect environment of righteousness.	2 Peter 3:13

Kingdom of Light	A kingdom of Christ, who is the light of the world (John 8:12).	Colossians 1:12
Paradise of God	A paradise of joy and delight.	Revelation 2:7
New Jerusalem	This will be the capital of heaven.	Revelation 21:12-14

CROSS-REFERENCES
The Spirit Departs the Body
At death, Jesus committed His spirit to the Father—Luke 23:46
At death, Stephen prayed for Jesus to receive his spirit—Acts 7:59
Away from the body; at home with the Lord—2 Corinthians 5:8
Better to depart and be with Christ—Philippians 1:21-24
Immaterial part separates from material part—Genesis 35:18; John 19:30
In paradise—Luke 23:43
Souls under God's altar—Revelation 6:9-10
Spirit returns to God who gave it—Ecclesiastes 12:7

3. We Will Be Resurrected with Awesome Bodies

The apostle Paul had a remarkable gift for teaching. His unique ability to craft vivid word pictures helped Christians to grasp complex spiritual concepts with ease. One example of this is how he describes the death of our mortal bodies and our subsequent resurrection: "Our earthly bodies are planted in the ground when we die, but they will be raised to live forever. Our bodies are buried in brokenness, but they will be raised in glory. They are buried in weakness, but they will be raised in strength" (1 Corinthians 15:42-43 NLT).

These expressions are full of depth and meaning. Much like planting a seed in the ground, our mortal bodies are symbolically "sown" when they're placed in the ground. In time, our bodies decay and turn to dust. But this is far from the final chapter. The day will come when our bodies undergo a remarkable physical resurrection!

Our present bodies are characterized by brokenness. As we journey through life, we relentlessly fight off threatening infections and do everything in our power to maintain our health. However, the harsh reality remains—we will all succumb to sickness at some point. And as the sands of time slip away, so too does our finite existence.

In contrast to this dismal state of affairs, our resurrection bodies will be glorious and imperishable. All susceptibility to disease and mortality will cease to exist. We will no longer be haunted by the fear of infection or the inevitability of death.

What does Paul mean when he says that our present bodies are "buried in weakness"? As the sands of time slip through our fingers, our once youthful vigor wanes, disease creeps upon us, and the inevitable embrace of old age leaves us with wrinkles and weakness. In the twilight of our lives, we may find ourselves helpless, struggling to perform even the most mundane tasks. But again, this is not the end of the story.

Our dead bodies "will be raised in strength." We will be eternally free from the merciless grasp of aging, decay, and death. Our resurrected bodies will be full of vigor, forever banishing the lament, "I'm too tired." We will stride and leap with newfound zeal, our health and vitality never faltering or diminishing.

Imagine a body that no longer suffers from cholesterol buildup, heart disease, kidney failure, diabetes, or blindness and deafness. Imagine yourself with ageless, wrinkle-free skin, experiencing eternal youth, filled with boundless vitality and energy. The very thought of this extraordinary existence is breathtaking!

FAST FACTS ON THE RESURRECTION BODY BEING STURDY AS A BUILDING

- Paul came up with another incredible word picture.
- He compared our present earthly bodies to mere tents and our eternal resurrection bodies to sturdy buildings (2 Corinthians 5:1-4).
- The temporary tabernacle of Israel's nomadic wanderings in the wilderness was a huge tent-like structure that was later replaced by a sturdy stone temple upon their arrival in the Promised Land.
- Paul skillfully uses the stark contrast between the transient tabernacle and the permanent stone temple to emphasize the amazing difference between our present mortal bodies and our future resurrected bodies.
- If Paul were speaking to people in our modern world today, he would probably illustrate this comparison with a towering skyscraper next to a humble camping tent.

The impermanent "tent" (our mortal body) that we currently inhabit is destined to succumb to death. But it will be replaced by an eternal body which Paul likens to a solid, sturdy building (1 Corinthians 15:42, 53-54). How can we not be excited by this prospect? Let us embrace life with a heightened sense of anticipation, knowing that what awaits us in the afterlife is beyond our wildest dreams.

As we age, we all eventually experience increasing weakness, nagging backaches, nagging joint pains, and other physical symptoms. It is through the ongoing process of aging that God increasingly instills in us a longing for this ultimate physical transformation! God uses our aging experiences to gently shift our attention from this world to the things of heaven.

FREQUENTLY ASKED QUESTION
Will our pets be in heaven?

It is possible. I say this because the *whole creation* is destined to be redeemed through the work of Christ. Romans 8:21 tells us that "the creation itself will be set free from its bondage to corruption and obtain the freedom of the glory of the children of God." Since our animals are a part of "the creation" that will be "set free from its bondage to corruption," some theologians reason that perhaps our pets will be in heaven.

CROSS-REFERENCES
Our Coming Resurrection

Believers will be resurrected—Job 19:25-27; Psalm 49:15; Isaiah 26:19; John 6:39-40, 44, 54; 1 Corinthians 6:14; 1 Thessalonians 4:13-17; Revelation 20:4-6

Eternal bodies made for us by God—2 Corinthians 5:1

Glorious bodies—Philippians 3:21

If Christ is not risen, faith is in vain—1 Corinthians 15:12-21

Jesus is the resurrection and the life—John 11:24-25
Perishable body becomes imperishable—1 Corinthians 15:42
Resurrection will swallow up death—Isaiah 25:8
We will all be changed—1 Corinthians 15:50-52

Living Righteously

We have seen that one life-changing result of studying Bible prophecy is that it ignites in us an exhilarating sense of anticipation for what lies ahead. But it doesn't stop there. The study of prophecy also serves as a powerful catalyst for walking in righteousness and purity in daily life.

Numerous prophetic Bible verses are immediately followed by a call to personal righteousness and purity. Studying these verses can profoundly affect our lives and reshape our actions. Our behavior can be guided by these teachings, as masterfully exemplified in the writings of Paul, Peter, John, and Daniel.

THE LESSONS WE LEARN FROM PAUL

The apostle Paul shows us the important connection between prophecy and purity in Romans 13:11-14:

> You know the time, that the hour has come for you to wake from sleep. For salvation is nearer to us now than when we first believed. The night is far gone; the day is at hand. So then let us cast off the works of darkness and put on the armor of light. Let us walk properly as in the daytime, not in orgies and drunkenness, not in sexual immorality and sensuality, not in quarreling and jealousy. But put on the Lord Jesus Christ, and make no provision for the flesh, to gratify its desires.

Paul is alluding to the rapture of the church in this passage, especially in his affirmation that "salvation is nearer to us now than when we first believed." He teaches that because the rapture is imminent and could occur at any moment, we should strive to purify our lives and zealously pursue righteousness. It is our responsibility to eliminate all traces of sin and embrace the Lord

Jesus Christ wholeheartedly. In essence, we must live our lives as if the rapture could happen today!

THE LESSONS WE LEARN FROM PETER

Like Paul, Peter sheds light on the intimate connection between prophecy and righteousness. As we navigate the rise of the end times, Peter emphasizes the importance of self-control, prayer, cultivating love, offering hospitality to others, and using our spiritual gifts in service to others:

> The end of all things is at hand; therefore be self-controlled and sober-minded for the sake of your prayers. Above all, keep loving one another earnestly, since love covers a multitude of sins. Show hospitality to one another without grumbling. As each has received a gift, use it to serve one another, as good stewards of God's varied grace. (1 Peter 4:7-10)

Peter later admonishes us in 2 Peter 3:10-14:

> The day of the Lord will come like a thief, and then the heavens will pass away with a roar, and the heavenly bodies will be burned up and dissolved, and the earth and the works that are done on it will be exposed.
>
> Since all these things are thus to be dissolved, what sort of people ought you to be in lives of holiness and godliness, waiting for and hastening the coming of the day of God, because of which the heavens will be set on fire and dissolved, and the heavenly bodies will melt as they burn! But according to his promise we are waiting for new heavens and a new earth in which righteousness dwells.
>
> Therefore, beloved, since you are waiting for these, be diligent to be found by him without spot or blemish, and at peace.

In this latter passage, Peter paints a vivid, wide-ranging picture that extends from the day of the Lord—encompassing the tribulation period—all the way to the final establishment of the new heavens and the new earth. With such a glorious future awaiting Christians, Peter exclaims, "What sort of people ought you to be in lives of holiness and godliness!"

THE LESSONS WE LEARN FROM JOHN

John echoes the sentiments of Paul and Peter in emphasizing the connection between prophetic revelation and the pursuit of righteousness:

> Beloved, we are God's children now, and what we will be has not yet appeared; but we know that when he appears we shall be like him, because we shall see him as he is. And everyone who thus hopes in him purifies himself as he is pure (1 John 3:2-3).

John seems to be alluding to the imminent return of Christ at the rapture. Can you imagine the glory of that moment?

> *"The hope of the rapture, when we will meet the Savior, should be a sanctifying force in our lives. We will be made completely like Him then; so we should endeavor with His help to serve Him faithfully now and to lead lives of purity."*
>
> —John F. Walvoord[1]

It is imperative that we seize every moment to live passionately for the Lord. Let us use our time wisely and make every second count.

USE YOUR TIME WISELY

> "Look carefully then how you walk, not as unwise but as wise, making the best use of the time, because the days are evil" (Ephesians 5:15-16).

> "Walk in wisdom toward outsiders, making the best use of the time" (Colossians 4:5).

> "Teach us to number our days that we may get a heart of wisdom" (Psalm 90:12).

> "O Lord, make me know my end and what is the measure of my days; let me know how fleeting I am" (Psalm 39:4).

*God tells us about the **future** so that we can live well in the **present**.*

THE LESSONS WE LEARN FROM DANIEL

Daniel, the author of the biblical book that bears his name, reveals God's prophetic plan not only for the Gentiles (chapters 2–7) but also for Israel (chapters 8–12). His visions delve into the end-times revival of the Roman Empire, the reign of the antichrist, the desecration of a future Jewish temple during the tribulation period, and the relentless persecution of the Jews.

Daniel's awareness of the prophetic future played a crucial role in shaping his life of unwavering integrity. His inspiring story serves as a guiding light for each of us, encouraging us to embrace and live our lives according to prophetic wisdom.

Obedient to God

Daniel's life was marked by unwavering obedience to God. For example, when King Darius decreed that no one should pray to any god but him for a month, Daniel courageously defied the ban. Instead, he chose to worship the one true God and ignored the king's command. As a result, Daniel faced the terrible punishment of being thrown into a den of lions. However, his fierce obedience was rewarded when God intervened and rescued him from certain death (Daniel 6).

Another inspiring example is found in the story of Daniel's three devout friends who stood up to King Nebuchadnezzar. They refused to bow down and worship his golden statue, standing firm in their faith even though they knew it could mean death. As punishment, they were thrown into a fiery furnace; yet remarkably, God protected them in the inferno (Daniel 3).

The unwavering faithfulness of Daniel and his companions is inspiring! Sadly, there seems to be a stark contrast with many contemporary Christians who often choose convenience over commitment when it comes to following God's commands. This tendency to waver and compromise reveals a lack of understanding of what true obedience entails.

Let us recognize that obedience to God is not only necessary, but ultimately beneficial to us in both the short and long term. Throughout Scripture, we see that those who choose to follow God's way will reap bountiful rewards, including:

- Blessing (Luke 11:28)
- Long life (1 Kings 3:14; John 8:51)
- Happiness (Psalms 112:1; 119:56)

- Peace (Proverbs 1:33)
- Well-being (Jeremiah 7:23)

Walking by Faith

Daniel consistently walked by faith and not by sight. A prime example is when the king had Daniel thrown into the lions' den. From the perspective of "walking by sight," death was certain. But Daniel kept faith, and God rewarded that faith by rescuing him from the lions (Daniel 6).

Daniel's three Hebrew friends illustrate the same truth. From a "walking by sight" perspective, being thrown into a fiery furnace is a sure death sentence. But they kept faith, and God rescued them from the fire (Daniel 3).

> As we move further into the prophetic end times, let's follow Daniel's example by walking by faith and not by sight.

> *The following verses will help you:* Psalms 40:4; 118:8; Proverbs 3:5; Jeremiah 17:7; Matthew 15:28; 21:21-22; Luke 17:5-6; Romans 10:17; 2 Corinthians 5:7; 1 Timothy 1:19; Hebrews 10:35; 11:1; 1 Peter 1:7.

A Good Reputation

For Daniel, the relentless pursuit of a spotless reputation was of immense importance, even among the pagans of Babylon. From the first days of his captivity, his reputation shone like a beacon and remained unblemished until his last breath. This extraordinary regard for his character not only earned him audiences with royalty, but also immense respect and admiration.

> As we continue our journey through the prophetic end times, let's commit ourselves to emulating Daniel—a paragon of virtue—by cultivating an excellent reputation among all people.

> *The following verses will help you:* 1 Samuel 2:1-5; 29:3; Psalms 86:2; 87:3; 109:4; Proverbs 22:1; Acts 17:11.

Integrity

Throughout his life, Daniel consistently demonstrated a remarkable sense of integrity (Daniel 1:7-9; 6:10). This unwavering moral strength was evident to everyone he encountered, including the likes of King Nebuchadnezzar and King Darius. Undoubtedly, Daniel would have resonated deeply with the sentiments expressed by Paul in 2 Corinthians 8:21: "We aim at what is honorable not only in the Lord's sight but also in the sight of man."

> ➤ We should all be inspired by Daniel's exemplary lifestyle and embody integrity in our daily lives, especially as we face the end times.

> ➤ *The following verses will help you:* Psalms 25:21; 26:1; Proverb 11:3; 19:1; 20:7; 28:6; Micah 6:8; Acts 24:16; Titus 2:1-14; Hebrews 13:18; James 1:22-25.

Walking in Humility

Daniel was a humble man who constantly focused his attention on God rather than on his own abilities (Daniel 2:27-28). His humble attitude echoed that of John the Baptist, who said of Jesus, "He must increase, but I must decrease" (John 3:30).

Daniel seemed to recognize the divine favor given to those who embrace humility. The Bible affirms this by saying, "Humble yourselves before the Lord, and he will exalt you" (James 4:10; see also Proverbs 15:33; 22:4; 29:23; Luke 1:52; 1 Peter 5:5-6). Throughout his life, Daniel demonstrated humility, and time and again, God exalted and honored him. It is incumbent upon us to follow in Daniel's footsteps and embrace a life of humility.

FREQUENTLY ASKED QUESTION

Is one motivation for walking in righteousness the fact that departed believers are watching our behavior from the balcony of heaven?

Some Christians interpret the reference to "a great crowd of witnesses" in Hebrews 12:1 to mean that Christians look out from the balcony of heaven and observe people and events on earth. They are said to be like "spectators in a great arena" who are "watching our progress." Some Christians see this as a motivation to live righteously.

However, a correct interpretation of Hebrews 12:1 is found by looking at the book's previous chapter, Hebrews 11. The main idea of Hebrews 12:1 is that because we have been preceded by superheroes of the faith (great "witnesses" or "testifiers" that are listed in Hebrews 11—people like Enoch, Noah, and Abraham), we should seek to imitate their behavior and follow their example in righteous, godly conduct. One commentator writes of these witnesses, "This [verse] does not mean that they are spectators of what goes on earth. Rather they witness to us by their lives of faith and endurance and set a high standard for us to duplicate."[2] Therefore, as the writer to the Hebrews exhorts, "Let us throw off everything that hinders and the sin that so easily entangles, and let us run with perseverance the race marked out for us."

Maintaining Christian Unity

In the midst of the turbulence often seen among Christians who hold to different prophetic views (such as pretribulationism, midtribulationism, and posttribulationism), I want to conclude this chapter by emphasizing the importance of unity within the Christian community despite our different perspectives. That's one way we can walk the path of righteousness.

I begin with the observation that while Christians love to debate many of the finer points of Bible prophecy, they do agree on the **big picture**:

> Christ is coming again.
> Christians will receive incredible body upgrades (resurrection bodies).
> Christians will be held accountable in a future judgment for how they lived on earth.
> Christians will live face to face with God forever.
> There will be no more sin, suffering, Satan, or death in heaven.

Despite our differences, I think it is wise to keep the big picture in mind. And as we debate the finer points of Bible prophecy, let's avoid divisive attitudes. Embracing humility, as Daniel did, can help us counteract tendencies toward dogmatism.

It is perfectly acceptable—and even *good*—to be committed to our interpretations of Bible prophecy and even be confident in their accuracy. However, we must refrain from using these nonessential doctrines as standards of orthodoxy or as barriers to Christian fellowship. As someone who is firmly committed to pretribulationism, I count numerous posttribulationists as friends—and I intend to keep it that way. I will continue to love them, despite our disagreements.

FAST FACTS ON AVOIDING A DIVISIVE ATTITUDE

- It's entirely possible to be accurate in your speech and still be offensive in your delivery.

- Jesus was a relentless defender of truth, declaring, "You will know the truth, and the truth will set you free" (John 8:32). However, He also emphasized that love is a defining characteristic of a true Christian (John 13:35), rather than simply upholding the truth.

- A person can be right in what he says and wrong in how he says it.

- As Christians, we must strive to be as compassionate as we are truthful.

- The apostle Paul skillfully captured this balance in his advice to the Ephesians: "Speak the truth in love" (Ephesians 4:15).

- YES—Engage in stimulating debate in a spirit of love.

- NO—Never let it divide us.

Living with an Eternal Perspective

The word *motivation* may be defined as "the reason or reasons one has for acting or behaving in a particular way." One of the most powerful forms of motivation comes from Bible prophecy, which inspires us to live with a sense of hopeful anticipation and to walk the righteous path. This motivation also fuels our desire to focus our attention on eternal matters. Adopting such a perspective requires keeping our eyes fixed on heaven, maintaining an awareness of our mortality, and committing ourselves to living a life that honors God in the face of eternal realities.

Eyes Focused on Heaven

Heaven is not just a concept that concerns our fate after death. Heaven has great significance in our present lives. In fact, thinking about heaven can dramatically change our daily outlook.

A key verse in the Bible that underscores this is Colossians 3:1-2: "If then you have been raised with Christ, seek the things that are above, where Christ is, seated at the right hand of God. Set your minds on things that are above, not on things that are on earth."

This inspiring passage has always resonated with me, especially because of its intensity in the original Greek language. It conveys the idea, "with determination, zeal, and unwavering focus, set your mind on heavenly things."

The Greek text also uses the present tense. This suggests continuous action and conveys the idea: "*Continuously* immerse your mind in contemplating the truths of heaven…Make this a constant practice."

We could combine these lexical insights into an enhanced translation of Colossians 3:1-2: "Continually immerse your mind in the captivating truths of heaven with steadfast focus and determination. Never waver in this pursuit. Persistently strive to keep the wonders of heaven at the center of your mind."

This attitude is appropriate, for "our citizenship is in heaven, and from it we await a Savior, the Lord Jesus Christ" (Philippians 3:20).

WHY FOCUS ON HEAVEN?

> Heaven, our true home, awaits us with open arms (John 14:2-3).

> Our names are written in its eternal records (Luke 10:20).

> A glorious inheritance awaits us there (1 Peter 1:4).

> There we will be reunited with our dearly departed Christian loved ones (Hebrews 12:23).

> No wonder Hebrews 11:13 describes God's people as mere "strangers and exiles on the earth."

> We are all pilgrims on our way to a better country—"a heavenly one" (Hebrews 11:16).

The Puritans serve as an inspiration for us, demonstrating the art of maintaining an eternal perspective throughout life.

The puritans saw themselves as "God's pilgrims, traveling home through rough country; God's warriors, battling the world, the flesh, and the devil; and God's servants, under orders to worship, fellowship, and do all the good they could as they went along."

—J.I. Packer[1]

These ideas may seem alien to contemporary Christianity, much to our detriment. Personally, I'm convinced that the Puritans had it right. The following trio of observations perfectly captures the essence of their perspective:

1. The "lack of long, strong thinking about our promised hope of glory is a major cause of our plodding, lackluster lifestyle."

2. "It is the heavenly Christian that is the lively Christian."

3. We "run so slowly, and strive so lazily, because we so little mind the prize...So let Christians animate themselves daily to run the race set before them by practicing heavenly meditation."

—Cited by J.I. Packer[2]

Richard Baxter, a beloved Puritan figure to both Packer and me, had an attitude worth emulating:

- Baxter's recommended daily habit was to "dwell on the glory of the heavenly life to which one was going."

- Baxter practiced daily to hold "heaven at the forefront of his thoughts and desires." The hope of heaven gave him joy, and that joy gave him strength.

- Baxter once said, "A heavenly mind is a joyful mind; this is the nearest and truest way to live a life of comfort...A heart in heaven will be a most excellent preservative against temptations, a powerful means to kill thy corruptions."[3]

MAINTAIN AN AWARENESS OF YOUR MORTALITY

> Christian author Philip Yancey once said that our time on earth is but a mere "dot in eternity."

> That dot in eternity passes quickly. It will soon be over.

> Whether we realize it or not, we are all literally hurtling toward eternity at a dizzying pace.

> If life on earth is a dot, then eternal life in heaven is a line.

> Live for the line, not the dot.

Although it is unhealthy to be morbid, it is wise to maintain a healthy awareness of our mortality. Each of us should pray with the psalmist:

- "Teach us to number our days that we may get a heart of wisdom" (Psalm 90:12).

- "O LORD, make me know my end and what is the measure of my days; let me know how fleeting I am" (Psalm 39:4).

Despite our fleeting existence in this temporal world, our hearts are filled with whispers of eternal life. We are naturally drawn to the concept of eternity. We can't help but sense a vast expanse of time waiting beyond the horizon of this life. Our souls long for heaven; our hearts are inclined toward the hereafter. It is wondrous to even think about it. We are heaven-bent; our hearts have an inner inclination upward.

Once we get to heaven, we will live forever in an environment free of pain, aging, and death. Looking back on life on earth will seem like a brief moment in time.

"Not only is it certain that this life will end, but it is certain that from the perspective of eternity it will be seen to have passed in a flash."

—John Wenham[4]

Since writing these insightful words, Wenham has since passed into eternity. You and I will soon join him.

As we turn the pages of Scripture, we find godly men and women who demonstrated that eternity permeated their hearts. We read of Abel, Enoch, Noah, Abraham, and David, all of whom desired to spend eternity with God. They were each "seeking a homeland. If they had been thinking of that land from which they had gone out, they would have had opportunity to return. But as it is, they desire a better country, that is, a heavenly one. Therefore God is not ashamed to be called their God, for he has prepared for them a city" (Hebrews 11:14-16). That city is in heaven—the New Jerusalem (Revelation 21:10-21).

The psalms contain rich words of yearning for the eternal:

- Psalm 42:1-2 is one of my favorites: "As a deer pants for flowing streams, so pants my soul for you, O God. My soul thirsts for God, for the living God. When shall I come and appear before God?" (You and I will be able to "appear before God" following the moment of our death or following the rapture, whichever comes first.)

- I like the way David put it: "I shall dwell in the house of the LORD forever" (Psalm 23:6).

LONGING FOR THE AFTERLIFE

"We are of good courage, and we would rather be away from the body and at home with the Lord."	2 Corinthians 5:8
"My desire is to depart and be with Christ, for that is far better."	Philippians 1:23
"In your presence there is fullness of joy; at your right hand are pleasures forevermore."	Psalm 16:11

Living in Light of Eternity

Whenever I talk about heaven and an eternal perspective, I never fail to mention the extraordinary revivalist, orator, philosopher, and theologian Jonathan Edwards (1703–1758). Edwards followed to the Puritan practice of making spiritual resolutions to guide and strengthen his devotion as a Christian. Through these resolutions, he constantly reminded himself of the inevitability of death. He also considered how he would live if he knew he had only one hour remaining before he crossed the threshold of mortality. For Edwards, life was a remarkable journey toward heaven—one so crucial that every other aspect of life should be secondary in comparison. Take a moment to appreciate some of his inspiring resolutions:

- "Resolved, to endeavor to obtain for myself as much happiness, in the other world, as I possibly can."
- "Resolved, that I will live so as I shall wish I had done when I come to die."
- "Resolved, to endeavor to my utmost to act as I can think I should do, if I had already seen the happiness of heaven and hell's torments."

If the Holy Spirit is speaking to your heart as you read these words, why not make Edwards' resolutions your own? And why not start today?

Comments Worthy of Meditation

Many who have lived before me have brought me tremendous blessings with their insights into the need to live with an eternal perspective. I have included a sampling below. Please allow these words to sink deep into your soul:

God hath given to man a short time here upon earth, and yet upon this short time eternity depends.

> Jeremy Taylor (1613-1667), clergyman, Church of England

Time is short. Eternity is long. It is only reasonable that this short life be lived in the light of eternity.

> Charles Spurgeon (1834-1892), pastor,
> New Park Street Chapel, London

We are refugees from the sinking ship of this present world order, so soon to disappear; our hope is fixed in the eternal order, where the promises of God are made good to his people in perpetuity.

> F.F. Bruce (1910-1990), Bible scholar

Eternity to the godly is a day that has no sunset; eternity to the wicked is a night that has no sunrise.

> Thomas Watson (1620-1686), Puritan preacher, author

In our sad condition, our only consolation is the expectancy of another life. Here below all is incomprehensible.

> Martin Luther (1483-1546), professor of theology, reformer

Take courage. We walk in the wilderness today and in the Promised Land tomorrow.

> Dwight L. Moody (1837-1899), evangelist

However big and pressing the questions related to our present short life on earth may seem, they shrink into littleness compared with this timeless, measureless concern of death and the vast hereafter. How long earthly life looks to questing youth! How quickly fled it seems to the aged!

> J. Sidlow Baxter (1903-1999), pastor, theologian

It ought to be the business of every day to prepare for our last day.

Matthew Henry (1662–1714), Bible commentator, minister

This world is the land of the dying; the next is the land of the living.

Tryon Edwards (1809–1894), theologian

Let thy hope of heaven master thy fear of death.

William Gurnall (1617–1679), English author

Lord, make me to know that I am so frail that I may die at any time—early morning, noon, night, midnight, cockcrow. I may die in any place. If I am in the house of sin, I may die there. If I am in the place of worship, I may die there. I may die in the street. I may die while undressing tonight. I may die in my sleep, die before I get to my work tomorrow morning. I may die in any occupation.

Charles Spurgeon (1834–1892), pastor,
New Park Street Chapel, London

Our pleasant communion with our kind Christian friends is only broken off for a small moment, and is soon to be eternally resumed. These eyes of ours shall once more look upon their faces, and these ears of ours shall once more hear them speak...Blessed and happy indeed will that meeting be—better a thousand times than the parting! We parted in sorrow, and we shall meet in joy; we parted in stormy weather, and we shall meet in a calm harbor; we parted amidst pains and aches, and groans and infirmities: we shall meet with glorious bodies, able to serve our Lord forever without distraction.

J.C. Ryle (1816–1900), Anglican bishop, Liverpool

Lord, may we never forget these words!

The Grand Reversal

Few things are more exciting than understanding what Scripture says about the future. In the words of my late friend Walter Martin, "I read the last chapter of the book, *and we win!*" Martin helped us understand that we can know with certainty that we will end up in heaven and spend eternity with God and our Christian loved ones.

Our prophetic hope keeps us going even when the world around us seems to be going down the drain. Today, we see a great drift away from the truth, a wide acceptance of doctrinal error, a pervasive disregard for the Bible, a severe moral decline, an increase in the acceptance of evil and the labeling of evil as good, and an increase in a wide range of sexual sins and perversions, all with no end in sight. Also, we witness ever-increasing persecution of God's people around the world, an ever-escalating conflict in the Middle East, wars and threats of war around the world, the stage being set for a massive invasion of Israel by Russia and a group of Muslim nations, and so much more.

Despite all of this, we are not afraid because we understand where it's all leading. Regardless of current events, we have a firm conviction that God is bringing about a "grand reversal" for us. There's no better way to end our time together than by meditating on this grand reversal:

- "In the beginning, God created the heavens and the earth" (Genesis 1:1). In the eternal state, new heavens and a new earth await us (Revelation 21:1-2).

- In the beginning, the sun and the moon were created as "two great lights" (Genesis 1:16-17). The eternal state entails an eternal city where such lights are no longer needed, for the glory of God illuminates the eternal city of the redeemed (Revelation 21:23; 22:5).

- In the beginning, God created the night (Genesis 1:5). The eternal state involves a nightless eternity (Revelation 22:5).

- In the beginning, God created the seas (Genesis 1:10). The new earth in the eternal state will no longer have a sea (Revelation 21:1).

- In the beginning, human beings succumbed to Satan's temptations (Genesis 3:1-4). In the eternal state, Satan will be eternally quarantined from the people of God (Revelation 20:10).

- In the beginning, God pronounced a curse following humankind's fall into sin (Genesis 3:17). In the eternal state, there will be no more curse (Revelation 22:3).

- In the beginning, a Redeemer is promised (Genesis 3:15). In the eternal state, the victorious Redeemer reigns (Revelation 20:1-6; 21:22-27; 22:3-5).

- In the beginning, paradise was lost (Genesis 3:23-24). In the eternal state, paradise will be gloriously restored for the redeemed (Revelation 2:7).

- In the beginning, Adam and Eve were barred from the tree of life (Genesis 3:22-24). In the eternal state, redeemed humans will enjoy restoration to the tree of life (Revelation 2:7; 22:2, 14, 19).

- In the beginning, tears, death, and mourning entered human existence (Genesis 2:17; 29:11; 37:34). In the eternal state, tears, death, and mourning will be forever absent from the redeemed (Revelation 21:4).

- In the beginning, a bride is found for the first Adam (Genesis 2:18). In the eternal state, we witness the bride of Christ (the church) of the Last Adam, who is Jesus Christ (Revelation 19:9).

What a magnificent turnabout it will be! And it's all grounded in our acceptance of Christ for salvation. The verse with which I opened this book serves as its proper conclusion:

*To him who loves us and has freed us from our sins by his blood
and made us a kingdom, priests to his God and Father,
to him be glory and dominion forever and ever.
Amen.*

Behold, he is coming with the clouds,
and every eye will see him,
even those who pierced him,
and all tribes of the earth will wail on account of him.
Even so. Amen.

Revelation 1:5-7

A Concise Outline of the End Times in Chronological Order

1. The Course of the Present Age

a. God Has a Divine Purpose for the Present Age

  i. God's purpose for Israel

    1. Since the first century, Israel has experienced judicial blindness and hardening as God's judgment, when the Jews rejected Christ (Romans 11:25).

    2. As a result, Israel has lost its privileged position before God.

    3. The gospel was then preached to the Gentiles to make the Jews jealous and eventually be saved (Romans 11:11).

    4. Israel's hardening and casting off are only temporary.

    5. At Armageddon, the Jewish remnant will finally recognize their Messiah (Jesus) and turn to Him for deliverance from the forces of the antichrist (Zechariah 12:10; see also Romans 10:13-14).

    6. A remnant will thereby be saved.

  ii. God's purpose for the church. Members of the church are called to:

    1. be witnesses for Christ (Luke 24:45-49; Acts 1:7-8)

    2. build up the body of Christ (Ephesians 4:11-13)

    3. do good to all people (Galatians 6:10; Titus 3:14)

    4. exercise spiritual gifts (Romans 12:6-8)

    5. financially support God's work (1 Corinthians 16:1-3)

    6. help brothers and sisters in need (1 John 3:16-18)

7. love one another (Hebrews 13:1-3, 16)

8. make disciples of all nations (Matthew 28:19-20)

9. extend hospitality to one another (1 Peter 4:9-11)

10. and preach the Word of God (Mark 16:15-16; 1 Timothy 4:6, 13)

iii. The course of the present age

1. Christ reveals the characteristics of the period between the first and second comings of Christ in the parables recorded in Matthew 13.

2. The parable of the sower shows that people will respond to the gospel in different ways (Matthew 13:1-23).

3. The parable of the tares warns that the true sowing of the gospel seed will be imitated by a false counter-sowing (Matthew 13:24-30).

4. The parable of the mustard seed shows that God's spiritual kingdom would start small but eventually spread throughout the world (Matthew 13:31-32).

5. The parable of the leaven reveals that the kingdom will experience continual growth and expansion throughout history (Matthew 13:33-43).

6. The parable of the hidden treasure emphasizes the incredible value of the true kingdom of heaven in contrast to counterfeit belief systems (Matthew 13:44).

b. Israel's Rebirth as a Nation

i. Israel's rebirth as a nation in 1948 was a direct fulfillment of Bible prophecy (Ezekiel 37).

ii. Since then, Jews have been streaming back to the Holy Land from virtually every nation in the world, just as prophesied (Ezekiel 36:24).

c. Apostasy Will Continue to Increase as We Move Deeper into the End Times

i. "In later times some will depart from the faith by devoting themselves to deceitful spirits and teachings of demons" (1 Timothy 4:1).

   ii. "The time is coming when people will not endure sound teaching, but having itching ears they will accumulate for themselves teachers to suit their own passions, and will turn away from listening to the truth and wander off into myths" (2 Timothy 4:3).

   iii. Apostasy will reach a fever pitch during the tribulation period (Matthew 24:9-12).

d. The United States Will Apparently Weaken as We Move Deeper into the End Times

   i. During the first half of the tribulation period, the antichrist's revived Roman Empire will rise to the status of a political and economic superpower (Daniel 2; 7).

   ii. The United States will likely weaken either prior to or during this same period

      1. It is noteworthy that the United States is not directly mentioned in a single Bible prophecy. *Why not?* Is it because the United States has become so weak that it is no longer a "major player" on the world scene?

      2. The United States does not come to Israel's defense in the Ezekiel invasion (see Ezekiel 38:13). *Why not?* Is it because the United States is no longer strong enough to help defend Israel?

   iii. The United States could be weakened by:

      1. a moral implosion,

      2. a nuclear detonation in a major city,

      3. an EMP attack,

      4. an economic collapse,

      5. or possibly even the rapture.

2. The Rapture of the Church

a. The Church Will Be Raptured *Before* the Tribulation Period

   i. No New Testament or Old Testament passage about the tribulation period mentions the church (Deuteronomy 4:29-30; Jeremiah 30:4-11; Daniel 8:24-27; 12:1-2; Matthew 13:30, 39-42, 48-50; 24:15-31; 1 Thessalonians 1:9-10; 5:4-9; 2 Thessalonians 2:1-11; Revelation 4–18).

   ii. Jesus promised to protect the church from the "hour of trial" that will come upon the entire world (Revelation 3:10).

   iii. Jesus assured believers that He would deliver them from the wrath to come (1 Thessalonians 1:9).

   iv. The church is not appointed to wrath (Romans 5:9; 1 Thessalonians 5:9).

   v. God typically delivers His people before judgment falls (see 2 Peter 2:5-9).

b. As a Result of the Rapture, the Divine Restrainer Will Be Removed

   i. God (the Holy Spirit) is the only person who is capable of restraining Satan, who energizes the antichrist (2 Thessalonians 2:9; 1 John 4:4).

   ii. It is therefore reasonable to assume that the restrainer is the Holy Spirit, who indwells every believer in the church (1 Corinthians 3:16; 6:19).

   iii. The influence of the Holy Spirit through the church will be removed when the church is raptured, thereby allowing for the quick emergence of the antichrist (2 Thessalonians 2:7).

c. Following the Rapture, Christians Will Possess Heavenly (Glorified) Bodies

   i. The bodies of both dead and living believers will be imperishable, glorious, and powerful (1 Corinthians 15:42-43).

   ii. These glorified bodies are comparable to strong buildings, unlike our present mortal bodies that are comparable to tents that are easily torn down (2 Corinthians 5:1-4).

The Complete Reference Guide to Bible Prophecy

3. The Church Will Be with Christ in Heaven

a. After the Rapture, Christians Will Face the Judgment Seat of Christ in Heaven

   i. Each believer's life will be examined regarding deeds done while on earth (Romans 14:12; 1 Corinthians 3:13; 2 Corinthians 5:10).

   ii. Personal motives and intentions will also be weighed (Romans 14:8-10; 1 Corinthians 3:11-15; 9:24-27).

   iii. This judgment concerns the acquiring or losing of rewards for how one has lived on earth since becoming a Christian (1 Corinthians 3:12-15; 1 Peter 5:4; James 1:12; 2 Timothy 4:8).

b. The Marriage Between the Church and the Lamb Will Take Place in Heaven

   i. Jesus often referred to Himself as a bridegroom (Matthew 9:15; 22:2-14; 25:1-13; Mark 2:19-20; Luke 5:34-35; 14:15-24; John 3:29).

   ii. The church is portrayed as a virgin bride awaiting the coming of her heavenly Bridegroom (2 Corinthians 11:2).

   iii. The marriage of the Lamb and the church will occur in heaven sometime after the rapture.

4. Israel Will Be Invaded by a Northern Military Coalition—Likely After the Rapture but Before the Tribulation Period

a. Israel Will Be Living at Peace in Her Own Land

   i. This is a prerequisite for the Ezekiel invasion, when Russia and some Muslim nations invade Israel (Ezekiel 38:11).

   ii. Some prophecy scholars believe that Israel is currently secure because of its strong military.

   iii. This view suggests that the Ezekiel invasion could occur in the not-too-distant future.

b. The Northern Military Coalition Invades Israel

   i. The nations that make up this military alliance include (Ezekiel 36:1-6 NASB 1995):

    1. Rosh (Russia)

    2. Magog (the former southern Soviet republics of Kazakhstan, Kyrgyzstan, Uzbekistan, Turkmenistan, and Tajikistan)

    3. Meshech and Tubal (Turkey)

    4. Persia (the Islamic Republic of Iran)

    5. Ethiopia (Sudan)

    6. Put (Libya)

    7. Gomer (another reference to Turkey)

    8. and Beth-Togarmah (yet another reference to Turkey)

   ii. There is good reason to believe that this invasion will occur sometime after the rapture but before the tribulation period begins. (There will apparently be a gap of time between the rapture and the beginning of the tribulation period.)

5. The Tribulation Period Begins: The Emergence of the Antichrist

a. The Beginning of the Tribulation Period Will Be Marked by the Signing of a Covenant Between the Antichrist and Israel

   i. The antichrist will make a seven-year covenant with Israel (Daniel 9:27).

   ii. After three and a half years, however, he will break the covenant and put an end to the sacrifices and offerings in the rebuilt Jewish temple (compare with Matthew 24:15).

b. The Antichrist Will Rise Rapidly on the World Stage During the First Half of the Tribulation

   i. He will be a genius in:

    1. intellect (Daniel 8:23)

    2. commerce (Daniel 11:43; Revelation 13:16-17)

    3. war (Revelation 6:2; 13:2)

    4. speech (Daniel 11:36)

    5. politics (Revelation 17:11-12)

  ii. He will be energized by Satan (2 Thessalonians 2:9).

  iii. He will seek to establish his own global kingdom (Revelation 13).

  iv. He will elevate himself to godhood and demand worship (2 Thessalonians 2:4).

6. Early in the Tribulation Period: The Rebuilt Temple and Signs of the End

a. The Jewish Temple Will Be Rebuilt Early in the Tribulation Period—We Know This Because:

  i. The Jews will be allowed to offer temple sacrifices during the first half of the tribulation period (Daniel 9:27); and

  ii. The antichrist will desecrate the temple at the midpoint of the tribulation by placing an image of himself within it (Matthew 24:15-16; 2 Thessalonians 2:4).

b. The Signs of the Times Will Confirm that the End Times Have Arrived

  i. A "sign of the times" is an event of prophetic significance that indicates the end times.

  ii. These signs include:

    1. Apostasy, Departure from the faith—Matthew 24:3, 10; 2 Timothy 4:3-4; 1 Timothy 4:1

    2. Earthquakes—Matthew 24:7; Mark 13:8

    3. False Christs—Matthew 24:24-25; Mark 13:5, 21-23; Luke 21:8; John 5:41-44

    4. False prophets—Matthew 24:11; Mark 13:6, 21-23

    5. False signs and miracles—Matthew 24:24; Mark 13:22; Luke 21:8; 2 Thessalonians 2:9-10; Revelation 19:20

    6. Famines—Matthew 24:7; Mark 13:8; Revelation 6:5-6

7. Increase of evil—Matthew 24:12; 2 Timothy 3:1-5; 2 Peter 3:3-4

8. International strife—Matthew 24:7; Mark 13:8; Luke 21:10; Revelation 6:3-4

9. Lawlessness—Matthew 24:12

10. Many fall away—Matthew 24:10

11. Persecution of believers—Matthew 24:8-9; Mark 13:9-11, 13; Luke 21:12-17; 2 Timothy 3:1-5, 10-13; Revelation 6:9-11; 12:17; 20:4

12. Martyrdom of believers—Matthew 24:9

13. Pestilence—Luke 21:11; Revelation 6:7-8

14. Unprecedented distress—Matthew 24:21; Mark 13:17-19; Luke 21:23

15. Wars, rumors of wars—Matthew 24:6; Mark 13:7; Luke 21:9

16. Worldwide preaching of the gospel—Matthew 24:14; Mark 13:10; Revelation 14:6-7

iii. The appearance of these and other signs will confirm the end times.

7. Early in the Tribulation Period: The Lamb and His Witnesses

a. The Lamb (Christ) Will Receive a Seven-Sealed Scroll During the First Half of the Tribulation

  i. Only Christ in heaven is worthy to receive this scroll (Revelation 5).

  ii. When the seals are opened, the plagues of the seals will be released on the earth. (This will happen shortly.)

b. 144,000 Jewish Evangelists Will Begin Their Ministry

  i. These are Jewish men who come to faith in Jesus sometime after the rapture of the church (Revelation 7; 14).

  ii. These witnesses will be "sealed" by God (divinely protected) as they carry out their service for Him during the tribulation (Revelation 14:1-4; see also 2 Corinthians 1:22; Ephesians 1:13; 4:30).

    iii. They will fulfill the mandate originally given to the Jewish nation to share the good news of God with people all around the world (see Isaiah 42:6; 43:10).

    iv. They will preach the gospel of the kingdom (Matthew 24:14).

  c. God's Two Prophetic Witnesses Will Also Engage in Ministry

    i. God's two prophetic witnesses will testify to the one true God with astonishing power, similar to that of Elijah (1 Kings 17; Malachi 4:5) and Moses (Exodus 7–11).

    ii. In Bible times, two witnesses were required to confirm a testimony (Deuteronomy 17:6; 19:15; Matthew 18:16; John 8:17; Hebrews 10:28).

    iii. The efforts of the two prophets and the 144,000 Jewish evangelists will yield a "great multitude" of conversions (Revelation 7:9-17).

8. During the First Half of the Tribulation: Judgments, Martyrdom, and Apostasy

  a. The Seven Seal Judgments Will Be Unleashed

    i. This is the first set of judgments to be unleashed during the tribulation period.

    ii. These include the rise of the antichrist, the outbreak of war, widespread famine, massive casualties, God's people being killed, a devastating earthquake, and even worse judgments (Revelation 6).

    iii. Things will go from bad to worse.

  b. Martyrdom Will Increase

    i. While all Christians on earth will be raptured before the tribulation (1 Thessalonians 1:10; 4:13-17; 5:9; Revelation 3:10), many people who were "left behind" will become believers during these seven years (Matthew 25:31-46; Revelation 7:9-10).

      ii. Many of these individuals will be martyred (Revelation 6:9-11).

      iii. Christ tells His followers to stand firm and not to fear martyrdom (Revelation 2:10).

  c. The Trumpet Judgments Will Begin

      i. Things will continue to go from bad to worse during the tribulation period.

      ii. The trumpet judgments will include hail and fire falling on the earth, a fiery mountain plummeting into the sea, a star (asteroid) falling from heaven and making a deep impact on the earth, various cosmic disturbances, hideous demons tormenting humans, fallen angels killing one third of humankind, and even worse judgments.

  d. Meanwhile, Religious New Babylon Will Dominate the World During the First Half of the Tribulation Period

      i. The false religion associated with New Babylon will exert global influence (Revelation 17:15).

      ii. She will be utterly unfaithful to the truth and therefore be a spiritual "harlot" (17:1, 5, 15-16).

      iii. She will also wield powerful political influence among the nations of the world (17:12-13).

      iv. She will appear outwardly glorious while being inwardly corrupt (implied in 17:4).

      v. She will persecute believers (Christians) during the tribulation period (17:6).

9. The Midpoint of the Tribulation

  a. The Little Scroll Will Be Opened

      i. In Revelation 10, we read of an angel with a mysterious little scroll.

      ii. John obeyed the angel's instruction to eat the scroll, and although it was sweet as honey in his mouth, it quickly soured in his stomach.

    1. The scroll seems to represent Scripture.

    2. God's Word was sweet to John, containing many promises to believers.

    3. The message was also bitter because it contained stern warnings of woe and judgment for unbelievers.

    4. The book of Revelation contains much of this woe and judgment.

b. The Antichrist Will Be Wounded and Appear to Be Resurrected (Revelation 13:1-3)

    i. Some Bible scholars believe the antichrist will suffer a fatal head wound, die, and then be resurrected.

    ii. Others believe he will be wounded, but not fatally, and he will feign a resurrection from the dead.

    iii. Either way, the world will think he has been raised from the dead and will worship him.

c. Satan Will Be Cast Out of Heaven

    i. Satan will indwell or fully energize the antichrist once Satan is cast out of heaven at the midpoint of the tribulation period (Revelation 12:12-13; 2 Thessalonians 2:9).

    ii. Satan will be furious because he knows his time is short—only 1,260 days left, the last three-and-a-half years of the tribulation.

    iii. The ferocity of Satan will be expressed through the person of the antichrist.

    iv. Things on earth will continue to go from bad to much worse.

d. The False Religion Associated with New Babylon Will Be Destroyed

    i. The antichrist, along with the ten kings under his authority, will destroy the false religious system associated with New Babylon at the midpoint of the tribulation period (Revelation 17:16-18).

    ii. The antichrist will then establish global dominance in politics *and* religion, demanding worship as God (Daniel 11:36-38; 2 Thessalonians 2:4; Revelation 13:8, 15).

    iii. The final world religion will involve worship of the antichrist alone (Revelation 13:12).

    iv. There will be no room for competing religious systems.

  e. God's Two Prophetic Witnesses Will Be Executed and Then Resurrected

    i. The two prophets will serve during the first half of the tribulation, and once their service is complete, the antichrist will martyr them (Revelation 11:7-8).

    ii. All the unbelievers on earth will celebrate their deaths (11:10).

    iii. Three-and-a-half days later, the two witnesses will resurrect from the dead and ascend into heaven, and the people's celebration will turn to dread (11:11-13).

  f. The Antichrist Will Break His Covenant with Israel

    i. The covenant was intended to remain in effect for seven years (Daniel 9:27).

    ii. But the antichrist will break the covenant at the three-and-a-half-year mark and shut down Israel's temple sacrifices.

    iii. From that point forward, the antichrist will demand that worship be confined to him alone (Revelation 13:12).

  g. The Abomination of Desolation Will Occur

    i. The antichrist will desecrate the Jewish temple at the midpoint of the tribulation by enthroning himself in it and then placing an image of himself in it (2 Thessalonians 2:4; Revelation 13:15).

    ii. This will desecrate and desolate the temple in an abominable way (Matthew 24:15).

    iii. The antichrist now shows his true colors:

      1. He starts out as *Israel's protector* (with a signed covenant) but will become *Israel's persecutor*.

      2. He turns from being *Israel's defender* to being *Israel's defiler*.

  h. The False Prophet Will Carry Out His Diabolical Ministry

    i. Satan will empower the false prophet to engage in "Grade-B" miracles (Revelation 13:13-15)—lesser than God's miracles but still impressive (compare with Exodus 7:11; 2 Timothy 3:8).

   ii. The false prophet will perform miracles to induce people to worship Satan's substitute for Christ—*the antichrist* (Daniel 9:27; 11:31; 12:11; Matthew 24:15).

i. The Antichrist Will Blaspheme God

   i. The antichrist will engage in gross self-exaltation and self-deification.

   ii. He "opposes and exalts himself against every so-called god or object of worship, so that he takes his seat in the temple of God, proclaiming himself to be God" (2 Thessalonians 2:4).

   iii. "He shall exalt himself and magnify himself above every god, and shall speak astonishing things against the God of gods" (Daniel 11:36).

   iv. There is no greater blasphemy than this.

   v. The antichrist truly is *anti*-Christ, putting himself in Christ's place, appropriating the worship that belongs to Christ alone.

   vi. He will "utter blasphemies against God, blaspheming his name" (Revelation 13:6).

j. The Jewish Remnant Will Flee from Israel

   i. Jesus told the Jews in Jerusalem that when these terrible things happen, they should forget about getting their personal belongings and leave Jerusalem as soon as possible (Matthew 24:15-20).

   ii. They must run for their lives.

   iii. Time spent gathering things might mean the difference between life and death.

   iv. Jesus warned that the persecution of the Jews would now increase dramatically and rapidly (Matthew 24:16-22; Revelation 12:56).

k. The Antichrist Will Make War on the Saints

   i. The beast (antichrist) will be allowed to "make war on the saints and to conquer them" (Revelation 13:7).

      ii. He "made war with the saints and prevailed over them" (Daniel 7:21).

         1. Notice the past tense in this verse.

         2. This emphasizes the certainty of the antichrist's victory over believers.

   l. Midtribulational Announcements Will Be Uttered from Heaven

      i. These divine announcements include details about the impending bowl judgments—the worst judgments of all (Revelation 14).

      ii. There will also be words of assurance, encouragement, and comfort for God's people amid the tribulation.

10. The Second Half of the Tribulation

   a. The "Great Tribulation" Begins

      i. The last three-and-a-half years of the tribulation period are called the "great tribulation" (Matthew 24:15-21; see also Daniel 9:27).

      ii. It will be the worst period in human history.

   b. The Great Tribulation Will Be Limited to Three-and-a-Half Years

      i. God sovereignly decreed that the great tribulation will be strictly limited to three-and-a-half years (Matthew 24:21-22; see also Daniel 7:25).

      ii. Otherwise, humanity would not survive.

   c. The Mark of the Beast Will Be Enforced

      i. The antichrist and the false prophet will subjugate the entire world so that anyone who does not receive the mark of the beast cannot buy or sell (Revelation 13:16-18).

      ii. This mark will be a passport to commerce.

     iii. This means that those who refuse the mark of the beast will have a hard time getting food. Famine will be widespread.

   d. Deception Will Continue to Escalate

      i. Jesus warned that during the tribulation period, there will be numerous false prophets who will lead people astray (Matthew 24:11).

ii. The apostle Paul spoke of end-times "wicked deception" rooted in lies (2 Thessalonians 2:9-11).

iii. Revelation 12:9 tells us that Satan—"the deceiver of the whole world"—will be very active during this time.

iv. The antichrist's first lieutenant, the false prophet, "deceives those who dwell on earth" (Revelation 13:14).

e. The Bowl Judgments Will Be Unleashed

i. The worst judgments of all are now unleashed on the world.

ii. People will be inflicted with painful sores, the sea will become like blood, rivers and springs of water will also become like blood, the sun will scorch people with fire, the world will be plunged into utter darkness, the Euphrates River will dry up (preparing the way for the outbreak of Armageddon), and more (Revelation 16:1-21).

f. The Gospel of the Kingdom Will Continue to Be Proclaimed

i. Jesus prophesied that "the Good news about the Kingdom will be preached throughout the whole world" (Matthew 24:14).

ii. There will be a "great multitude" of conversions (Revelation 14:9-17).

iii. God's light will continue to shine even in the darkest period of human history.

11. The End of the Tribulation

a. The Campaign of Armageddon Will Ignite

i. Armageddon will explode on the scene at the end of the tribulation period (Revelation 16:14-16; see also Daniel 11:40-45; Joel 3:9-17; Zechariah 14:1-3).

ii. The worst escalation of conflict ever to hit planet earth will cause millions of deaths.

iii. There will be eight stages of Armageddon.

b. *Stage One of Armageddon:* The Antichrist's Allies Will Assemble for War

    i. These allies will gather for one purpose: the final destruction of the Jews (Revelation 16:12-16).

    ii. This attack will be demonically inspired.

c. *Stage Two of Armageddon:* Commercial Babylon Will Be Destroyed

    i. This destruction will demonstrate God's mighty wrath (Jeremiah 50:13-14).

    ii. Babylon will become a desert wasteland.

    iii. It will be "like Sodom and Gomorrah when God overthrew them" (Isaiah 13:19; Jeremiah 50:40).

    iv. The destruction will be comprehensive and permanent.

d. *Stage Three of Armageddon:* Jerusalem Will Fall

    i. Zechariah 14:1-2 reveals that "all the nations" will be gathered to fight "against Jerusalem."

    ii. The city of Jerusalem will be ravaged by this overwhelming attack.

e. *Stage Four of Armageddon:* The Antichrist Will Move South Against the Jewish Remnant

    i. The antichrist will then move south against the remnant of Jews who fled from Jerusalem at the midpoint of the tribulation.

    ii. These Jews will seek refuge in the deserts and mountains (Matthew 24:16), perhaps in Bozrah/Petra, about 80 miles south of Jerusalem.

    iii. From an earthly perspective, this remnant of Jews will be completely defenseless.

f. *Stage Five of Armageddon:* The Jews Will Be Endangered and Will Experience National Regeneration

    i. The Jewish remnant will experience supernatural national regeneration by turning to their Messiah, Jesus Christ (Hosea 6:1-3; see also Joel 2:28-29).

    ii. They will finally recognize their former blindness, their spiritual eyes will be opened, and they will repent of their rejection of Jesus.

    iii. They will see Messiah Jesus for who He truly is and cry out to Him for deliverance (see Zechariah 12:10; Matthew 23:37-39; see also Isaiah 53:1-9).

g. *Stage Six of Armageddon:* Jesus Christ Will Return in Glory

    i. Jesus will immediately answer the prayers of the born-again Jewish remnant.

    ii. The divine Messiah will personally return to rescue His people from peril.

    iii. Christ will come as the King of kings and Lord of lords, and no one will withstand Him (Revelation 19:11-16).

    iv. Every eye will see Him (Revelation 1:7; Matthew 24:30).

h. *Stage Seven of Armageddon:* The Final Battle Will Erupt

    i. Jesus will confront the antichrist and his military forces and will slay them with the "breath" of His mouth: "The lawless one will be revealed, whom the Lord Jesus will kill with the breath of his mouth and bring to nothing by the appearance of his coming" (2 Thessalonians 2:8).

    ii. In popular parlance, this means that Jesus will essentially say "drop dead," and the forces of the antichrist will experience instant death.

    iii. They will be no match for the King of kings and Lord of lords (Revelation 19:16).

i. *Stage Eight of Armageddon:* Christ Will Victoriously Ascend to the Mount of Olives

    i. "On that day his feet shall stand on the Mount of Olives that lies before Jerusalem on the east, and the Mount of Olives shall be split in two from east to west by a very wide valley, so that one half of the Mount shall move northward, and the other half southward" (Zechariah 14:4).

    ii. What an extraordinary moment that will be.

12. After the Tribulation, Before the Millennial Kingdom

a. There Will Be a 75-Day Transitional Period Between the End of the Tribulation and the Beginning of the Millennium (Daniel 12:11-12)

    i. Daniel 12:12 states, "Blessed is he who waits and arrives at the 1,335 days."

    ii. The second half of the tribulation period is three-and-a-half years, which is 1,260 days.

    iii. This means Daniel's 1,335 days extend 75 days beyond the end of the tribulation period.

    iv. The math is simple: 1,335 minus 1,260 equals 75.

    v. During this 75-day interim period, eight significant events will take place (12b–12i).

b. The Nations Will Be Judged

    i. The nations are comprised of the sheep and the goats, representing the saved and the lost among the Gentiles (Matthew 25:31-46).

    ii. They are intermingled and require separation by a special judgment.

    iii. They are judged based on how they treated Christ's "brothers"—the 144,000 Jewish witnesses.

    iv. Only the "sheep" (saved Gentiles) will help these 144,000.

    v. The "sheep" will then be invited into Christ's millennial kingdom in their mortal bodies (not yet resurrected).

c. The Jews Will Be Judged

    i. The judgment of the Jews is described in Ezekiel 20:34-38.

    ii. It will occur after the Lord has gathered the Jews from around the earth to Israel.

    iii. Jewish rebels who have refused to turn to Christ for salvation will be purged by Christ.

    iv. Believers from among this group will enter Christ's millennial kingdom, where they will then enjoy the blessings of the new covenant (verse 37; see also Jeremiah 31:31).

   v. These saved Jews will enter the millennial kingdom in their mortal bodies (not yet resurrected).

d. The Antichrist and the False Prophet Will Be Cast into the Lake of Fire (Revelation 19:20)

e. Satan Will Be Bound in Spirit Prison from This Point Till the Very End of the Millennial Kingdom (Revelation 20:1-3)

f. Old Testament Saints Will Be Resurrected from the Dead (Daniel 12:2)

g. Saints Who Died During the Tribulation Will Be Resurrected from the Dead (Revelation 20:4)

h. The Government Structure of the Millennial Kingdom Will Be Set Up (2 Timothy 2:12; Revelation 3:21; 5:10: 20:4, 6; 22:5)

i. The Marriage Supper of the Lamb Will Be Celebrated

   i. The marriage feast of Christ and the church will be the highlight of this two-and-a-half-month period.

   ii. Hebrew weddings included three phases:

      1. The bride became betrothed to the bridegroom,

      2. the bridegroom came to retrieve his bride,

      3. and the marriage supper was celebrated—a feast lasting up to a week.

   iii. All three phases are seen in Christ's relationship to the church, the bride of Christ.

13. The Millennial Kingdom

a. The Millennial Kingdom Begins

   i. Following the second coming of Christ, Jesus will establish His kingdom on earth (Revelation 20:2-7; see also Psalm 2:6-9; Isaiah 65:18-23; Jeremiah 31:12-14, 31-37; Ezekiel 34:25-29; 37:1-13; 40–48; Daniel 2:35; 7:13-14; Joel 2:21-27; Amos 9:13-14; Micah 4:1-7; Zephaniah 3:9-20).

    ii. "Millennium" comes from two Latin words:

        1. *mille*, which means "thousand,"

        2. and *annum*, which means "year."

        3. The millennial kingdom of Christ will last 1,000 years (Revelation 20:3-6).

b. The Tribulation Saints Enter the Millennial Kingdom

    i. The Gentiles who are found to be believers at the judgment of the nations (Matthew 25:31-46) will be invited into Christ's millennial kingdom in their mortal bodies.

    ii. The redeemed Jews will also be invited to enter the millennial kingdom in their mortal bodies (Ezekiel 20:34-38).

c. Israel Is Restored and Possesses the Land

    i. Israel will not only experience regeneration in fulfillment of the new covenant (Jeremiah 31:31-34) but will also be regathered.

    ii. The land covenant recorded in Deuteronomy 29–30 is eternal and unconditional.

    iii. Even though Israel would be scattered all over the world, God promised that He would gather them and restore them to the land (see Isaiah 43:5-7; Jeremiah 16:14-18).

    iv. Christ's millennial kingdom brings the fulfillment of these prophecies.

d. A Millennial Temple Will Be Built

    i. Prophetic Scripture affirms that a millennial temple will be built (Ezekiel 40–48; Isaiah 2:3; 60:13; Joel 3:18).

    ii. Millennial animal sacrifices will be instituted (Isaiah 56:7; 60:7; Jeremiah 33:17-18; Zechariah 14:19-21).

        1. The purpose of the sacrifices is to remove ceremonial uncleanness from the temple, and to prevent defilement from polluting the purity of the temple environment.

        2. This will be necessary because Yahweh will once again dwell on the earth among sinful (and therefore unclean) mortal people.

      3. Remember that these people survived the tribulation period and entered the millennial kingdom in their mortal bodies, retaining their sinful natures.

      4. The sacrifices will thus remove any ceremonial uncleanness in the temple.

  iii. The sacrifices, therefore, should not be viewed as a return to the Mosaic Law.

  iv. The law has been abolished forever through the death and resurrection of Jesus Christ (Romans 6:14-15; 7:1-6; 1 Corinthians 9:20-21; 2 Corinthians 3:7-11; Galatians 4:1-7; 5:18; Hebrews 8:13; 10:1-14).

e. Christ Will Reign from the Davidic Throne

  i. God promised David that one of his descendants would rule forever on his throne (2 Samuel 7:12-13; 22:51).

  ii. This is an unconditional covenant. It was not dependent on David for its fulfillment.

  iii. This covenant finds its ultimate fulfillment in Jesus Christ, who was born from the line of David (Matthew 1:1; see also Micah 4:1-5; Zephaniah 3:14-20; Zechariah 14).

f. Resurrected Saints Will Reign with Christ

  i. Scripture promises that the saints will reign with Christ.

  ii. The apostle Paul instructs, "If we endure, we will also reign with him" (2 Timothy 2:12).

  iii. Believers "shall reign on the earth" (Revelation 5:10).

  iv. "They will reign with him for a thousand years" (Revelation 20:6).

  v. The privilege of reigning with Christ extends beyond the millennial kingdom and into the eternal state: "They will reign forever and ever" (Revelation 22:5).

g. Christ Will Bring Physical Blessings to the Millennial Kingdom

  i. People will live in an enhanced and blessed environment (Isaiah 35:1-2).

  ii. There will be abundant rain and food (Isaiah 30:23-24).

iii. Animals will live in harmony with humans and with each other (Isaiah 11:6-7).

iv. Longevity will be increased (Isaiah 29:18).

v. Infirmities and illnesses will be removed from the body (Isaiah 29:18).

vi. Prosperity will prevail, resulting in joy and gladness (Jeremiah 31:12-14).

h. Christ Will Institute a Perfect Government in the Millennial Kingdom

i. Christ's government will be global (Psalm 2:6-9).

ii. Jerusalem will serve as the capital of Christ's future world government (Isaiah 2:2-4; Jeremiah 3:17; Ezekiel 48:30-35; Joel 3:16-17; Micah 4:1, 6-8; Zechariah 8:2-3).

iii. Christ's government will be perfect and effective (Isaiah 9:6-7).

iv. Christ's government will achieve lasting global peace (Micah 4:3-4)

i. Christ Will Bestow Great Spiritual Blessing During the Millennial Kingdom

i. All believers will experience the presence and indwelling of the Holy Spirit (Isaiah 44:3; Ezekiel 37:14; Joel 2:28-29).

ii. Righteousness will prevail throughout the world (Isaiah 46:13; 51:5; 60:21).

iii. Obedience to the Lord will prevail (Psalm 22:27; Jeremiah 31:33).

iv. Holiness will prevail (Isaiah 35:8-10; Joel 3:17).

v. Faithfulness will prevail (Psalm 85:10-11; Zechariah 8:3).

vi. All the inhabitants of the world will worship the Messiah (Malachi 1:11; Zechariah 8:23).

vii. God will make His presence known (Ezekiel 37:27-28; Zechariah 2:10-13).

14. After the Millennial Kingdom

a. Satan Will Lead a Final Revolt

    i. At the end of the millennial kingdom, "Satan will be released from his prison and will come out to deceive the nations that are at the four corners of the earth" (Revelation 20:7-8).

    ii. Satan's activities have always been characterized by deception (John 8:44).

    iii. Remember that only believers will be allowed to enter Christ's millennial kingdom (Matthew 25:31-46).

        1. But some children, grandchildren, and great-grandchildren of these believers *will not* become believers.

        2. Some of these will join Satan in this rebellion.

    iv. The satanic uprising will be directed against Jerusalem, the seat of Christ's rule throughout the millennial kingdom (Isaiah 2:1-5).

    v. Fire will quickly devour the invaders (Revelation 20:9).

    vi. The insurrection will be met with immediate defeat.

b. Satan Will Be Cast into the Lake of Fire

    i. Following this final revolt against Christ, Satan will be "thrown into the lake of fire and sulfur where the beast and the false prophet were, and they will be tormented day and night forever and ever" (Revelation 20:10).

    ii. The satanic trinity of Satan, the antichrist, and the false prophet will all face the same ignominious fate in the lake of fire.

c. The Second Resurrection Will Occur

    i. The "first resurrection" is the resurrection of believers.

    ii. The "second resurrection" is the resurrection of the wicked who will face Christ at the great white throne judgment.

d. The Wicked Dead Will Be Judged

    i. Unbelievers face a horrific judgment that leads to their

being cast into the lake of fire. This is the great white throne judgment (Revelation 20:11-15).

   ii. The unsaved dead from all eras shall be judged by Christ Himself.

   iii. This judgment will occur after the millennial kingdom.

   iv. Once the wicked are before the divine Judge, they are judged according to their works...

   1. not only to justify their condemnation

   2. but to determine the degree to which each person should be punished throughout eternity (Matthew 10:15; 16:27; Luke 12:47-48; Revelation 20:12-13; 22:12)

   v. There are different levels of punishment in hell just as there are different levels of reward in heaven. Christ the Judge is perfectly fair.

   vi. When Christ opens the book of life, no name of anyone present at the great white throne judgment is in it (Revelation 20:15).

   vii. Their names do not appear in the book of life because they have rejected the source of life—Jesus Christ (see John 14:6).

e. The Lake of Fire Will Be Populated

   i. The lake of fire will be the permanent residence of Satan, demons, the antichrist, the false prophet, and unbelievers throughout history (Revelation 19:20; 20:10-15).

   ii. All residents will be tormented day and night forever and ever.

   iii. The "lake of fire" is a term used to describe hell.

   iv. The Bible employs a variety of descriptive terms to describe the calamities of hell:

   1. unquenchable fire (Mark 9:47-48)

   2. the fiery lake of burning sulfur (Revelation 19:20)

   3. eternal fire (Matthew 18:8)

   4. eternal punishment (Matthew 25:46)

   5. destruction (Matthew 7:13)

    6. everlasting destruction (2 Thessalonians 1:8-9)

    7. the place of weeping and gnashing of teeth (Matthew 13:42)

    8. the second death (Revelation 20:14)

15. The Eternal State Begins

a. The Old Heavens and Earth Will Be Destroyed

    i. The earth was cursed by God after Adam and Eve sinned (Genesis 3:17-18).

    ii. The universe was subjected to futility and is now in bondage to decay (Romans 8:20-22).

    iii. Satan has also long carried out his evil schemes on earth (Ephesians 2:2).

    iv. Therefore, the earth must be cleansed of the curse and all the stains of Satan's prolonged presence.

    v. The earth and the first and second heavens—the earth's atmosphere (Job 35:5) and the stellar universe (Genesis 1:17; Deuteronomy 17:3)—must be renewed. The old must make room for the new.

    vi. Scripture therefore speaks of the passing of the old heavens and earth (Psalm 102:25-26; Isaiah 51:6; Matthew 24:35; 2 Peter 3:7-13).

b. The New Heaven and New Earth Will Be Created

    i. When God creates a new heaven and a new earth, all vestiges of the curse and Satan's presence will be forever removed.

    ii. Everything will be made new.

    iii. All creation will be cleansed of all evil, sin, suffering, and death.

    iv. The Greek word used to designate the newness of the cosmos is not *neos* but *kainos*.

        1. *Neos* means "new in time" or "new in origin."

        2. *Kainos* means "new in nature" or "new in quality."

v. The phrase "new heavens and a new earth" does not refer to a universe that differs significantly from the one we currently inhabit.

  1. The new cosmos will stand in continuity with the present cosmos.

  2. But it will be utterly renewed and renovated.

vi. This means that a *resurrected people* will live in a *resurrected universe*!

c. The New Jerusalem Will Set Upon the New Earth

  i. The New Jerusalem is the eternal city in which the saints of all ages will live (Revelation 21).

  ii. It is a city of extraordinary grandeur.

  iii. It is called "the holy city" (21:2).

  iv. The heavenly city measures approximately 1,500 miles by 1,500 miles by 1,500 miles (21:16).

  v. The city is transparent, and the glory of God shines through it (21:23).

  vi. The city will feature the river of the water of life and the tree of life (22:1-5).

  vii. It will rest upon the new earth for all eternity.

  viii. It will be glorious!

~ ~ ~ Come soon, Lord! ~ ~ ~

APPENDIX B:

A Simplified Glossary of Prophetic Terms

666—the number of the beast, or antichrist (Revelation 13:18). Bible scholars have different ideas about what this means. It may not make full sense until the antichrist appears on the scene.

144,000—Jewish men who are described as being "from every tribe of the sons of Israel"—12,000 from each of the 12 tribes (Revelation 7:4-8). These redeemed Jews will be worldwide evangelists for Christ during the tribulation period (Matthew 24:14).

Abomination of Desolation—the desecration of the Jewish temple by the antichrist, who will set up an image of himself within it at the midpoint of the tribulation period (Daniel 9:27; Matthew 24:15).

Abrahamic Covenant—an unconditional covenant in which God promised to give Abraham's descendants (Israel) a land with specific boundaries (Genesis 12:1-3; 15:18-21).

Advent—another word for "coming." The first coming of Christ is the "first advent." The second coming of Christ is the "second advent."

Amillennialism—the view that there will be no literal millennial kingdom. Prophetic verses referring to Christ's reign metaphorically refer to Christ's present spiritual rule from heaven during the church age. Old Testament predictions about Israel are seen as being fulfilled by the New Testament church.

Antichrist—a "man of lawlessness" (2 Thessalonians 2:3, 8-9), also called "the beast" (Revelation 13:1-10), who will rise to global power during the tribulation period. He will seek to be worshiped as God and will persecute God's people. He will be empowered by Satan (2 Thessalonians 2:9) to carry out an anti-God agenda.

Apocalypse—literally means "revelation," "uncovering," "unveiling," or "disclosure of the truth." It is an alternative way of referring to the book of Revelation, which unveils the future.

Apostasy—comes from the Greek word *apostasia*, meaning "to fall away." The term refers to a determined, willful departure from the faith or the abandonment of the faith. Apostasy will increase dramatically in the end times (1 Timothy 4:1-2; 2 Timothy 4:3-4).

Armageddon—a word that literally means "Mount of Megiddo," a location about 60 miles north of Jerusalem. This will be the site of the final horrific battles of humankind before the second coming of Jesus Christ (Revelation 16:16).

Babylon—a paganized city that will be rebuilt and flourish during the tribulation period. It will be the operational center of a worldwide false religion during the first half of the tribulation period (Revelation 17) and will transition into a global commercial center during the second half (Revelation 18). It is often called "New Babylon" in prophecy circles.

Beast—a term describing the character of the antichrist (Revelation 13:1). The antichrist, as a beast, is in contrast to Jesus Christ, the Lamb of God. The Lamb saves sinners, but the beast persecutes and executes the saints. The Lamb is gentle, but the beast is ferocious. The Lamb is loving, but the beast is heartless and cruel.

Beginning of the Birth Pains—just as birth pangs increase in intensity and frequency, so will the trials of the tribulation period increase in intensity and frequency (Matthew 24:8).

Beth-Togarmah—a reference to a region in present-day Turkey.

Bottomless Pit—also known as the abyss, it currently serves as a place of imprisonment for some demonic spirits (Luke 8:31; 2 Peter 2:4).

Bowl Judgments—the worst (and the last) of God's judgments that will fall upon the world near the end of the tribulation period. People will suffer painful sores, the sea will become like blood, rivers and springs of water will also become like blood, the sun will scorch people with fire, the world will plunge into utter darkness, and the Euphrates River will dry up—preparing the way for the onset of Armageddon (Revelation 16:2-21).

Church Age—an extended period of time during which the church is on earth. It began on the day of Pentecost (Acts 2) and will end with the rapture (1 Thessalonians 4:13-18).

Conditional Covenant—a covenant with an "if" attached. Conditions had to be met for the promises to be fulfilled.

Covenant—an agreement between two parties.

Cush—the territory south of Egypt on the Nile River, now known as Sudan (Ezekiel 38:5).

Daniel's Seventieth Week—another term for the tribulation period. More specifically, the final "week" of seven years will begin for Israel in the end-times future when the antichrist confirms a "covenant" for seven years (Daniel 9:27). When this peace pact is signed, this will signal the beginning of the tribulation period. That signature marks the beginning of a seven-year countdown to the second coming of Christ, which follows the tribulation period.

Davidic Covenant—an unconditional covenant in which God promised David that one of his descendants would rule forever (2 Samuel 7:12-13; 22:51). This will be fulfilled when Christ reigns during the millennial kingdom.

Day of the Lord—a term used in several senses in Scripture. The Old Testament prophets sometimes used the term for an event to be fulfilled in the near future. At other times, they used the term for an event in the distant eschatological future (the future tribulation period). The immediate context of the term usually indicates which sense is intended. In both cases, the day of the Lord is characterized by God's active supernatural intervention to bring judgment against sin in the world. The day of the Lord is a time when God actively controls and governs history in a direct way, rather than working through secondary causes. Among the New Testament writers, the term is commonly used to refer to the judgment that will culminate in the future seven-year tribulation period (2 Thessalonians 2:2; Revelation 16–18), as well as the judgment that will usher in the new earth in the end times (2 Peter 3:10-13; Revelation 20:7–21:1; see also Isaiah 65:17-19; 66:22; Revelation 21:1). It is this theme of judgment against sin that runs like a thread through the many references to the day of the Lord.

Dispensationalism—a system of theology that views the world as a "household" run by God. In this household, God delegates duties and assigns specific responsibilities to human beings. If people obey God during that dispensation, He promises blessing; if they disobey, He promises judgment. In each dispensation, we see a pattern involving the testing of humankind, the failure of humankind, and the resulting judgment. As things unfold, God provides progressive revelation relating to His plan for history. The present dispensation is the church age. Before that was the dispensation of the law. A future dispensation will be the millennial kingdom (see Ephesians 1 and 3; John 1:17; Romans 6:14; Galatians 3:19-25). These three dispensations can be categorized as Old Testament, New Testament, and Kingdom. Dispensationalism recognizes that God deals with people differently in different ages, as illustrated by how God dealt with people in Moses' day, in our day, and in the future millennium.

End Times—a general term that includes events that take place in the eschatological last days. Included are the rapture, the judgment seat of Christ (for Christians), the tribulation period, the second coming of Christ, the millennial kingdom, the great white throne judgment (for the wicked), a destiny in hell for the wicked, and a destiny in heaven for believers.

Eschatology—derives from two Greek words: *eschatos*, meaning "last" or "last things," and *logos*, meaning "study of." Eschatology is the study of last things.

Eternal State—the eternal state of Christians is heaven (Revelation 21:1-8), while the eternal state of unbelievers is the lake of fire (verses 11-15).

Ezekiel Invasion—an all-out invasion of Israel in the end times by a massive northern assault force comprising Russia and some Muslim nations, including modern Iran, Sudan, Turkey, and Libya. Their goal will be to eradicate the Jews. The paradoxical outcome is that the invaders will themselves be eradicated by God.

False Prophet, The—a religious leader who will emerge during the tribulation period. He will be the antichrist's right-hand man—his "first lieutenant" (Revelation 13:11-18). The antichrist will be a military and political leader, but the false prophet will be a religious leader.

Four Horsemen of the Apocalypse—Christ's metaphorical way of describing four prophecies that will unfold early during the tribulation period (Revelation 6:1-6).

Gehenna—a term sometimes used metaphorically to refer to hell. The term originally referred to a valley that was used as a public dumping ground for all the filth of Jerusalem—including the dead bodies of criminals. Jesus used this word 11 times as a metaphorical way of describing the eternal place of suffering of unsaved humanity.

Globalism—an agenda that places the interests of the entire world above those of individual nation-states. The antichrist will rise to global political and religious power during the tribulation period (Revelation 13:3, 7-8, 12, 16-18).

Gog—literally means "high," "supreme," "a height," or "a high mountain." The term refers to a king-like role—such as pharaoh, caesar, czar, or president. Gog will be the leader of the Ezekiel invasion of Israel (Ezekiel 38:3).

Gog-Magog War—another term for the Ezekiel invasion.

Gomer—a reference to modern-day Turkey (Ezekiel 38:6).

Great Multitude—the countless people from many different ethnic groups who trust in the Lord for salvation during the tribulation period (Revelation 7:9-10).

Great Tribulation, The—the second half of the tribulation period, which will be unimaginably horrific (Matthew 24:21-22).

Great White Throne Judgment—the judgment of the wicked dead following Christ's millennial kingdom (Revelation 20:11-15). Degrees of punishment will be handed out at this judgment (20:11-15; 22:12). The wicked dead will then be cast into the lake of fire.

Hades—the New Testament counterpart to *Sheol* in the Old Testament. The rich man, during the intermediate state, endured great suffering in Hades (Luke 16:19-31). Hades, however, is a temporary abode and will one day be cast into the lake of fire (Revelation 20:14).

Hell—not part of God's original creation, which He called "good" (Genesis 1). Hell was created later to accommodate the banishment of Satan and his fallen angels who rebelled against God (Matthew 25:41). Human beings who reject Christ will join Satan and his fallen angels in this infernal place of suffering. In the New Testament, hell is described in a wide variety of different ways—including the lake of burning sulfur (Revelation 19:20) and eternal fire (Matthew 18:8).

Imminent—a word often used in association with the rapture, meaning "ready to take place" or "impending." The rapture is a signless event that can occur at any moment (Romans 13:11-12; James 5:7-9). Nothing must be fulfilled prophetically before the rapture occurs (1 Corinthians 1:7; 16:22; Philippians 3:20; 4:5; 1 Thessalonians 1:10; Titus 2:13; Hebrews 9:28; James 5:7-9; 1 Peter 1:13; Jude 21).

Judgment of the Nations—a judgment following the second coming of Christ that will determine which individual Gentiles are believers. They will be granted entry into Christ's millennial kingdom.

Judgment Seat of Christ—all believers will face Christ and either receive or forfeit rewards, based on how they lived during their earthly lives (Romans 14:8-10; 1 Corinthians 3:11-15; 9:24-27). These rewards are described as crowns (James 1:12; Revelation 2:10; 1 Peter 5:4; 1 Corinthians 9:25; 2 Timothy 4:8).

Lake of Fire—the eternal abode of Satan, the antichrist, the false prophet, and unbelievers from all ages (Revelation 19:20; 20:10-15). All inhabitants will be tormented day and night forever. The lake of fire is another term for hell.

Last Days—several New Testament passages use the terms "last days," "last times," and "last time" to refer to the present church age in which we now live (Hebrews 1:1-2; 1 Peter 1:20). The Old Testament, however, uses these terms specifically to refer to the time encompassing the tribulation period and the coming of the Messiah to set up His millennial kingdom on earth (Deuteronomy 4:30).

Little Horn—a reference to the antichrist who will appear small and insignificant at first but will rise to enormous power and influence in the world (Daniel 7:8).

Magog—the area now occupied by the former southern Soviet republics of Kazakhstan, Kyrgyzstan, Uzbekistan, Turkmenistan, Tajikistan, and possibly even northern parts of modern Afghanistan. This entire region is Muslim dominated.

Mark of the Beast—a visible mark on the skin (perhaps a tattoo) that serves as a passport to commerce during the tribulation period. The mark is a sign of allegiance to the antichrist. People cannot buy or sell anything without the mark (Revelation 13:16-17).

Meshech and Tubal—the geographical territory south of the Black and Caspian Seas. Today much of this area is modern Turkey.

Midtribulationism—the view that Christ will rapture the church at the midpoint of the tribulation period.

Millennium—comes from two Latin words: *mille*, meaning "thousand," and *annum*, meaning "year." Christ's millennial kingdom will last 1,000 years (Revelation 20:3-6).

Mystery—a truth that was unknown to the people of Old Testament times but was revealed in New Testament times (Matthew 13:17; Colossians 1:26). In this sense, the rapture is a mystery (1 Corinthians 15:51-55).

New Babylon—a literal rebuilt city of Babylon that will be the operational center of a worldwide false religion during the first half of the tribulation period. It will transition into a global economic center during the second half of the tribulation period (Revelation 17–18).

New Covenant—an unconditional covenant God made with humankind in which He promised to provide the forgiveness of sins, based entirely on the sacrificial death and resurrection of Jesus Christ (Jeremiah 31:31-34).

New Heavens and a New Earth—the earth and the "heavens" (the earth's atmosphere and interstellar space) will be completely renewed and renovated, with all traces of sin and all stains left by Satan removed forever. The new heavens and the new earth will be brought into perfect harmony with all that God is—in a state of fixed bliss and absolute perfection.

New Jerusalem—a heavenly city that will be the eternal dwelling place of the saints of all ages (Revelation 21:9-27). The city is beautiful beyond description (Revelation 21:18-21). Christ Himself is its architect (John 14:1-3). Key features of the city include the river of the water of life and the tree of life (Revelation 22:1-2).

Newspaper Exegesis—taking the headlines of a newspaper and then forcing them into Bible prophecy. Such a strategy is unworthy of serious students of prophecy.

Olivet Discourse—a prophetic sermon delivered by Jesus on the Mount of Olives (Matthew 24:3).

Parable—the word literally means "a placing alongside of" for the purpose of comparison. A parable is a teaching tool that uses stories. By comparing a story to a spiritual truth, people can better understand spiritual teachings. Parables always point to a literal truth.

Partial-Rapture Theory—the view that only faithful and watchful Christians will be raptured. Unfaithful Christians will be "left behind" to be purged during the tribulation period.

Persia—modern Iran. Persia officially became Iran in 1935. Later, during the Iranian Revolution in 1979, the name was changed to the Islamic Republic of Iran.

Postmillennialism—a metaphorical view that claims that the world will be "Christianized" through the progressive influence of the church before Christ returns. The kingdom of God is supposedly now being extended in the world through the preaching of the gospel.

Posttribulationism—the view that Christ will rapture the church after the tribulation period, at the second coming of Christ.

Pre-Wrath Rapture Theory—the view that the rapture will occur toward the end of the tribulation period before the great wrath of God is unleashed.

Premillennialism—the view that Christ will establish a literal kingdom of perfect peace and righteousness after His second coming. The kingdom will last 1,000 years. This view is consistent with a literal approach to understanding Bible prophecy.

Preterism—derives from the Latin *preter*, meaning "past." In this view, the Bible prophecies in the book of Revelation (especially chapters 6–18) and Christ's Olivet Discourse (Matthew 24–25) have already been fulfilled in the past. This view relies heavily on allegorism.

Pretribulationism—the view that Christ will rapture the church before the tribulation period.

Prophecy—God's specific revelations about future events and personalities. Prophecy can be described as "history written in advance."

Prophet—the word prophet comes from the Hebrew word *nabi*, which carries the idea of "God's spokesman." There are both major and minor prophets in the Bible—the "big wheels" and the "small fries." The major prophets were Isaiah, Jeremiah, Ezekiel, and Daniel. The minor prophets were Hosea, Joel, Amos, Obadiah, Jonah, Micah, Nahum, Habakkuk, Zephaniah, Haggai, Zechariah, and Malachi.

Put—a land located to the west of Egypt that is modern-day Libya (Ezekiel 38:5).

Rapture—that glorious event when Christ descends from heaven to earth, the dead in Christ are raised, and living Christians are immediately translated into their glorified bodies. Both groups will be caught up to meet Christ in the air and taken back to heaven (1 Thessalonians 4:13-17; John 14:1-3; 1 Corinthians 15:51-54).

Religious Babylon—called a "great prostitute," religious Babylon refers to the idolatrous false religion that will predominate during the first half of the tribulation period (Jeremiah 3:6-9; Ezekiel 20:30; Hosea 4:15; 5:3; 6:10; 9:1).

Replacement Theology—a view that holds that the church replaces Israel. All the promises made to Israel in Scripture are fulfilled allegorically by the church. God is said to have no further prophetic plans for Israel.

Resurrections, First and Second—the "first resurrection" (Revelation 20:5) is also called the "resurrection of life" (John 5:29), the "resurrection of the righteous" (Luke 14:14), and the "better resurrection" (Hebrews 11:35). This is the resurrection of believers. The second resurrection is the last resurrection (Revelation 20:5), appropriately called the "resurrection of judgment" (John 5:29; see also Daniel 12:2; Acts 24:15). This is the resurrection of the wicked.

Rosh—modern Russia. There are two primary reasons for making this identification: (1) Rosh is identified as being located in "the uttermost parts of the north" (Ezekiel 39:2). Russia is to the uttermost north of Israel. (2) A place known as Rosh—sometimes with alternate spellings such as Rus, Ros, Rox, Rash, Rashu, and Reshu—was well known in the ancient world. It was located in the area now occupied by Russia.

Satan—formerly known as Lucifer, Satan is a fallen angel who is aligned against God and His purposes. He leads a vast company of demons who are also aligned against God and His purposes. He is called the "ruler of this world" (John 12:31), "the god of this world" (2 Corinthians 4:4), and the "prince of the power of the air" (Ephesians 2:2). He is also said to deceive the whole world (Revelation 12:9; 20:3). He is portrayed as having power in the governmental realm (Matthew 4:8-9; 2 Corinthians 4:4), the physical realm (Luke 13:11, 16; Acts 10:38), the angelic realm (Jude 9; Ephesians 6:11-12), and the ecclesiastical (church) realm (Revelation 2:9; 3:9). He will empower the antichrist (2 Thessalonians 2:9).

Seal Judgments—the first set of God's wrathful judgments to be unleashed on the earth during the tribulation period. These will include the rise of the antichrist, the outbreak of war, widespread famine, massive casualties, a devastating earthquake, and even worse judgments (Revelation 6).

Second Coming—that glorious event in which Jesus Christ, the King of kings and Lord of lords, will return to the earth in clouds of glory at the end of the present age and set up His kingdom (Revelation 19:11-16). This will involve a visible, physical, bodily coming of the glorified Jesus. The event will be a universal experience, as all will witness it (Revelation 1:7).

Sheol—sometimes the word means "grave," and other times refers to the place of departed people in contrast to the state of living people. The Old Testament portrays Sheol as a place of horror (Psalm 30:9), weeping (Isaiah 38:3), and punishment (Job 24:19).

Signs of the Times—events of prophetic significance that point to the end times. These signs will be fulfilled during the tribulation period, but even now, as illustrated by the current efforts to rebuild the Jewish temple, we can see the foreshadowing of these prophecies in our own day.

Ten Kings—the rulers of ten kingdoms over which the antichrist will gain power and control. They will form the nucleus of the antichrist's world empire (see Revelation 12:3).

Time of Jacob's Trouble—a term pointing to the suffering of Israel in the great tribulation (Jeremiah 30:7; Daniel 12:1-4).

Times of the Gentiles—refers to an extended period of Gentile rule over Jerusalem (Luke 21:24). This period began with the Babylonian captivity of the Jewish people, which began in 605 BC. The dominating powers over Jerusalem throughout biblical history include Babylon, the Medo-Persian Empire, Greece, and Rome. Gentile dominion over Jerusalem will continue through the tribulation period and will be terminated at the second coming of Christ.

Tribulation Period—a definite period of tribulation at the end of the age (Matthew 24:29-35). It will be of such severity that no period in history—past or future—will equal it (Matthew 24:21). It is called the time of Jacob's trouble because it is a judgment on Messiah-rejecting Israel (Jeremiah 30:7; Daniel 12:1-4). The nations will also be judged for their sin and rejection of Christ (Isaiah 26:21; Revelation 6:15-17). This seven-year period will be so bad that people will want to hide and even die (Daniel 9:24, 27; Revelation 6:16).

Trumpet Judgments—the second set of God's wrathful judgments that will be unleashed on the earth during the tribulation period. These will include hail and fire falling on the earth, a fiery mountain crashing into the sea, a star (asteroid) falling from the sky and making a deep impact on the earth, various cosmic disturbances, hideous demons tormenting people, fallen angels killing one-third of humankind, and even worse judgments (Revelation 8:6–9:21).

Unconditional Covenant—a covenant that has no conditions attached for its fulfillment. There are no "ifs" attached.

Vision of the Dry Bones—Ezekiel 37 describes the Lord miraculously bringing scattered bones back together into a skeleton, which then becomes wrapped in muscles, tendons, and flesh. God then breathes life into the body. We know this chapter is about Israel because we read that "these bones are the whole house of Israel" (verse 11). Israel is portrayed as becoming a living, breathing nation, brought back from the dead.

Wormwood—refers to a "star" (probably a meteor or asteroid) that will plummet through the atmosphere and strike the earth (Revelation 8:10-12). It will turn one-third of the waters bitter so that people who drink it will die.

Bibliography

Alcorn, Randy. *Heaven*. Wheaton: Tyndale House, 2004.

Ankerberg, John, and Dillon Burroughs. *Middle East Meltdown*. Eugene: Harvest House, 2007.

Baxter, Richard. *Saints' Everlasting Rest*. Philadelphia: Lippincott, 1859.

Benware, Paul N. *Understanding End Times Prophecy: A Comprehensive Approach*. Chicago: Moody, 1995.

Campbell, Donald K. *Daniel: God's Man in a Secular Society*. Grand Rapids: Discovery House, 1988.

DeMar, Gary. *End Times Fiction*. Nashville: Thomas Nelson, 2001.

Dyer, Charles. *The Rise of Babylon: Sign of the End Times*. Chicago: Moody, 2003.

Feinberg, Charles. *A Commentary on Revelation*. Winona Lake: BMH, 1985.

———. *Premillennialism or Amillennialism?* Grand Rapids: Zondervan, 1936.

———. *The Prophecy of Ezekiel*. Eugene: Wipf and Stock, 2003.

Fruchtenbaum, Arnold. *The Footsteps of the Messiah*. San Antonio: Ariel, 2004.

Geisler, Norman. *Systematic Theology: Church/Last Things*, vol. 4. St. Paul: Bethany House, 2005.

Habermas, Gary R. and J.P. Moreland. *Immortality: The Other Side of Death*. Nashville: Thomas Nelson, 1992.

Hamilton, Floyd. *The Basis of the Millennial Faith*. Grand Rapids: Eerdmans, 1955.

Hampson, Todd. *The Non-Prophet's Guide to the Book of Revelation: Bible Prophecy for Everyone*. Eugene: Harvest House, 2019.

———. *The Non-Prophet's Guide to the End Times: Bible Prophecy for Everyone*. Eugene: Harvest House, 2018.

Heitzig, Skip. *You Can Understand the Book of Revelation*. Eugene: Harvest House, 2011.

Hindson, Ed. *Future Glory: Living in the Hope of the Rapture, Heaven, and Eternity*. Eugene: Harvest Prophecy, 2021.

———. *Revelation: Unlocking the Future*. Chattanooga: AMG, 2002.

Hitchcock, Mark. *55 Answers to Questions About Life After Death*. Sisters: Multnomah, 2005.

———. *Bible Prophecy*. Wheaton: Tyndale House, 1999.

———. *The End*. Wheaton: Tyndale Momentum, 2018.

Hoyt, Herman. *The End Times*. Chicago: Moody, 1969.

Ice, Thomas, and Randall Price. *Ready to Rebuild: The Imminent Plan to Rebuild the Last Days Temple*. Eugene: Harvest House, 1992.

Ice, Thomas, and Timothy Demy. *Prophecy Watch*. Eugene: Harvest House, 1998.

———. *When the Trumpet Sounds*. Eugene: Harvest House, 1995.

Jeremiah, David. *Escape the Coming Night: An Electrifying Tour of the World as It Races Toward Its Final Days*. Dallas: Word, 1990.

———. *The Coming Economic Armageddon: What Bible Prophecy Warns About the New Global Economy*. New York: FaithWords, 2010.

Kinley, Jeff. *Aftershocks: Christians Entering a New Era of Global Crisis*. Eugene: Harvest Prophecy, 2021.

———. *As It Was in the Days of Noah: Warnings from Bible Prophecy About the Coming Global Storm*. Eugene: Harvest House, 2014.

Kinley, Jeff, and Todd Hampson. *The Prophecy Pros' Illustrated Guide to Tough Questions About the End Times*. Eugene: Harvest Prophecy, 2021.

LaHaye, Tim, and Ed Hindson. *Global Warning: Are We on the Brink of World War III?* Eugene: Harvest House, 2007.

LaHaye, Tim, and Jerry Jenkins. *Are We Living in the End Times?* Wheaton: Tyndale, 1999.

LaHaye, Tim, and Thomas Ice. *Charting the End Times*. Eugene: Harvest House, 2001.

LaHaye, Tim. *Revelation Illustrated and Made Plain*. Grand Rapids: Zondervan, 1975.

Lindsey, Hal. *There's a New World Coming: A Prophetic Odyssey*. Santa Ana: Vision House, 1973.

Lutzer, Erwin W. *Your Eternal Reward: Triumph and Tears at the Judgment Seat of Christ*. Chicago: Moody, 1998.

Miller, Steve. *Foreshadows: 12 Megaclues That Jesus' Return Is Nearer Than Ever*. Eugene: Harvest Prophecy, 2022.

Morris, Henry. *The Revelation Record*. Wheaton: Tyndale, 1983.

Newell, William. *Revelation Chapter-by-Chapter*. Grand Rapids: Kregel, 1994.

Pache, Rene. *The Future Life*. Chicago: Moody, 1980.

Pentecost, J. Dwight. *Prophecy for Today*. Grand Rapids: Discovery House, 1989.

———. *Things to Come*. Grand Rapids: Zondervan, 1964.

Phillips, John. *Exploring Revelation*. Grand Rapids: Kregel, 1974.

———. *Exploring the Future: A Comprehensive Guide to Bible Prophecy*. 3rd ed. Grand Rapids: Kregel, 2003.

Pink, Arthur W. *The Antichrist: A Study of Satan's Christ*. Blacksburg: Wilder, 2008.

Price, Randall. *Jerusalem in Prophecy*. Eugene: Harvest House, 1998.

———. *Unholy War*. Eugene: Harvest House, 2001.

Price, Walter K. *The Coming Antichrist*. Neptune: Loizeaux Brothers, 1985.

Prophecy Study Bible, ed. Tim LaHaye. Chattanooga: AMG, 2001.

Reagan, David. *The Man of Lawlessness: The Antichrist in the Tribulation*. Princeton: Lamb & Lion Ministries, 2012.

Richardson, Joel. *The Islamic Antichrist*. Los Angeles: WND, 2009.

Rosenberg, Joel. *Epicenter: Why Current Rumblings in the Middle East Will Change Your Future*. Carol Stream: Tyndale House, 2006.

Ryle, J.C. *Heaven*. Great Britain: Christian Focus, 2001.

Ryrie, Charles. *Come Quickly, Lord Jesus: What You Need to Know About the Rapture*. Eugene: Harvest House, 1996.

———. *Dispensationalism Today*. Chicago: Moody, 1965.

Showers, Renald. *Maranatha: Our Lord Come!* Bellmawr: Friends of Israel, 1995.

Smith, Wilbur M. *The Biblical Doctrine of Heaven*. Chicago: Moody, 1974.

Stanton, Gerald. *Kept from the Hour*. Grand Rapids: Zondervan, 1956.

The Popular Bible Prophecy Commentary, eds. Tim LaHaye and Ed Hindson. Eugene: Harvest House, 2006.

The Popular Encyclopedia of Bible Prophecy, eds. Tim LaHaye and Ed Hindson. Eugene: Harvest House, 2004.

Toussaint, Stanley. *Behold the King: A Study of Matthew*. Grand Rapids: Kregel, 2005.

Walvoord, John F. and John E. Walvoord. *Armageddon, Oil, and the Middle East Crisis*. Grand Rapids: Zondervan, 1975.

Walvoord, John F. *Daniel: The Key to Prophetic Revelation*. Chicago: Moody Press, 1971.

————. *The Millennial Kingdom*. Grand Rapids: Zondervan, 1975.

————. *The Prophecy Knowledge Handbook*. Wheaton: Victor, 1990.

————. *The Rapture Question*. Grand Rapids: Zondervan Publishers, 1979.

Wiersbe, Warren. *Be Victorious: Revelation*. Colorado Springs: David C. Cook, 2008.

Willmington, H.L. *The King Is Coming: A Compelling Study of the Last Days*. Wheaton: Tyndale House Publishers, 1973.

Scripture Copyright Notifications

Notes

Chapter 1—Demystifying Prophets and Prophecy

1. C.S. Lewis, cited at "History is a Story Written by the Finger of God," *HistoricalUSA* website, https://historicalus.com/2021/11/26/history-is-a-story-written-by-the-finger-of-god/, November 26, 2021.

2. Robert P. Lightner, *Evangelical Theology* (Grand Rapids, MI: Baker Books, 1986), 57.

3. Mark Hitchcock, *The Amazing Claims of Bible Prophecy* (Eugene, OR: Harvest House, 2010), Kindle.

Chapter 2—The Vital Importance of Prophecy

1. Mark Hitchcock, *Seven Signs of the End Times* (Sisters, OR: Multnomah, 2009), Kindle.

Chapter 4—Essential Prophetic Passages You Need to Know

1. Warren Wiersbe, *Be Victorious: Revelation* (Colorado Springs, CO: David C. Cook, 2008), 176.

Chapter 5—A Mini-Survey of 16 Debated Issues

1. J. Dwight Pentecost, *Things to Come* (Grand Rapids, MI: Zondervan, 1964), iBooks edition.

Chapter 6—Why a Literal Approach Is Best

1. David Cooper; cited in Arnold Fruchtenbaum, *The Footsteps of the Messiah* (San Antonio, TX: Ariel Ministries, 2003), n.p.

2. Charles C. Ryrie, *The Basis of the Premillennial Faith* (Dubuque, IA: ECS Ministries, 2005), n.p.

3. Charles Feinberg, *Premillennialism or Amillennialism?* (Grand Rapids, MI: Zondervan, 1936), 39, insert added for clarification.

4. Floyd Hamilton, *The Basis of the Millennial Faith* (Grand Rapids, MI: Eerdmans, 1955), 38.

Chapter 7—Fundamentals of Prophecy Interpretation

1. Arnold Fruchtenbaum, *The Footsteps of the Messiah* (San Antonio, TX: Ariel Ministries, 2003), n.p.

2. Bernard Ramm, cited in Ron Rhodes, *1001 Unforgettable Quotes About God, Faith, and the Bible* (Eugene, OR: Harvest House Publishers, 2011).

3. Gordon Lewis, cited in Ron Rhodes, *1001 Unforgettable Quotes About God, Faith, and the Bible* (Eugene, OR: Harvest House Publishers, 2011).

Chapter 8—The Striking Connection Between Jesus, Paul, and John

1. John F. Walvoord, *Jesus Christ Our Lord* (Chicago, IL: Moody, 1980), 254-55.

2. See, for example, Robert L. Reymond, *Jesus, Divine Messiah: The Old Testament Witness* (Scotland: Christian Focus Publications, 1990), 101.

3. Quoted in Robert Jamieson, A.R. Fausset, and David Brown, *The Bethany Parallel Commentary on the New Testament* (Minneapolis, MN: Bethany House, 1983), 1368; see also Erich Sauer, *From Eternity to Eternity* (Grand Rapids, MI: Eerdmans, 1979), 45.

4. Millard J. Erickson, *Christian Theology* (Grand Rapids, MI: Baker, 1987), 765.

5. R.C.H. Lenski, *First Peter* (Minneapolis, MN: Augsburg, 1961), 46.

6. Thomas Schultz, quoted in Josh McDowell and Bart Larson, *Jesus: A Biblical Defense of His Deity* (San Bernardino, CA: Here's Life, 1983), 54.

Chapter 9—Distinguishing Israel and the Church

1. Harold Lindsell, quoted in Ron Rhodes, *1001 Unforgettable Quotes About God, Faith, and the Bible* (Eugene, OR: Harvest House Publishers, 2011), Apple Books.

2. Jim Wallis, quoted in Rhodes, *1001 Unforgettable Quotes About God, Faith, and the Bible.*

Chapter 10—Clarifying Misunderstood Verses About Israel and the Church

1. Thomas Constable, "Notes on Galatians," *Constable's Expository Notes on the Bible*, www.soniclight.com/constable/notes/pdf/galatians.pdf.

2. Scot McKnight, *NIV Application Commentary*, BibleGateway, "Galatians 3:29."

3. William MacDonald, *Believer's Bible Commentary*, ed. Art Farstad (Nashville, TN: Thomas Nelson Publishers, 2016), The Bible Study App.

4. Robert P. Lightner, in *Bible Knowledge Commentary*, eds. John F. Walvoord and Roy B. Zuck, Philippians 3:3, The Bible Study App, OliveTree Software.

5. Jon Courson, *Courson's Application Commentary*, The Bible Study App, Olive Tree Software, "Philippians 3:3."

6. F.F. Bruce, *The Epistle to the Galatians* (Grand Rapids, MI: Eerdmans Publishers, 1982), 275.

7. William MacDonald, *Believer's Bible Commentary*, ed. Art Farstad (Nashville, TN: Thomas Nelson Publishers, 2016), The Bible Study App.

Chapter 12—The Remarkable Rebirth of Israel

1. Joel Rosenberg, *Epicenter: Why the Current Rumblings in the Middle East Will Change Your Future* (Carol Stream, IL: Tyndale House, 2006), 27.

Chapter 13—Deciphering the Signs of the Times

1. Kyle Morris and Sam Dorman, "Over 63 Million Abortions Have Occurred in the US Since Roe V. Wade Decision in 1973," *Fox News* (May 4, 2022), https://www.foxnews.com/politics/abortions-since-roe-v-wade.

2. Elizabeth Wildsmith, Jennifer Manlove, Elizabeth Cook, "Dramatic Increase in the Proportion of Births Outside of Marriage in the United States from 1990 to 2016," *ChildTrends* (August 8, 2018), https://www.childtrends.org/publications/dramatic-increase-in-percentage-of-births-outside-marriage-among-whites-hispanics-and-women-with-higher-education-levels#.

Chapter 14—The Rebuilding of the Jewish Temple

1. John F. Walvoord, "Revelation," in *The Bible Knowledge Commentary*, in The Bible Study App, Olive Tree Software, insert added.

2. Arutz Sheva Staff, "Preparation for Temple No Longer a Dream," *Temple Mount*, August 8, 2016, online edition.

3. Thomas Ice, "Is It Time for the Temple?" article posted at *Pre-Trib Research Center*, www.pretrib.org/.

4. Arnold Fruchtenbaum, *Ariel Ministries Newsletter*, Fall 2004/Winter 2005.

5. "New 'Sanhedrin' Plans Rebuilding of Temple: Israeli Rabbinical Body Calls for Architectural Blueprint," *WorldNetDaily.com*, June 8, 2005.

6. "New 'Sanhedrin' Plans Rebuilding of Temple…"

7. "New 'Sanhedrin' Plans Rebuilding of Temple…"

Chapter 15—The Rising Tide of Apostasy

1. The Barna Group, *The Bible in America: The Changing Landscape of Bible Perceptions and Engagement* (Ventura, CA: Barna Group, 2016), 19.

2. George Barna, *America at the Crossroads* (Grand Rapids, MI: Baker Books, 2016), 41.

3. David Kinnaman and Gabe Lyons, *Good Faith: Being a Christian When Society Thinks You're Irrelevant and Extreme* (Grand Rapids, MI: Baker Books, 2016), 12-13.

4. George Barna, *America at the Crossroads* (Grand Rapids, MI: Baker Books, 2016), 41.

5. Barna, *America at the Crossroads*, 33, 67.

6. Barna, *America at the Crossroads*, 33, 67.

7. Ron Rhodes, *1001 Unforgettable Quotes About God, Faith, and the Bible* (Eugene, OR: Harvest House Publishers, 2011), Apple Books edition.

Chapter 16—The Decline of the United States

1. Most of these statistics are derived from George Barna, *America at the Crossroads* (Grand Rapids, MI: Baker Books, 2016), 126.

Chapter 17—Millions Vanish in the Blink of an Eye

1. Ed Hindson, *Future Glory* (Eugene, OR: Harvest Prophecy, 2021), Kindle edition.

2. Mark Hitchcock, *101 Answers to the Most Asked Questions about the End Times* (Colorado Springs, CO: Multnomah Books, 2001), Apple Books edition.

Chapter 18—Exploring Alternative Perspectives on the Rapture

1. The exception is full preterists, who believe that references to the second coming in prophetic Scripture refer to AD 70 when General Titus and his Roman army overran Jerusalem and its temple. Christ allegedly *spiritually* came in judgment against Israel at that time.

Chapter 19—Investigating Historical Claims About the Origin of the Rapture

1. *John Gill Commentary*, in e-Sword Bible Software, designed by Rick Meyers, "1 Thessalonians 4:13-17."

2. Thomas Ice and Timothy Demy, *When the Trumpet Sounds* (Eugene, OR: Harvest House Publishers, 1995), 119, 121.

3. Paul N. Benware, *Understanding End Times Prophecy: A Comprehensive Approach* (Chicago, IL: Moody Press, 1995), 197-98.

4. Irenaeus, cited in William Watson, "The Rapture, Antichrist, and Rebirth of Israel in Medieval Manuscripts," article posted at the *Pretrib Research Center*, https://www.pre-trib.org/dr-robert-thomas/message/the-rapture-antichrist-and-rebirth-of-israel-in-medieval-manuscripts/read.

5. The *Shepherd of Hermas* (CrossReach Publications, 2014), 1.4.2.

6. Francis X. Gumerlock, "The Rapture in the Apocalypse of Elijah," *Bibliotheca Sacra* (October–December, 2013), 422.

7. Lee Brainard, "Recent Pre-Trib Rapture Findings in the Early Church," article posted at the Pretrib Research Center, https://www.pre-trib.org/dr-robert-thomas/message/prophecy-in-deuteronomy/read.

8. Aspringius of Beja, cited in Watson, "The Antichrist, Rebirth of Israel, and Rapture in the Fathers and Medieval Manuscripts."

9. Norman Geisler and Ron Rhodes, *Conviction Without Compromise* (Eugene, OR: Harvest House Publishers, 2008), Kindle edition.

10. Charles C. Ryrie, *Dispensationalism* (Chicago, IL: Moody Publishers, 2007), Kindle edition.

11. Thomas A. Howe, *What the Bible Really Says* (Eugene, OR: Wipf & Stock, 2009), 15.

12. John Calvin, "Prefatory Address to King Francis," in *Institutes of the Christian Religion* (London: Wolfe & Harison, 1561), 4, cited in Ryrie, *Dispensationalism*.

13. See Thomas Ice, "Myths of the Origin of Pretribulationism"—Part 2, article posted at the *Pretrib Research Center*, https://www.pre-trib.org/articles/all-articles/message/myths-of-the-origin-of-pretribulationism-part-2.

14. Ice, "Myths of the Origin of Pretribulationism"—Part 2.

15. *The Harvest Handbook of Bible Prophecy*, eds. Ed Hindson, Mark Hitchcock, and Tim LaHaye (Eugene, OR: Harvest House Publishers, 2020), Kindle edition.

16. J. Barton Payne, *The Imminent Appearing of Christ* (Grand Rapids, MI: Eerdmans Publishers, 1962), 102.

17. John F. Walvoord, *The Rapture Question* (Grand Rapids, MI: Zondervan Publishers, 1979), Kindle edition.

18. Walvoord.

Chapter 20—Frequently Asked Questions About the Rapture

1. C.S. Lewis, *Mere Christianity* (San Francisco, CA: HarperOne, 2015), 134.

2. J.I. Packer, ed. *Alive to God: Studies in Spirituality* (Downers Grove, IL: InterVarsity, 1992), 162.

3. Packer, 171.

Chapter 21—The Mysterious Withdrawal of "He Who Now Restrains"

1. *The Bible Knowledge Commentary*, eds. John F. Walvoord and Roy B. Zuck (Colorado Springs, CO: David C. Cook, 2002), The Bible Study App, Olive Tree Software.

2. Mal Couch, "Restrainer," in *The Popular Encyclopedia of Bible Prophecy*, eds. Tim LaHaye and Ed Hindson (Eugene, OR: Harvest House, 2004), 325.

3. John Phillips; cited in David Jeremiah, *The Coming Economic Armageddon* (New York, NY: Faith Words, 2010), 114.

4. Paul Feinberg, "2 Thessalonians 2 and the Rapture," in *When the Trumpet Sounds*, eds. Thomas Ice and Timothy Demy (Eugene, OR: Harvest House, 1995), 308.

Chapter 23—The Sacred Union: The Marriage of the Lamb

1. John F. Walvoord, *Revelation*, The John Walvoord Prophecy Commentaries, eds. Philip E. Rawley and Mark Hitchcock (Chicago, IL: Moody, 2011), in The Bible Study App, Olive Tree Software.

2. Arnold Fruchtenbaum, *The Footsteps of the Messiah* (Tustin: Ariel Ministries, 2003), 597.

3. Thomas Constable, *Dr. Constable's Expository Notes*, 2010 edition, "Revelation 19:8," in The Bible Study App, Olive Tree Software.

4. John MacArthur, *The MacArthur Study Bible* (Nashville, TN: Thomas Nelson, 2006), n.p.

Chapter 25—The Timing of the Invasion

1. Arnold Fruchtenbaum, *The Footsteps of the Messiah* (San Antonio, TX: Ariel, 2004), 121.

2. Mark Hitchcock, "The Battle of Gog and Magog." Available online at www.pre-trib.org.

Chapter 26—The Epic Defeat of the Invaders

1. John F. Walvoord and John E. Walvoord, *Armageddon, Oil, and the Middle East Crisis* (Grand Rapids, MI: Zondervan, 1975), 125.

2. Charles Feinberg, *The Prophecy of Ezekiel* (Eugene, OR: Wipf and Stock, 2003), 220-21.

3. Mark Hitchcock, *The Coming Islamic Invasion of Israel* (Sisters, OR: Multnomah, 2002), 106.

4. John F. Walvoord and Roy B. Zuck, eds., *The Bible Knowledge Commentary* (Wheaton, IL: Victor, 1985), Logos Bible Software.

5. Joel Rosenberg, *Epicenter* (Carol Stream, IL: Tyndale, 2006), 163-64.

Chapter 27—The Rise of a Revived Roman Empire

1. Mark Hitchcock, *101 Answers to the Most Asked Questions about the End Times* (Sisters, OR: Multnomah Books, 2001), Apple Books edition.

2. "Birth of a Superstate," documentary, cited in *The Harvest Handbook of Bible Prophecy: A Comprehensive Survey from the World's Foremost Experts*, eds. Ed Hindson, Mark Hitchcock, and Tim LaHaye (Eugene, OR: Harvest House Publishers, 2018), 377-79.

3. *The Harvest Handbook of Bible Prophecy*, 377-79.

4. Ed Hindson, *15 Future Events That Will Shake the World* (Eugene, OR: Harvest House Publishers, 2014), Apple Books edition.

5. Mark Hitchcock, *The Amazing Claims of Bible Prophecy* (Eugene, OR: Harvest House Publishers, 2010), Apple Books edition.

Chapter 28—Menacing Features of the Tribulation Period

1. Randall Price, "An Overview of the Tribulation," *Rapture Ready*, http://www.raptureready.com/2015/01/16/an-overview-of-the-tribulation-by-randall-price/.

Chapter 29—The Stranglehold of Religious New Babylon on the World

1. Mark Hitchcock, *101 Answers to Questions About the Book of Revelation* (Eugene, OR: Harvest House, 2012), Apple Books edition.

Chapter 30—The 144,000 Courageous Jewish Evangelists

1. William Macdonald and Arthur L. Farstad, *The Believer's Bible Commentary*, e-Sword Bible Software, Rick Meyers, 2022.

2. Stanley Toussaint, *Behold the King: A Study of Matthew* (Grand Rapids, MI: Kregel, 2005), 291.

3. Merrill F. Unger, *Beyond the Crystal Ball* (Chicago, IL: Moody, 1978), 134-35.

4. J. Dwight Pentecost, *The Words and Works of Jesus Christ* (Grand Rapids, MI: Zondervan, 1978), 410; insert added for clarification. See also J. Dwight Pentecost, *Things to Come* (Grand Rapids, MI: Zondervan, 1978), 418.

5. *The Bible Knowledge Commentary*, New Testament, eds. Roy B. Zuck and John F. Walvoord (Wheaton, IL: Victor, 1983), 81.

Chapter 34—The Emergence of the Insidious False Prophet

1. J. Dwight Pentecost, *Things to Come* (Grand Rapids, MI: Zondervan, 2000), 336-37.

2. David Reagan, "The Rise and Fall of the Antichrist," Article posted at *Rapture Ready* website.

3. John F. Walvoord, "Revelation," in *The Bible Knowledge Commentary*, Accordance, Oaktree Software, insert added.

4. Ed Hindson, "False Prophet," in *The Popular Encyclopedia of Bible Prophecy*, eds. Tim LaHaye and Ed Hindson (Eugene, OR: Harvest House, 2004), 103.

5. John MacArthur, *Revelation: The MacArthur New Testament Commentary*, Accordance, Oaktree Software.

6. John Phillips, cited in Mark Hitchcock, *The Complete Book of Bible Prophecy* (Wheaton, IL: Tyndale House, 1999), 135.

7. J. Hampton Keathley, III, "The Beast and the False Prophet (Rev 13:1-18)," study posted at Bible.org.

8. Keathley, "The Beast and the False Prophet (Rev 13:1-18)."

Chapter 35—The Wounding and "Resurrection" of the Antichrist

1. Arnold Fruchtenbaum, *The Footsteps of the Messiah* (San Antonio, TX: Ariel Ministries, 2020), Logos Bible Software.

2. *The Bible Knowledge Commentary*, eds. John Walvoord and Roy Zuck (Colorado Springs, CO: David C Cook, 2002), E-Sword Bible Software, Rick Meyers, 2022.

3. Tim LaHaye and Jerry Jenkins, *Are We Living in the End Times?* (Wheaton, IL: Tyndale House, 1999), 281.

4. Walter K. Price, *The Coming Antichrist* (Neptune, NJ: Loizeaux Brothers, 1985), 145.

5. Price, 146-47.

6. Mark Hitchcock, *The Complete Book of Bible Prophecy* (Wheaton, IL: Tyndale House, 1999), 199-200.

Chapter 36—666 and the Mark of the Beast

1. Thomas Ice and Timothy Demy, *The Coming Cashless Society* (Eugene, OR: Harvest House Publishers, 1996), 125-26.

2. Arnold Fruchtenbaum, *Footsteps of the Messiah* (San Antonio, TX: Ariel Ministries, 2003), Logos Bible Software. See also Mark Hitchcock, *Cashless: Bible Prophecy, Economic Chaos, & the Future Financial Order* (Eugene, OR: Harvest House, 2010), 163-64.

3. Robert Thomas, cited in Thomas Ice and Timothy Demy, *Fast Facts on Bible Prophecy from A to Z* (Eugene, OR: Harvest House, 2004), 129, insert added for clarification.

4. John MacArthur, *The MacArthur Study Bible* (Nashville, TN: Thomas Nelson, 2003), Logos Bible Software.

5. David Jeremiah, *The Coming Economic Armageddon: What Bible Prophecy Warns About the New Global Economy* (New York, NY: FaithWords, 2010), 146.

6. John F. Walvoord, *The Prophecy Knowledge Handbook* (Wheaton, IL: Victor, 1990), Logos Bible Software.

7. Mark Hitchcock, *Cashless: Bible Prophecy, Economic Chaos, & the Future Financial Order* (Eugene, OR: Harvest House, 2010), 43.

Chapter 37—Religious New Babylon Falls, Commercial New Babylon Rises

1. Thomas Constable, *Dr. Constable's Expository Notes*, "Revelation," The Bible Study App, Olive Tree Software.

2. Warren Wiersbe, *The Wiersbe Bible Commentary: New Testament* (Colorado Springs, CO: David C Cook, 2007), in The Bible Study App, Olive Tree Software.

3. Mark Hitchcock, *The Second Coming of Babylon* (Sisters, OR: Multnomah, 2003), 147-150.

Chapter 39—Darkness Descends: The Antichrist Is Worshiped

1. Renald Showers, *Maranatha: Our Lord Come!* (Bellmawr, NJ: Friends of Israel, 1995), 43.

Chapter 40—The Onset of the "Great Tribulation"

1. Henry C. Thiessen, cited in Renald Showers, *Maranatha: Our Lord Come!* (Bellmawr, NJ: Friends of Israel, 1995), 50.

2. Renald Showers, *Maranatha: Our Lord Come!* (Bellmawr, NJ: Friends of Israel, 1995), 50.

Chapter 42—Armageddon Ignites

1. John F. Walvoord, "Revelation," in *The Bible Knowledge Commentary*, The Bible Study App, Olive Tree Software.

2. Charles Ryrie, *The Ryrie Study Bible* (Chicago, IL: Moody Press, 2011).

3. Arnold G. Fruchtenbaum, "The Campaign of Armageddon," article posted at *Rapture Ready* website, published July 19, 2016, https://www.raptureready.com/category/dr-arnold-g-fruchtenbaum/.

4. Thomas Ice, "Armageddon," *The Harvest Handbook of Bible Prophecy* (Eugene, OR: Harvest House, 2020), Apple Books edition.

Chapter 43—The Collapse of Commercial New Babylon

1. Thomas Ice and Timothy Demy, *Prophecy Watch* (Eugene, OR: Harvest House, 1998), 191.

Chapter 45—The Glorious Appearing

1. William F. Arndt and F. Wilbur Gingrich, *A Greek-English Lexicon of the New Testament* (Chicago, IL: University of Chicago Press, 1957), 814.

2. Joseph Thayer, *Greek-English Lexicon of the New Testament* (Grand Rapids, MI: Zondervan Publishers, 1963), 616.

3. W.E. Vine, *Expository Dictionary of New Testament Words* (Nashville, TN: Thomas Nelson Publishers, 1985), 913.

Chapter 46—The Subsequent 75-Day Transition Period

1. Renald Showers, *Maranatha: Our Lord Come!* (Bellmawr, NJ: Friends of Israel, 1995), 57-58.

Chapter 48—Satan's Dramatic Final Act: The Climactic Uprising

1. Mark Hitchcock, *101 Answers to Questions About the Book of Revelation* (Eugene, OR: Harvest House Publishers, 2012), Apple Books.

2. Henry Morris, *The Revelation Record* (Wheaton, IL: Tyndale, 1983), 419-20.

Chapter 49—The Divine Reckoning: The Wicked Face the Great White Throne Judgment

1. C.S. Lewis, *The Great Divorce* (San Francisco, CA: HarperOne, 2009), 26.

Chapter 51—The Majestic New Heavens—the Pristine New Earth

1. Albert Barnes, "Revelation," *Notes on the New Testament* (Grand Rapids, MI: Baker, 1996), 454.

2. John MacArthur, *The Glory of Heaven* (Wheaton, IL: Crossway, 1996), 90.

3. William Hendrickson, cited in J. Oswald Sanders, *Heaven: Better by Far* (Grand Rapids, MI: Discovery House, 1993), 131.

4. Sanders, 134.

5. John Piper, cited in Randy Alcorn, *Heaven* (Wheaton, IL: Tyndale, 2004), 125.

Chapter 52—The Resplendently Glorious New Jerusalem

1. John F. Walvoord, "Revelation," in *The Bible Knowledge Commentary*, eds. John F. Walvoord and Roy Zuck (Wheaton, IL: Victor, 1985), Logos Bible Software.

2. Millard Erickson, *Christian Theology* (Grand Rapids, MI: Baker, 1987), 1229.

3. Jonathan Edwards, cited in George Marsden, *Jonathan Edwards: A Life* (New Haven, CT: Yale University, 2003), 98.

4. A.T. Pierson, cited in John F. Walvoord, *The Revelation of Jesus Christ* (Chicago, IL: Moody Press, 1989), 332.

5. Anne Graham Lotz, *Heaven: My Father's House* (Nashville, TN: Thomas Nelson, 2001), 48.

6. Lehman Strauss, cited in Tim LaHaye, *Revelation: Illustrated and Made Plain* (Grand Rapids, MI: Zondervan, 1975), 315.

Chapter 54—Living Righteously

1. John F. Walvoord, *End Times* (Nashville, TN: Word, 1998), 219.

2. W. MacDonald and A. Farstad, *Believer's Bible Commentary* (Nashville, TN: Nelson, 1997), in Logos Bible Software, insert added.

Chapter 55—Living with an Eternal Perspective

1. J.I. Packer, ed., *Alive to God: Studies in Spirituality* (Downers Grove, IL: InterVarsity, 1992), 163.

2. Packer, *Alive to God: Studies in Spirituality*, 171.

3. Richard Baxter, cited in Packer, 167.

4. John Wenham, *The Enigma of Evil: Can We Believe in the Goodness of God?* (Grand Rapids, MI: Zondervan, 1985), 55.

Other Great Harvest House Books by Ron Rhodes

Basic Bible Prophecy

40 Days Through Genesis

40 Days Through Daniel

40 Days Through Revelation

40 Days Through Bible Prophecy

The Big Book of Bible Answers

Commonly Misunderstood Bible Verses

Find It Fast in the Bible

A Popular Survey of Apologetics for Today

The Popular Dictionary of Bible Prophecy

Understanding the Bible from A to Z

8 Great Debates of Bible Prophecy

Bible Prophecy Under Siege

Cyber Meltdown

New Babylon Rising

End Times Super Trends

Jesus and the End Times

The End Times in Chronological Order

Northern Storm Rising

Unmasking the Antichrist

Spiritual Warfare in the End Times

Israel on High Alert

Secret Life of Angels

What Happens After Life?

Why Do Bad Things Happen If God Is Good?

Wonder of Heaven

Reasoning from the Scriptures with the Jehovah's Witnesses

Reasoning from the Scriptures with Mormons

To learn more about our
Harvest Prophecy resources, please visit:

www.HarvestProphecyHQ.com

HARVEST PROPHECY
An Imprint of Harvest House Publishers